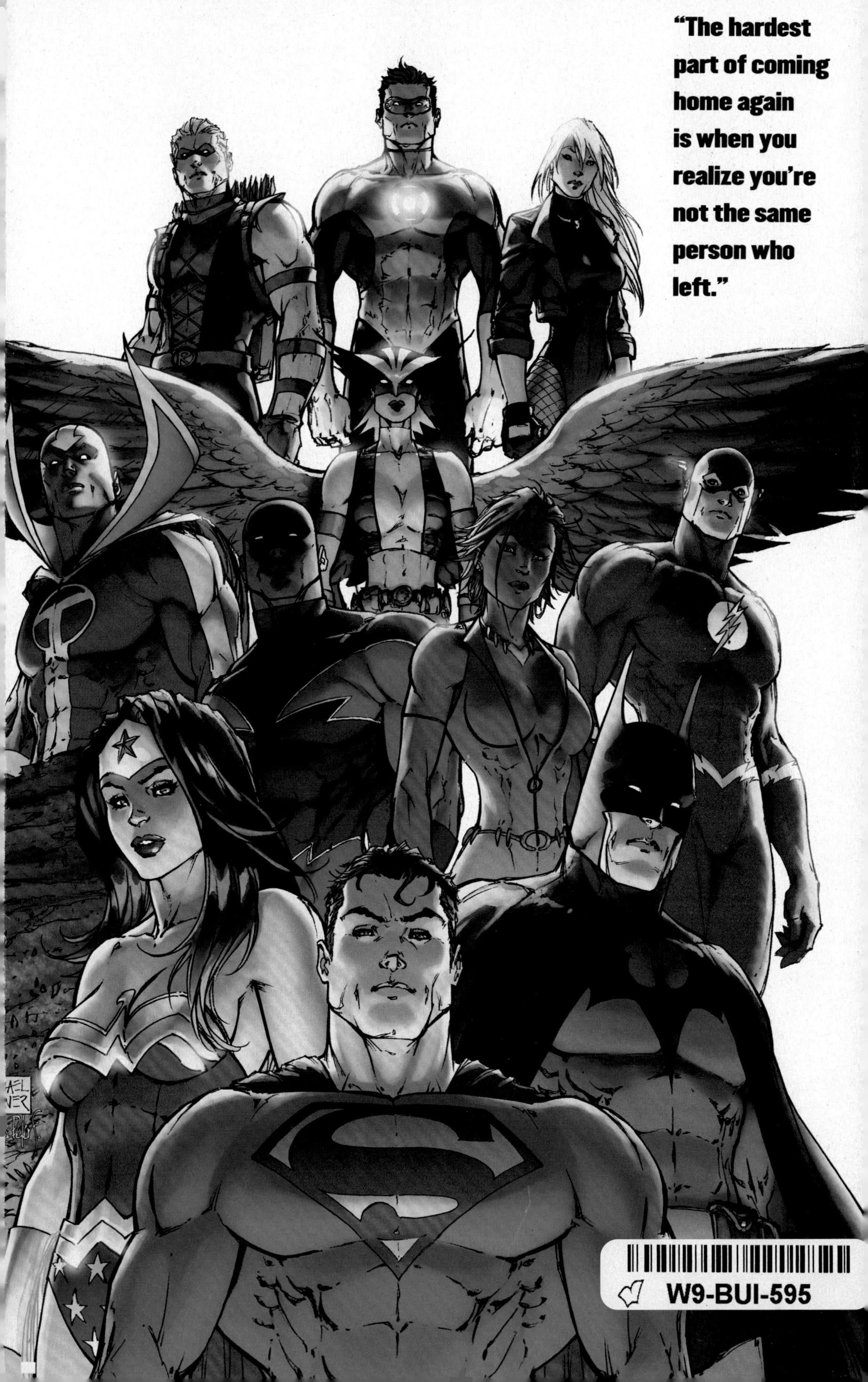
"The hardest part of coming home again is when you realize you're not the same person who left."

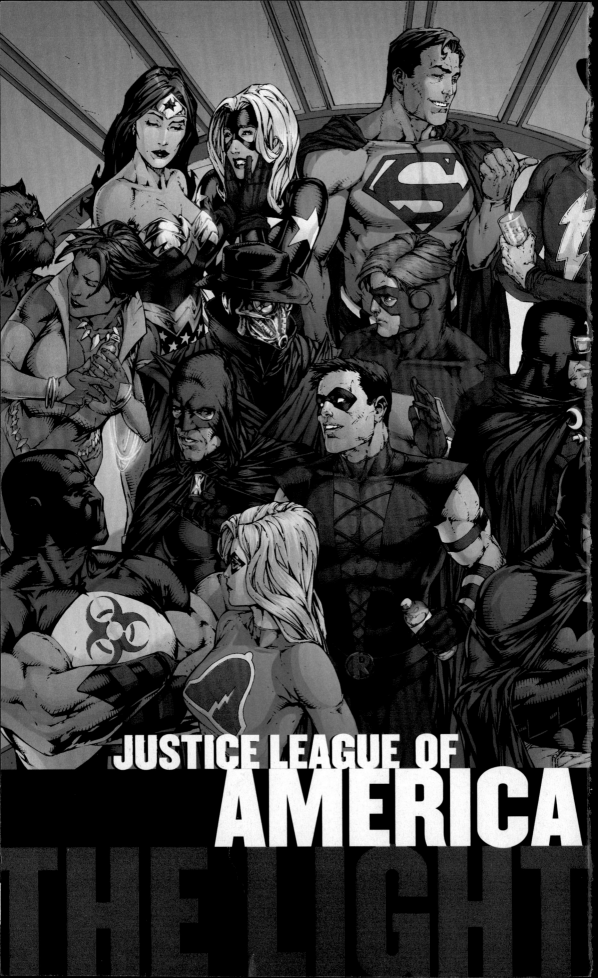

JUSTICE LEAGUE OF
AMERICA
THE LIGHT

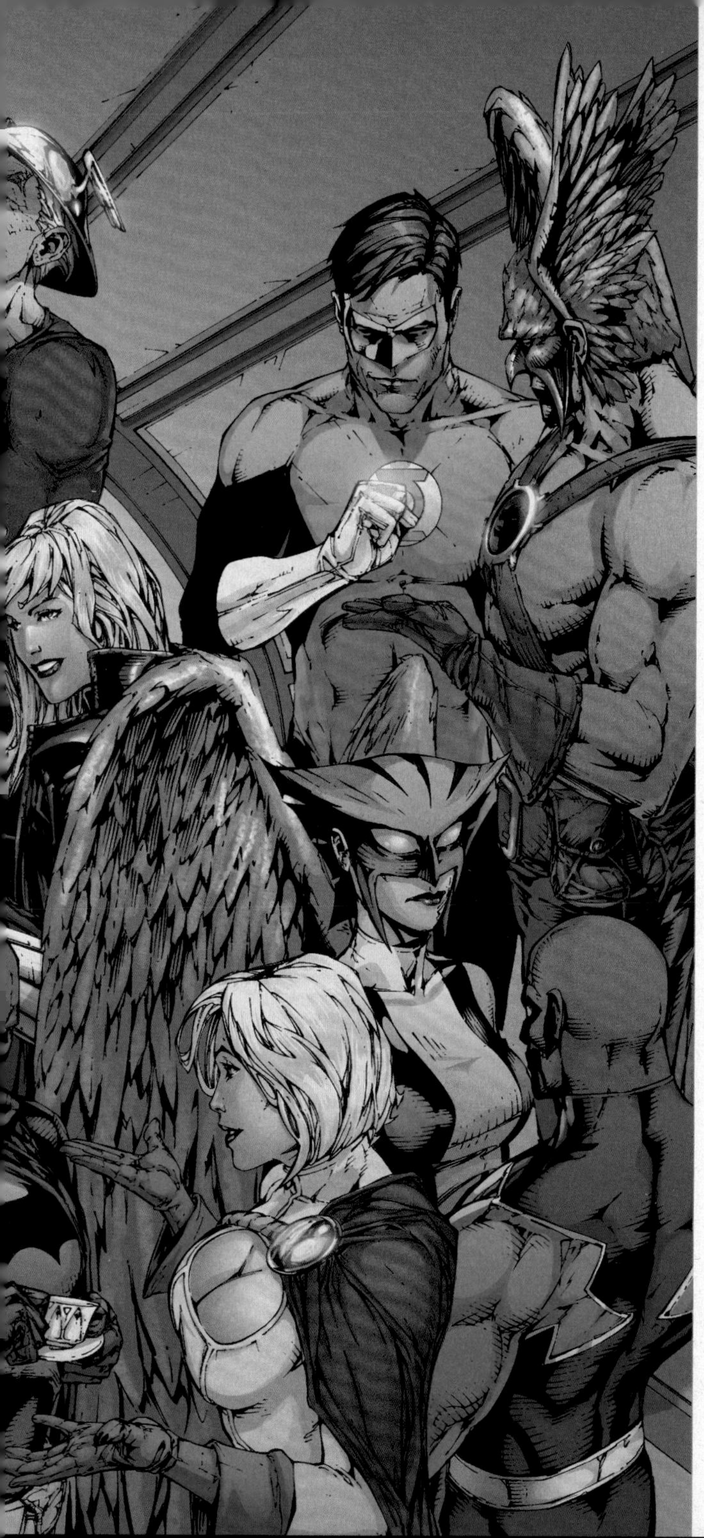

The Lightning Saga

Chapter 1
Brad Meltzer
Writer
Shane Davis
Penciller
Matt Banning
Inker

Chapter 2
Geoff Johns
Writer
Fernando Pasarin
Artist

Chapter 3
Brad Meltzer
Writer
Ed Benes
Artist

Chapter 4
Geoff Johns
Writer
Dale Eaglesham
Penciller
Ruy Jose
Inker

Chapter 5
Brad Meltzer
Writer
Ed Benes
Penciller
Sandra Hope
Inker

Walls
Brad Meltzer
Writer
Gene Ha
Artist

Monitor Duty
Brad Meltzer
Writer
Ed Benes
Eric Wight
Pencillers
Sandra Hope
Inker

Rob Leigh
Letterer

Alex Sinclair
Jeromy Cox
Art Lyon
Pete Pantazis
Colorists

Special thanks to
Joe Prado

Introduction by
Patton Oswalt

NING SAGA

Dan DiDio Senior VP-Executive Editor
Eddie Berganza Editor-original series
Adam Schlagman Jeanine Schaefer
Assistant Editors-original series
Bob Harras Editor-collected edition
Robbin Brosterman Senior Art Director
Paul Levitz President & Publisher
Georg Brewer VP-Design & DC Direct Creative
Richard Bruning Senior VP-Creative Director
Patrick Caldon Executive VP-Finance & Operations
Chris Caramalis VP-Finance
John Cunningham VP-Marketing
Terri Cunningham VP-Managing Editor
Alison Gill VP-Manufacturing
David Hyde VP-Publicity
Hank Kanalz VP-General Manager, WildStorm
Jim Lee Editorial Director-WildStorm
Paula Lowitt Senior VP-Business & Legal Affairs
MaryEllen McLaughlin VP-Advertising & Custom Publishing
John Nee VP-Business Development
Gregory Noveck Senior VP-Creative Affairs
Sue Pohja VP-Book Trade Sales
Steve Rotterdam Senior VP-Sales & Marketing
Cheryl Rubin Senior VP-Brand Management
Jeff Trojan VP-Business Development, DC Direct
Bob Wayne VP-Sales

Cover by Michael Turner
Logo designed by Ken Lopez

Justice League of America:
The Lightning Saga

Published by DC Comics. Cover, introduction, text and compilation
copyright © 2008 DC Comics. All Rights Reserved.

Originally published in single magazine form in JUSTICE LEAGUE
OF AMERICA 0, 8-12 and JUSTICE SOCIETY OF AMERICA 5-6.
Copyright © 2006, 2007 DC Comics. All Rights Reserved. All characters, their distinctive likenesses and related elements featured
in this publication are trademarks of DC Comics. The stories,
characters and incidents featured in this publication are entirely
fictional. DC Comics does not read or accept unsolicited submissions
of ideas, stories or artwork.

DC Comics, 1700 Broadway, New York, NY 10019
A Warner Bros. Entertainment Company
Printed in Canada. First Printing.

HC: 978-1-4012-1652-8
SC: 978-1-4012-1869-0

For Noah Kuttler,
the best damn superfriend ever.

INTRODUCTION BY PATTON OSWALT

Comic books suck these days, and this book is a shining example why.

Used to be, you could buy a single issue, say, of THE FLASH or *X-Men* or even *Richie Rich* and be told a zippy story with a beginning, middle and end. It'd take you ten to fifteen minutes to read, cost you a nickel (I am 117 years old as I write this), and you'd also get to see a cartoon, a newsreel, and a short subject. And oh, the sour candy! Whatever happened to Ray Bowlly? The radishes are dying in my victory garden!

Sorry, had to pop a glycerin pill. I'm all better now.

Brad Meltzer threw a flaming monkey wrench into the machinery when he wrote the IDENTITY CRISIS storyline for DC Comics. It brought darkness (tinged with hope), humanity (touched by the infinite), and a jarring, fast-cutting-between-storylines immediacy to the DC Universe, and especially to the JLA.

And now they've let Brad have the JLA all by himself. Yet another incarnation. A new roster. The Justice League is a sports dynasty, an orchestra, a theater company and a police precinct all in one. Members come and go, lineups change, but the idea goes on. And on.

And *this* collection, "THE LIGHTNING SAGA," is a perfect example of why comics suck.

Not comic books in general, and certainly not the multilayered, involved-but-rewarding story that gets told here. No, this one's a home run.

It's the *single issues* that are driving me crazy these days.

Like 100 BULLETS and Y: THE LAST MAN and PLANETARY and so many others (and, now that I think of it, TV shows like *The Wire* and *Deadwood* and *Friday Night Lights*), these are stories that are much more satisfying when gulped down in big, trade paperback-sized bites (or complete seasons on DVD).

Writers like Brad and Geoff Johns, who have massive, epic visions for their stories (and for the epic characters that crash-bang through them) make for frustrating, confusing single issues. Is it any wonder that most of Brian Michael Bendis's and Ed Brubaker's comics have "...the story thus far" blurbs at the beginning?

We're hurtling away, faster and faster, from the days of "Here's a new costumed villain with a gimmick, and the hero is down for the count mid-story and then finds a way to defeat said villain's gimmick" issues.

Not that Brad can't write a terrific, stand-alone story – as "WALLS" will attest to. Oh man, there's a moment of revelation that will, literally, make you flip...something.

Plus, you've got issue #0 included here, where you get to see Superman, Batman and Wonder Woman bicker and argue over who should and shouldn't be in the League. How many times will the world have been saved because Kal-El refused to be intimidated by Bruce's dismissive glower? And there's yet another terrific one-shot, "MONITOR DUTY," where two other members of the League, members with some real history and maybe a little resentment towards the "Big Three" (as well as some deep-as-the-ocean and wide-as-the-galaxy perspective) watch the new lineup, with humor and hope.

There's so much I don't want to tell you about this book. It's a grand story arc, stuffed to bursting with "wasn't it cool" scenes. Wasn't it cool when the JLA and JSA were playing capture the flag? How about when Meltzer reveals, mid-story, three major (and I mean serious) supervillains, and then has them *fade into the background to plot something even more evil and sinister for a later date*? And, I mean, on top of the JLA/JSA pairing, there's The Legion of Super-Heroes?

For me, having toured rock clubs with various incarnations of a loose-knit "league" of comedians these past three years, one element really hit home in these books. And that's how a team, no matter how well it works together, is still a collection of personalities, and how sometimes the biggest threat to a team's strength is the day-to-day intimate, mundane hassles of its members. Meltzer and Johns understand that, and then up the ante in this story. Not only do the League, Society and Legion have to contend with those pressures, but they've also got to deal with the massive, ongoing universal storm of fate and history, of things so much larger than any of them – even united as a team – can handle. But listen carefully for something Batman says, almost as an aside to himself, after the story's climax. It's precise and quiet, and hums under the colorful, action-packed surface of this story. And that's the awful realization that there's stinging, lonely heartbreak, even in the souls of heroes, when history is through with them.

That idea stayed with me the strongest after I finished this story. It hit harder than a Kryptonian punch, cut me to my truth better than any Themysciran lasso, and made the shadows darker than even a dark knight would want.

Thanks, Brad and Geoff. For making comics suck again.

-Patton Oswalt
October 2007

Patton Oswalt is an actor, writer, voiceover artist, and professional comedian who has garnered roles in many films, including *Magnolia* and *Ratatouille*, as well as appearing in the television series *The King of Queens*.

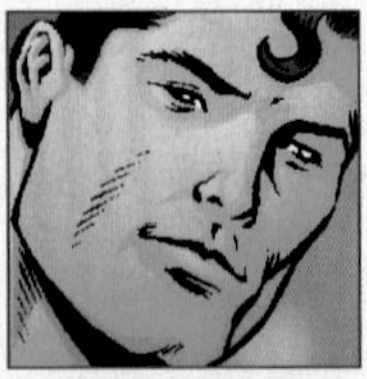
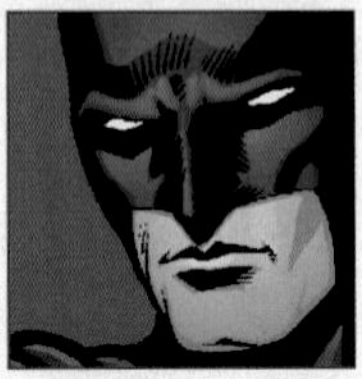
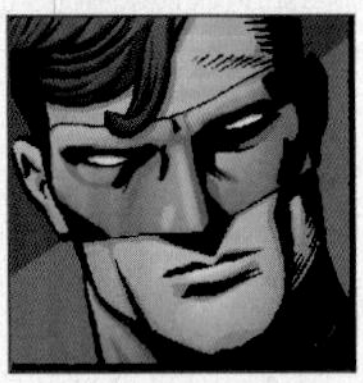
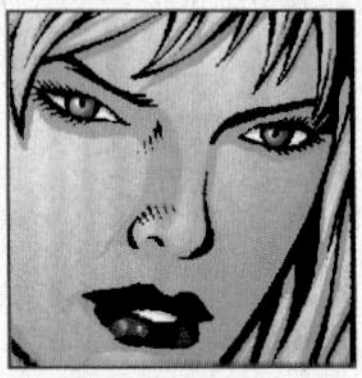
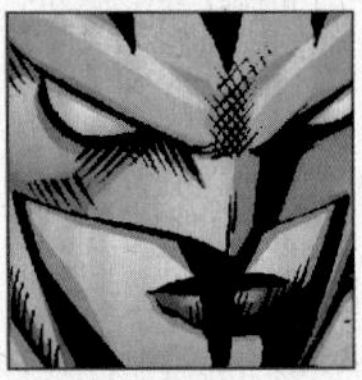
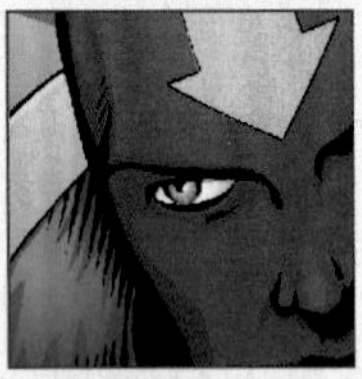
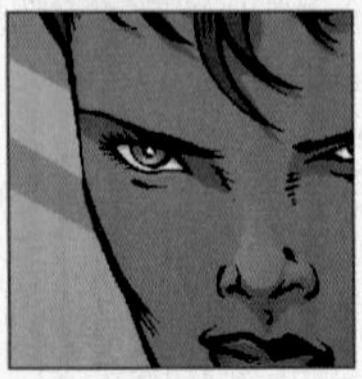
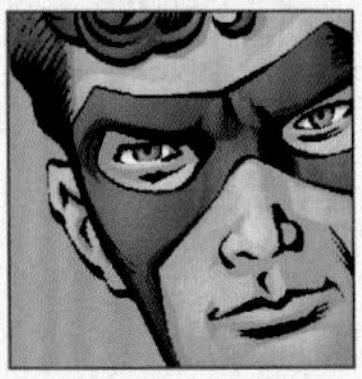

The world's greatest heroes gather together as the

JUSTICE LEAGUE of AMERICA

The world's first super-team trains the heroes of tomorrow as the

JUSTICE SOCIETY of AMERICA

After a bitter falling out, Batman, Superman and Wonder Woman discovered they could no longer trust each other, and the Justice League of America was dissolved.

But time heals all wounds, and the world needs a Justice League almost as much as its members need each other. With their friendships renewed, the "Big Three" came together once again to choose a new team.

But as the team selection was begun in secret in the Batcave, a new team consisting of Green Lantern, Black Canary, Red Arrow, Black Lightning, Hawkgirl, Vixen, Red Tornado and Geo-Force came together on their own. The League is bigger than any three members.

After defeating Solomon Grundy, this newly formed Justice League of America subdued a villain named Trident — and discovered that he's actually named Val Armorr — a hero from the 31st century, and a member of the Legion of Super-Heroes known as Karate Kid.

Coincidentally, the League's sister team, the Justice Society of America, has a new member — Starman — who also claims to be a hero from the 31st century. The Society was disinclined to believe him at first, as they discovered him living in and fighting crime out of a mental hospital.

But with the sudden appearance of Karate Kid, could Starman have been telling the truth?

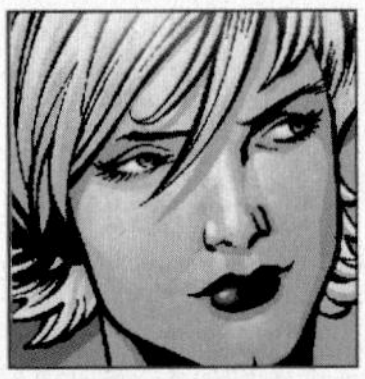
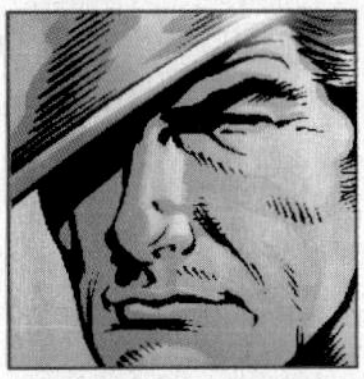
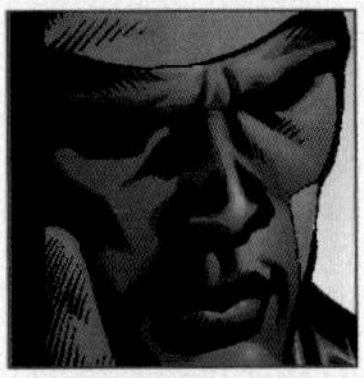
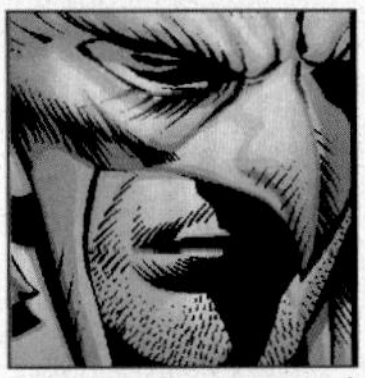
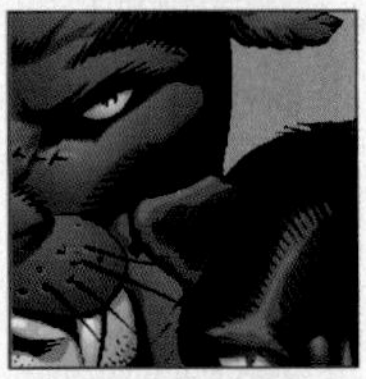
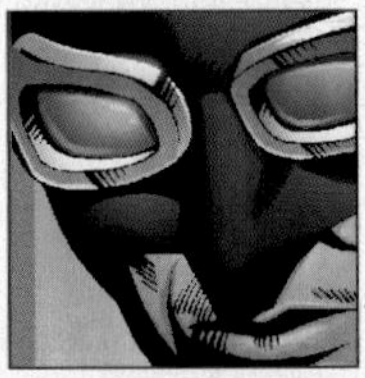
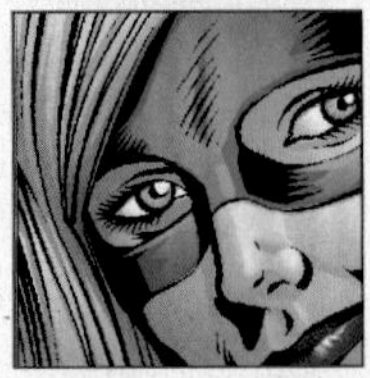
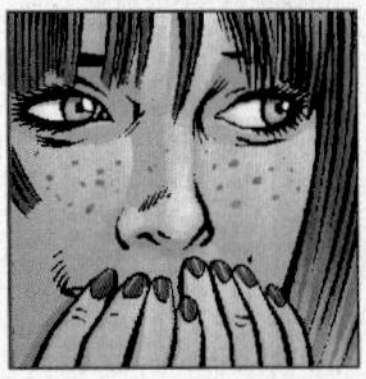

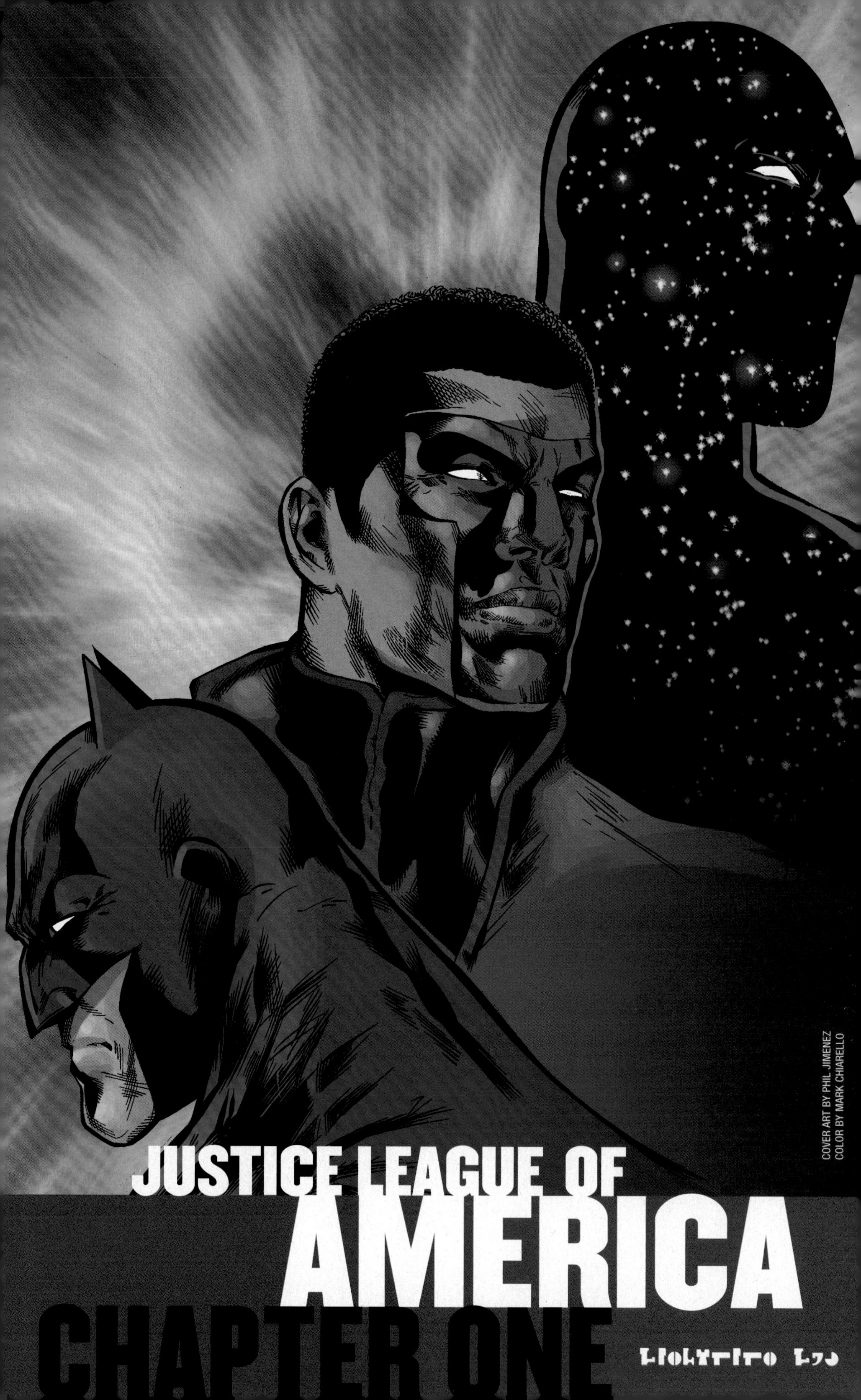
JUSTICE LEAGUE OF
AMERICA
CHAPTER ONE
COVER ART BY PHIL JIMENEZ
COLOR BY MARK CHIARELLO

"Only way to pull it off...

...is by splitting into teams."

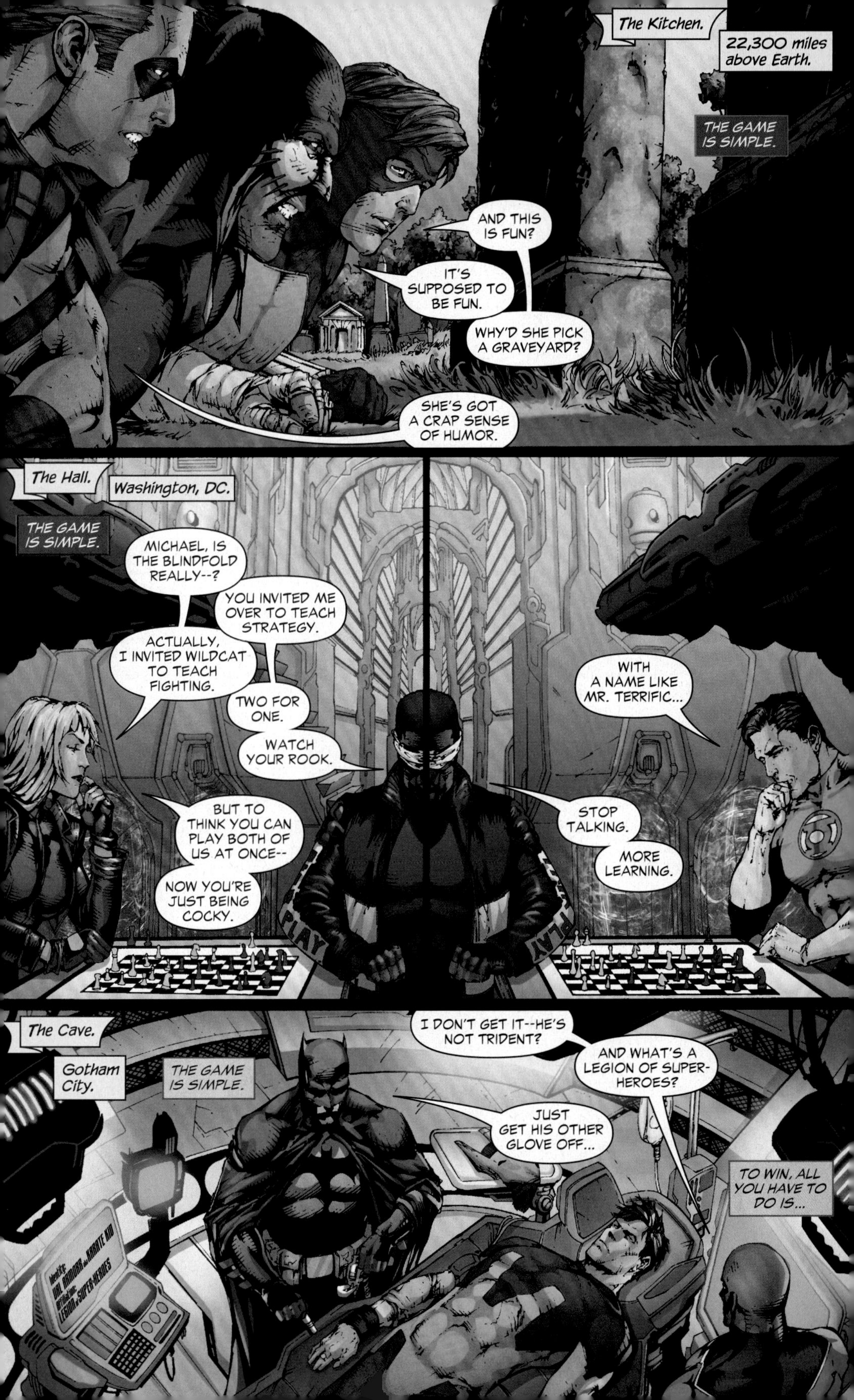

The Kitchen.
22,300 miles above Earth.
THE GAME IS SIMPLE.
AND THIS IS FUN?
IT'S SUPPOSED TO BE FUN.
WHY'D SHE PICK A GRAVEYARD?
SHE'S GOT A CRAP SENSE OF HUMOR.
The Hall.
Washington, DC.
THE GAME IS SIMPLE.
MICHAEL, IS THE BLINDFOLD REALLY--?
YOU INVITED ME OVER TO TEACH STRATEGY.
ACTUALLY, I INVITED WILDCAT TO TEACH FIGHTING.
TWO FOR ONE.
WATCH YOUR ROOK.
WITH A NAME LIKE MR. TERRIFIC...
BUT TO THINK YOU CAN PLAY BOTH OF US AT ONCE--
NOW YOU'RE JUST BEING COCKY.
STOP TALKING.
MORE LEARNING.
The Cave.
Gotham City.
THE GAME IS SIMPLE.
I DON'T GET IT--HE'S NOT TRIDENT?
AND WHAT'S A LEGION OF SUPER-HEROES?
JUST GET HIS OTHER GLOVE OFF...
Identity: VAL ARMORR aka KARATE KID
Affiliation: LEGION of SUPER-HEROES
TO WIN, ALL YOU HAVE TO DO IS...

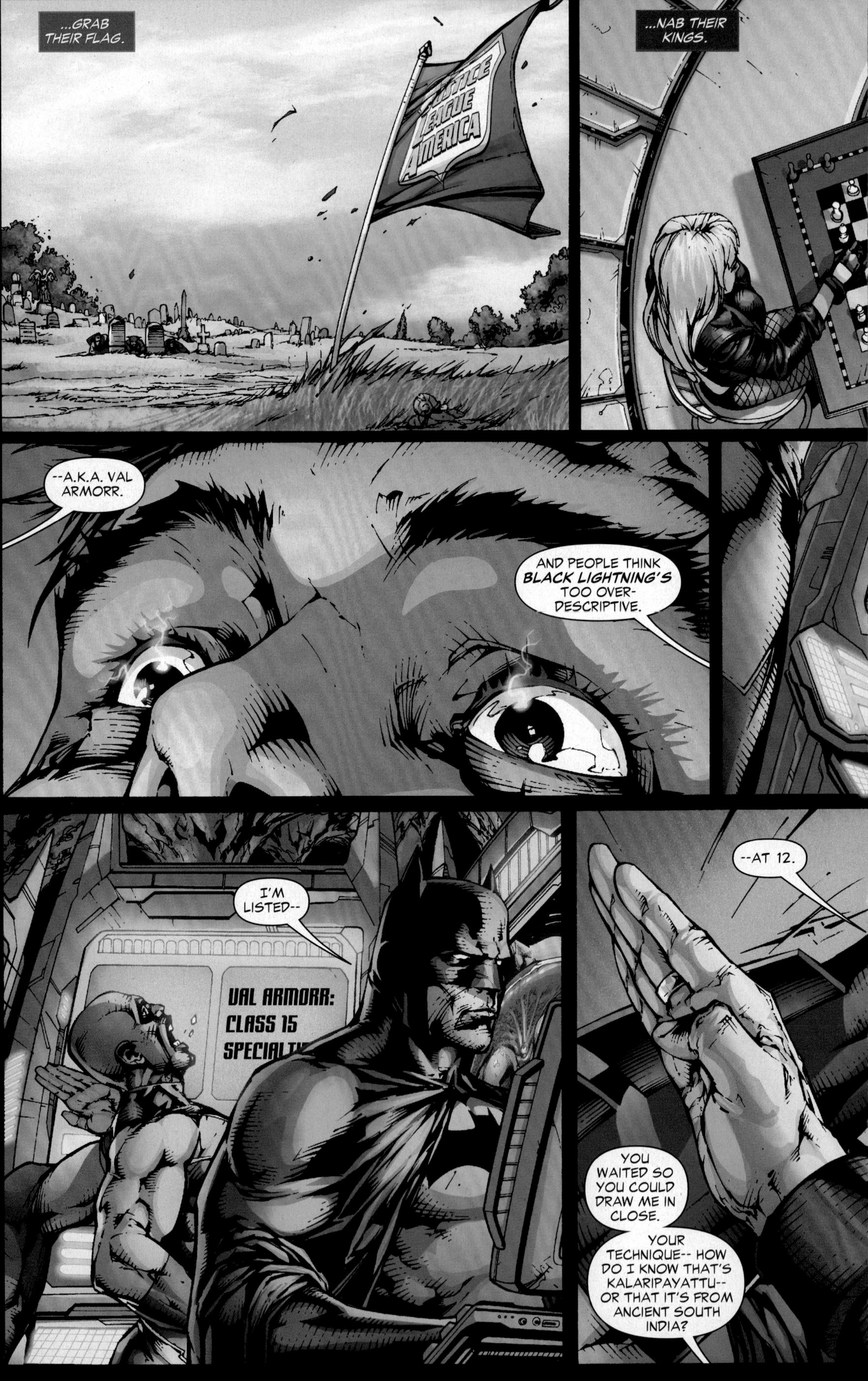
...GRAB THEIR FLAG.
JUSTICE LEAGUE AMERICA
...NAB THEIR KINGS.
--A.K.A. VAL ARMORR.
AND PEOPLE THINK BLACK LIGHTNING'S TOO OVER-DESCRIPTIVE.
I'M LISTED--
VAL ARMORR: CLASS 15
--AT 12.
YOU WAITED SO YOU COULD DRAW ME IN CLOSE.
YOUR TECHNIQUE-- HOW DO I KNOW THAT'S KALARIPAYATTU-- OR THAT IT'S FROM ANCIENT SOUTH INDIA?

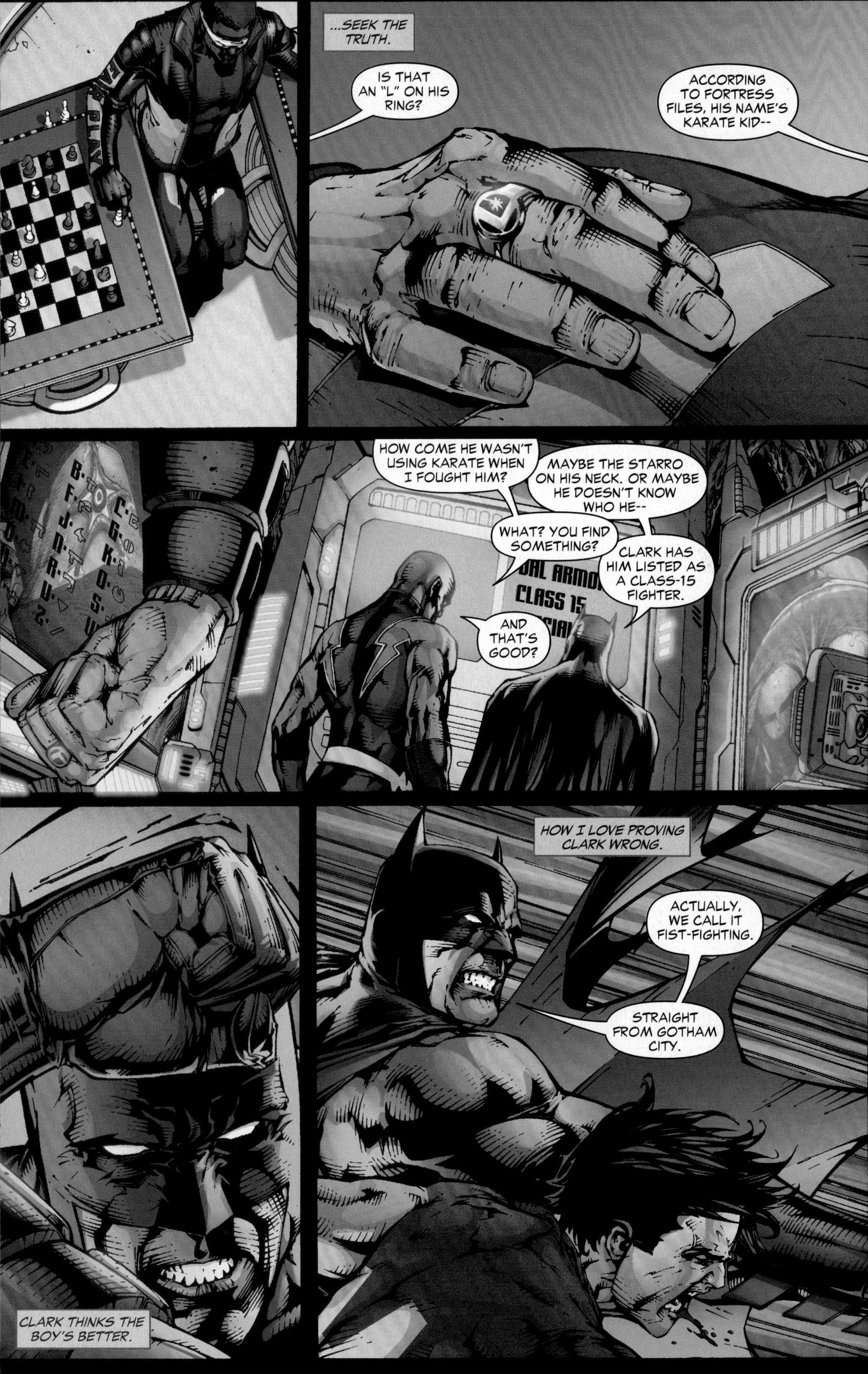
...SEEK THE TRUTH.
IS THAT AN "L" ON HIS RING?
ACCORDING TO FORTRESS FILES, HIS NAME'S KARATE KID--
HOW COME HE WASN'T USING KARATE WHEN I FOUGHT HIM?
MAYBE THE STARRO ON HIS NECK. OR MAYBE HE DOESN'T KNOW WHO HE--
WHAT? YOU FIND SOMETHING?
CLARK HAS HIM LISTED AS A CLASS-15 FIGHTER.
AND THAT'S GOOD?
CLARK THINKS THE BOY'S BETTER.
HOW I LOVE PROVING CLARK WRONG.
ACTUALLY, WE CALL IT FIST-FIGHTING.
STRAIGHT FROM GOTHAM CITY.

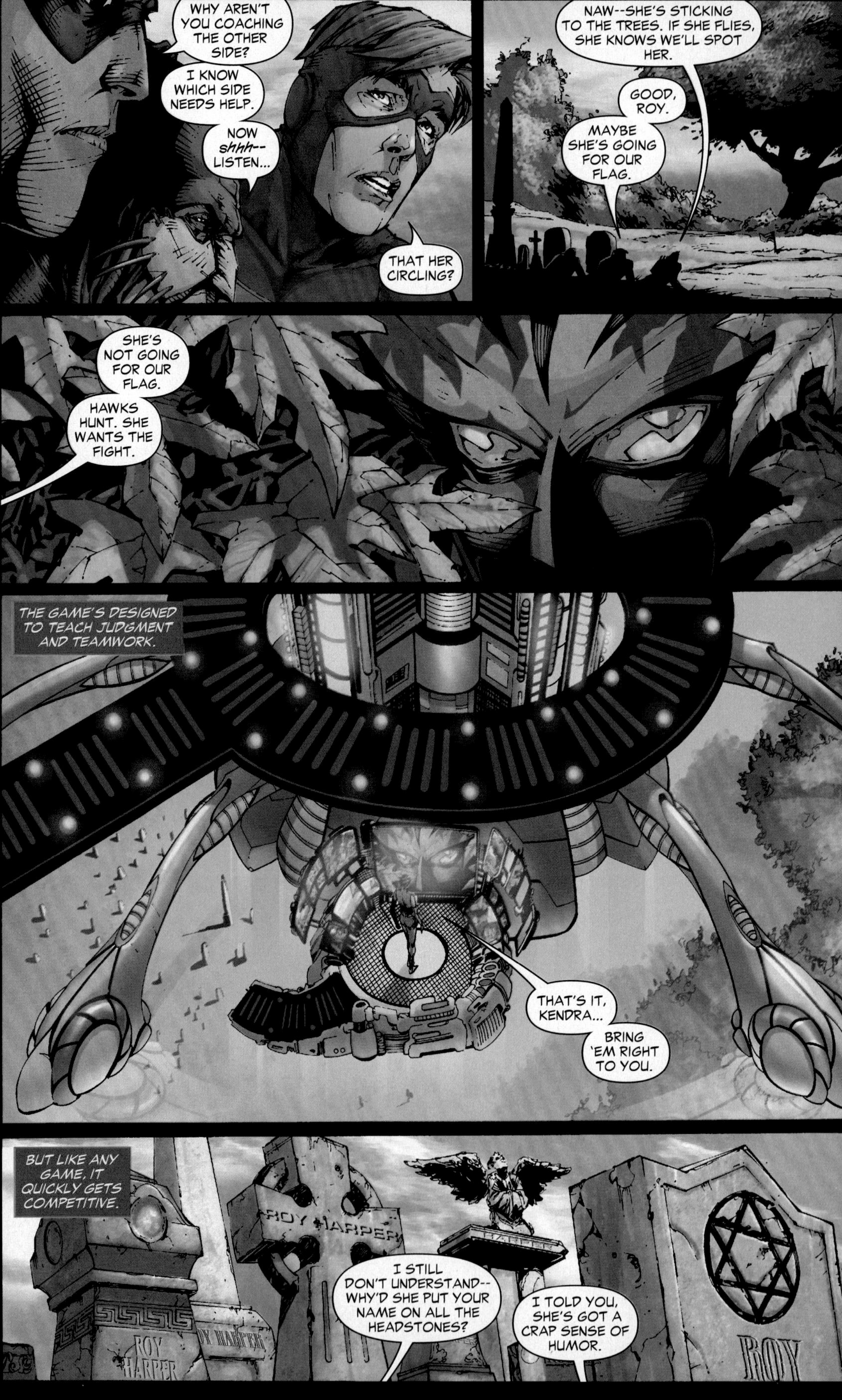
WHY AREN'T YOU COACHING THE OTHER SIDE?
I KNOW WHICH SIDE NEEDS HELP.
NOW shhh-- LISTEN...
THAT HER CIRCLING?
NAW--SHE'S STICKING TO THE TREES. IF SHE FLIES, SHE KNOWS WE'LL SPOT HER.
GOOD, ROY.
MAYBE SHE'S GOING FOR OUR FLAG.
SHE'S NOT GOING FOR OUR FLAG.
HAWKS HUNT. SHE WANTS THE FIGHT.
THE GAME'S DESIGNED TO TEACH JUDGMENT AND TEAMWORK.
THAT'S IT, KENDRA...
BRING 'EM RIGHT TO YOU.
BUT LIKE ANY GAME, IT QUICKLY GETS COMPETITIVE.
ROY HARPER
ROY HARPER
ROY HARPER
I STILL DON'T UNDERSTAND-- WHY'D SHE PUT YOUR NAME ON ALL THE HEADSTONES?
I TOLD YOU, SHE'S GOT A CRAP SENSE OF HUMOR.

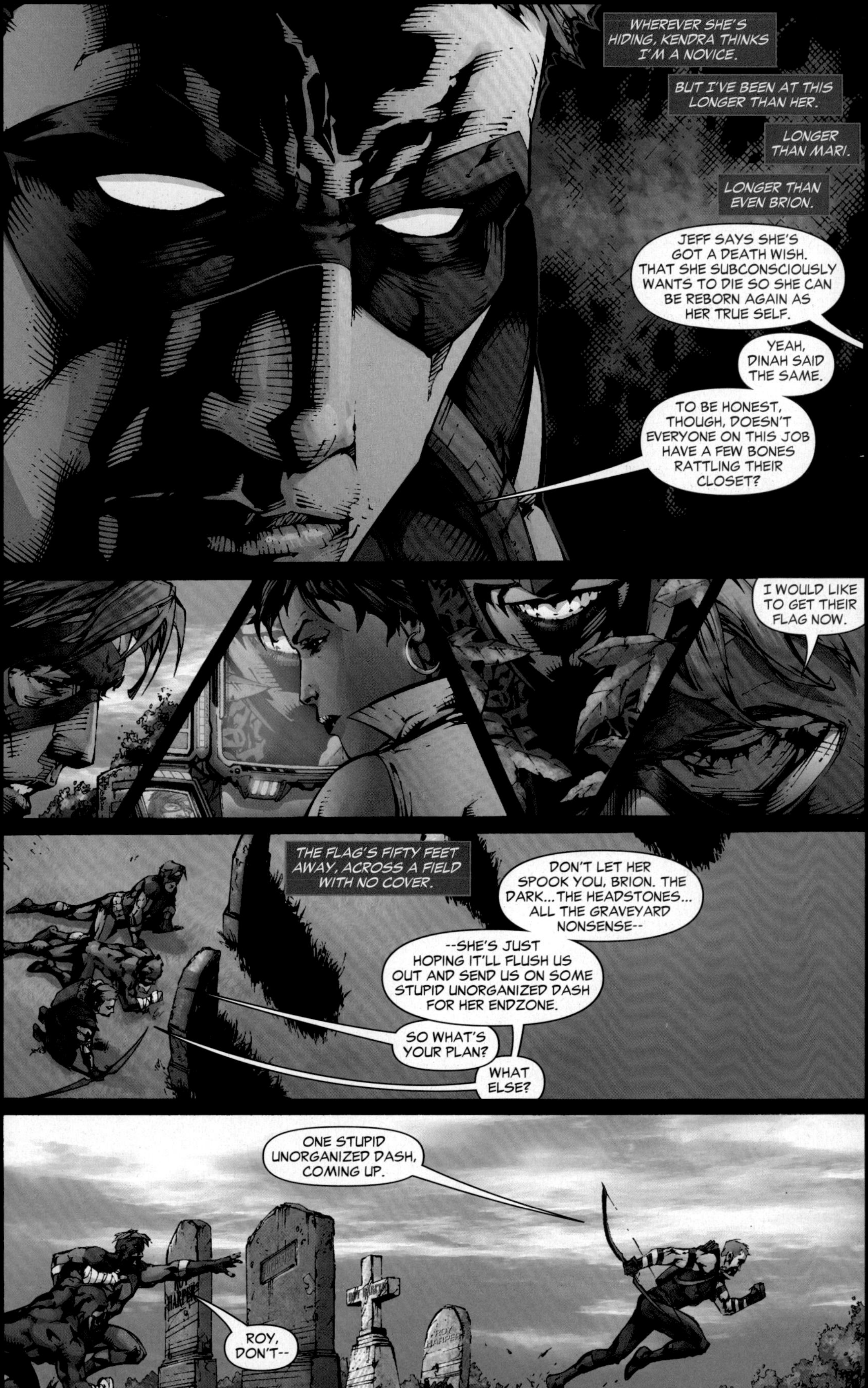

WHEREVER SHE'S HIDING, KENDRA THINKS I'M A NOVICE.
BUT I'VE BEEN AT THIS LONGER THAN HER.
LONGER THAN MARI.
LONGER THAN EVEN BRION.
JEFF SAYS SHE'S GOT A DEATH WISH. THAT SHE SUBCONSCIOUSLY WANTS TO DIE SO SHE CAN BE REBORN AGAIN AS HER TRUE SELF.
YEAH, DINAH SAID THE SAME.
TO BE HONEST, THOUGH, DOESN'T EVERYONE ON THIS JOB HAVE A FEW BONES RATTLING THEIR CLOSET?
I WOULD LIKE TO GET THEIR FLAG NOW.
THE FLAG'S FIFTY FEET AWAY, ACROSS A FIELD WITH NO COVER.
DON'T LET HER SPOOK YOU, BRION. THE DARK... THE HEADSTONES... ALL THE GRAVEYARD NONSENSE--
--SHE'S JUST HOPING IT'LL FLUSH US OUT AND SEND US ON SOME STUPID UNORGANIZED DASH FOR HER ENDZONE.
SO WHAT'S YOUR PLAN?
WHAT ELSE?
ONE STUPID UNORGANIZED DASH, COMING UP.
ROY, DON'T--

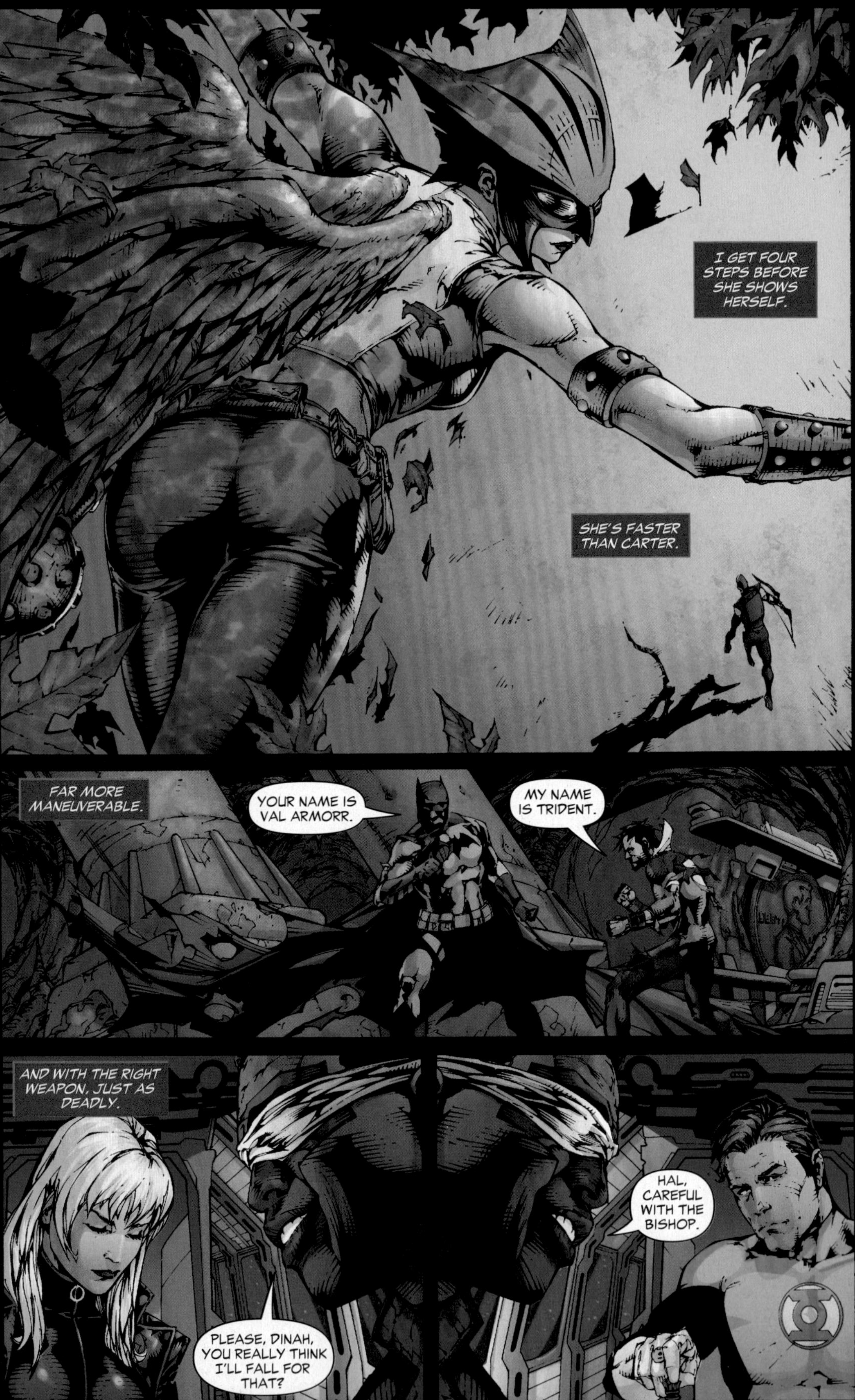
I GET FOUR STEPS BEFORE SHE SHOWS HERSELF.
SHE'S FASTER THAN CARTER.
FAR MORE MANEUVERABLE.
YOUR NAME IS VAL ARMORR.
MY NAME IS TRIDENT.
AND WITH THE RIGHT WEAPON, JUST AS DEADLY.
HAL, CAREFUL WITH THE BISHOP.
PLEASE, DINAH, YOU REALLY THINK I'LL FALL FOR THAT?

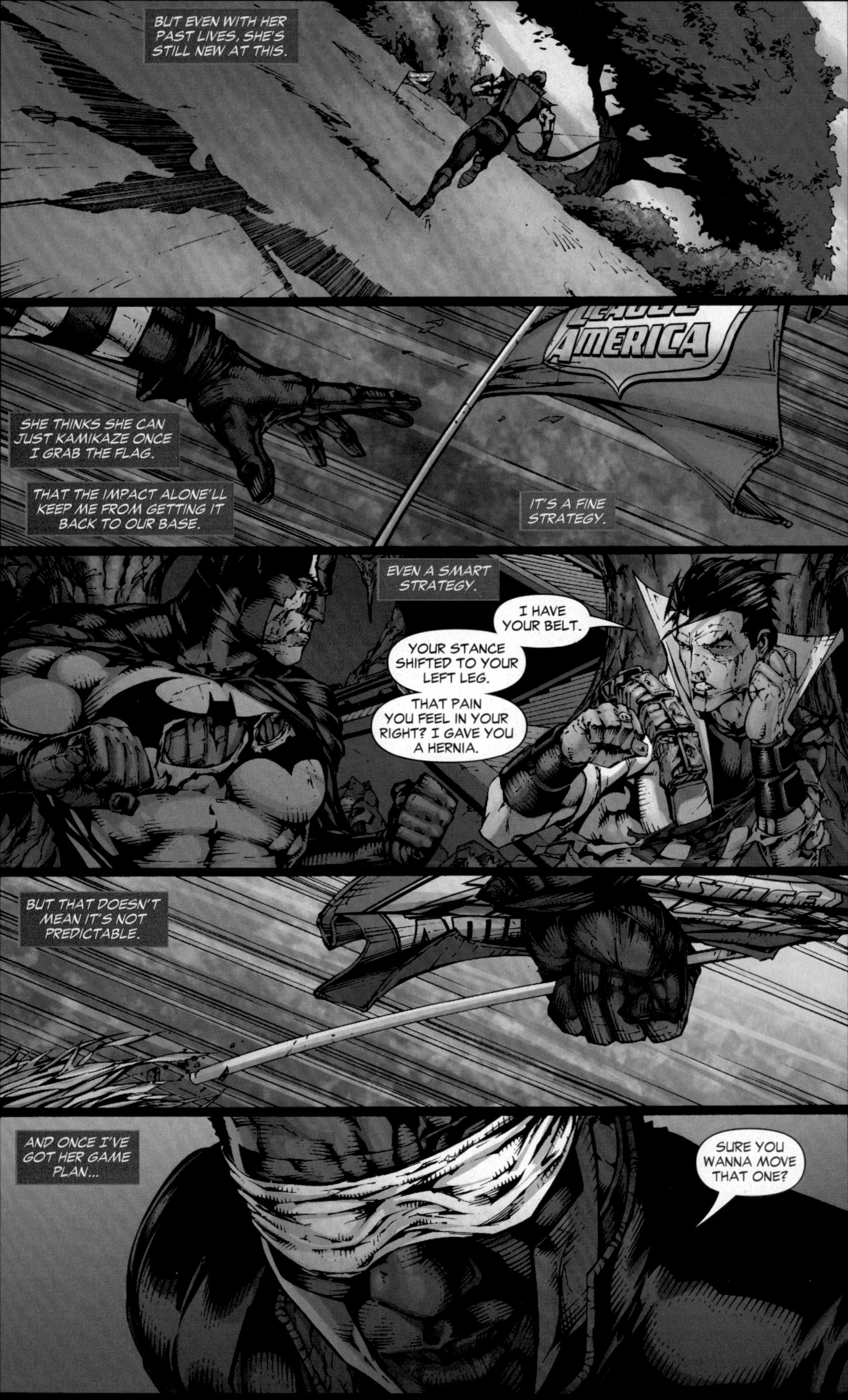

BUT EVEN WITH HER PAST LIVES, SHE'S STILL NEW AT THIS.
LEAGUE AMERICA
SHE THINKS SHE CAN JUST KAMIKAZE ONCE I GRAB THE FLAG.
THAT THE IMPACT ALONE'LL KEEP ME FROM GETTING IT BACK TO OUR BASE.
IT'S A FINE STRATEGY.
EVEN A SMART STRATEGY.
I HAVE YOUR BELT.
YOUR STANCE SHIFTED TO YOUR LEFT LEG.
THAT PAIN YOU FEEL IN YOUR RIGHT? I GAVE YOU A HERNIA.
BUT THAT DOESN'T MEAN IT'S NOT PREDICTABLE.
AND ONCE I'VE GOT HER GAME PLAN...
SURE YOU WANNA MOVE THAT ONE?

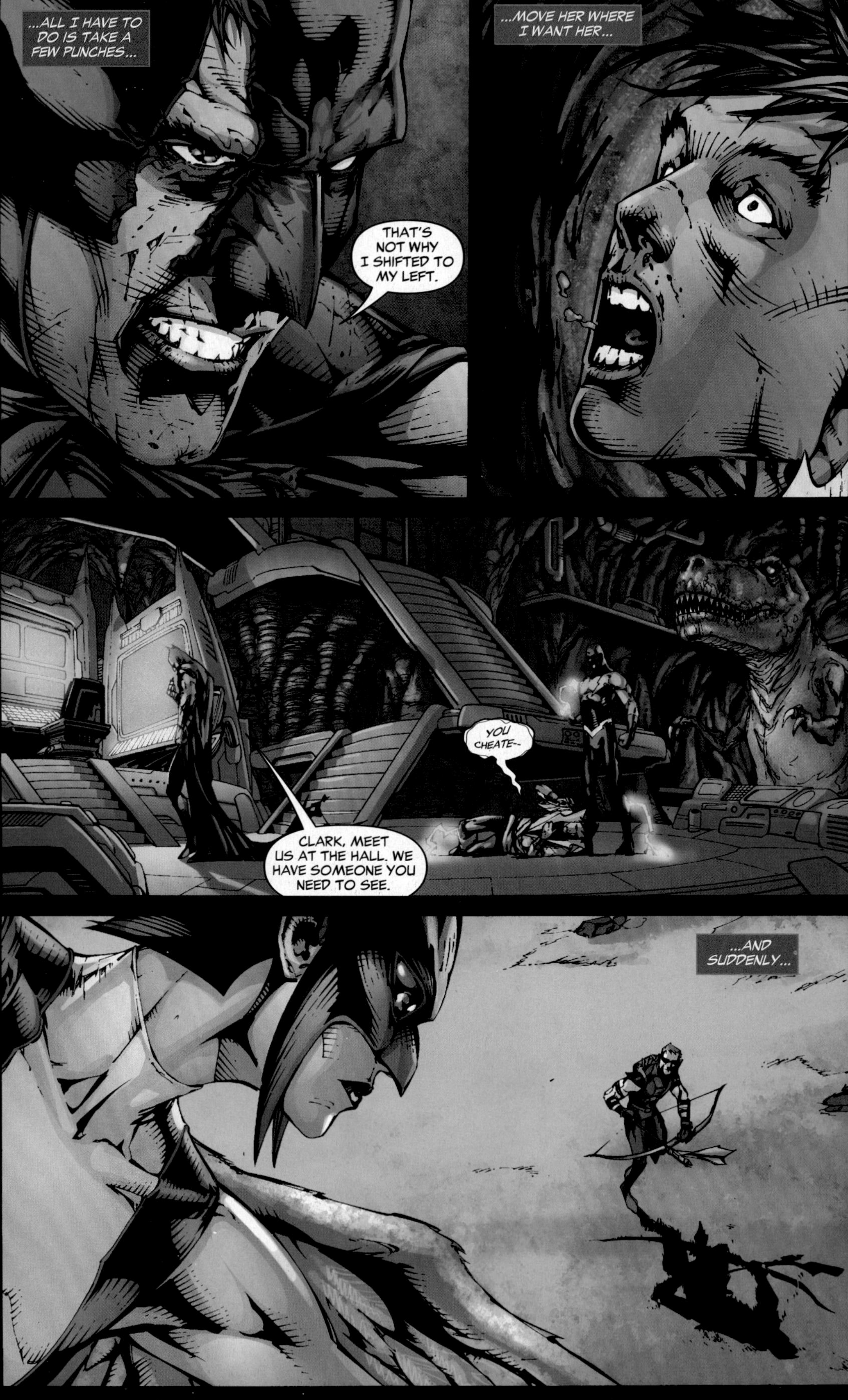
...ALL I HAVE TO DO IS TAKE A FEW PUNCHES...
THAT'S NOT WHY I SHIFTED TO MY LEFT.
...MOVE HER WHERE I WANT HER...
YOU CHEATE--
CLARK, MEET US AT THE HALL. WE HAVE SOMEONE YOU NEED TO SEE.
...AND SUDDENLY...

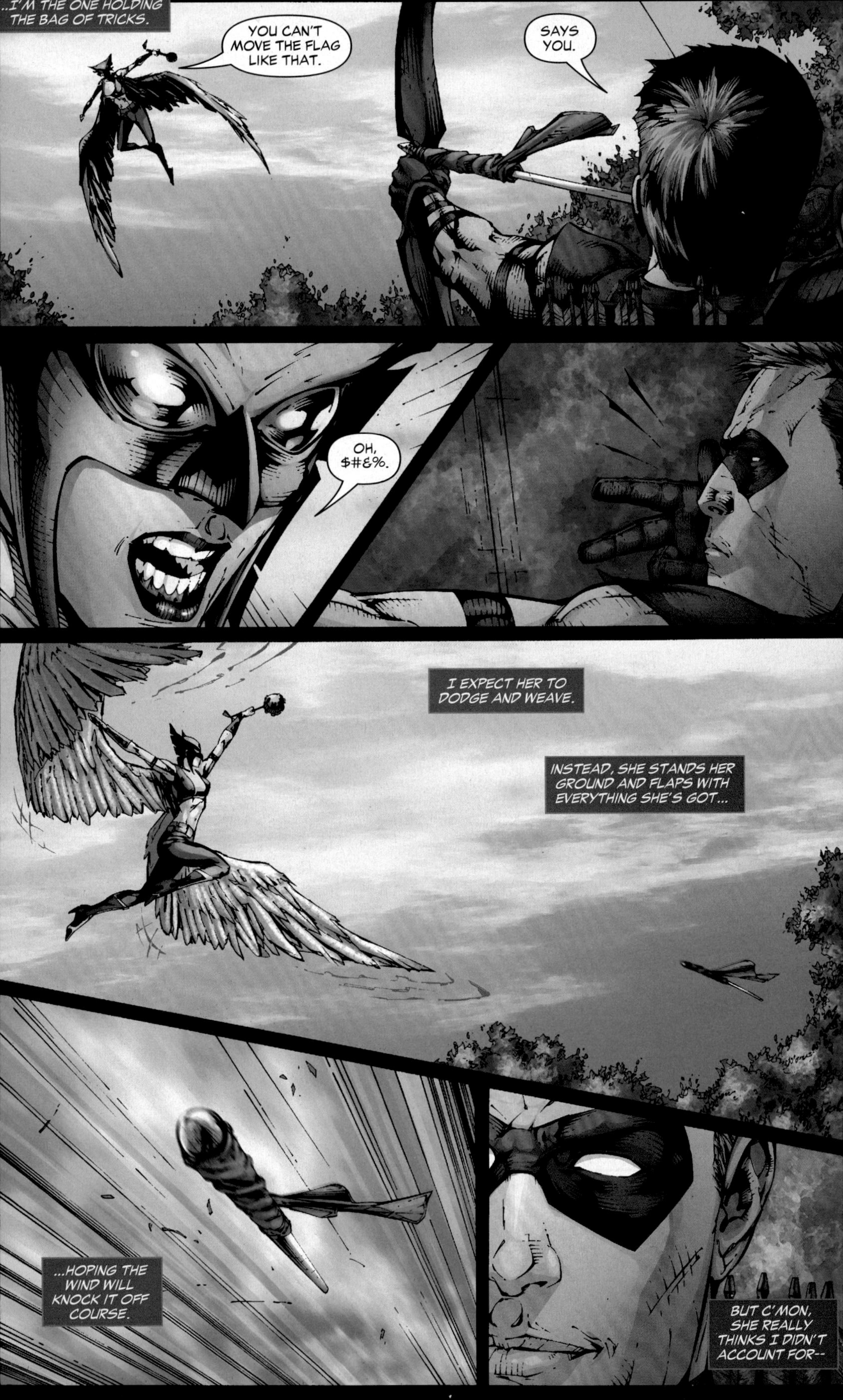
...I'M THE ONE HOLDING THE BAG OF TRICKS.
YOU CAN'T MOVE THE FLAG LIKE THAT.
SAYS YOU.
OH, $#&%.
I EXPECT HER TO DODGE AND WEAVE.
INSTEAD, SHE STANDS HER GROUND AND FLAPS WITH EVERYTHING SHE'S GOT...
...HOPING THE WIND WILL KNOCK IT OFF COURSE.
BUT C'MON, SHE REALLY THINKS I DIDN'T ACCOUNT FOR--

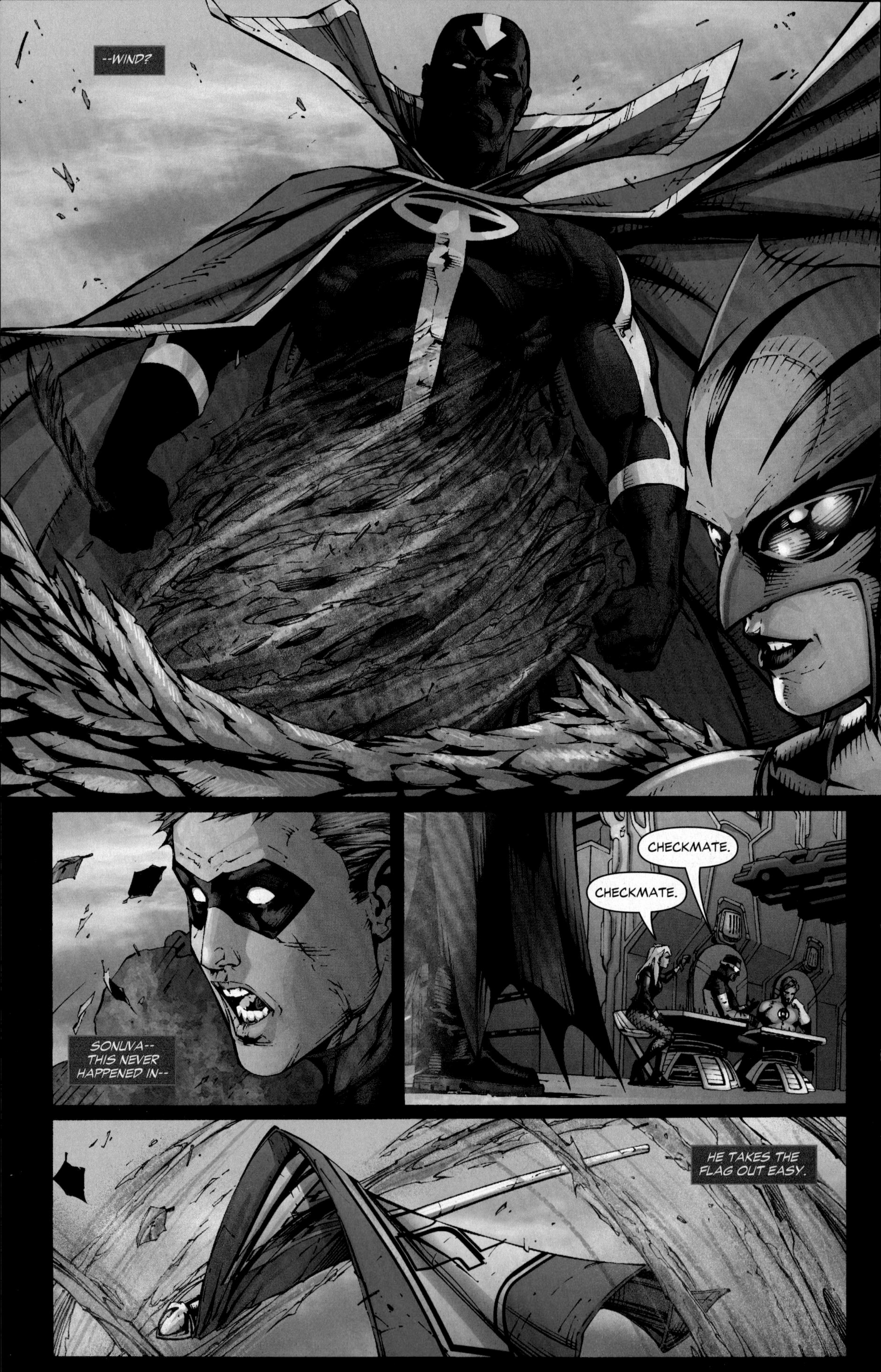

--WIND?
SONUVA-- THIS NEVER HAPPENED IN--
CHECKMATE.
CHECKMATE.
HE TAKES THE FLAG OUT EASY.

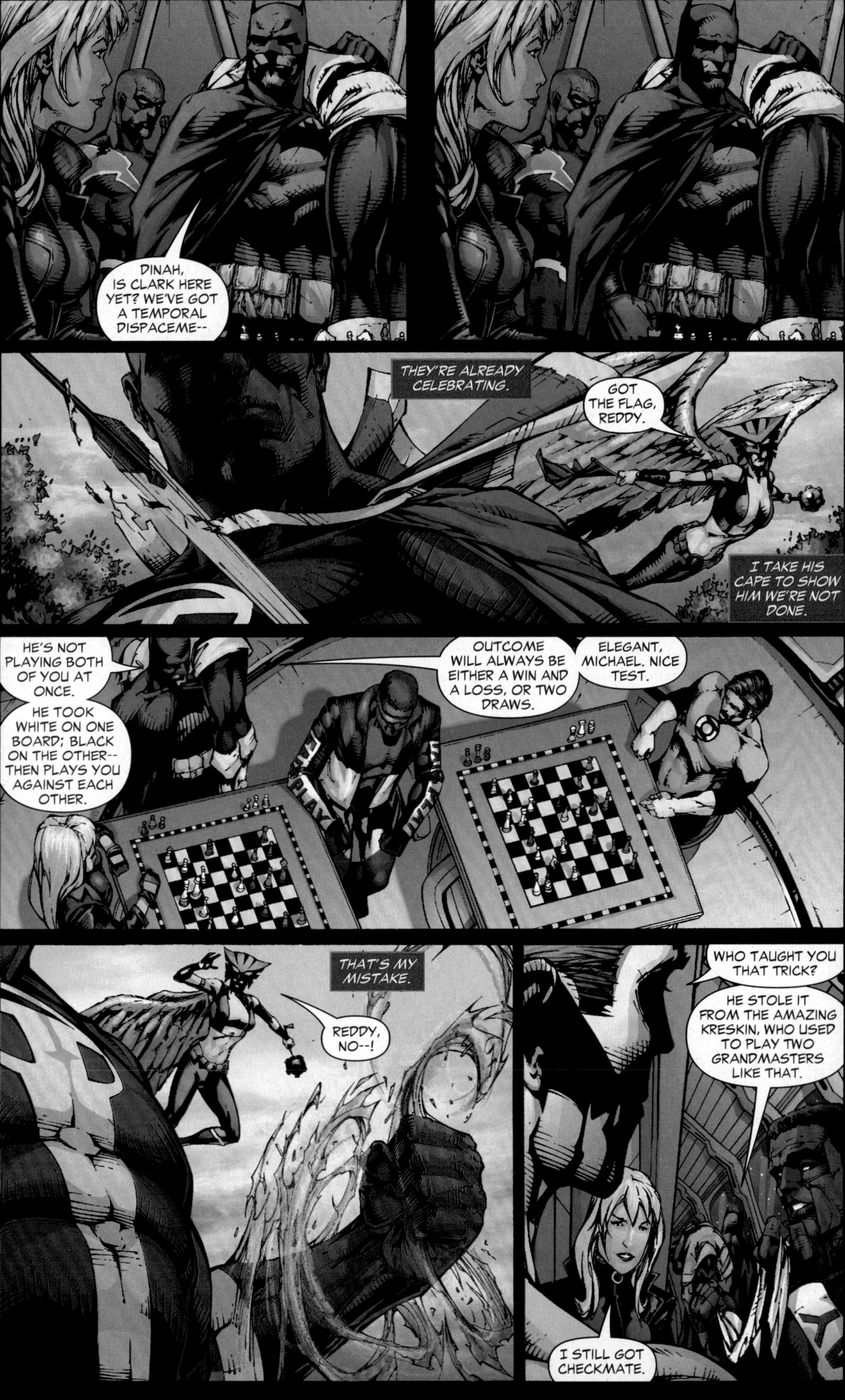

DINAH, IS CLARK HERE YET? WE'VE GOT A TEMPORAL DISPACEME--
THEY'RE ALREADY CELEBRATING.
GOT THE FLAG, REDDY.
I TAKE HIS CAPE TO SHOW HIM WE'RE NOT DONE.
HE'S NOT PLAYING BOTH OF YOU AT ONCE.
HE TOOK WHITE ON ONE BOARD; BLACK ON THE OTHER-- THEN PLAYS YOU AGAINST EACH OTHER.
OUTCOME WILL ALWAYS BE EITHER A WIN AND A LOSS, OR TWO DRAWS.
ELEGANT, MICHAEL. NICE TEST.
THAT'S MY MISTAKE.
REDDY, NO--!
WHO TAUGHT YOU THAT TRICK?
HE STOLE IT FROM THE AMAZING KRESKIN, WHO USED TO PLAY TWO GRANDMASTERS LIKE THAT.
I STILL GOT CHECKMATE.

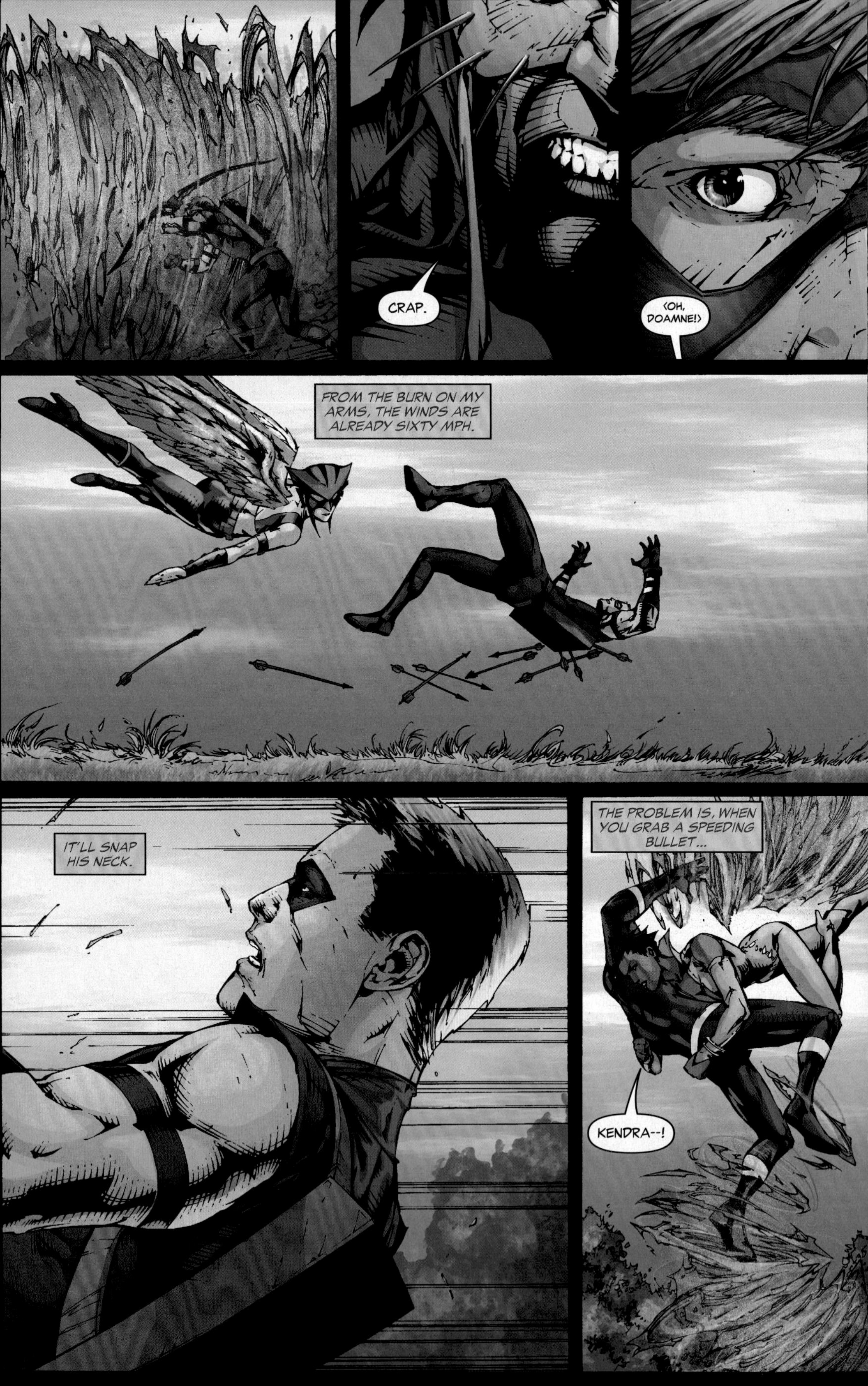
CRAP.
‹OH, DOAMNE!›
FROM THE BURN ON MY ARMS, THE WINDS ARE ALREADY SIXTY MPH.
IT'LL SNAP HIS NECK.
THE PROBLEM IS, WHEN YOU GRAB A SPEEDING BULLET...
KENDRA--!

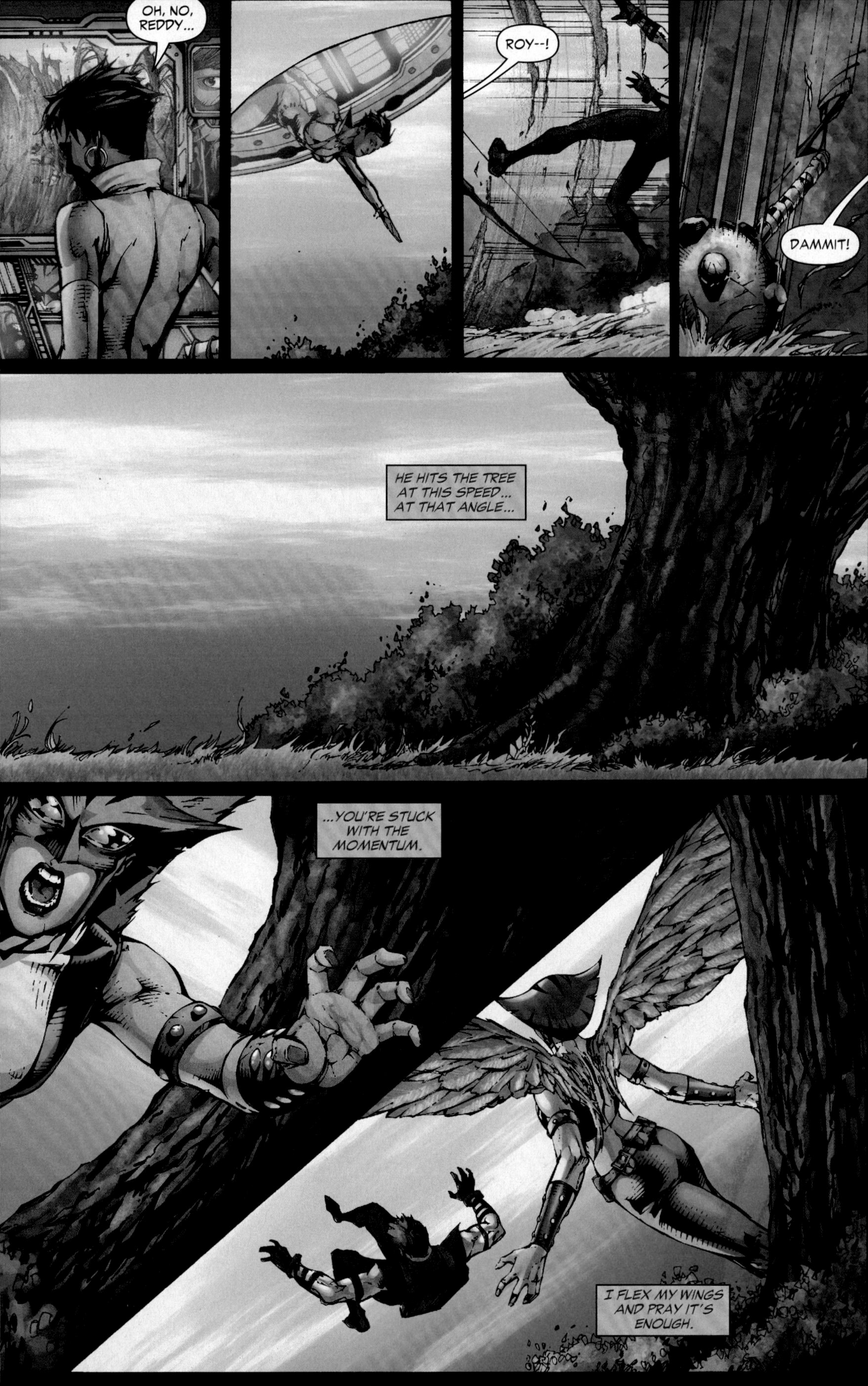
OH, NO, REDDY...
ROY--!
DAMMIT!
HE HITS THE TREE AT THIS SPEED... AT THAT ANGLE...
...YOU'RE STUCK WITH THE MOMENTUM.
I FLEX MY WINGS AND PRAY IT'S ENOUGH.

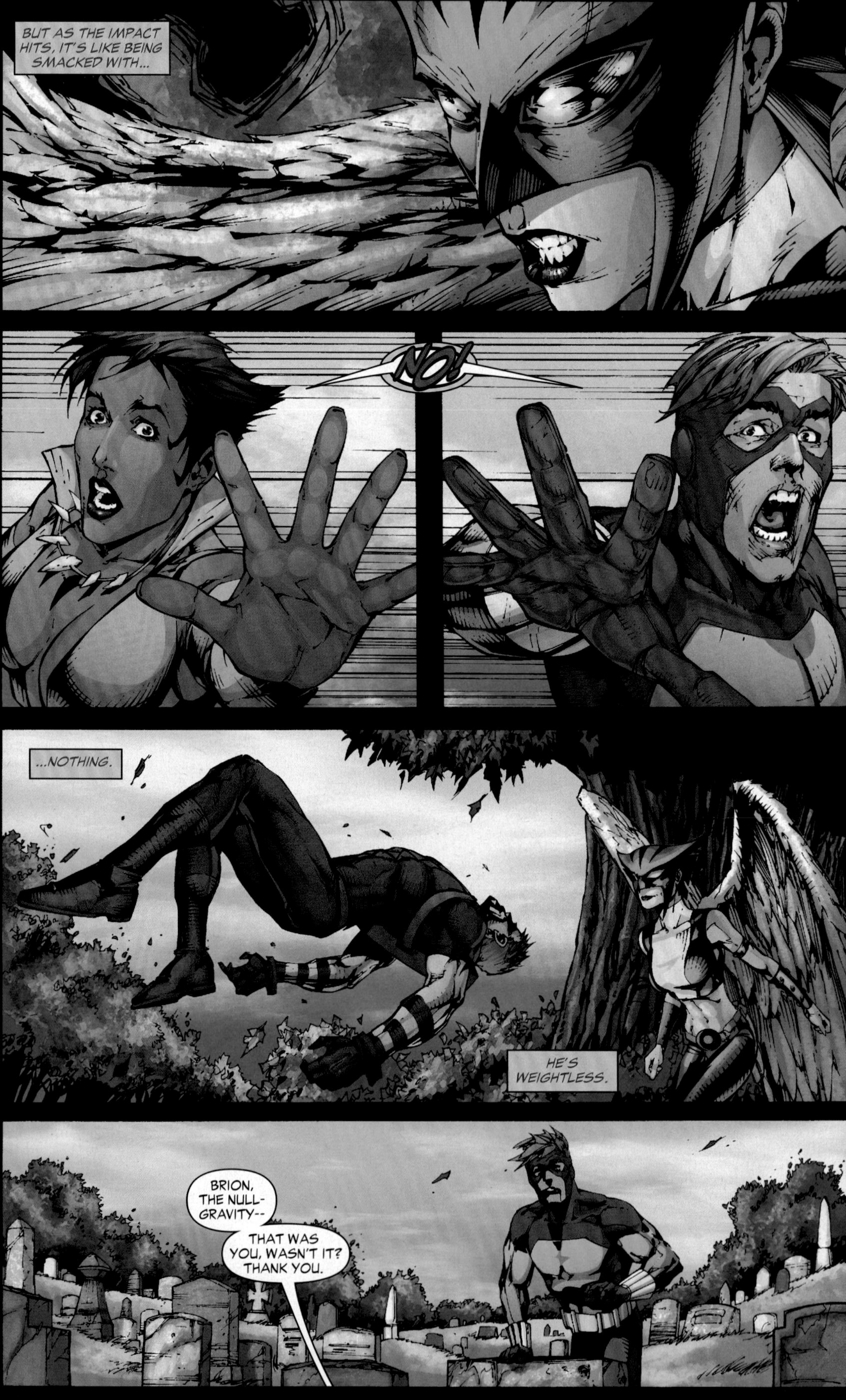
BUT AS THE IMPACT HITS, IT'S LIKE BEING SMACKED WITH...
NO!
...NOTHING.
HE'S WEIGHTLESS.
BRION, THE NULL-GRAVITY--
THAT WAS YOU, WASN'T IT? THANK YOU.

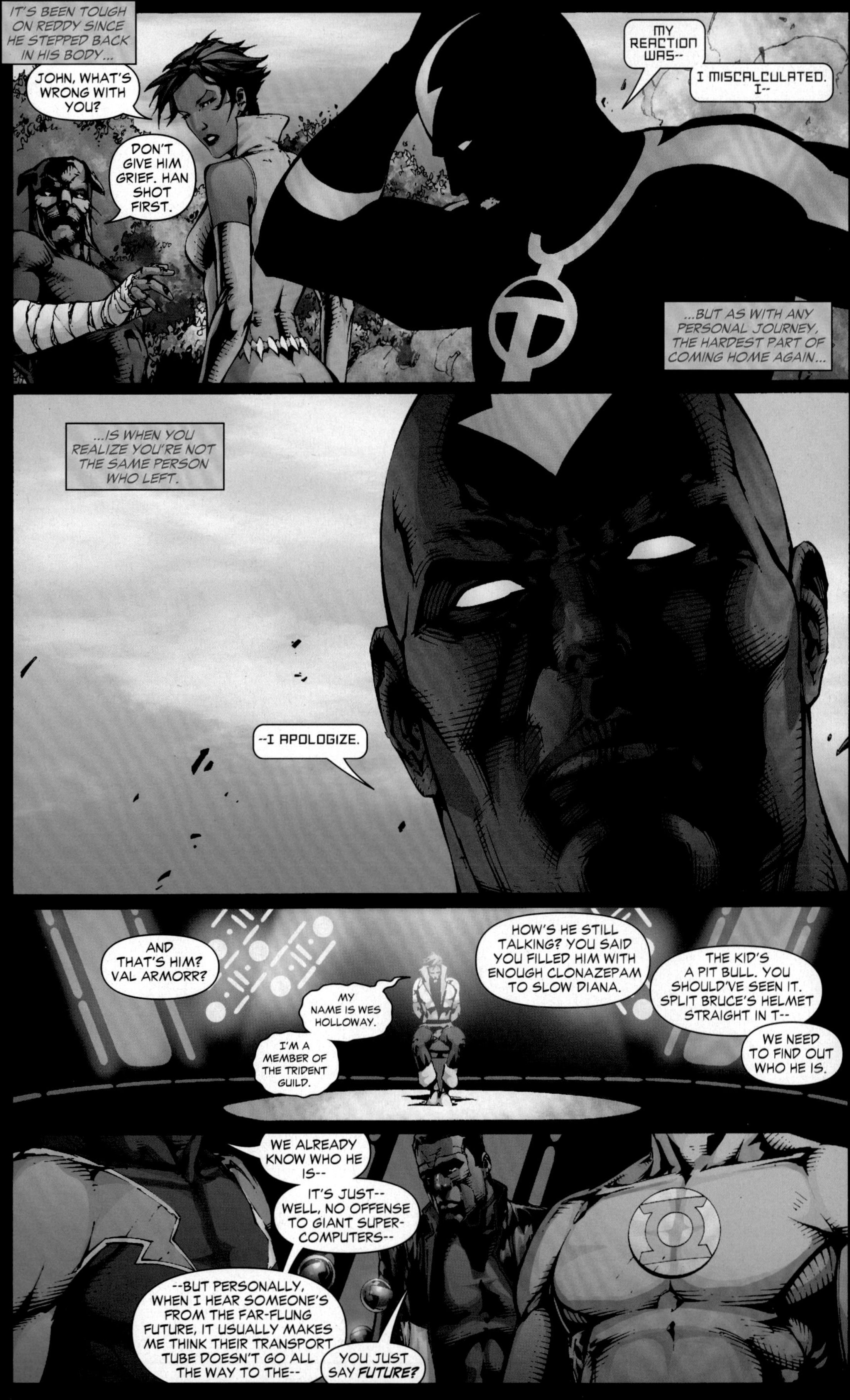
IT'S BEEN TOUGH ON REDDY SINCE HE STEPPED BACK IN HIS BODY...
JOHN, WHAT'S WRONG WITH YOU?
DON'T GIVE HIM GRIEF. HAN SHOT FIRST.
MY REACTION WAS--
I MISCALCULATED. I--
...BUT AS WITH ANY PERSONAL JOURNEY, THE HARDEST PART OF COMING HOME AGAIN...
...IS WHEN YOU REALIZE YOU'RE NOT THE SAME PERSON WHO LEFT.
--I APOLOGIZE.
AND THAT'S HIM? VAL ARMORR?
MY NAME IS WES HOLLOWAY.
I'M A MEMBER OF THE TRIDENT GUILD.
HOW'S HE STILL TALKING? YOU SAID YOU FILLED HIM WITH ENOUGH CLONAZEPAM TO SLOW DIANA.
THE KID'S A PIT BULL. YOU SHOULD'VE SEEN IT. SPLIT BRUCE'S HELMET STRAIGHT IN T--
WE NEED TO FIND OUT WHO HE IS.
WE ALREADY KNOW WHO HE IS--
IT'S JUST-- WELL, NO OFFENSE TO GIANT SUPER-COMPUTERS--
--BUT PERSONALLY, WHEN I HEAR SOMEONE'S FROM THE FAR-FLUNG FUTURE, IT USUALLY MAKES ME THINK THEIR TRANSPORT TUBE DOESN'T GO ALL THE WAY TO THE--
YOU JUST SAY *FUTURE?*

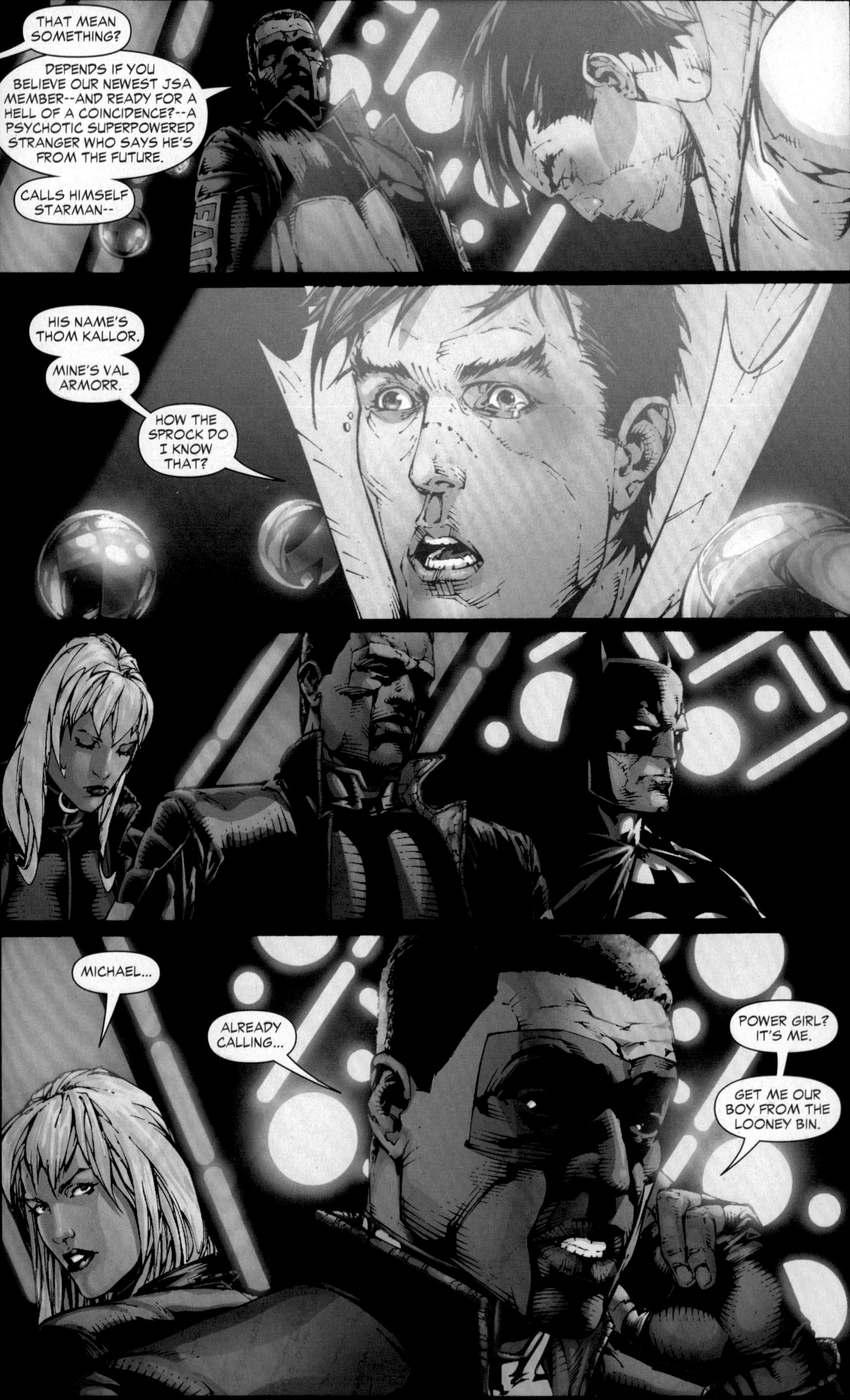

THAT MEAN SOMETHING?
DEPENDS IF YOU BELIEVE OUR NEWEST JSA MEMBER--AND READY FOR A HELL OF A COINCIDENCE?--A PSYCHOTIC SUPERPOWERED STRANGER WHO SAYS HE'S FROM THE FUTURE.
CALLS HIMSELF STARMAN--
HIS NAME'S THOM KALLOR.
MINE'S VAL ARMORR.
HOW THE SPROCK DO I KNOW THAT?
MICHAEL...
ALREADY CALLING...
POWER GIRL? IT'S ME.
GET ME OUR BOY FROM THE LOONEY BIN.

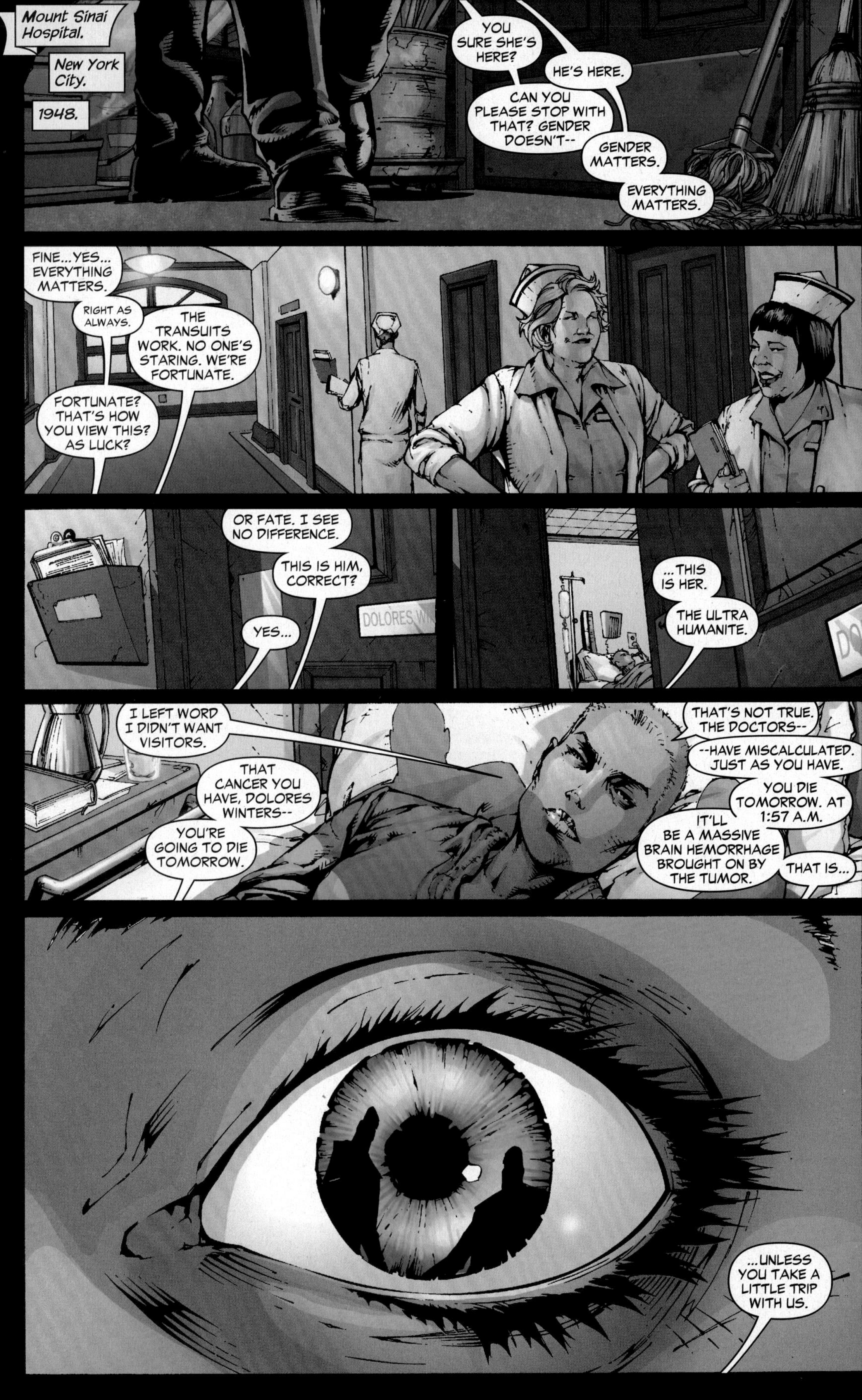

Mount Sinai Hospital.
New York City.
1948.
YOU SURE SHE'S HERE?
HE'S HERE.
CAN YOU PLEASE STOP WITH THAT? GENDER DOESN'T--
GENDER MATTERS.
EVERYTHING MATTERS.
FINE...YES... EVERYTHING MATTERS.
RIGHT AS ALWAYS.
THE TRANSUITS WORK. NO ONE'S STARING. WE'RE FORTUNATE.
FORTUNATE? THAT'S HOW YOU VIEW THIS? AS LUCK?
OR FATE. I SEE NO DIFFERENCE.
THIS IS HIM, CORRECT?
YES...
...THIS IS HER.
THE ULTRA HUMANITE.
I LEFT WORD I DIDN'T WANT VISITORS.
THAT CANCER YOU HAVE, DOLORES WINTERS--
YOU'RE GOING TO DIE TOMORROW.
THAT'S NOT TRUE. THE DOCTORS--
--HAVE MISCALCULATED. JUST AS YOU HAVE.
YOU DIE TOMORROW. AT 1:57 A.M.
IT'LL BE A MASSIVE BRAIN HEMORRHAGE BROUGHT ON BY THE TUMOR.
THAT IS...
...UNLESS YOU TAKE A LITTLE TRIP WITH US.

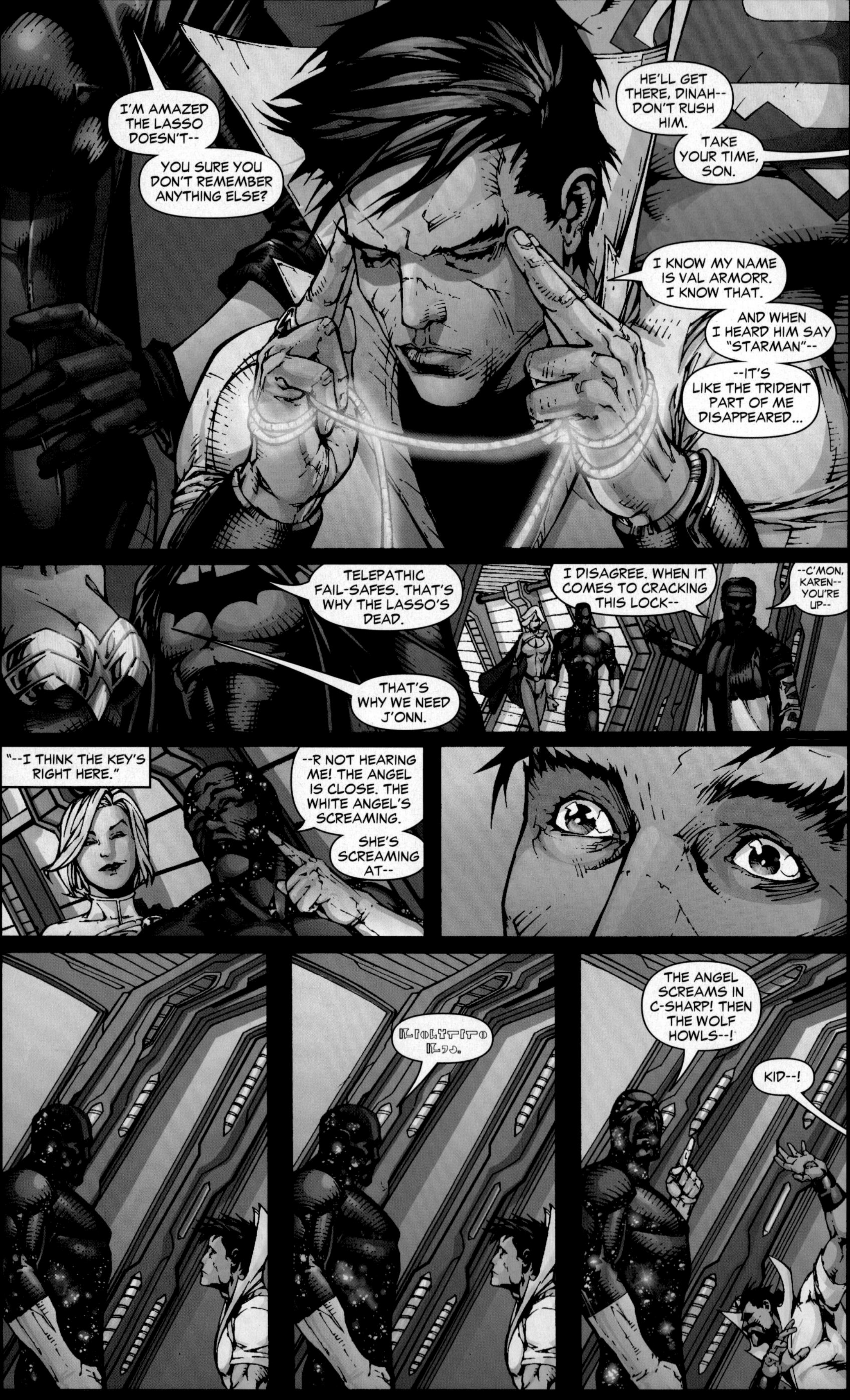
I'M AMAZED THE LASSO DOESN'T--
YOU SURE YOU DON'T REMEMBER ANYTHING ELSE?
HE'LL GET THERE, DINAH-- DON'T RUSH HIM.
TAKE YOUR TIME, SON.
I KNOW MY NAME IS VAL ARMORR. I KNOW THAT.
AND WHEN I HEARD HIM SAY "STARMAN"--
--IT'S LIKE THE TRIDENT PART OF ME DISAPPEARED...
TELEPATHIC FAIL-SAFES. THAT'S WHY THE LASSO'S DEAD.
THAT'S WHY WE NEED J'ONN.
I DISAGREE. WHEN IT COMES TO CRACKING THIS LOCK--
--C'MON, KAREN-- YOU'RE UP--
"--I THINK THE KEY'S RIGHT HERE."
--R NOT HEARING ME! THE ANGEL IS CLOSE. THE WHITE ANGEL'S SCREAMING.
SHE'S SCREAMING AT--
THE ANGEL SCREAMS IN C-SHARP! THEN THE WOLF HOWLS--!
KID--!

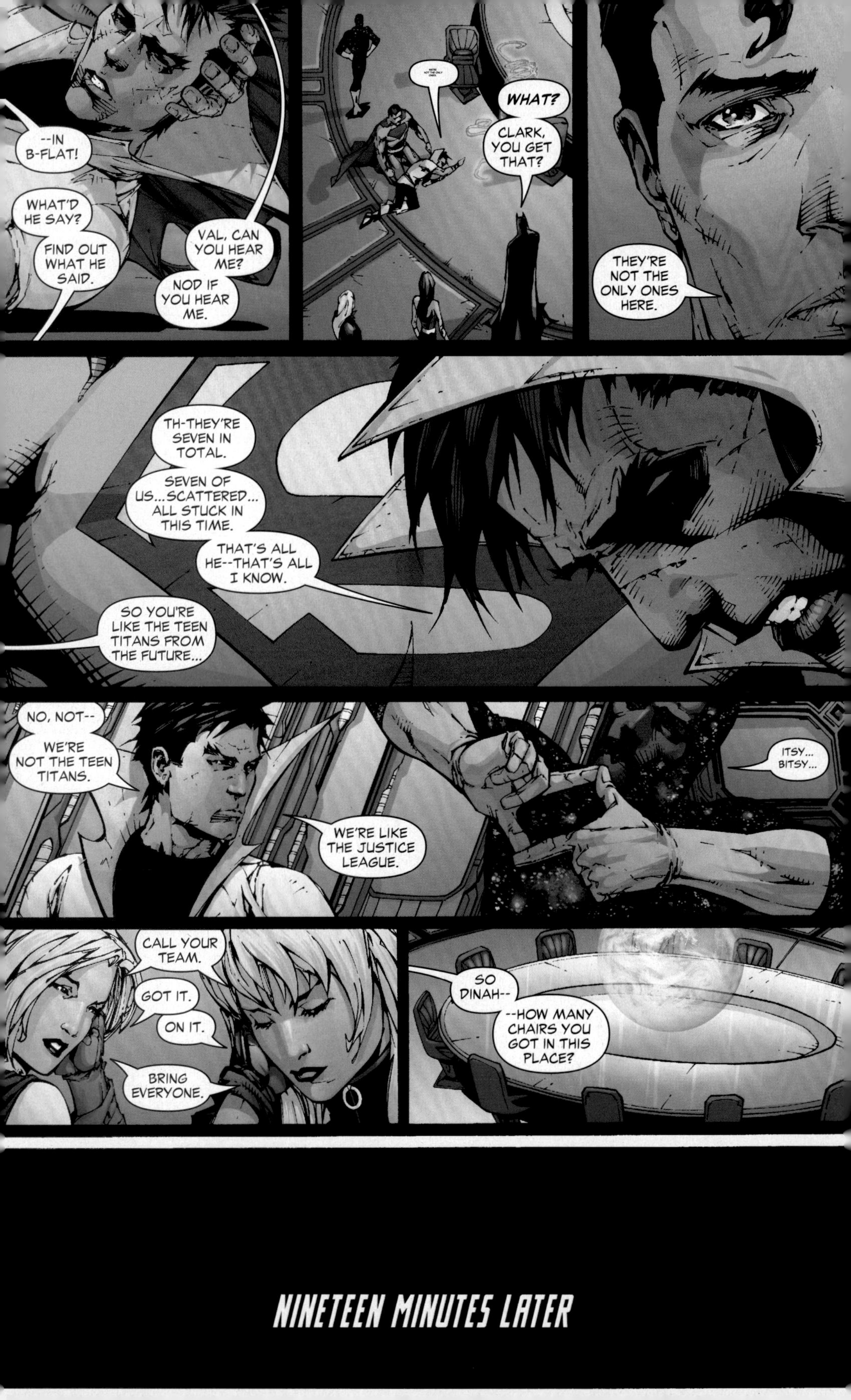
--IN B-FLAT!
WHAT'D HE SAY?
FIND OUT WHAT HE SAID.
VAL, CAN YOU HEAR ME?
NOD IF YOU HEAR ME.
WE'RE NOT THE ONLY ONES.
WHAT?
CLARK, YOU GET THAT?
THEY'RE NOT THE ONLY ONES HERE.
TH-THEY'RE SEVEN IN TOTAL.
SEVEN OF US...SCATTERED... ALL STUCK IN THIS TIME.
THAT'S ALL HE--THAT'S ALL I KNOW.
SO YOU'RE LIKE THE TEEN TITANS FROM THE FUTURE...
NO, NOT--
WE'RE NOT THE TEEN TITANS.
WE'RE LIKE THE JUSTICE LEAGUE.
ITSY... BITSY...
CALL YOUR TEAM.
GOT IT.
ON IT.
BRING EVERYONE.
SO DINAH--
--HOW MANY CHAIRS YOU GOT IN THIS PLACE?
NINETEEN MINUTES LATER

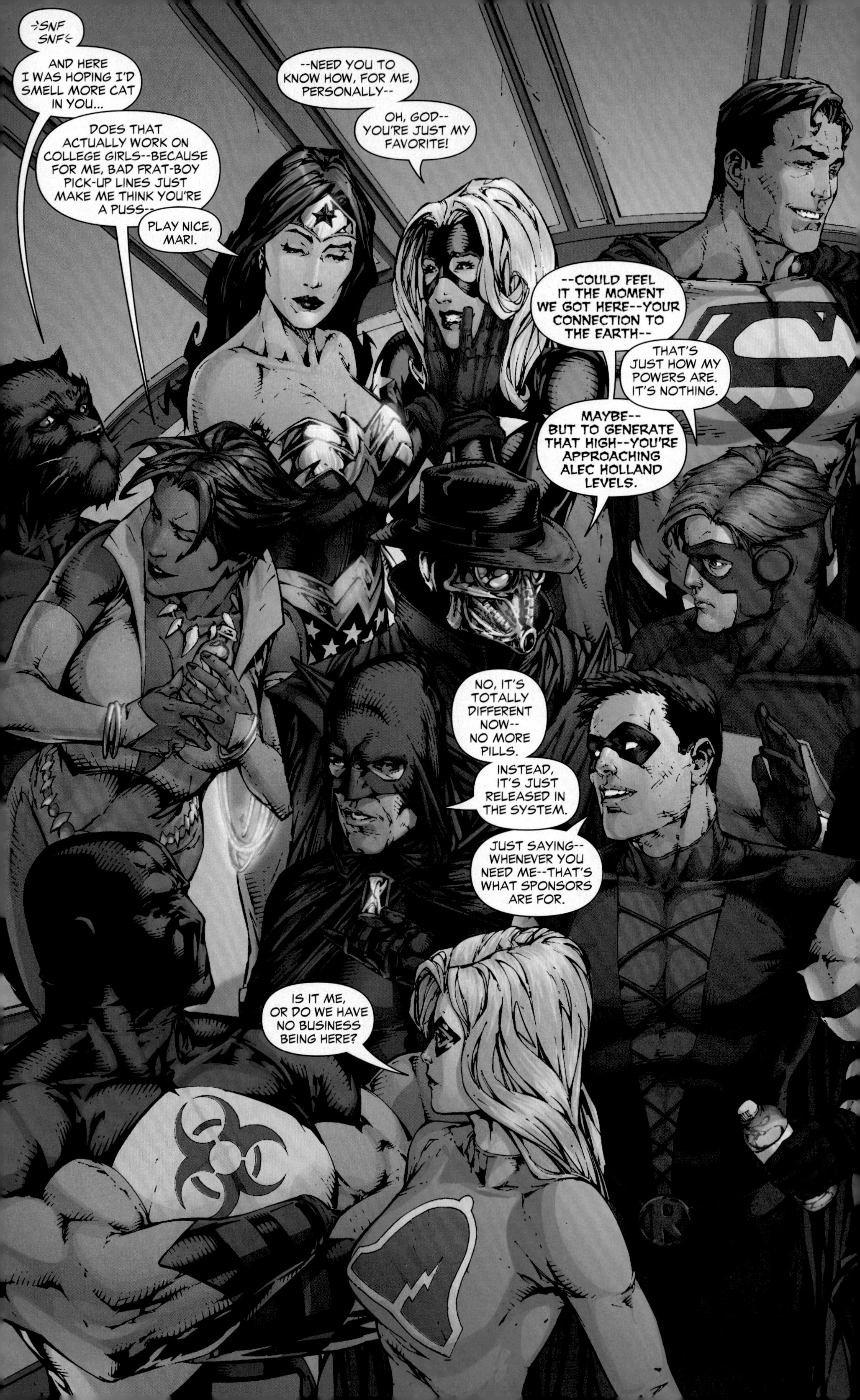

SNF SNF
AND HERE I WAS HOPING I'D SMELL MORE CAT IN YOU...
DOES THAT ACTUALLY WORK ON COLLEGE GIRLS--BECAUSE FOR ME, BAD FRAT-BOY PICK-UP LINES JUST MAKE ME THINK YOU'RE A PUSS--
PLAY NICE, MARI.
--NEED YOU TO KNOW HOW, FOR ME, PERSONALLY--
OH, GOD--YOU'RE JUST MY FAVORITE!
--COULD FEEL IT THE MOMENT WE GOT HERE--YOUR CONNECTION TO THE EARTH--
THAT'S JUST HOW MY POWERS ARE. IT'S NOTHING.
MAYBE--BUT TO GENERATE THAT HIGH--YOU'RE APPROACHING ALEC HOLLAND LEVELS.
NO, IT'S TOTALLY DIFFERENT NOW--NO MORE PILLS.
INSTEAD, IT'S JUST RELEASED IN THE SYSTEM.
JUST SAYING--WHENEVER YOU NEED ME--THAT'S WHAT SPONSORS ARE FOR.
IS IT ME, OR DO WE HAVE NO BUSINESS BEING HERE?

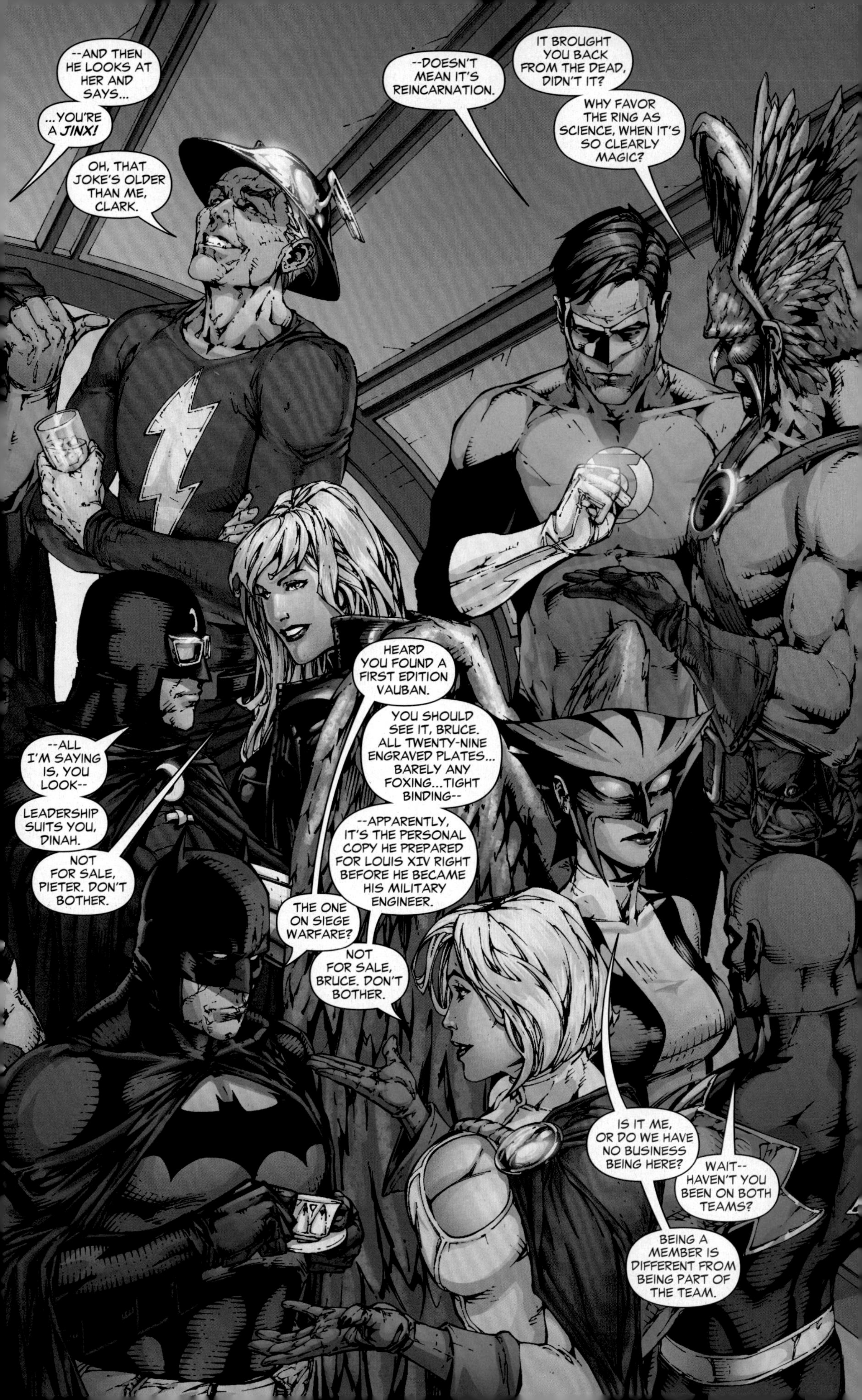
--AND THEN HE LOOKS AT HER AND SAYS...
...YOU'RE A JINX!
OH, THAT JOKE'S OLDER THAN ME, CLARK.
--DOESN'T MEAN IT'S REINCARNATION.
IT BROUGHT YOU BACK FROM THE DEAD, DIDN'T IT?
WHY FAVOR THE RING AS SCIENCE, WHEN IT'S SO CLEARLY MAGIC?
--ALL I'M SAYING IS, YOU LOOK--
LEADERSHIP SUITS YOU, DINAH.
NOT FOR SALE, PIETER. DON'T BOTHER.
HEARD YOU FOUND A FIRST EDITION VAUBAN.
YOU SHOULD SEE IT, BRUCE. ALL TWENTY-NINE ENGRAVED PLATES... BARELY ANY FOXING...TIGHT BINDING--
--APPARENTLY, IT'S THE PERSONAL COPY HE PREPARED FOR LOUIS XIV RIGHT BEFORE HE BECAME HIS MILITARY ENGINEER.
THE ONE ON SIEGE WARFARE?
NOT FOR SALE, BRUCE. DON'T BOTHER.
IS IT ME, OR DO WE HAVE NO BUSINESS BEING HERE?
WAIT-- HAVEN'T YOU BEEN ON BOTH TEAMS?
BEING A MEMBER IS DIFFERENT FROM BEING PART OF THE TEAM.

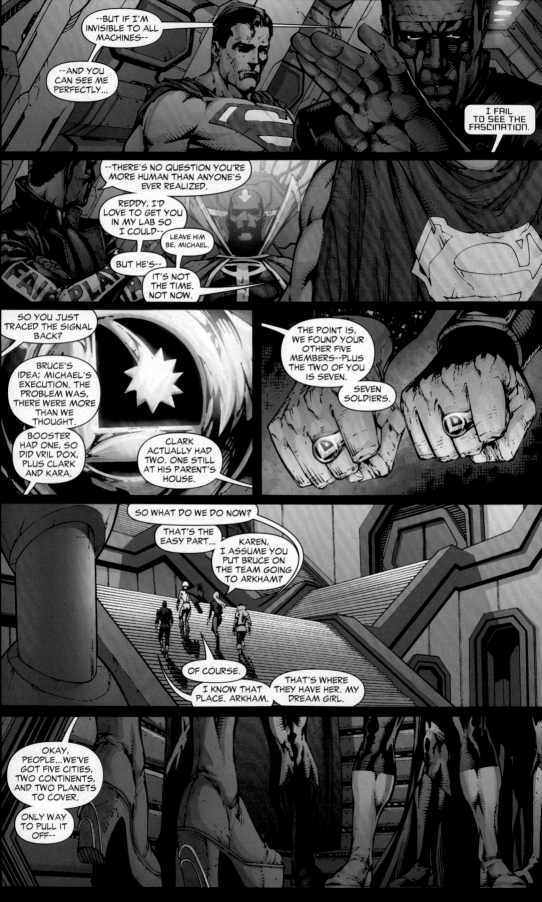

--BUT IF I'M INVISIBLE TO ALL MACHINES--

--AND YOU CAN SEE ME PERFECTLY...

I FAIL TO SEE THE FASCINATION.

--THERE'S NO QUESTION YOU'RE MORE HUMAN THAN ANYONE'S EVER REALIZED.

REDDY, I'D LOVE TO GET YOU IN MY LAB SO I COULD--

LEAVE HIM BE, MICHAEL.

BUT HE'S--

IT'S NOT THE TIME. NOT NOW.

SO YOU JUST TRACED THE SIGNAL BACK?

BRUCE'S IDEA; MICHAEL'S EXECUTION. THE PROBLEM WAS, THERE WERE MORE THAN WE THOUGHT.

BOOSTER HAD ONE, SO DID VRIL DOX, PLUS CLARK AND KARA.

CLARK ACTUALLY HAD TWO. ONE STILL AT HIS PARENT'S HOUSE.

THE POINT IS, WE FOUND YOUR OTHER FIVE MEMBERS--PLUS THE TWO OF YOU IS SEVEN.

SEVEN SOLDIERS.

SO WHAT DO WE DO NOW?

THAT'S THE EASY PART...

KAREN, I ASSUME YOU PUT BRUCE ON THE TEAM GOING TO ARKHAM?

OF COURSE.

I KNOW THAT PLACE. ARKHAM.

THAT'S WHERE THEY HAVE HER. MY DREAM GIRL.

OKAY, PEOPLE...WE'VE GOT FIVE CITIES, TWO CONTINENTS, AND TWO PLANETS TO COVER.

ONLY WAY TO PULL IT OFF--

30

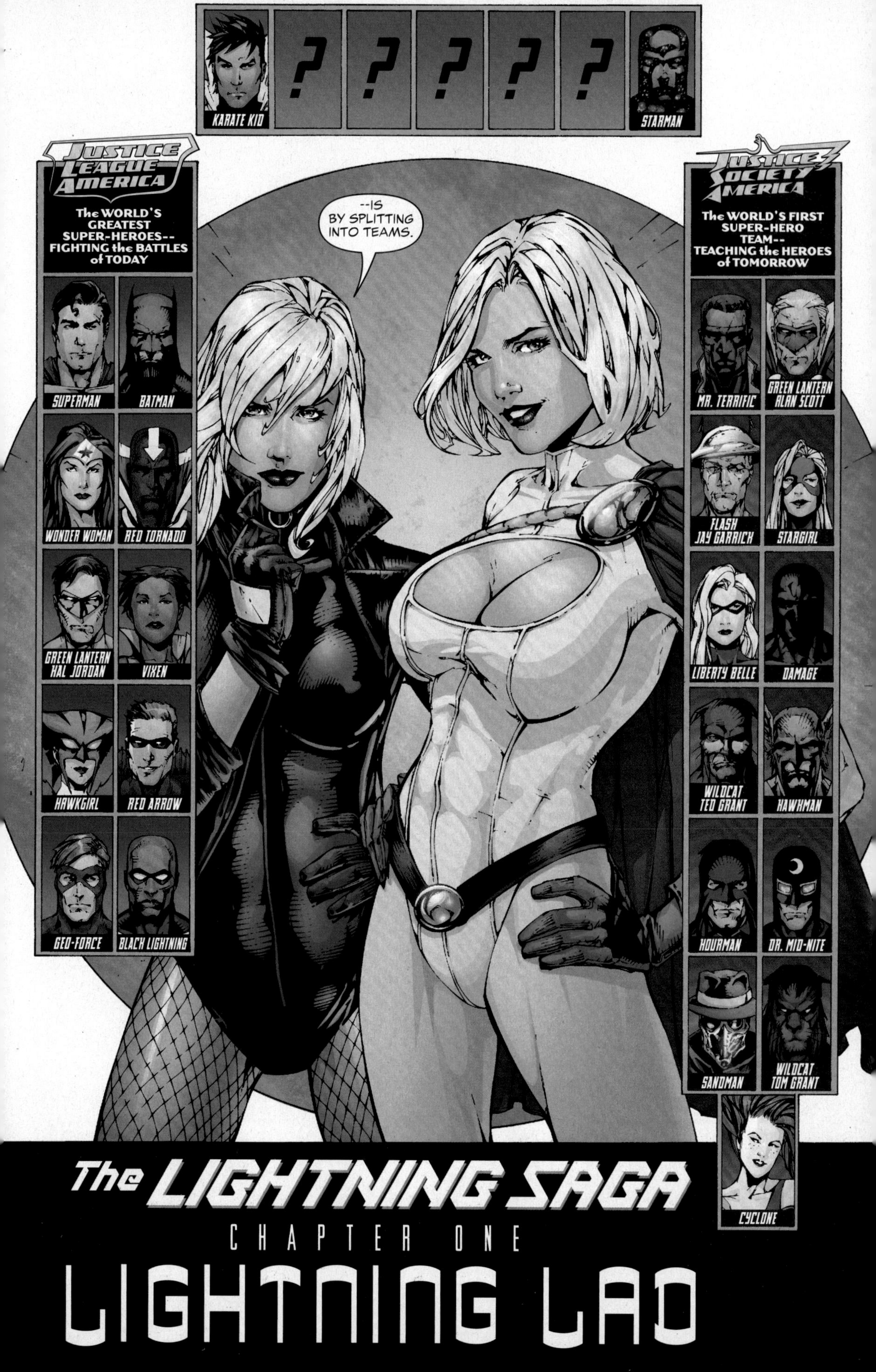
KARATE KID
?
?
?
?
?
STARMAN
JUSTICE LEAGUE AMERICA
The WORLD'S GREATEST SUPER-HEROES-- FIGHTING the BATTLES of TODAY
SUPERMAN
BATMAN
WONDER WOMAN
RED TORNADO
GREEN LANTERN HAL JORDAN
VIXEN
HAWKGIRL
RED ARROW
GEO-FORCE
BLACK LIGHTNING
--IS BY SPLITTING INTO TEAMS.
JUSTICE SOCIETY AMERICA
The WORLD'S FIRST SUPER-HERO TEAM-- TEACHING the HEROES of TOMORROW
MR. TERRIFIC
GREEN LANTERN ALAN SCOTT
FLASH JAY GARRICK
STARGIRL
LIBERTY BELLE
DAMAGE
WILDCAT TED GRANT
HAWKMAN
HOURMAN
DR. MID-NITE
SANDMAN
WILDCAT TOM GRANT
CYCLONE
The LIGHTNING SAGA
CHAPTER ONE
LIGHTNING LAD

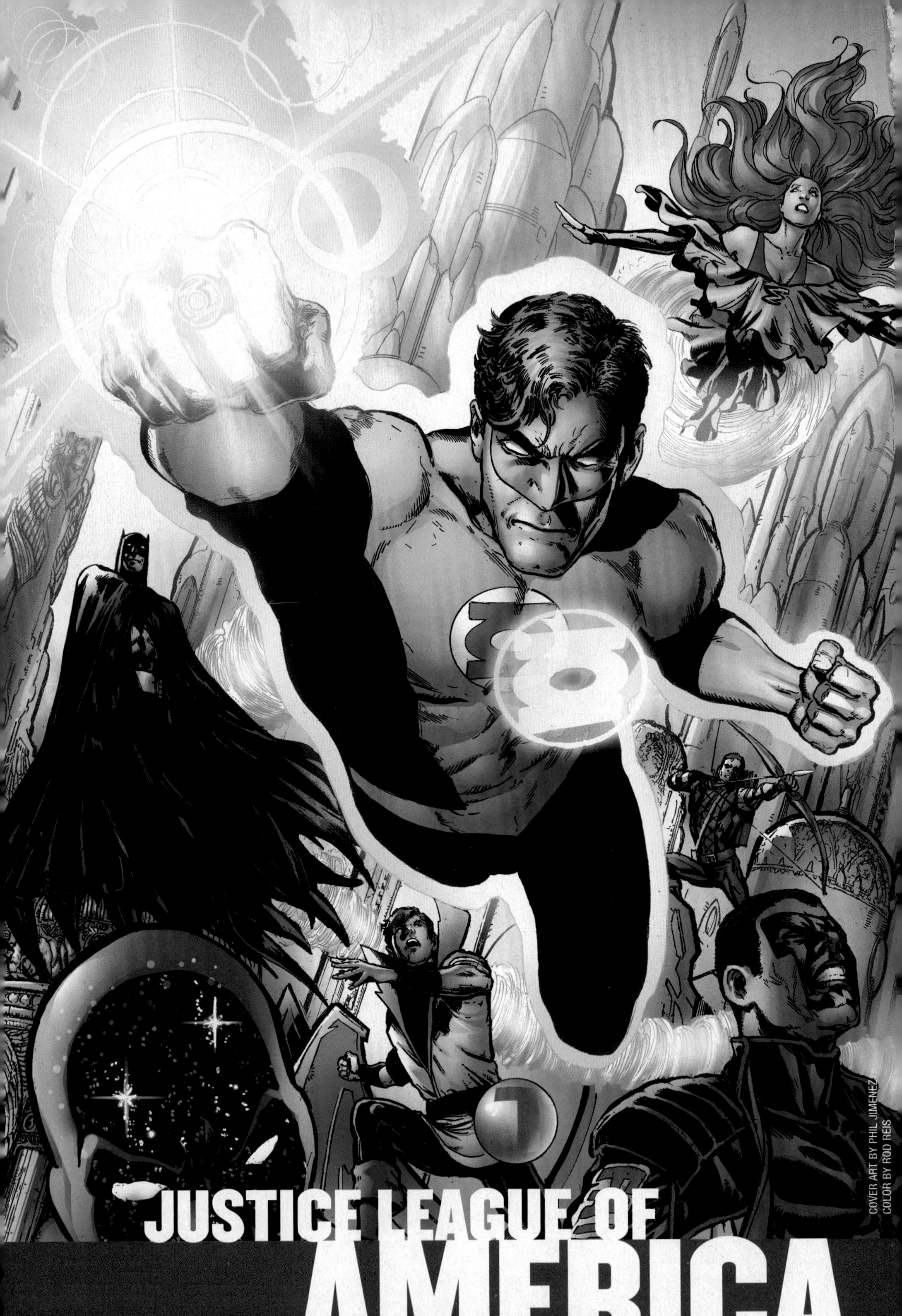
COVER ART BY PHIL JIMENEZ
COLOR BY ROD REIS

JUSTICE LEAGUE OF AMERICA

CHAPTER TWO

MOST PEOPLE GET AN OVERWHELMING SENSE OF RELIEF WHEN THEY WAKE UP FROM THEIR NIGHTMARES.

I DON'T.

GOTHAM CITY.

ARKHAM ASYLUM.

THEY SAW DARKSEID IN THERE.

WHO THE HELL'S DARKSEID?

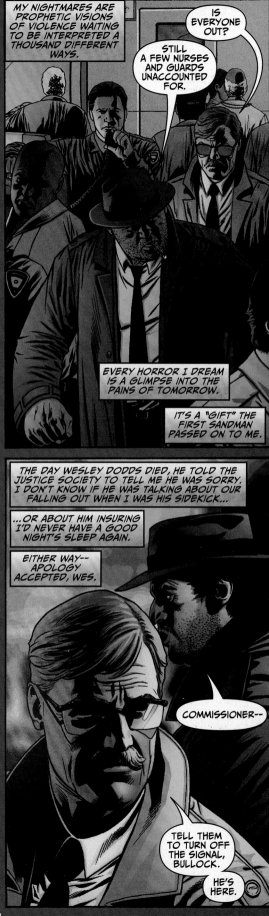

MY NIGHTMARES ARE PROPHETIC VISIONS OF VIOLENCE WAITING TO BE INTERPRETED A THOUSAND DIFFERENT WAYS.

IS EVERYONE OUT?

STILL A FEW NURSES AND GUARDS UNACCOUNTED FOR.

EVERY HORROR I DREAM IS A GLIMPSE INTO THE PAINS OF TOMORROW.

IT'S A "GIFT" THE FIRST SANDMAN PASSED ON TO ME.

THE DAY WESLEY DODDS DIED, HE TOLD THE JUSTICE SOCIETY TO TELL ME HE WAS SORRY. I DON'T KNOW IF HE WAS TALKING ABOUT OUR FALLING OUT WHEN I WAS HIS SIDEKICK...

...OR ABOUT HIM INSURING I'D NEVER HAVE A GOOD NIGHT'S SLEEP AGAIN.

EITHER WAY-- APOLOGY ACCEPTED, WES.

COMMISSIONER--

TELL THEM TO TURN OFF THE SIGNAL, BULLOCK.

HE'S HERE.

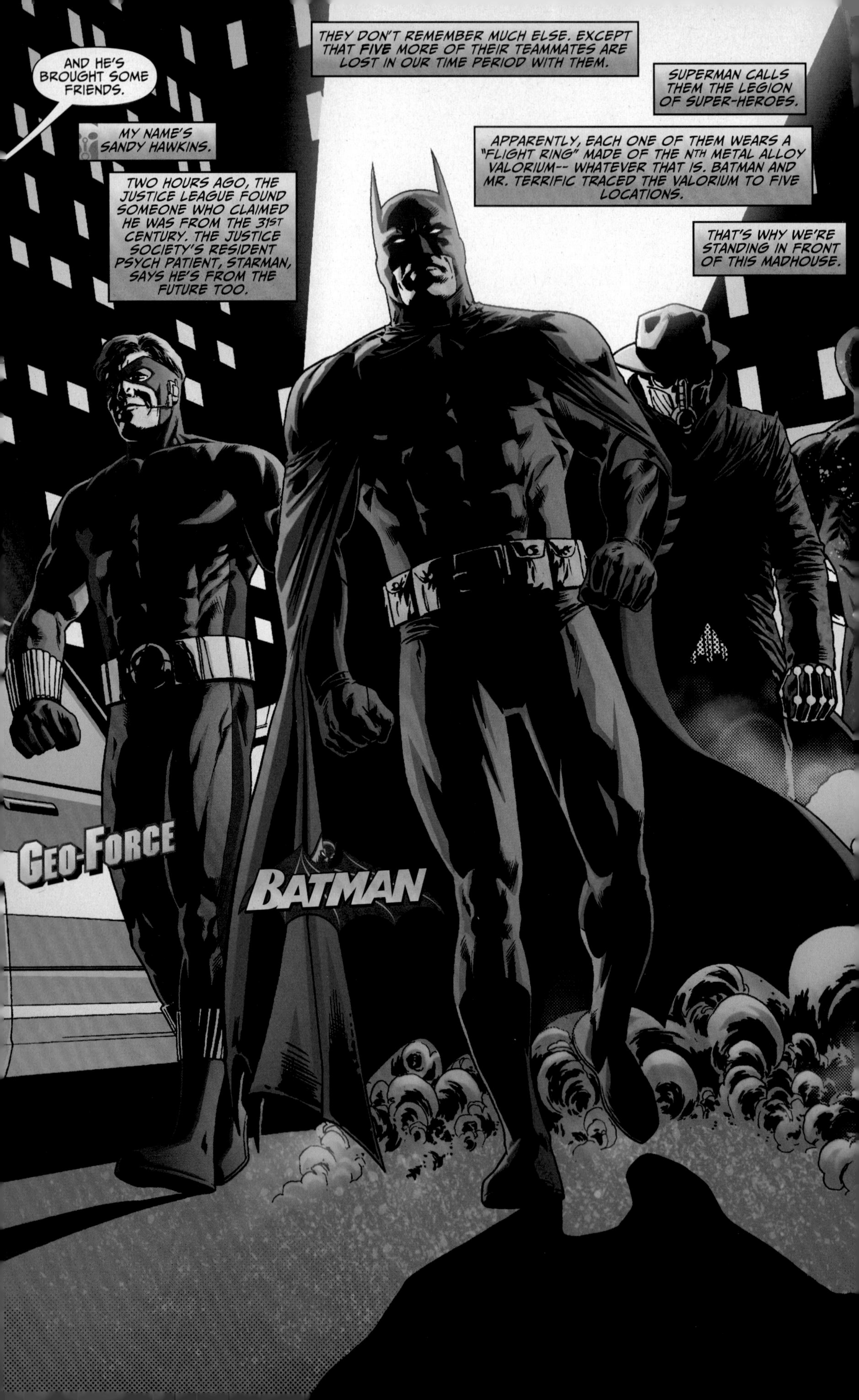

AND HE'S BROUGHT SOME FRIENDS.
MY NAME'S SANDY HAWKINS.
TWO HOURS AGO, THE JUSTICE LEAGUE FOUND SOMEONE WHO CLAIMED HE WAS FROM THE 31ST CENTURY. THE JUSTICE SOCIETY'S RESIDENT PSYCH PATIENT, STARMAN, SAYS HE'S FROM THE FUTURE TOO.
THEY DON'T REMEMBER MUCH ELSE. EXCEPT THAT FIVE MORE OF THEIR TEAMMATES ARE LOST IN OUR TIME PERIOD WITH THEM.
SUPERMAN CALLS THEM THE LEGION OF SUPER-HEROES.
APPARENTLY, EACH ONE OF THEM WEARS A "FLIGHT RING" MADE OF THE NTH METAL ALLOY VALORIUM-- WHATEVER THAT IS. BATMAN AND MR. TERRIFIC TRACED THE VALORIUM TO FIVE LOCATIONS.
THAT'S WHY WE'RE STANDING IN FRONT OF THIS MADHOUSE.
GEO-FORCE
BATMAN

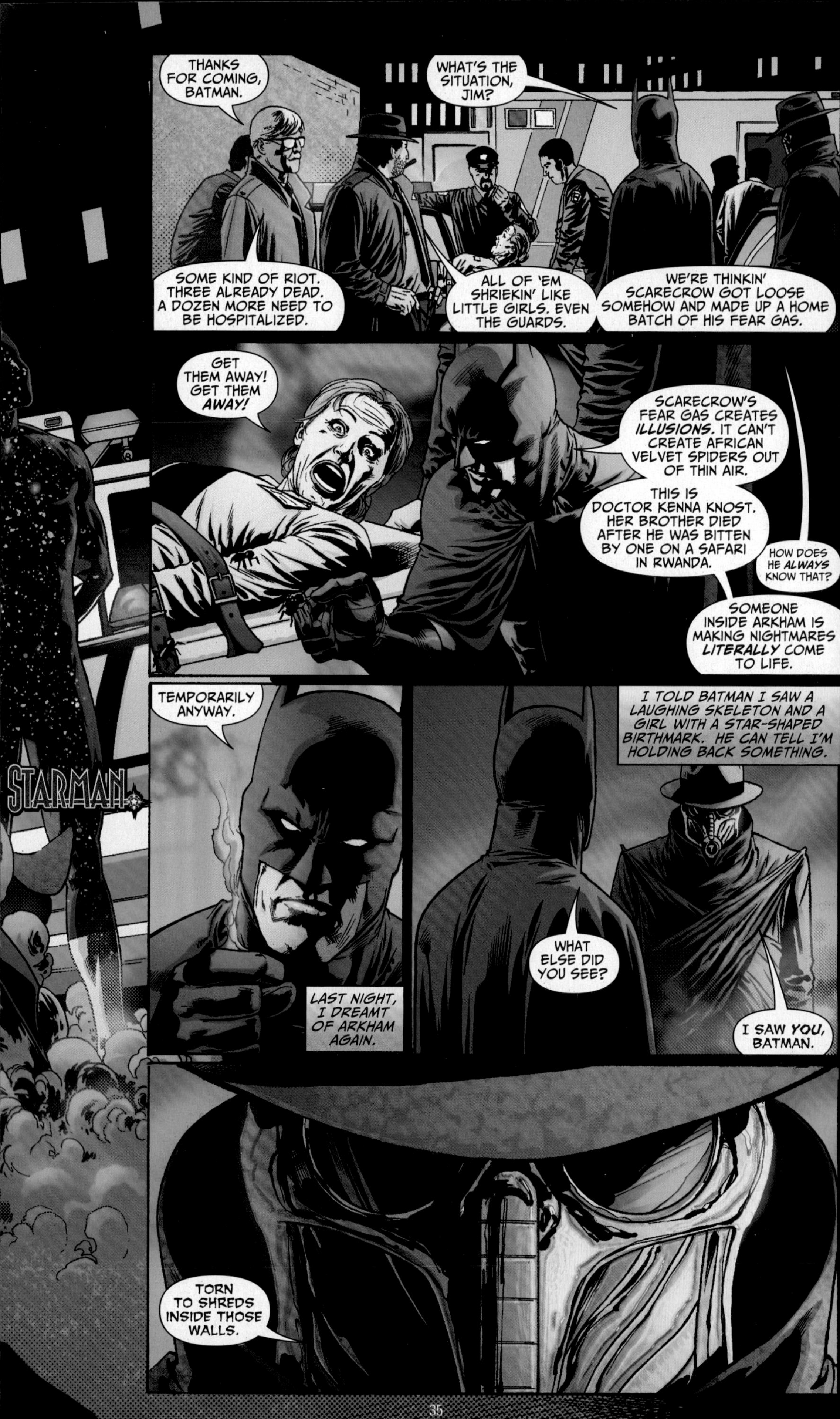
THANKS FOR COMING, BATMAN.
WHAT'S THE SITUATION, JIM?
SOME KIND OF RIOT. THREE ALREADY DEAD. A DOZEN MORE NEED TO BE HOSPITALIZED.
ALL OF 'EM SHRIEKIN' LIKE LITTLE GIRLS. EVEN THE GUARDS.
WE'RE THINKIN' SCARECROW GOT LOOSE SOMEHOW AND MADE UP A HOME BATCH OF HIS FEAR GAS.
GET THEM AWAY! GET THEM AWAY!
SCARECROW'S FEAR GAS CREATES ILLUSIONS. IT CAN'T CREATE AFRICAN VELVET SPIDERS OUT OF THIN AIR.
THIS IS DOCTOR KENNA KNOST. HER BROTHER DIED AFTER HE WAS BITTEN BY ONE ON A SAFARI IN RWANDA.
HOW DOES HE ALWAYS KNOW THAT?
SOMEONE INSIDE ARKHAM IS MAKING NIGHTMARES LITERALLY COME TO LIFE.
STARMAN
TEMPORARILY ANYWAY.
LAST NIGHT, I DREAMT OF ARKHAM AGAIN.
I TOLD BATMAN I SAW A LAUGHING SKELETON AND A GIRL WITH A STAR-SHAPED BIRTHMARK. HE CAN TELL I'M HOLDING BACK SOMETHING.
WHAT ELSE DID YOU SEE?
I SAW YOU, BATMAN.
TORN TO SHREDS INSIDE THOSE WALLS.

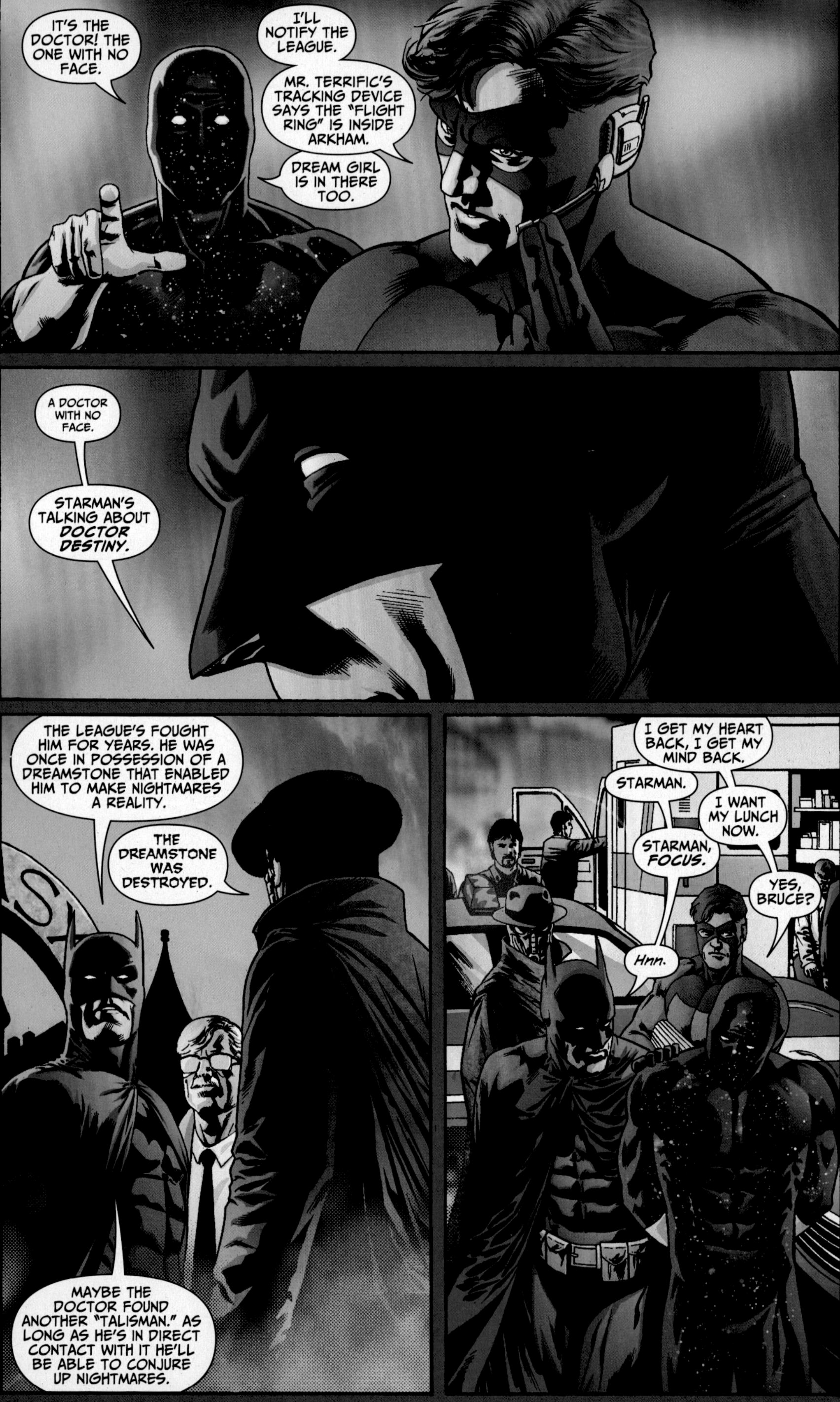
IT'S THE DOCTOR! THE ONE WITH NO FACE.
I'LL NOTIFY THE LEAGUE.
MR. TERRIFIC'S TRACKING DEVICE SAYS THE "FLIGHT RING" IS INSIDE ARKHAM.
DREAM GIRL IS IN THERE TOO.
A DOCTOR WITH NO FACE.
STARMAN'S TALKING ABOUT *DOCTOR DESTINY.*
THE LEAGUE'S FOUGHT HIM FOR YEARS. HE WAS ONCE IN POSSESSION OF A DREAMSTONE THAT ENABLED HIM TO MAKE NIGHTMARES A REALITY.
THE DREAMSTONE WAS DESTROYED.
MAYBE THE DOCTOR FOUND ANOTHER "TALISMAN." AS LONG AS HE'S IN DIRECT CONTACT WITH IT HE'LL BE ABLE TO CONJURE UP NIGHTMARES.
I GET MY HEART BACK, I GET MY MIND BACK.
STARMAN.
I WANT MY LUNCH NOW.
STARMAN, *FOCUS.*
YES, BRUCE?
Hnn.

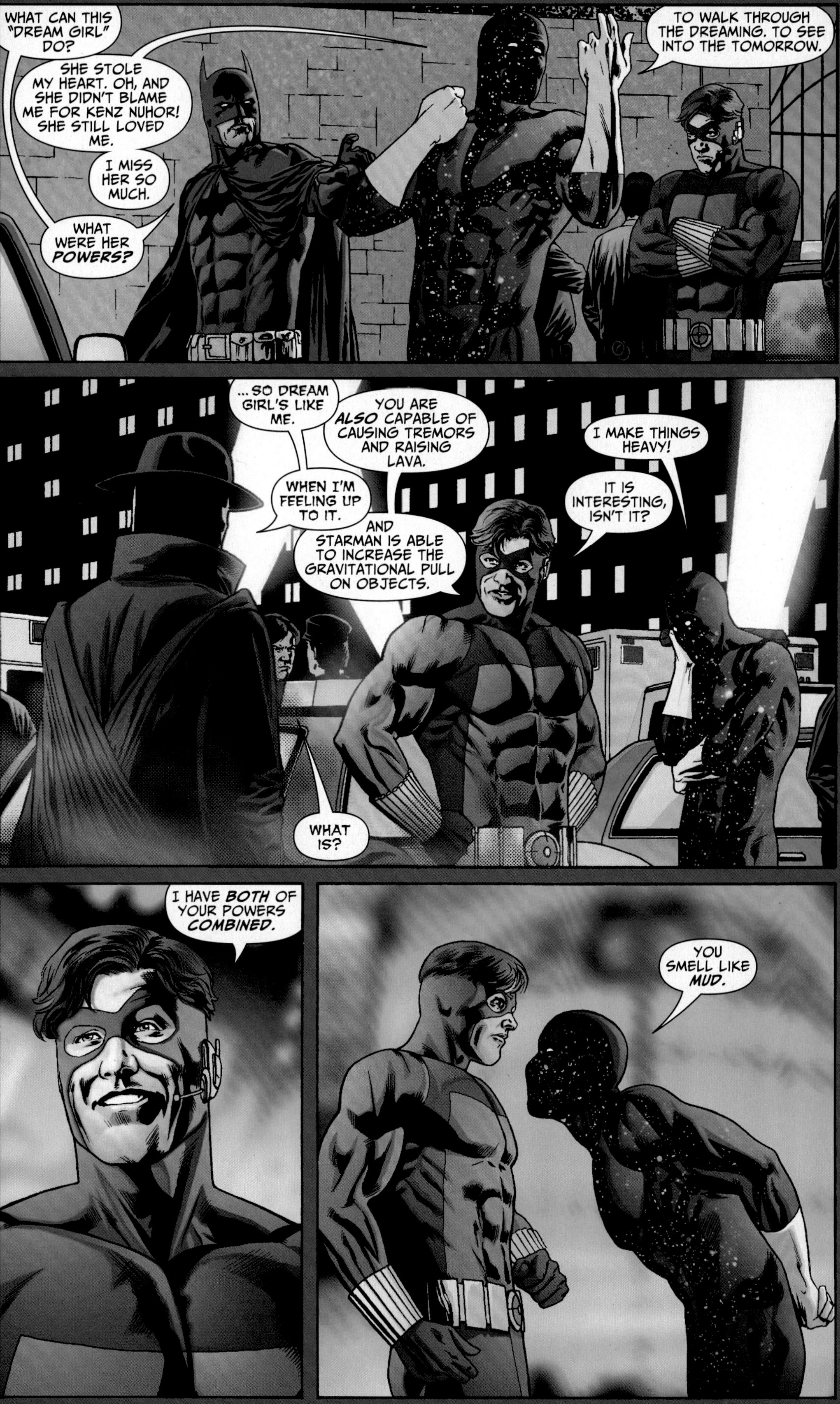
WHAT CAN THIS "DREAM GIRL" DO?
SHE STOLE MY HEART. OH, AND SHE DIDN'T BLAME ME FOR KENZ NUHOR! SHE STILL LOVED ME.
I MISS HER SO MUCH.
WHAT WERE HER POWERS?
TO WALK THROUGH THE DREAMING. TO SEE INTO THE TOMORROW.
...SO DREAM GIRL'S LIKE ME.
WHEN I'M FEELING UP TO IT.
YOU ARE ALSO CAPABLE OF CAUSING TREMORS AND RAISING LAVA.
AND STARMAN IS ABLE TO INCREASE THE GRAVITATIONAL PULL ON OBJECTS.
I MAKE THINGS HEAVY!
IT IS INTERESTING, ISN'T IT?
WHAT IS?
I HAVE BOTH OF YOUR POWERS COMBINED.
YOU SMELL LIKE MUD.

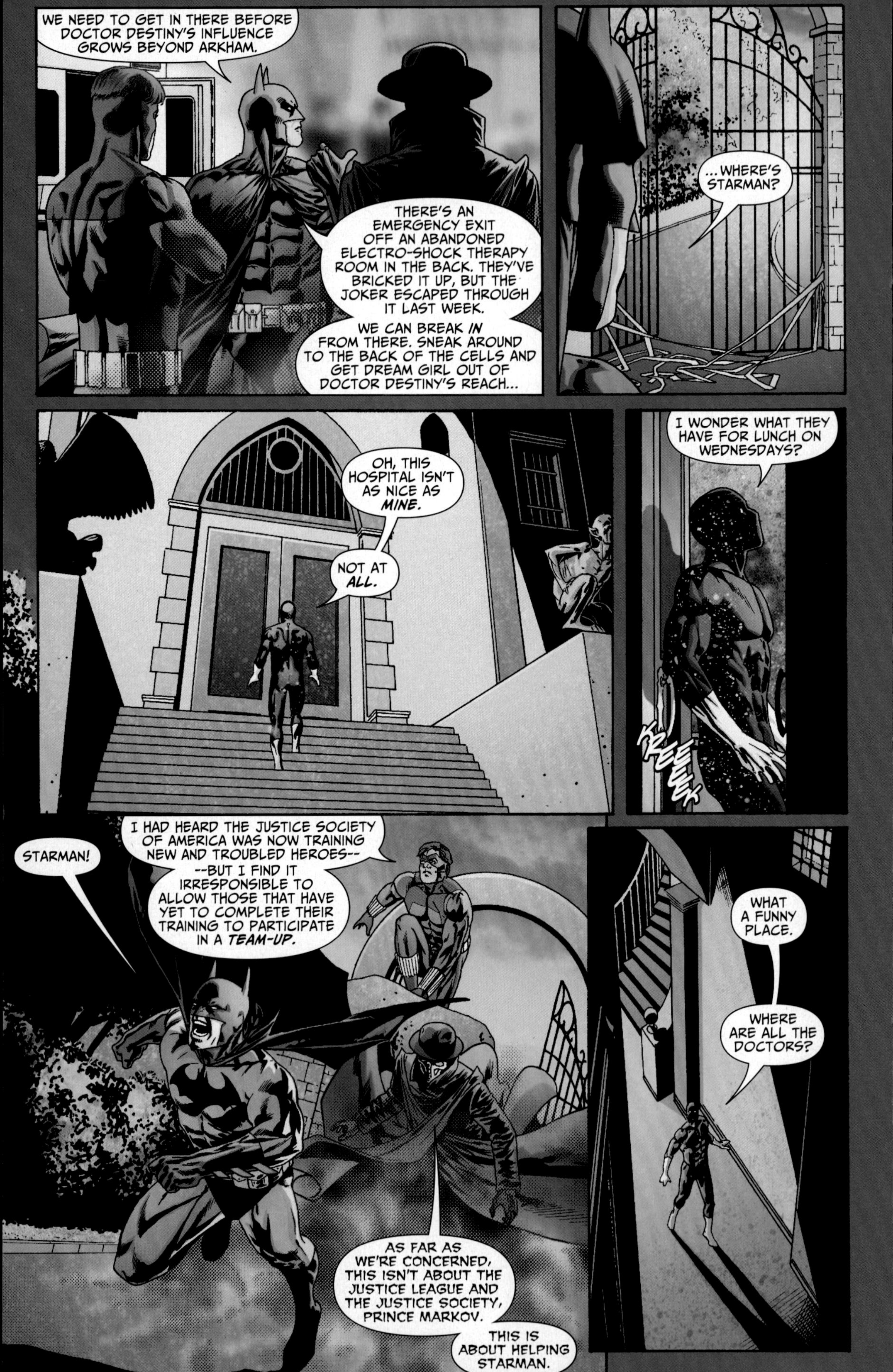
WE NEED TO GET IN THERE BEFORE DOCTOR DESTINY'S INFLUENCE GROWS BEYOND ARKHAM.
THERE'S AN EMERGENCY EXIT OFF AN ABANDONED ELECTRO-SHOCK THERAPY ROOM IN THE BACK. THEY'VE BRICKED IT UP, BUT THE JOKER ESCAPED THROUGH IT LAST WEEK.
WE CAN BREAK *IN* FROM THERE. SNEAK AROUND TO THE BACK OF THE CELLS AND GET DREAM GIRL OUT OF DOCTOR DESTINY'S REACH...
...WHERE'S STARMAN?
OH, THIS HOSPITAL ISN'T AS NICE AS **MINE.**
NOT AT **ALL.**
I WONDER WHAT THEY HAVE FOR LUNCH ON WEDNESDAYS?
KREEEK
STARMAN!
I HAD HEARD THE JUSTICE SOCIETY OF AMERICA WAS NOW TRAINING NEW AND TROUBLED HEROES--
--BUT I FIND IT IRRESPONSIBLE TO ALLOW THOSE THAT HAVE YET TO COMPLETE THEIR TRAINING TO PARTICIPATE IN A **TEAM-UP.**
AS FAR AS WE'RE CONCERNED, THIS ISN'T ABOUT THE JUSTICE LEAGUE AND THE JUSTICE SOCIETY, PRINCE MARKOV.
THIS IS ABOUT HELPING STARMAN.
WHAT A FUNNY PLACE.
WHERE ARE ALL THE DOCTORS?

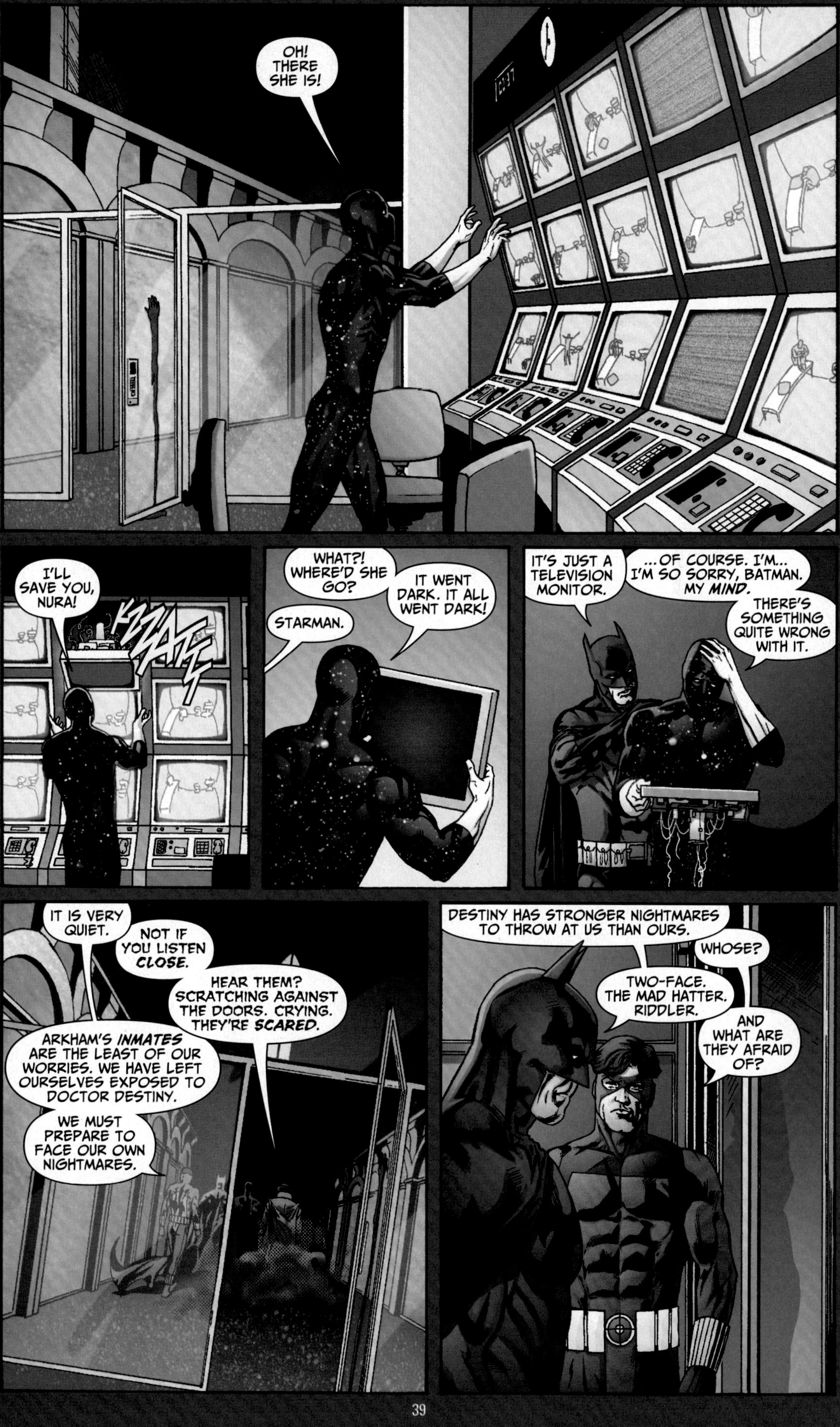
OH! THERE SHE IS!
I'LL SAVE YOU, NURA!
KZZAATZ
WHAT?! WHERE'D SHE GO?
IT WENT DARK. IT ALL WENT DARK!
STARMAN.
IT'S JUST A TELEVISION MONITOR.
...OF COURSE. I'M... I'M SO SORRY, BATMAN. MY MIND.
THERE'S SOMETHING QUITE WRONG WITH IT.
IT IS VERY QUIET.
NOT IF YOU LISTEN CLOSE.
HEAR THEM? SCRATCHING AGAINST THE DOORS. CRYING. THEY'RE SCARED.
ARKHAM'S INMATES ARE THE LEAST OF OUR WORRIES. WE HAVE LEFT OURSELVES EXPOSED TO DOCTOR DESTINY.
WE MUST PREPARE TO FACE OUR OWN NIGHTMARES.
DESTINY HAS STRONGER NIGHTMARES TO THROW AT US THAN OURS.
WHOSE?
TWO-FACE. THE MAD HATTER. RIDDLER.
AND WHAT ARE THEY AFRAID OF?

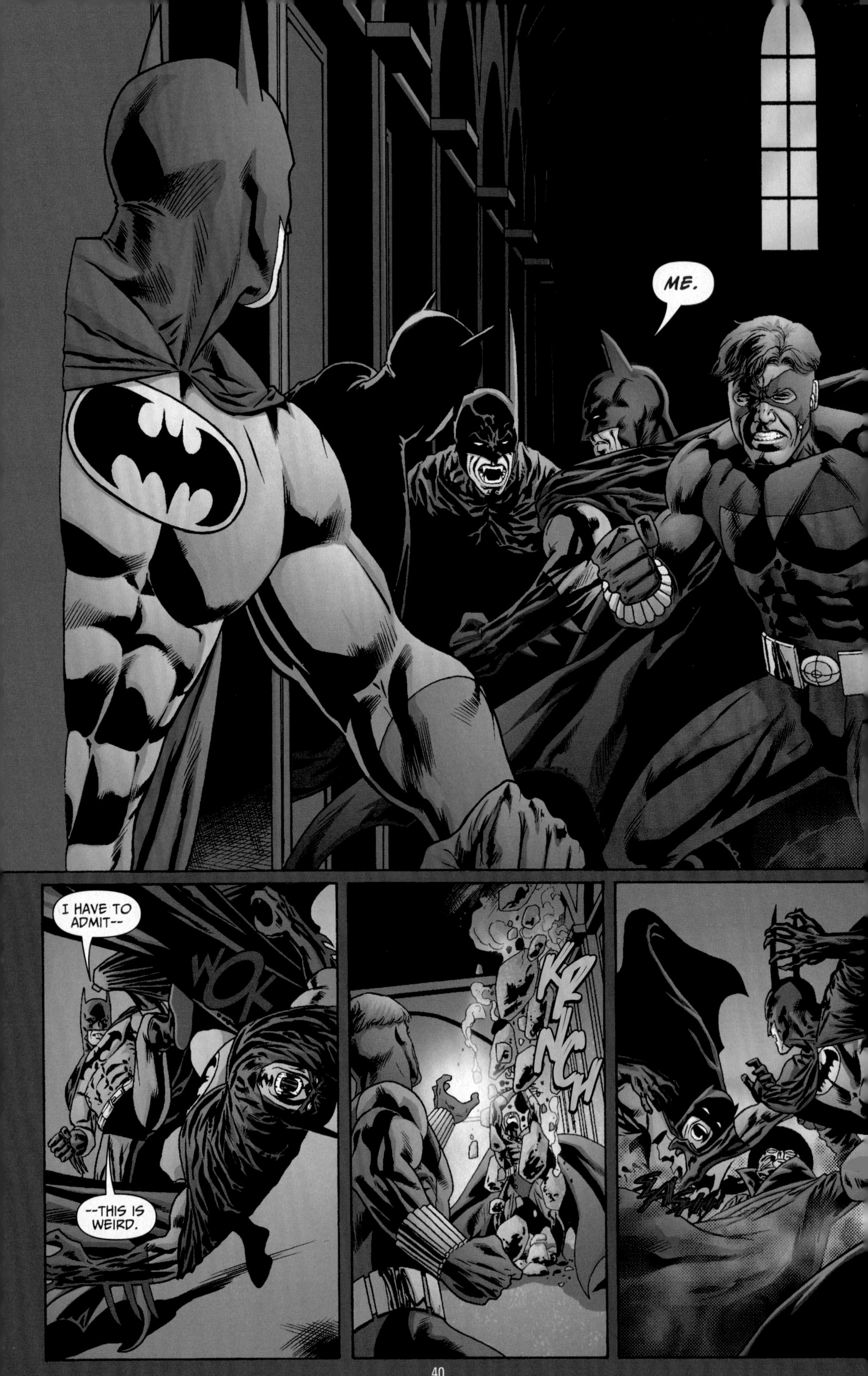
ME.
I HAVE TO ADMIT--
WOK
--THIS IS WEIRD.

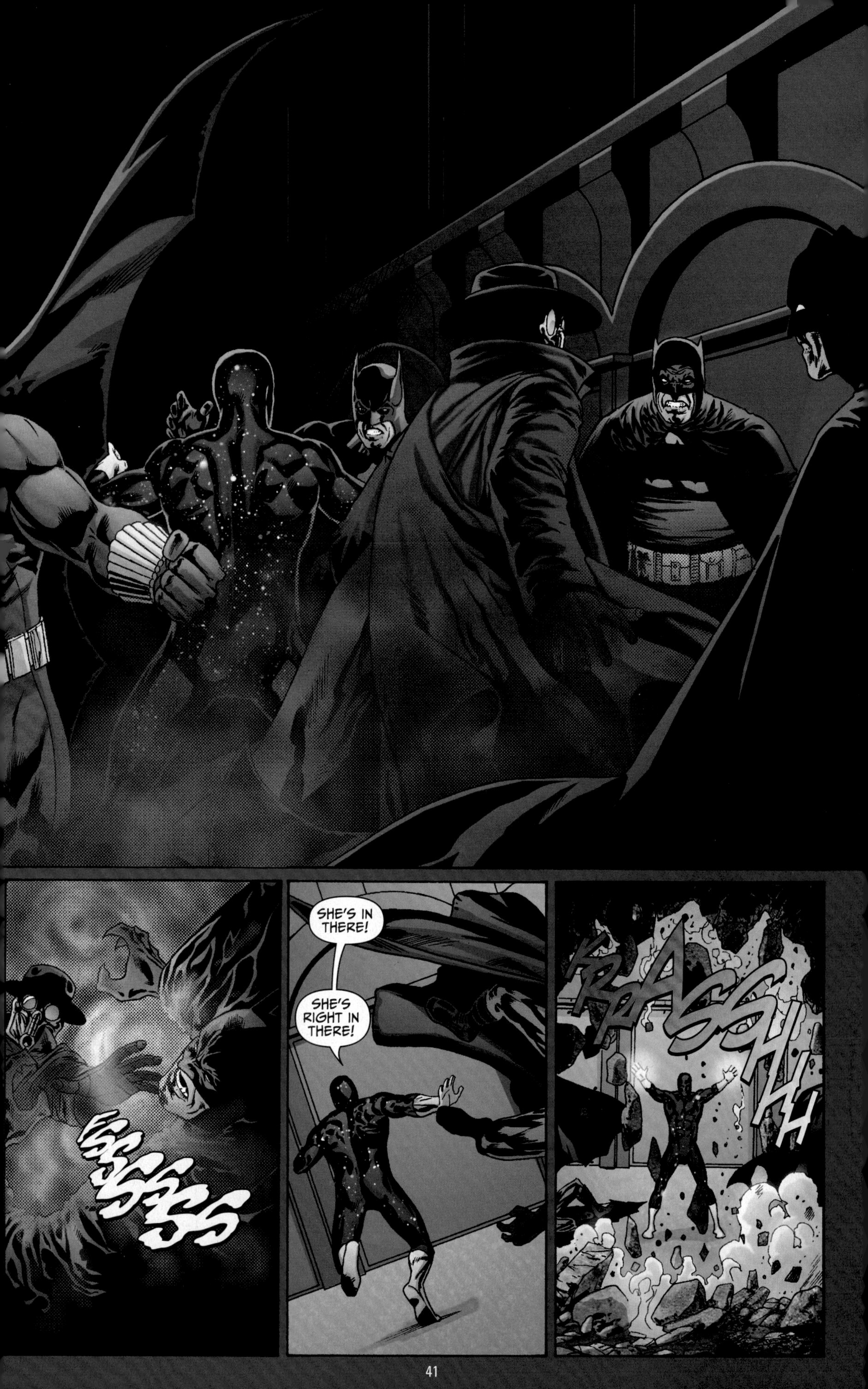
SHE'S IN THERE!
SHE'S RIGHT IN THERE!

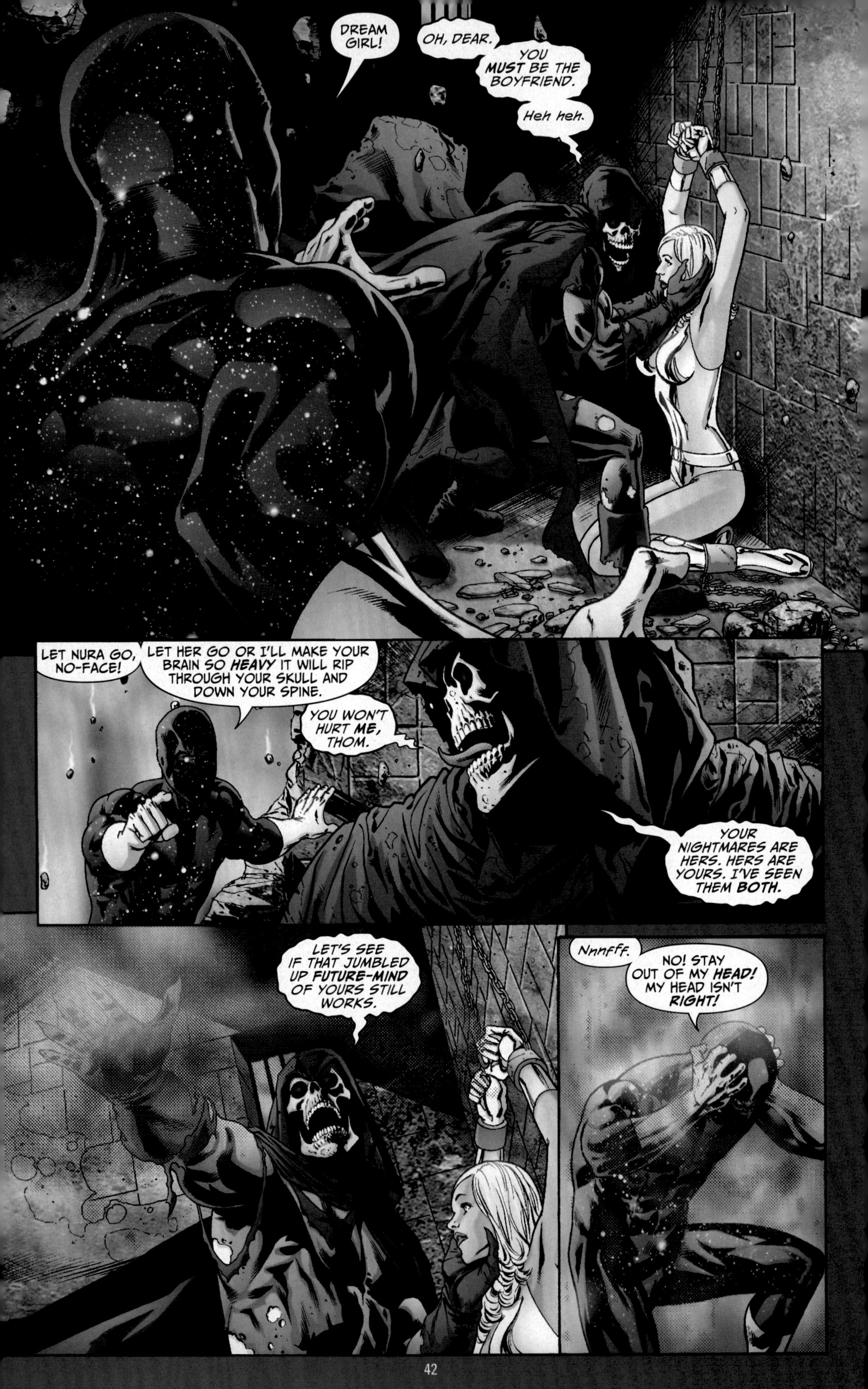
DREAM GIRL!
OH, DEAR.
YOU MUST BE THE BOYFRIEND.
Heh heh.
LET NURA GO, NO-FACE!
LET HER GO OR I'LL MAKE YOUR BRAIN SO HEAVY IT WILL RIP THROUGH YOUR SKULL AND DOWN YOUR SPINE.
YOU WON'T HURT ME, THOM.
YOUR NIGHTMARES ARE HERS. HERS ARE YOURS. I'VE SEEN THEM BOTH.
LET'S SEE IF THAT JUMBLED UP FUTURE-MIND OF YOURS STILL WORKS.
Nnnfff.
NO! STAY OUT OF MY HEAD! MY HEAD ISN'T RIGHT!

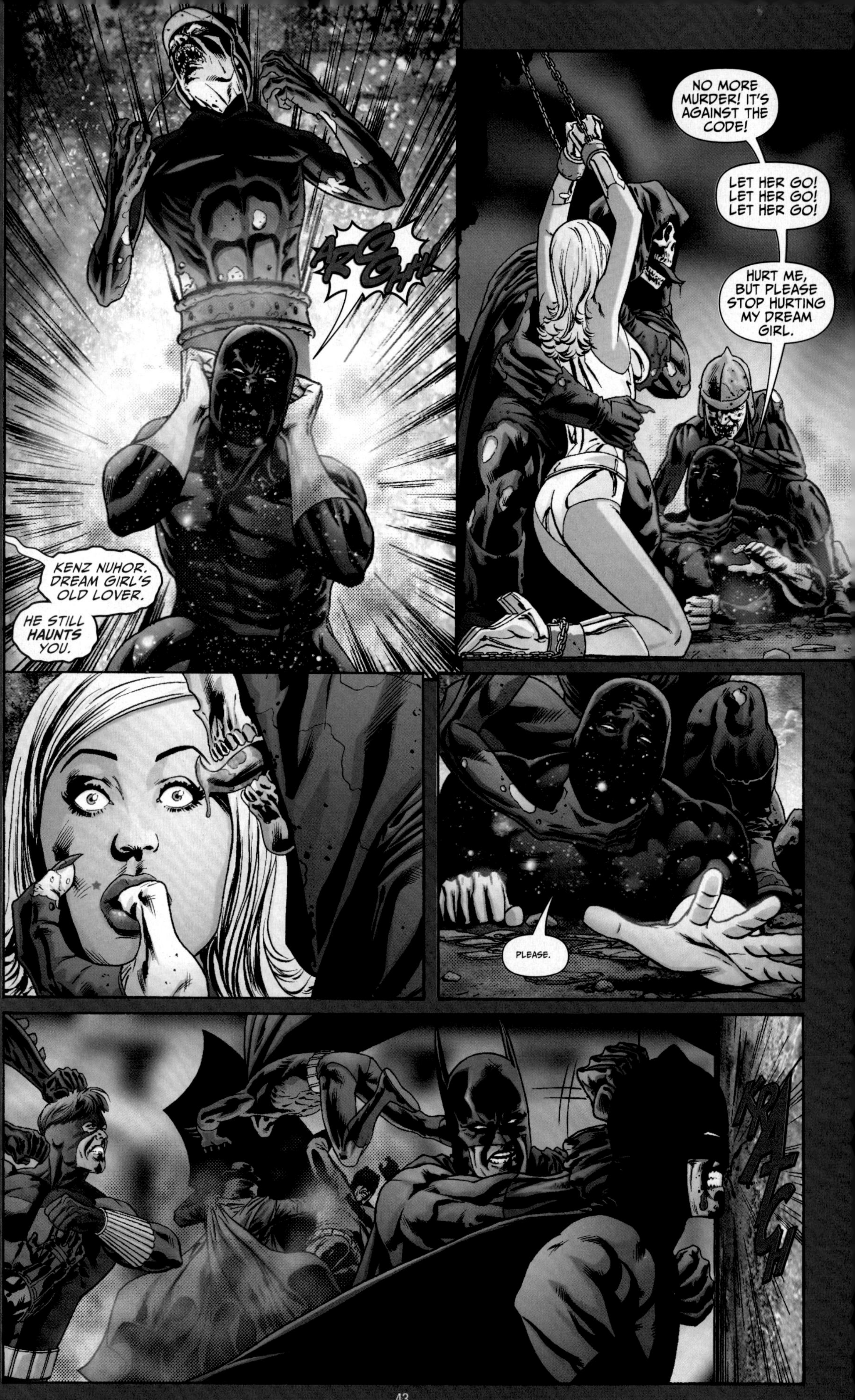
ARGGH!
KENZ NUHOR. DREAM GIRL'S OLD LOVER.
HE STILL HAUNTS YOU.
NO MORE MURDER! IT'S AGAINST THE CODE!
LET HER GO! LET HER GO! LET HER GO!
HURT ME, BUT PLEASE STOP HURTING MY DREAM GIRL.
PLEASE.
KRATCH

...THE WORD... THE WAKE UP WORD...

...ᒪᓄᒪᓮᓭ...

ᒪᓄᒪᓭᓮᓭᓮ ᒪᓄᓭ.

KRAKK

I'M AWAKE. AND THAT MEANS YOUR CONNECTION TO THE DREAMING IS CUT OFF.

WHAT?

I'VE SEEN YOUR FUTURE, DOCTOR DESTINY...

YOU'LL DIE IN A CELL IN YOUR SLEEP. TORTURED BY THE OWNER OF THE DREAMSTONE.

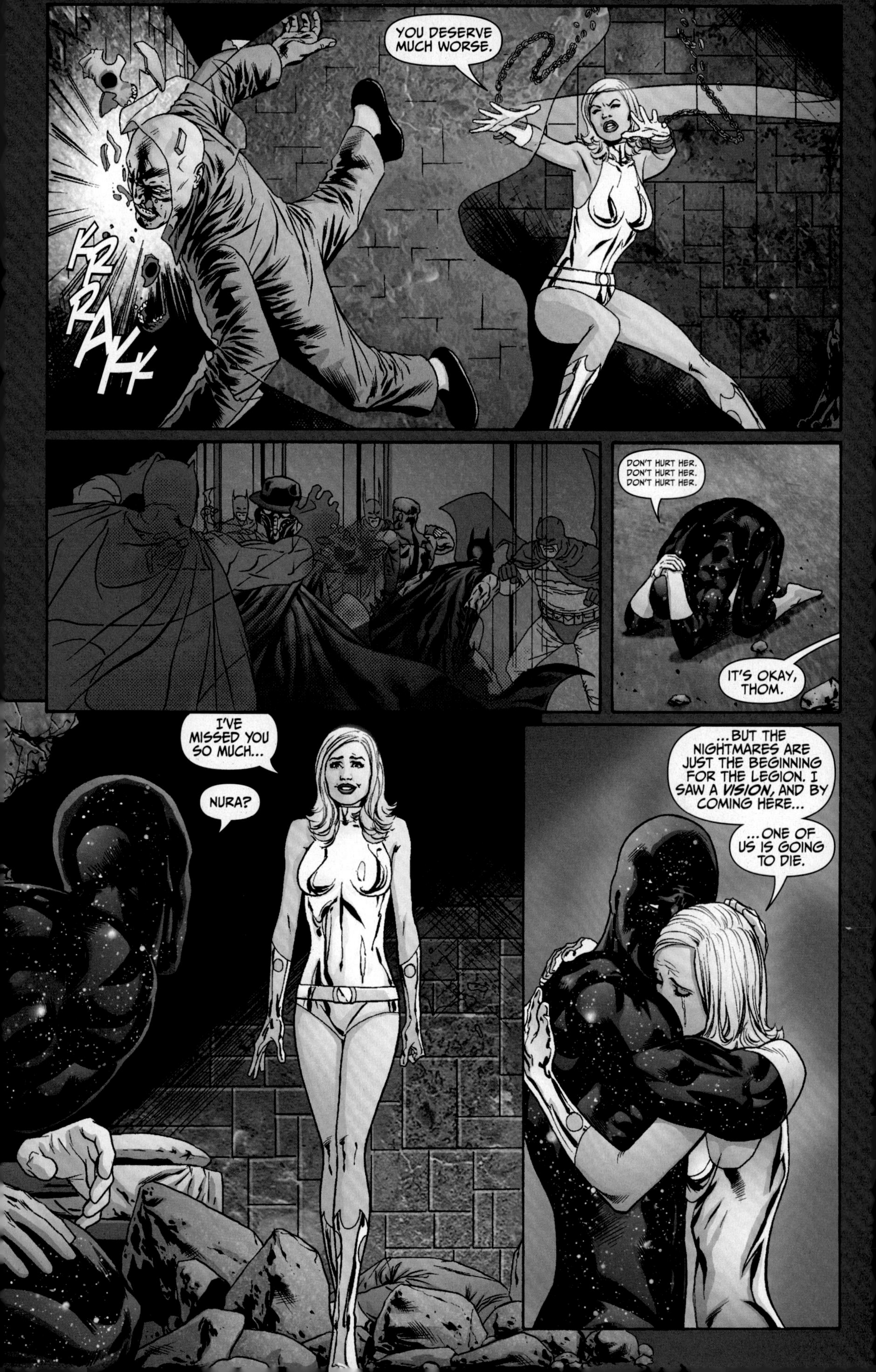
YOU DESERVE MUCH WORSE.
KRRAKK
DON'T HURT HER. DON'T HURT HER. DON'T HURT HER.
IT'S OKAY, THOM.
I'VE MISSED YOU SO MUCH...
NURA?
...BUT THE NIGHTMARES ARE JUST THE BEGINNING FOR THE LEGION. I SAW A *VISION*, AND BY COMING HERE...
...ONE OF US IS GOING TO DIE.

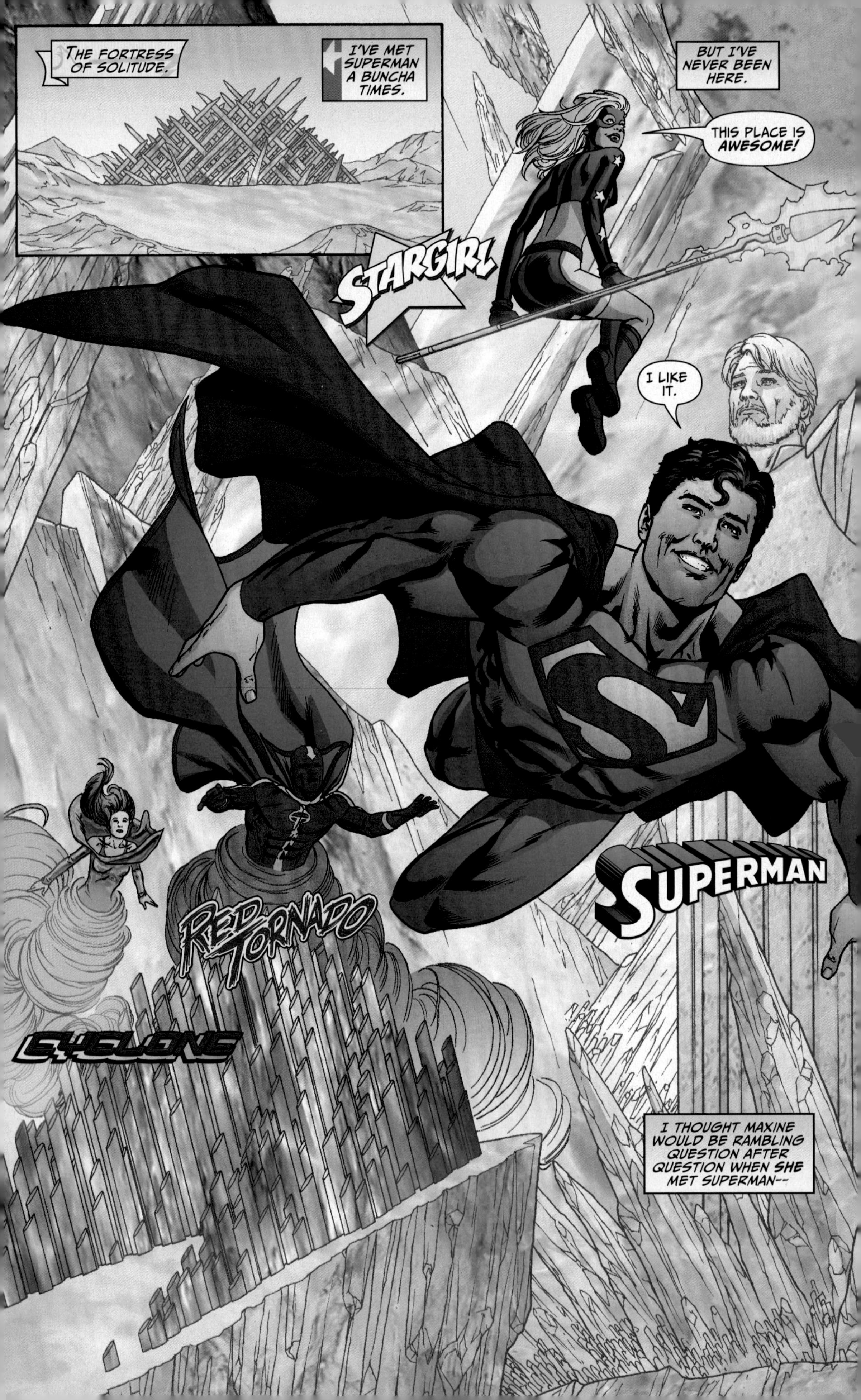
THE FORTRESS OF SOLITUDE.
I'VE MET SUPERMAN A BUNCHA TIMES.
BUT I'VE NEVER BEEN HERE.
THIS PLACE IS AWESOME!
STARGIRL
I LIKE IT.
SUPERMAN
RED TORNADO
CYCLONE
I THOUGHT MAXINE WOULD BE RAMBLING QUESTION AFTER QUESTION WHEN SHE MET SUPERMAN--

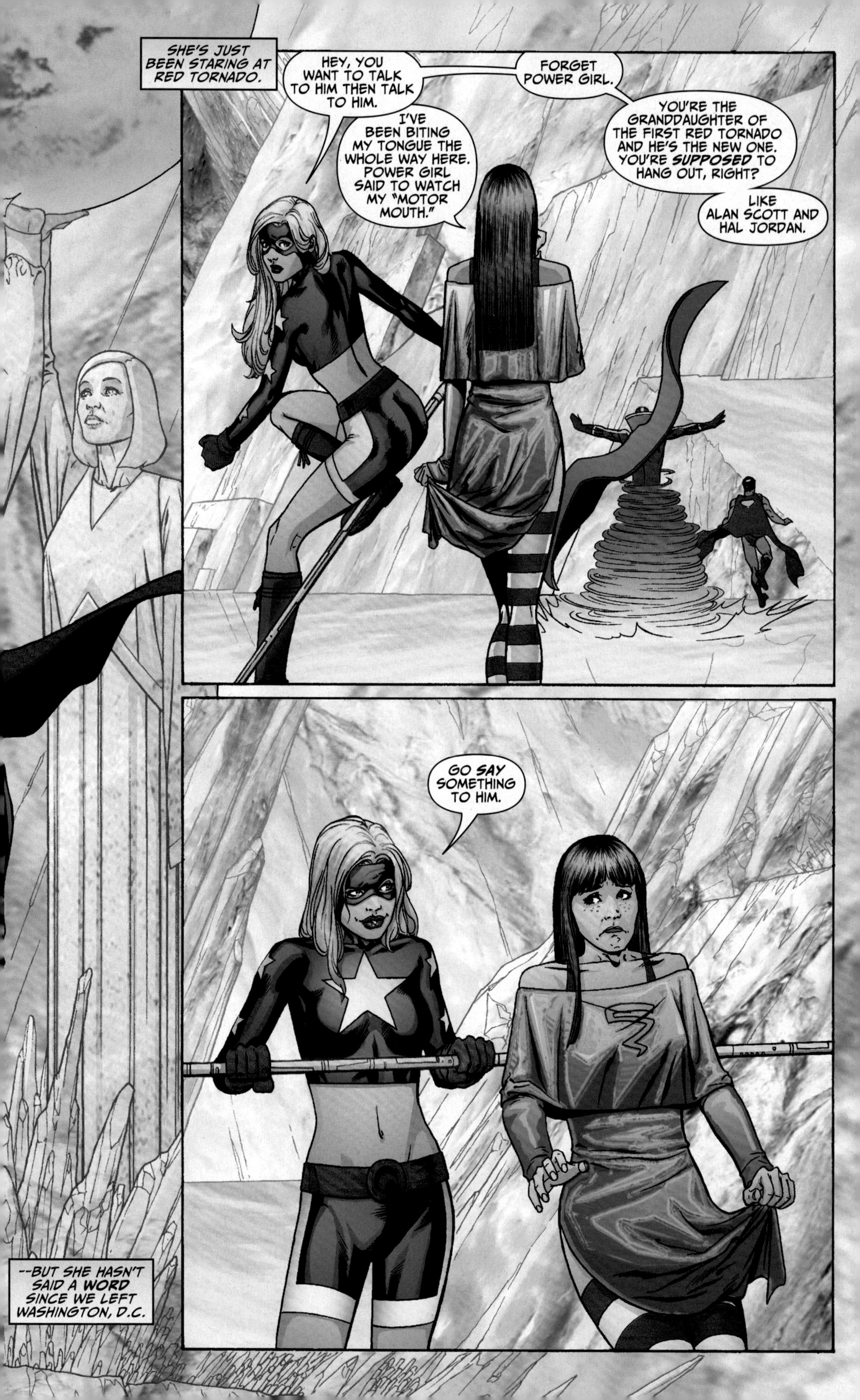
SHE'S JUST BEEN STARING AT RED TORNADO.
HEY, YOU WANT TO TALK TO HIM THEN TALK TO HIM.
I'VE BEEN BITING MY TONGUE THE WHOLE WAY HERE. POWER GIRL SAID TO WATCH MY "MOTOR MOUTH."
FORGET POWER GIRL.
YOU'RE THE GRANDDAUGHTER OF THE FIRST RED TORNADO AND HE'S THE NEW ONE. YOU'RE SUPPOSED TO HANG OUT, RIGHT?
LIKE ALAN SCOTT AND HAL JORDAN.
GO SAY SOMETHING TO HIM.
--BUT SHE HASN'T SAID A WORD SINCE WE LEFT WASHINGTON, D.C.

EXCUSE ME, *UM,* MR. TORNADO?

YES, CYCLONE?

MY REAL NAME'S MAXINE HUNKEL. YOU REMEMBER ME, DON'T YOU?

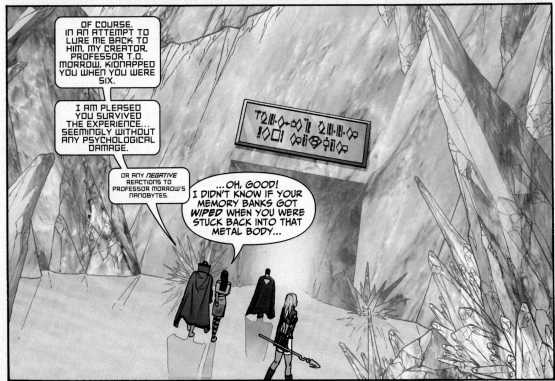

OF COURSE. IN AN ATTEMPT TO LURE ME BACK TO HIM, MY CREATOR, PROFESSOR T.O. MORROW, KIDNAPPED YOU WHEN YOU WERE SIX.

I AM PLEASED YOU SURVIVED THE EXPERIENCE... SEEMINGLY WITHOUT ANY PSYCHOLOGICAL DAMAGE.

OR ANY *NEGATIVE* REACTIONS TO PROFESSOR MORROW'S NANOBYTES.

...OH, GOOD! I DIDN'T KNOW IF YOUR MEMORY BANKS GOT *WIPED* WHEN YOU WERE STUCK BACK INTO THAT METAL BODY...

...I MEAN, NOT *STUCK,* JUST TRAPPED. OH, *TRAPPED* ISN'T RIGHT EITHER...

...IF IT MAKES YOU FEEL ANY BETTER, IT'S *NOT* EASY BEING HUMAN.

I WAS HUMAN LONG ENOUGH TO FIGURE THAT OUT.

HERE IT *IS.*

48

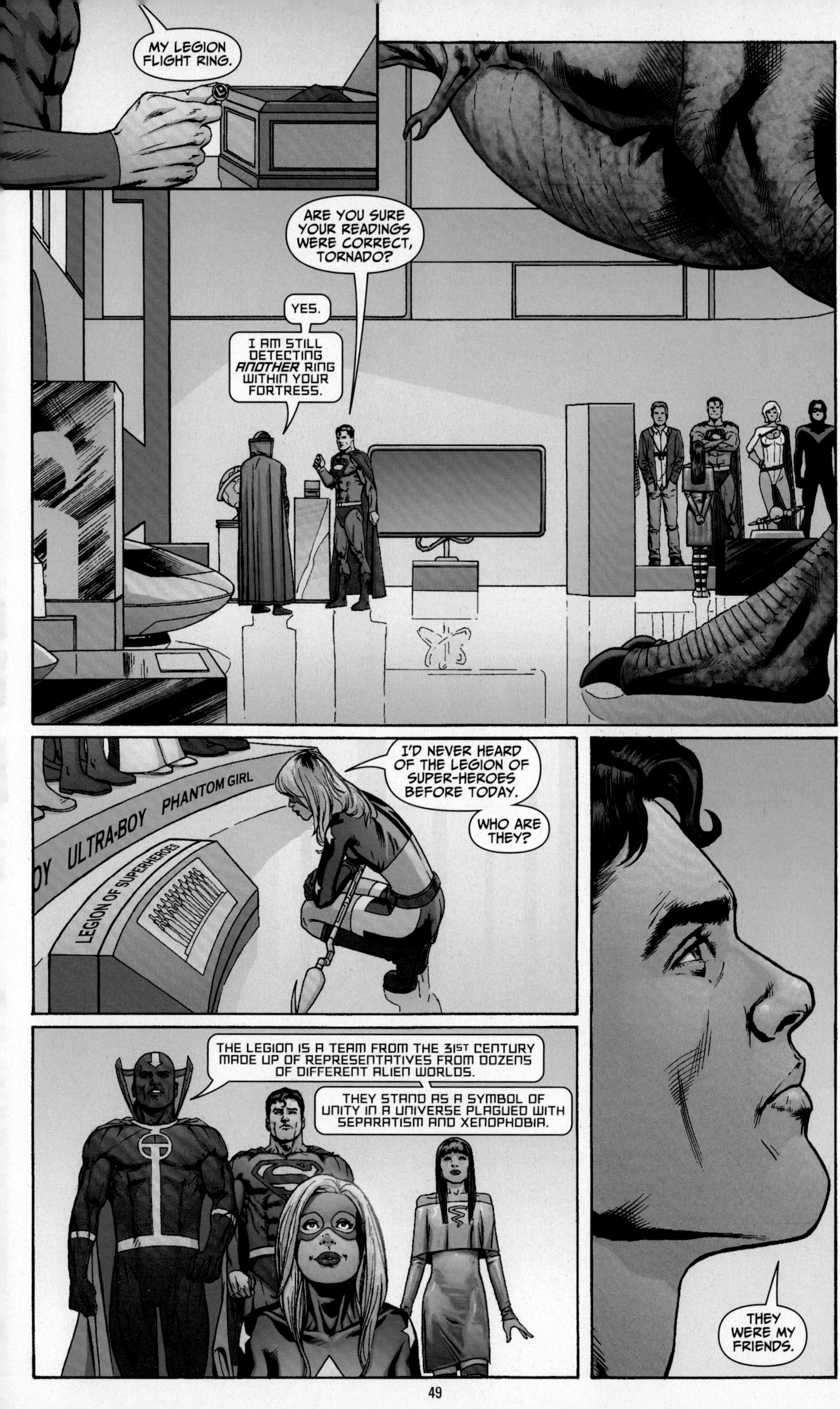
MY LEGION FLIGHT RING.
ARE YOU SURE YOUR READINGS WERE CORRECT, TORNADO?
YES.
I AM STILL DETECTING *ANOTHER* RING WITHIN YOUR FORTRESS.
PHANTOM GIRL
ULTRA-BOY
LEGION OF SUPERHEROES
I'D NEVER HEARD OF THE LEGION OF SUPER-HEROES BEFORE TODAY.
WHO ARE THEY?
THE LEGION IS A TEAM FROM THE 31ST CENTURY MADE UP OF REPRESENTATIVES FROM DOZENS OF DIFFERENT ALIEN WORLDS.
THEY STAND AS A SYMBOL OF UNITY IN A UNIVERSE PLAGUED WITH SEPARATISM AND XENOPHOBIA.
THEY WERE MY FRIENDS.

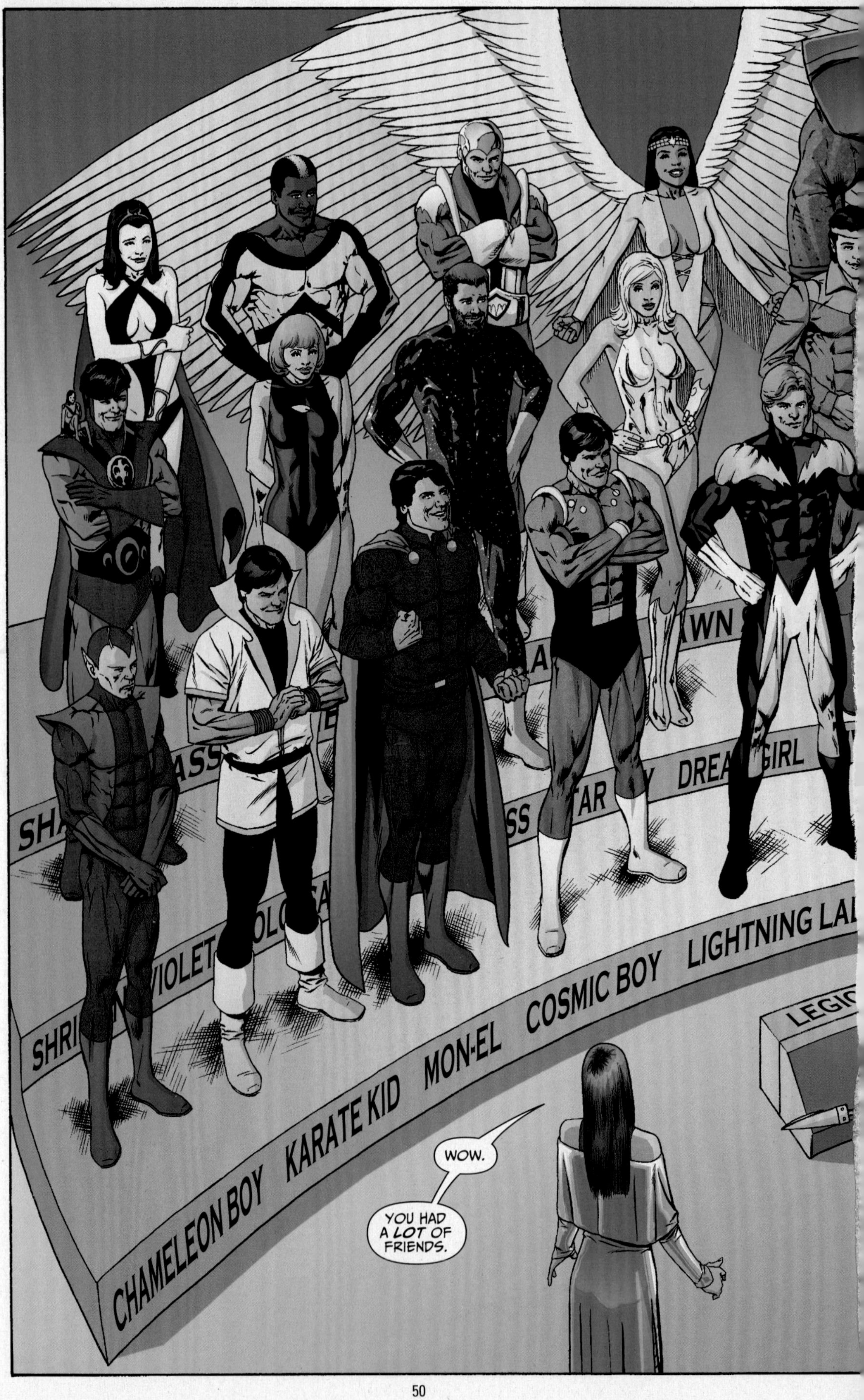
CHAMELEON BOY
KARATE KID
MON-EL
COSMIC BOY
VIOLET
WOW.
YOU HAD A *LOT* OF FRIENDS.

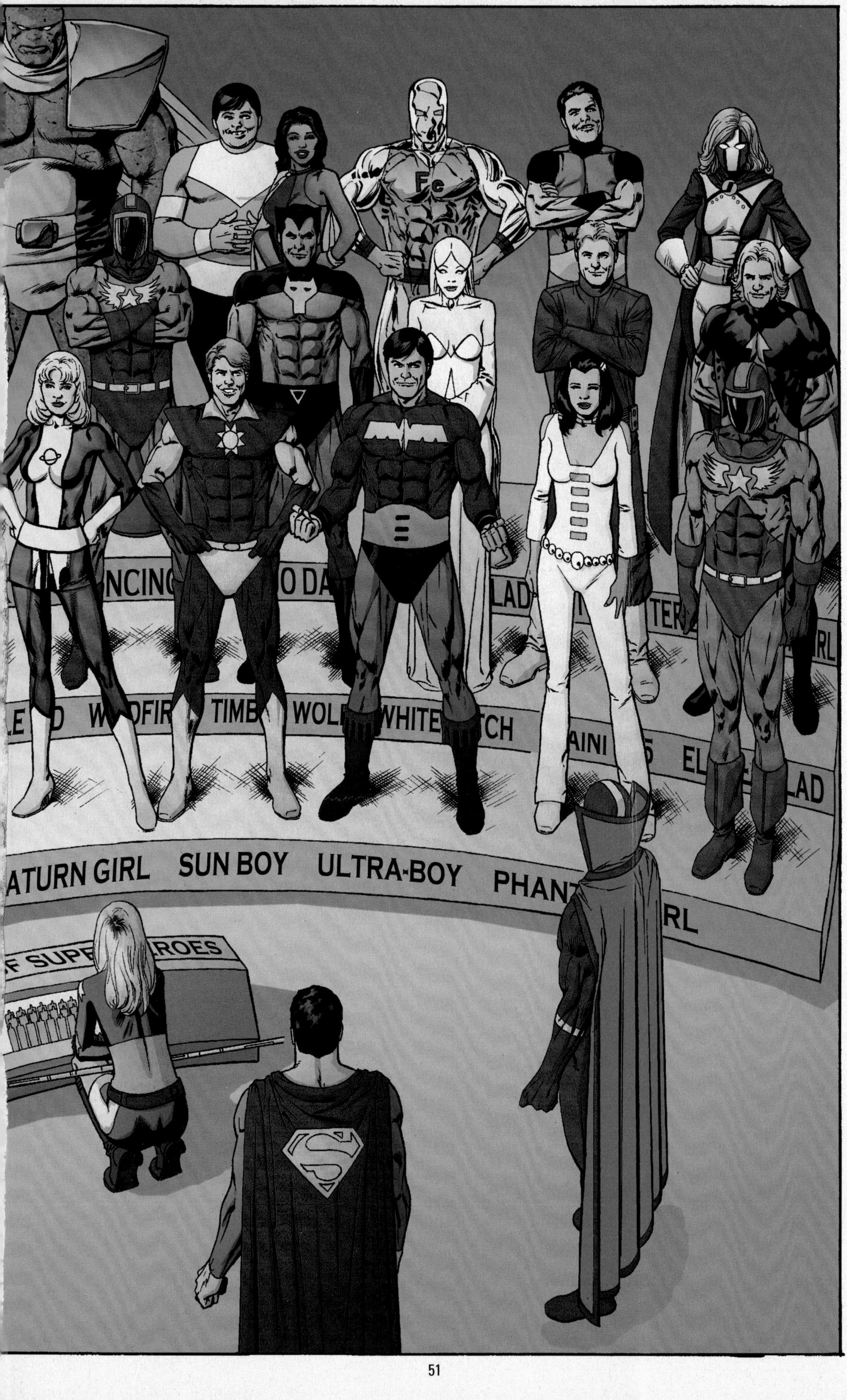
ATURN GIRL
SUN BOY
ULTRA-BOY

I DIDN'T FOR A LONG TIME.

WHEN *I* WAS YOUR AGE THERE WEREN'T ANY OTHER KIDS AROUND THAT COULD *FLY*.

YOU TWO ARE *LUCKY* TO HAVE EACH OTHER.

I CAN'T EVEN *IMAGINE* YOU AS A KID.

TOTALLY.

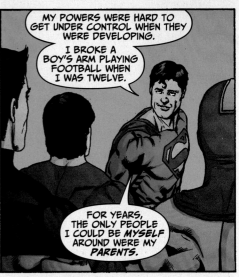

MY POWERS WERE HARD TO GET UNDER CONTROL WHEN THEY WERE DEVELOPING.

I BROKE A BOY'S ARM PLAYING FOOTBALL WHEN I WAS TWELVE.

FOR YEARS, THE ONLY PEOPLE I COULD BE *MYSELF* AROUND WERE MY *PARENTS*.

THEN ONE DAY AFTER SCHOOL, *THESE* THREE SHOWED UP.

SATURN GIRL?

COSMIC BOY TOLD ME WHEN I WAS OLDER I'D BECOME THE INSPIRATION THAT WOULD HELP FOUND THE LEGION.

E KID MON-EL COSMIC BOY LIGHTNING LAD SATURN GIRL SUN BOY ULTRA

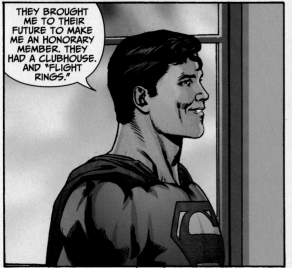

THEY BROUGHT ME TO THEIR FUTURE TO MAKE ME AN HONORARY MEMBER. THEY HAD A CLUBHOUSE. AND "FLIGHT RINGS."

EVERY SINGLE *ONE* OF THEM COULD *FLY*.

IN THE END I THINK THEY INSPIRED *ME* MORE THAN I INSPIRED *THEM*.

SO STARMAN'S A MEMBER OF THE LEGION?

HE *WAS*.

UNTIL HE KILLED A MAN NAMED KENZ NUHOR. IT WAS IN SELF-DEFENSE, BUT THE LEGION HAS A STRONG CODE *AGAINST* KILLING.

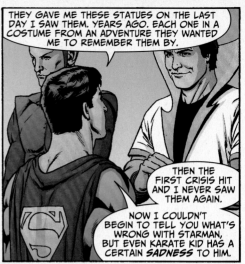

THEY GAVE ME THESE STATUES ON THE LAST DAY I SAW THEM. YEARS AGO. EACH ONE IN A COSTUME FROM AN ADVENTURE THEY WANTED ME TO REMEMBER THEM BY.

THEN THE FIRST CRISIS HIT AND I NEVER SAW THEM AGAIN.

NOW I COULDN'T BEGIN TO TELL YOU WHAT'S WRONG WITH STARMAN, BUT EVEN KARATE KID HAS A CERTAIN *SADNESS* TO HIM.

WHAT HAPPENED TO THE LEGION OF SUPER-HEROES WHEN THEY GREW UP?

SUPERMAN, I'VE LOCATED THE "FLIGHT RING" WE'VE BEEN TRACKING. ONE OF THESE STATUES IS *WEARING* IT.

HEY. HOW COME THERE'S *TWO* OF THAT *ORANGE GUY*?

ONE NEXT TO TIMBER WOLF AND ONE NEXT TO PHANTOM GIRL.

THAT ONE'S NOT A STATUE.

ᗡOᒪᔭᒥᑐ ᒪᔭ.

KRAKL

53

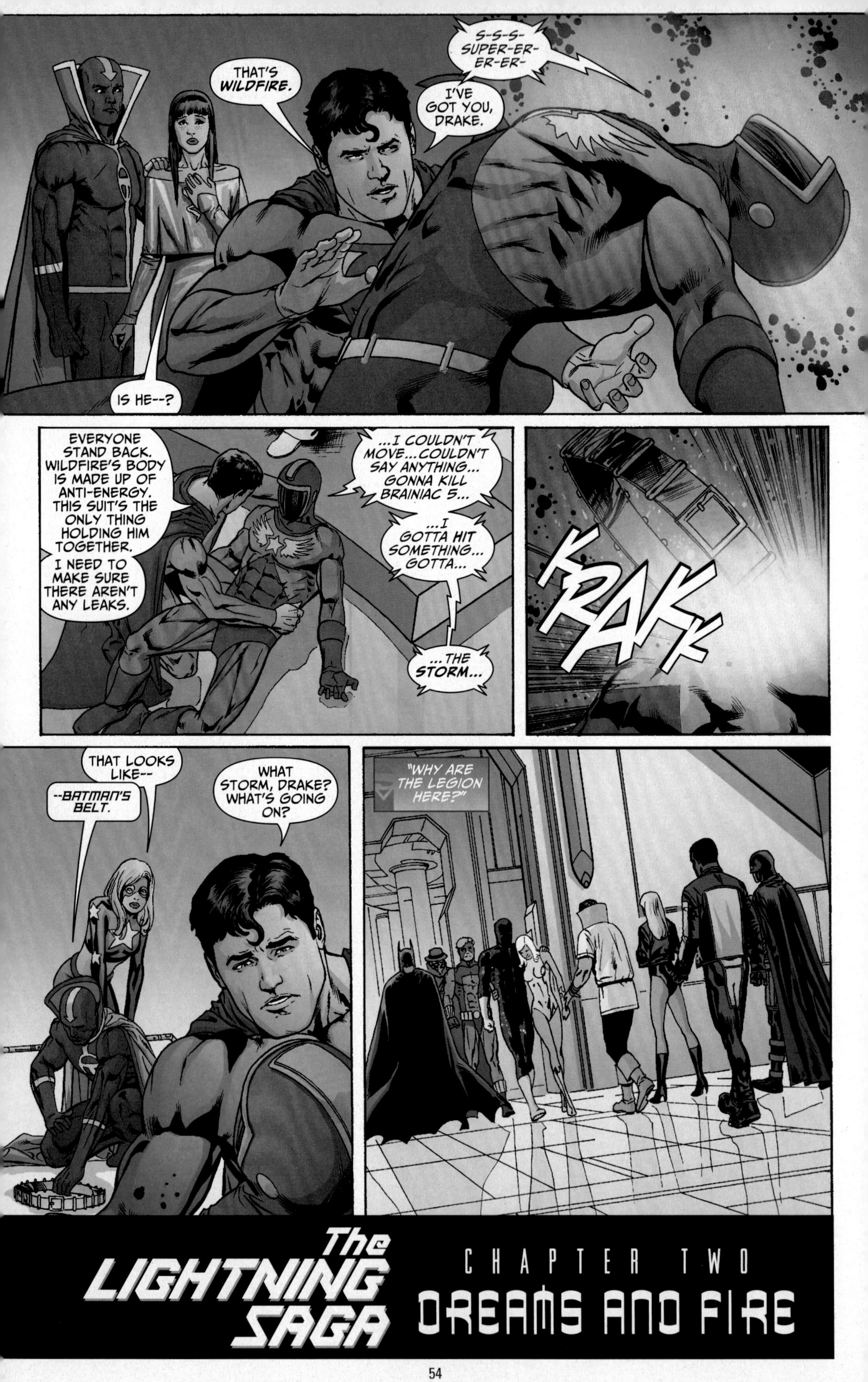
S-S-S-SUPER-ER-ER-ER-
THAT'S WILDFIRE.
I'VE GOT YOU, DRAKE.
IS HE--?
EVERYONE STAND BACK. WILDFIRE'S BODY IS MADE UP OF ANTI-ENERGY. THIS SUIT'S THE ONLY THING HOLDING HIM TOGETHER.
I NEED TO MAKE SURE THERE AREN'T ANY LEAKS.
...I COULDN'T MOVE...COULDN'T SAY ANYTHING... GONNA KILL BRAINIAC 5...
...I GOTTA HIT SOMETHING... GOTTA...
...THE STORM...
KRAKK
THAT LOOKS LIKE--
--BATMAN'S BELT.
WHAT STORM, DRAKE? WHAT'S GOING ON?
"WHY ARE THE LEGION HERE?"
The LIGHTNING SAGA
CHAPTER TWO
DREAMS AND FIRE

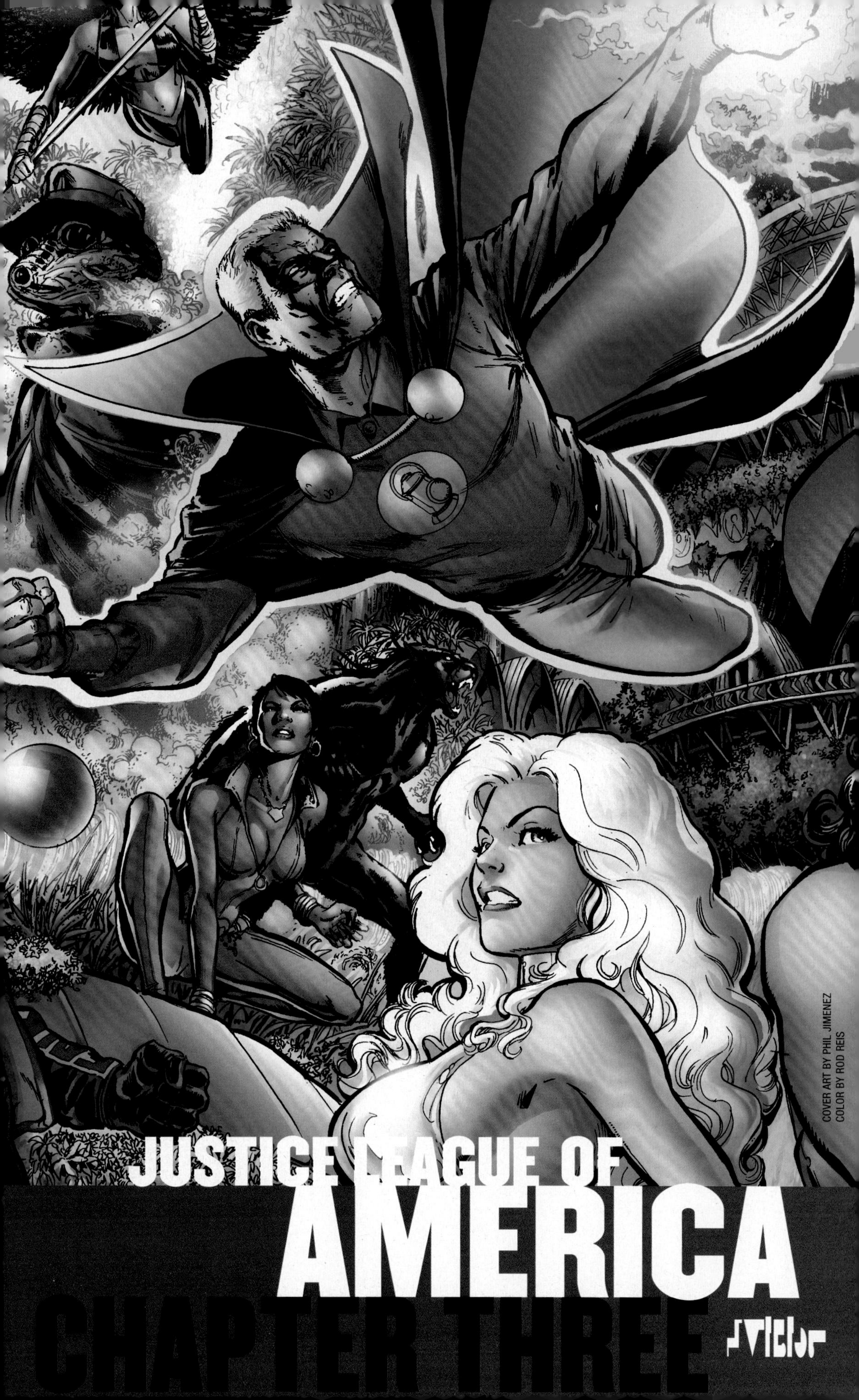
JUSTICE LEAGUE OF
AMERICA
CHAPTER THREE
COVER ART BY PHIL JIMENEZ
COLOR BY ROD REIS

"When the knife digs that deep,
it's usually coming from someone
right behind you. "

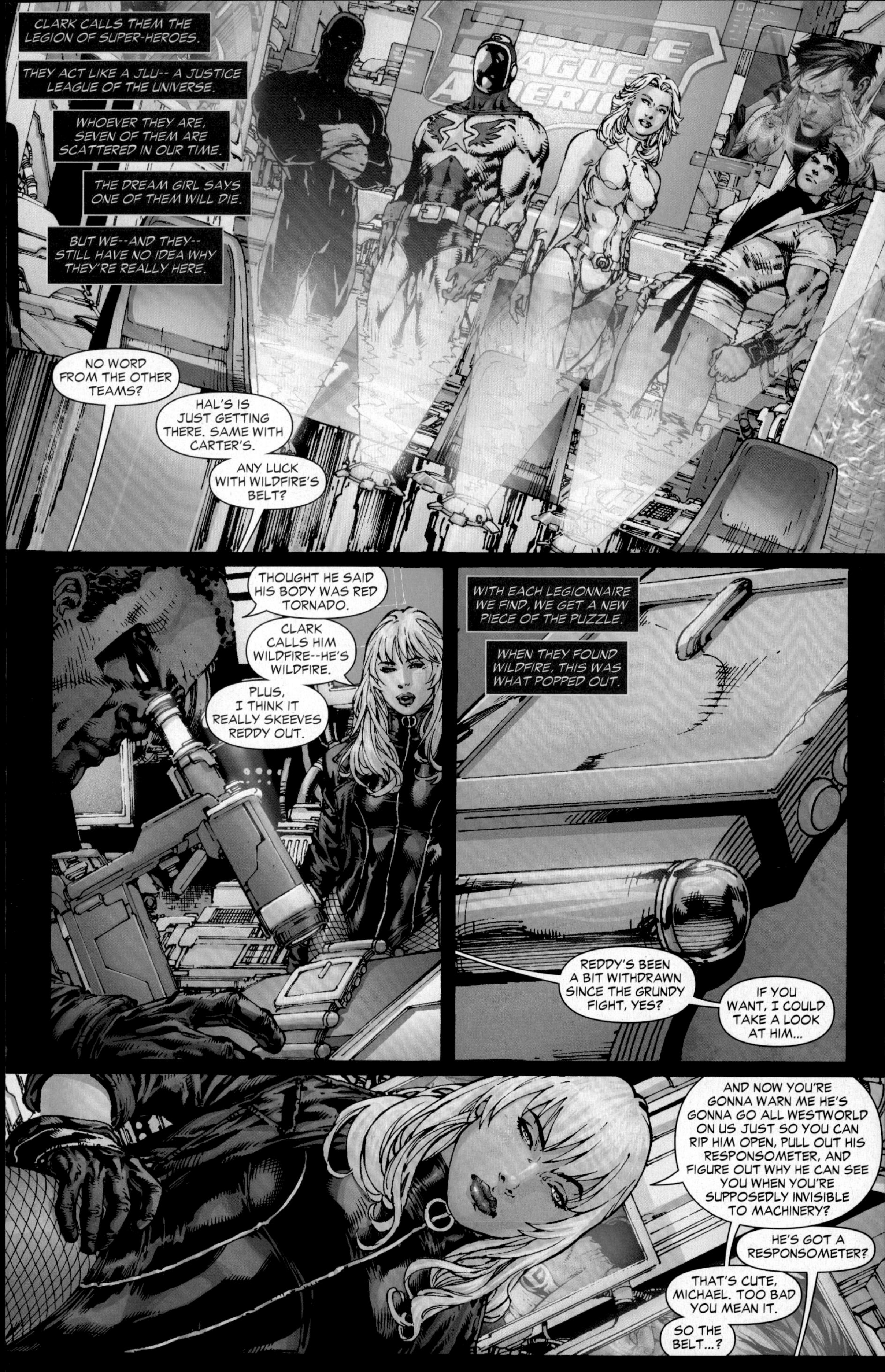
CLARK CALLS THEM THE LEGION OF SUPER-HEROES.
THEY ACT LIKE A JLU-- A JUSTICE LEAGUE OF THE UNIVERSE.
WHOEVER THEY ARE, SEVEN OF THEM ARE SCATTERED IN OUR TIME.
THE DREAM GIRL SAYS ONE OF THEM WILL DIE.
BUT WE--AND THEY-- STILL HAVE NO IDEA WHY THEY'RE REALLY HERE.
NO WORD FROM THE OTHER TEAMS?
HAL'S IS JUST GETTING THERE. SAME WITH CARTER'S.
ANY LUCK WITH WILDFIRE'S BELT?
THOUGHT HE SAID HIS BODY WAS RED TORNADO.
CLARK CALLS HIM WILDFIRE--HE'S WILDFIRE.
PLUS, I THINK IT REALLY SKEEVES REDDY OUT.
WITH EACH LEGIONNAIRE WE FIND, WE GET A NEW PIECE OF THE PUZZLE.
WHEN THEY FOUND WILDFIRE, THIS WAS WHAT POPPED OUT.
REDDY'S BEEN A BIT WITHDRAWN SINCE THE GRUNDY FIGHT, YES?
IF YOU WANT, I COULD TAKE A LOOK AT HIM...
AND NOW YOU'RE GONNA WARN ME HE'S GONNA GO ALL WESTWORLD ON US JUST SO YOU CAN RIP HIM OPEN, PULL OUT HIS RESPONSOMETER, AND FIGURE OUT WHY HE CAN SEE YOU WHEN YOU'RE SUPPOSEDLY INVISIBLE TO MACHINERY?
HE'S GOT A RESPONSOMETER?
THAT'S CUTE, MICHAEL. TOO BAD YOU MEAN IT.
SO THE BELT...?

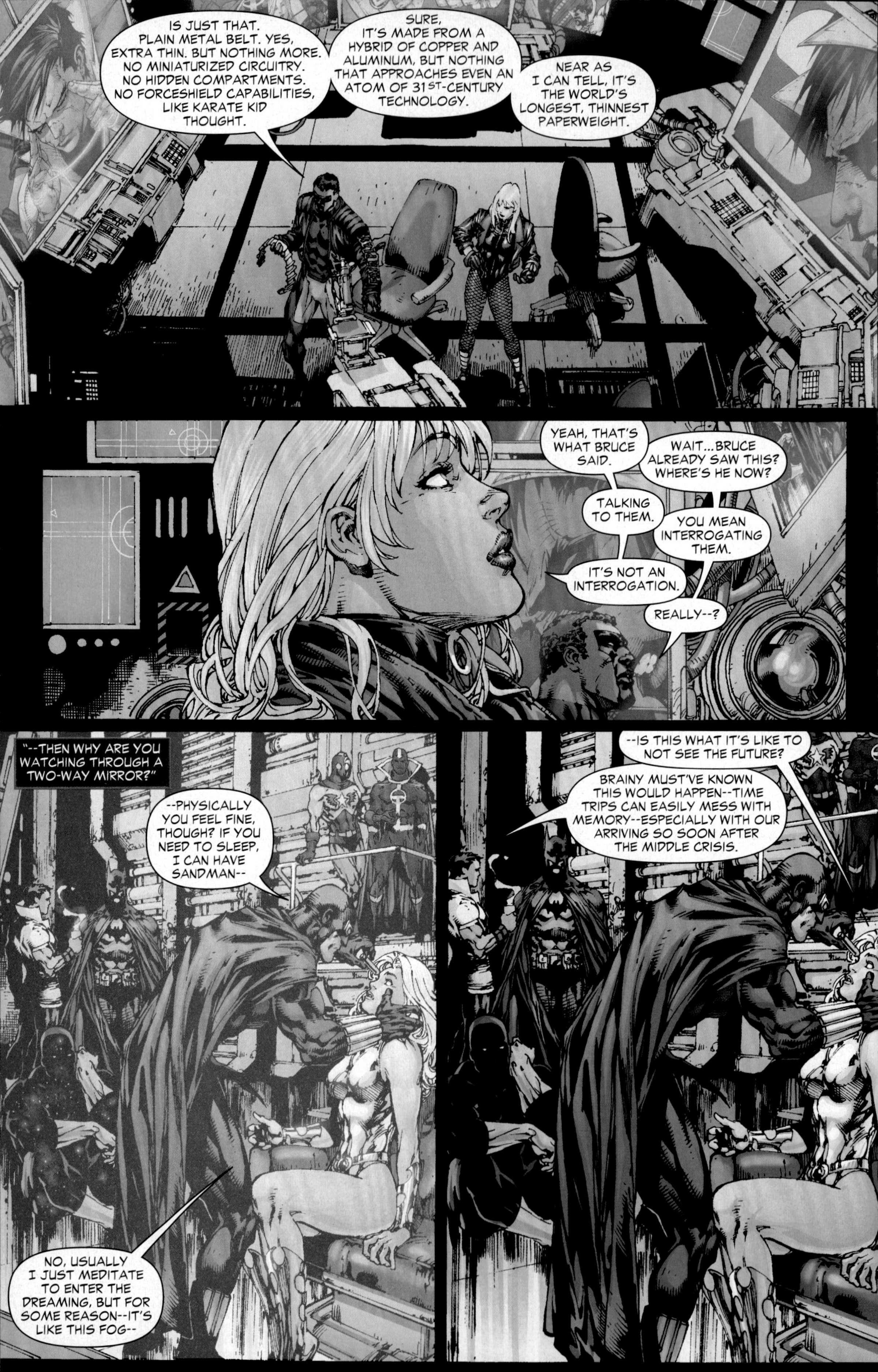
IS JUST THAT. PLAIN METAL BELT. YES, EXTRA THIN. BUT NOTHING MORE. NO MINIATURIZED CIRCUITRY. NO HIDDEN COMPARTMENTS. NO FORCESHIELD CAPABILITIES, LIKE KARATE KID THOUGHT.
SURE, IT'S MADE FROM A HYBRID OF COPPER AND ALUMINUM, BUT NOTHING THAT APPROACHES EVEN AN ATOM OF 31ST-CENTURY TECHNOLOGY.
NEAR AS I CAN TELL, IT'S THE WORLD'S LONGEST, THINNEST PAPERWEIGHT.
YEAH, THAT'S WHAT BRUCE SAID.
WAIT...BRUCE ALREADY SAW THIS? WHERE'S HE NOW?
TALKING TO THEM.
YOU MEAN INTERROGATING THEM.
IT'S NOT AN INTERROGATION.
REALLY--?
"--THEN WHY ARE YOU WATCHING THROUGH A TWO-WAY MIRROR?"
--PHYSICALLY YOU FEEL FINE, THOUGH? IF YOU NEED TO SLEEP, I CAN HAVE SANDMAN--
NO, USUALLY I JUST MEDITATE TO ENTER THE DREAMING, BUT FOR SOME REASON--IT'S LIKE THIS FOG--
--IS THIS WHAT IT'S LIKE TO NOT SEE THE FUTURE?
BRAINY MUST'VE KNOWN THIS WOULD HAPPEN--TIME TRIPS CAN EASILY MESS WITH MEMORY--ESPECIALLY WITH OUR ARRIVING SO SOON AFTER THE MIDDLE CRISIS.

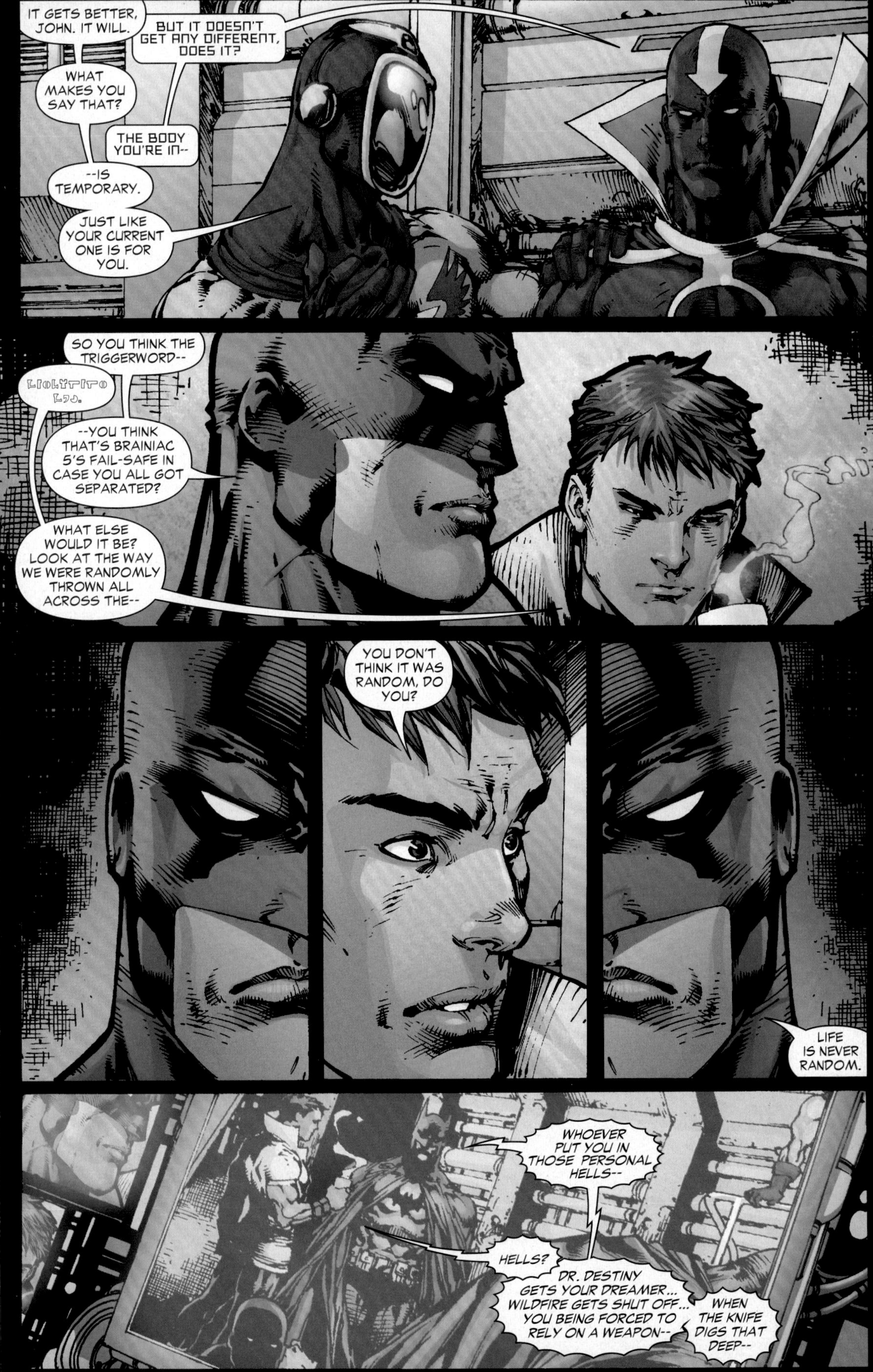
IT GETS BETTER, JOHN. IT WILL.
BUT IT DOESN'T GET ANY DIFFERENT, DOES IT?
WHAT MAKES YOU SAY THAT?
THE BODY YOU'RE IN--
--IS TEMPORARY.
JUST LIKE YOUR CURRENT ONE IS FOR YOU.
SO YOU THINK THE TRIGGERWORD--
--YOU THINK THAT'S BRAINIAC 5'S FAIL-SAFE IN CASE YOU ALL GOT SEPARATED?
WHAT ELSE WOULD IT BE? LOOK AT THE WAY WE WERE RANDOMLY THROWN ALL ACROSS THE--
YOU DON'T THINK IT WAS RANDOM, DO YOU?
LIFE IS NEVER RANDOM.
WHOEVER PUT YOU IN THOSE PERSONAL HELLS--
HELLS?
DR. DESTINY GETS YOUR DREAMER... WILDFIRE GETS SHUT OFF... YOU BEING FORCED TO RELY ON A WEAPON--
WHEN THE KNIFE DIGS THAT DEEP--

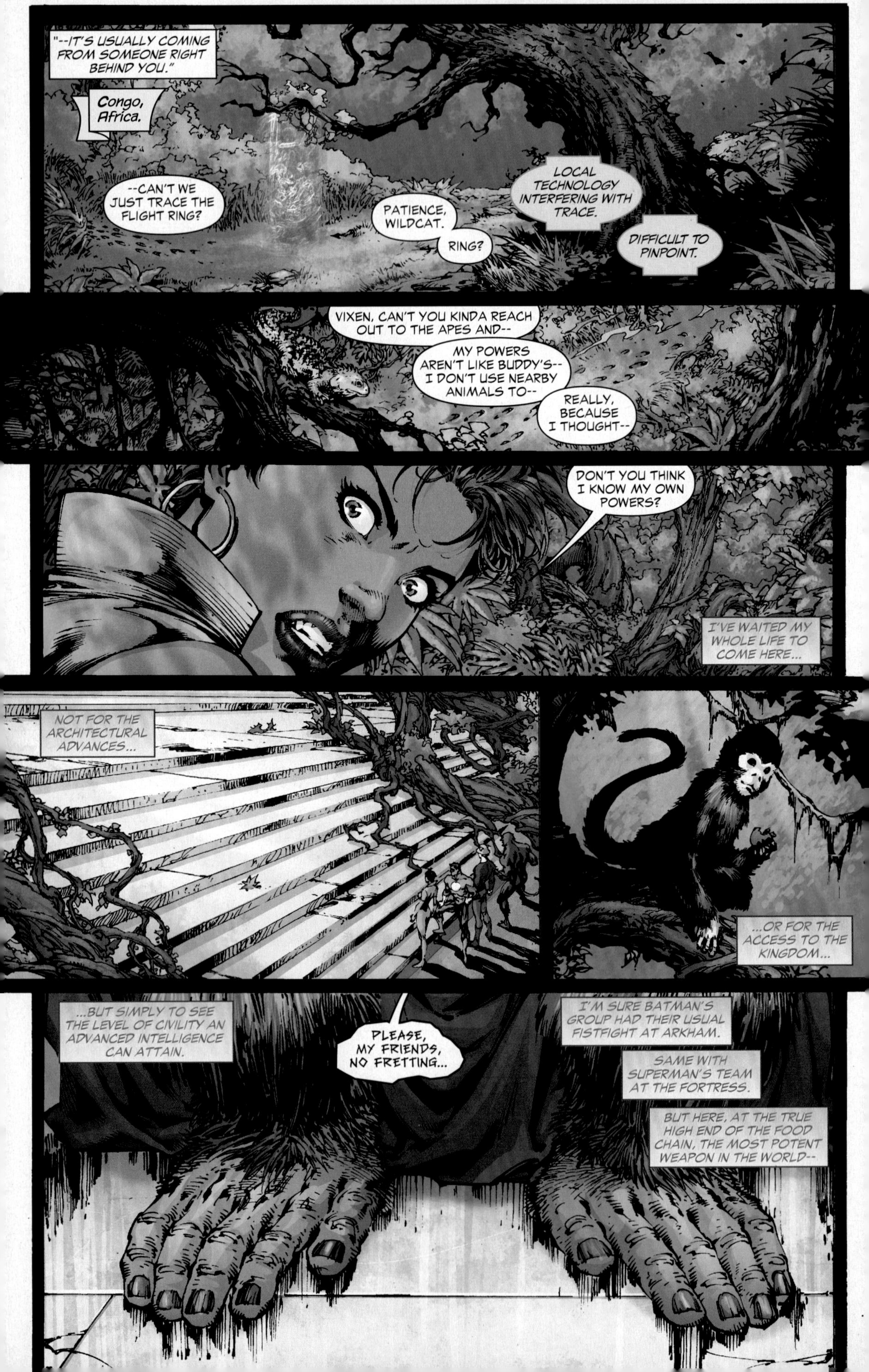
"--IT'S USUALLY COMING FROM SOMEONE RIGHT BEHIND YOU."
Congo, Africa.
--CAN'T WE JUST TRACE THE FLIGHT RING?
PATIENCE, WILDCAT.
RING?
LOCAL TECHNOLOGY INTERFERING WITH TRACE.
DIFFICULT TO PINPOINT.
VIXEN, CAN'T YOU KINDA REACH OUT TO THE APES AND--
MY POWERS AREN'T LIKE BUDDY'S-- I DON'T USE NEARBY ANIMALS TO--
REALLY, BECAUSE I THOUGHT--
DON'T YOU THINK I KNOW MY OWN POWERS?
I'VE WAITED MY WHOLE LIFE TO COME HERE...
NOT FOR THE ARCHITECTURAL ADVANCES...
...OR FOR THE ACCESS TO THE KINGDOM...
...BUT SIMPLY TO SEE THE LEVEL OF CIVILITY AN ADVANCED INTELLIGENCE CAN ATTAIN.
PLEASE, MY FRIENDS, NO FRETTING...
I'M SURE BATMAN'S GROUP HAD THEIR USUAL FISTFIGHT AT ARKHAM.
SAME WITH SUPERMAN'S TEAM AT THE FORTRESS.
BUT HERE, AT THE TRUE HIGH END OF THE FOOD CHAIN, THE MOST POTENT WEAPON IN THE WORLD--

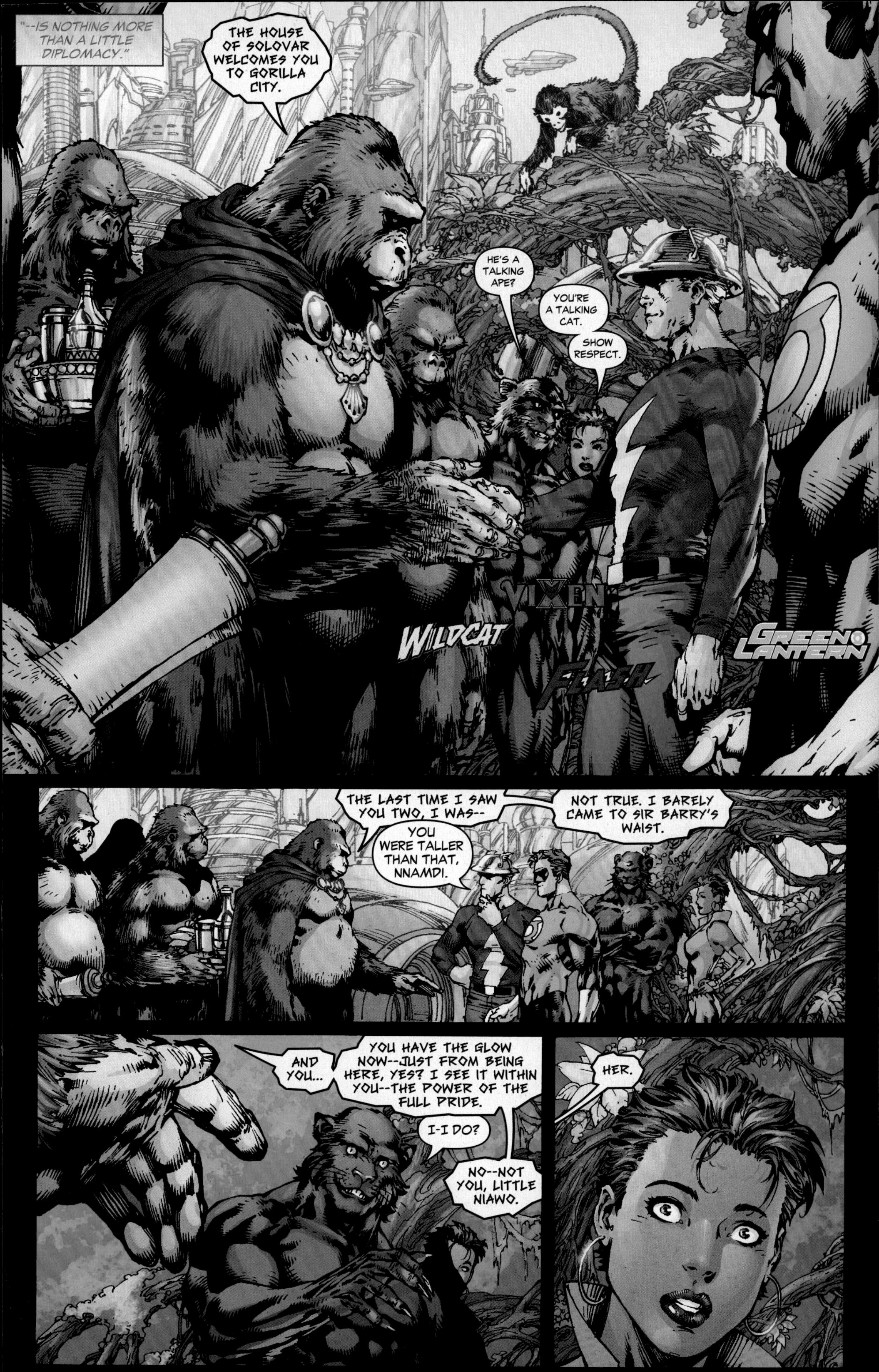
"--IS NOTHING MORE THAN A LITTLE DIPLOMACY."
THE HOUSE OF SOLOVAR WELCOMES YOU TO GORILLA CITY.
HE'S A TALKING APE?
YOU'RE A TALKING CAT.
SHOW RESPECT.
VIXEN
WILDCAT
FLASH
GREEN LANTERN
THE LAST TIME I SAW YOU TWO, I WAS--
YOU WERE TALLER THAN THAT, NNAMDI.
NOT TRUE. I BARELY CAME TO SIR BARRY'S WAIST.
AND YOU...
YOU HAVE THE GLOW NOW--JUST FROM BEING HERE, YES? I SEE IT WITHIN YOU--THE POWER OF THE FULL PRIDE.
I-I DO?
NO--NOT YOU, LITTLE NIAWO.
HER.

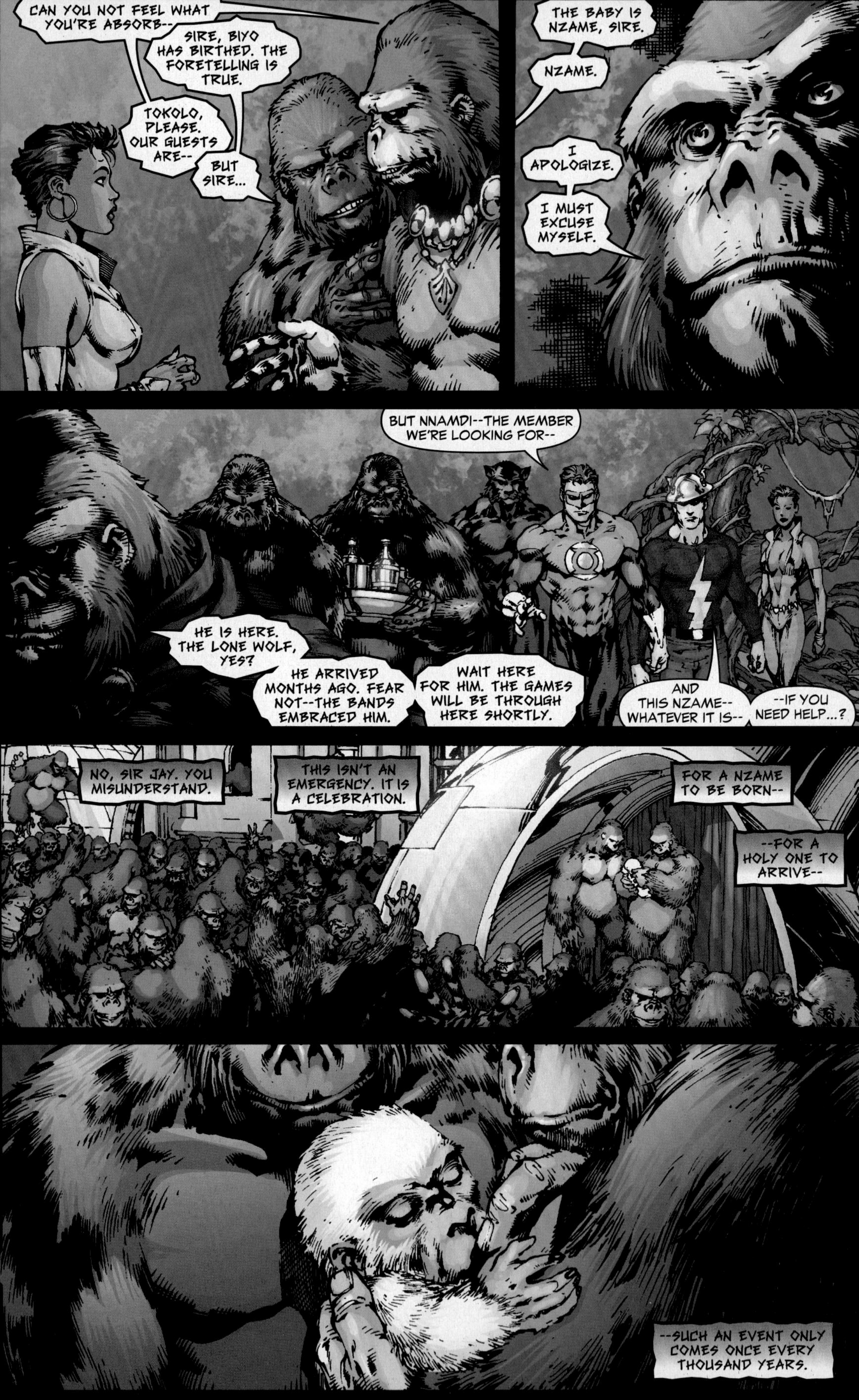
CAN YOU NOT FEEL WHAT YOU'RE ABSORB--
SIRE, BIYO HAS BIRTHED. THE FORETELLING IS TRUE.
TOKOLO, PLEASE. OUR GUESTS ARE--
BUT SIRE...
THE BABY IS NZAME, SIRE.
NZAME.
I APOLOGIZE.
I MUST EXCUSE MYSELF.
BUT NNAMDI--THE MEMBER WE'RE LOOKING FOR--
HE IS HERE. THE LONE WOLF, YES?
HE ARRIVED MONTHS AGO. FEAR NOT--THE BANDS EMBRACED HIM.
WAIT HERE FOR HIM. THE GAMES WILL BE THROUGH HERE SHORTLY.
AND THIS NZAME--WHATEVER IT IS--
--IF YOU NEED HELP...?
NO, SIR JAY. YOU MISUNDERSTAND.
THIS ISN'T AN EMERGENCY. IT IS A CELEBRATION.
FOR A NZAME TO BE BORN--
--FOR A HOLY ONE TO ARRIVE--
--SUCH AN EVENT ONLY COMES ONCE EVERY THOUSAND YEARS.

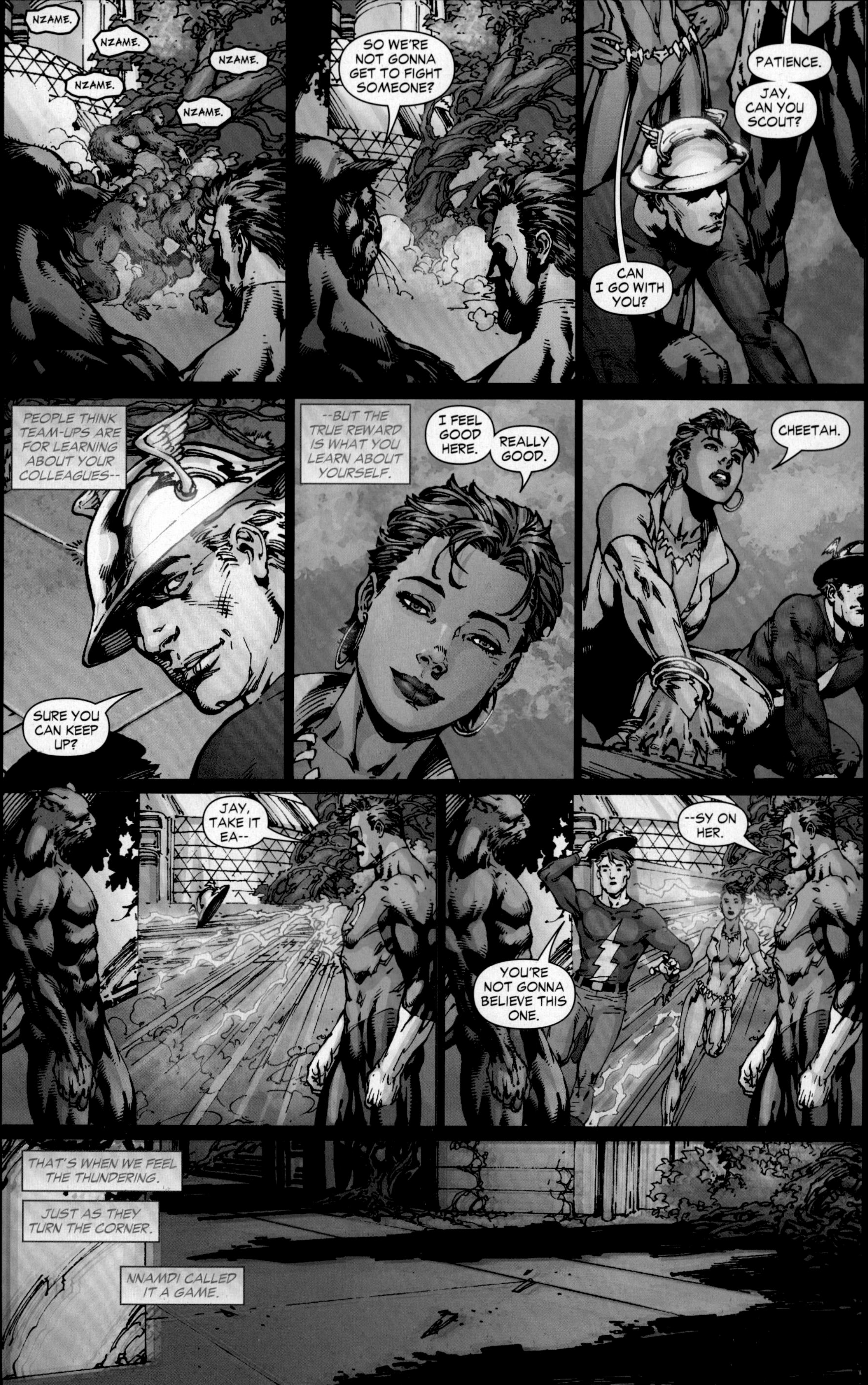
NZAME.
NZAME.
NZAME.
NZAME.
NZAME.
SO WE'RE NOT GONNA GET TO FIGHT SOMEONE?
PATIENCE.
JAY, CAN YOU SCOUT?
CAN I GO WITH YOU?
PEOPLE THINK TEAM-UPS ARE FOR LEARNING ABOUT YOUR COLLEAGUES--
SURE YOU CAN KEEP UP?
--BUT THE TRUE REWARD IS WHAT YOU LEARN ABOUT YOURSELF.
I FEEL GOOD HERE.
REALLY GOOD.
CHEETAH.
JAY, TAKE IT EA--
--SY ON HER.
YOU'RE NOT GONNA BELIEVE THIS ONE.
THAT'S WHEN WE FEEL THE THUNDERING.
JUST AS THEY TURN THE CORNER.
NNAMDI CALLED IT A GAME.

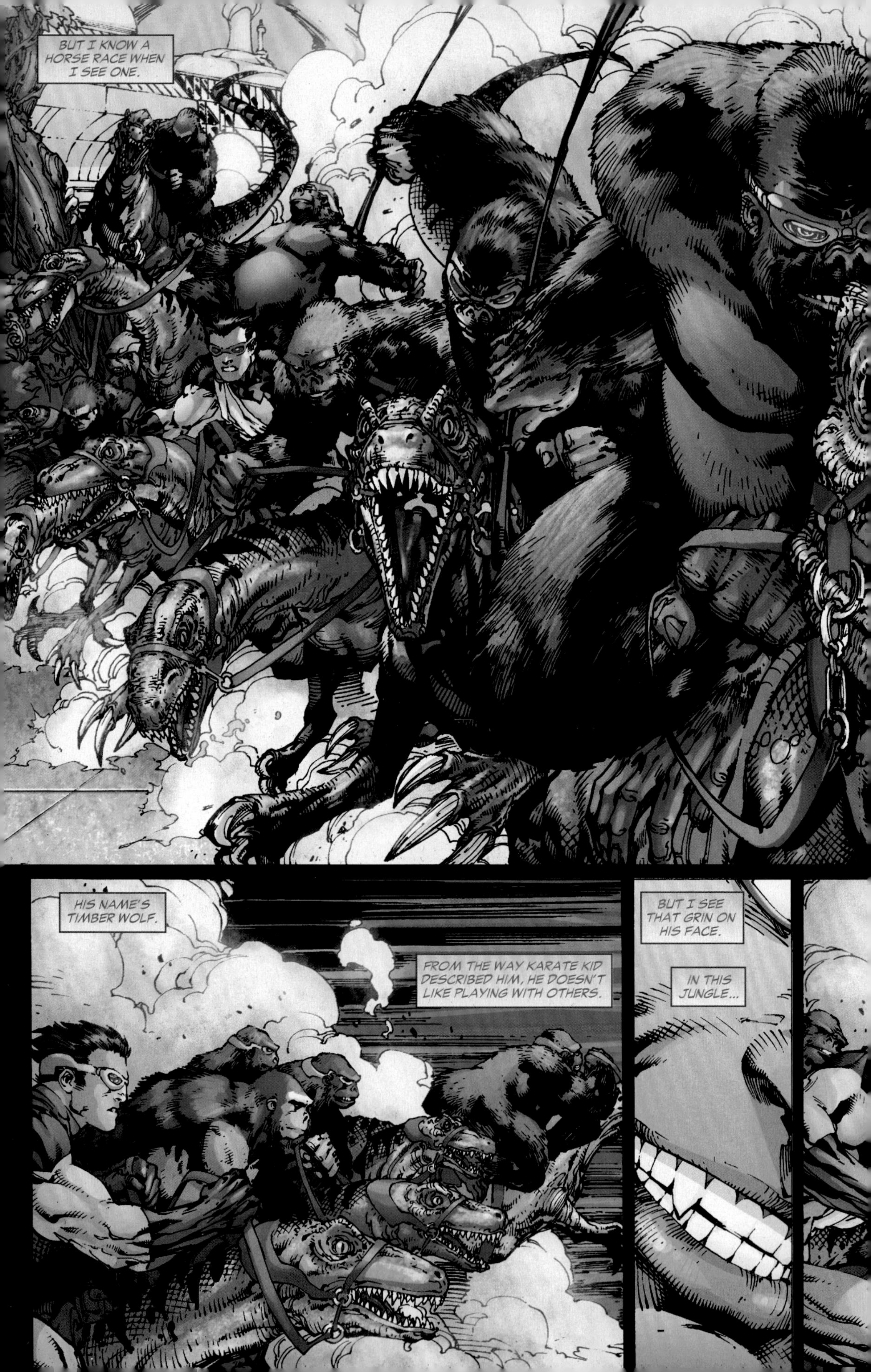
BUT I KNOW A HORSE RACE WHEN I SEE ONE.
HIS NAME'S TIMBER WOLF.
FROM THE WAY KARATE KID DESCRIBED HIM, HE DOESN'T LIKE PLAYING WITH OTHERS.
BUT I SEE THAT GRIN ON HIS FACE.
IN THIS JUNGLE...

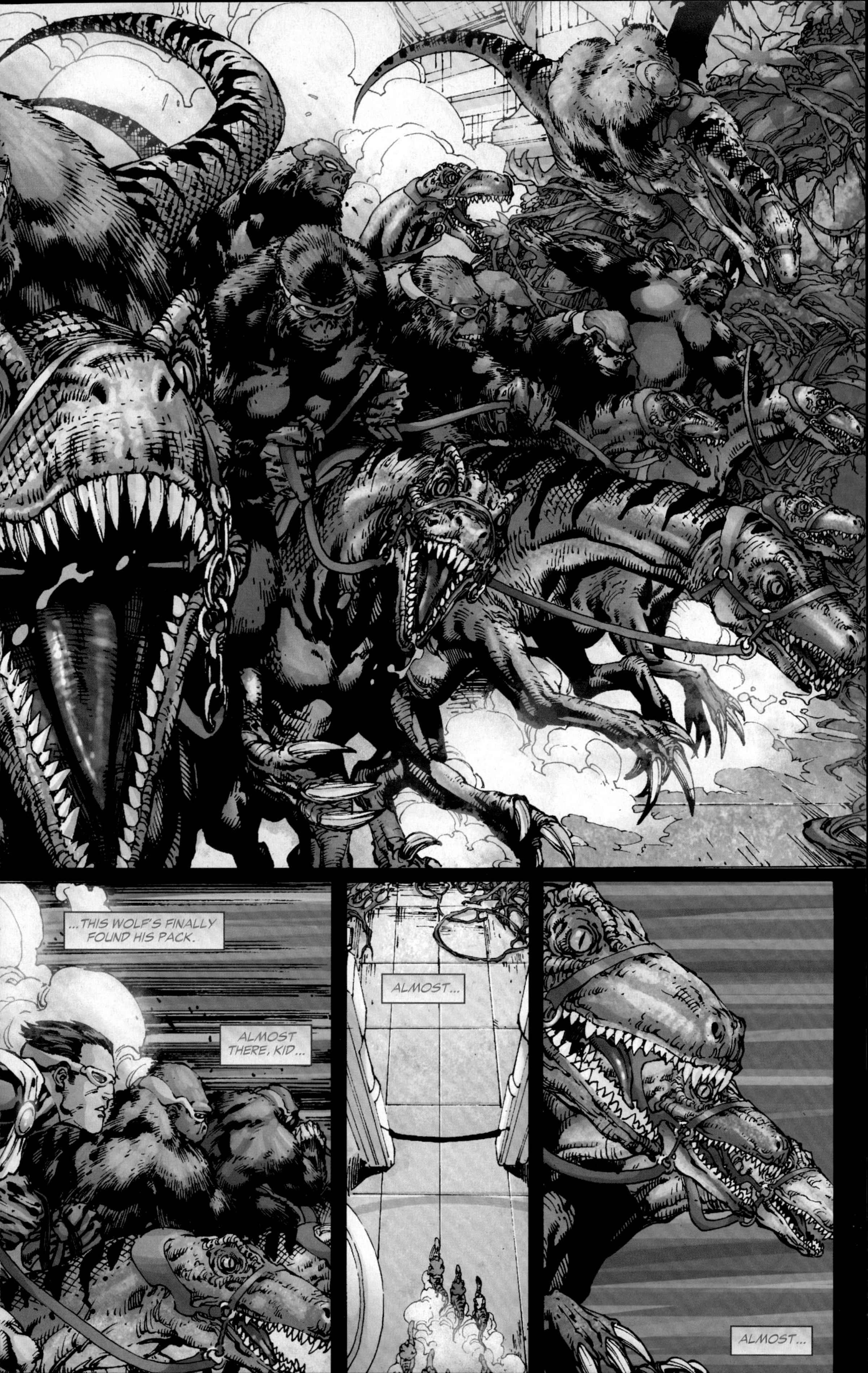
...THIS WOLF'S FINALLY FOUND HIS PACK.
ALMOST THERE, KID...
ALMOST...
ALMOST...

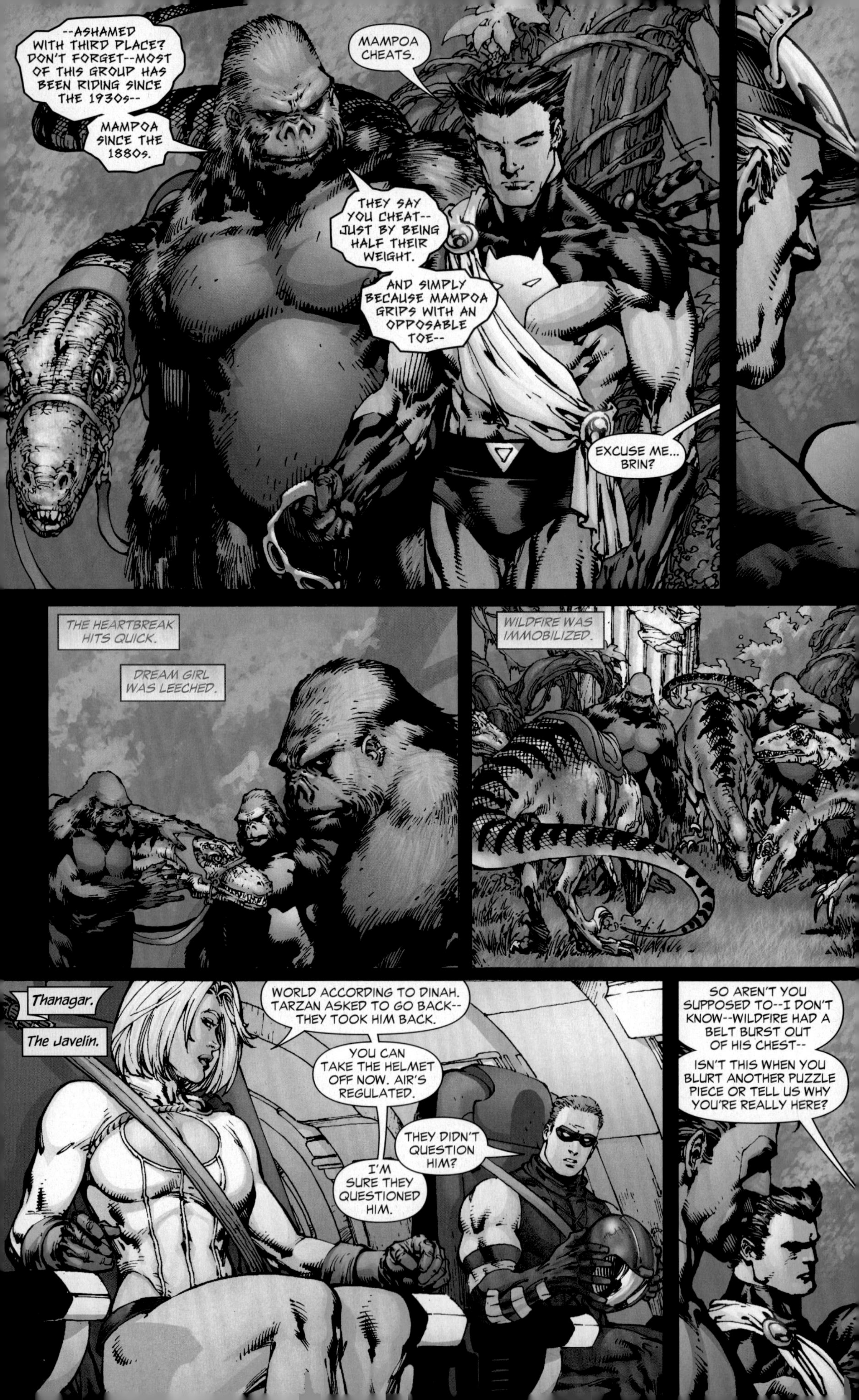
--ASHAMED WITH THIRD PLACE? DON'T FORGET--MOST OF THIS GROUP HAS BEEN RIDING SINCE THE 1930s--
MAMPOA SINCE THE 1880s.
MAMPOA CHEATS.
THEY SAY YOU CHEAT--JUST BY BEING HALF THEIR WEIGHT.
AND SIMPLY BECAUSE MAMPOA GRIPS WITH AN OPPOSABLE TOE--
EXCUSE ME... BRIN?
THE HEARTBREAK HITS QUICK.
DREAM GIRL WAS LEECHED.
WILDFIRE WAS IMMOBILIZED.
Thanagar.
The Javelin.
WORLD ACCORDING TO DINAH. TARZAN ASKED TO GO BACK--THEY TOOK HIM BACK.
YOU CAN TAKE THE HELMET OFF NOW. AIR'S REGULATED.
THEY DIDN'T QUESTION HIM?
I'M SURE THEY QUESTIONED HIM.
SO AREN'T YOU SUPPOSED TO--I DON'T KNOW--WILDFIRE HAD A BELT BURST OUT OF HIS CHEST--
ISN'T THIS WHEN YOU BLURT ANOTHER PUZZLE PIECE OR TELL US WHY YOU'RE REALLY HERE?

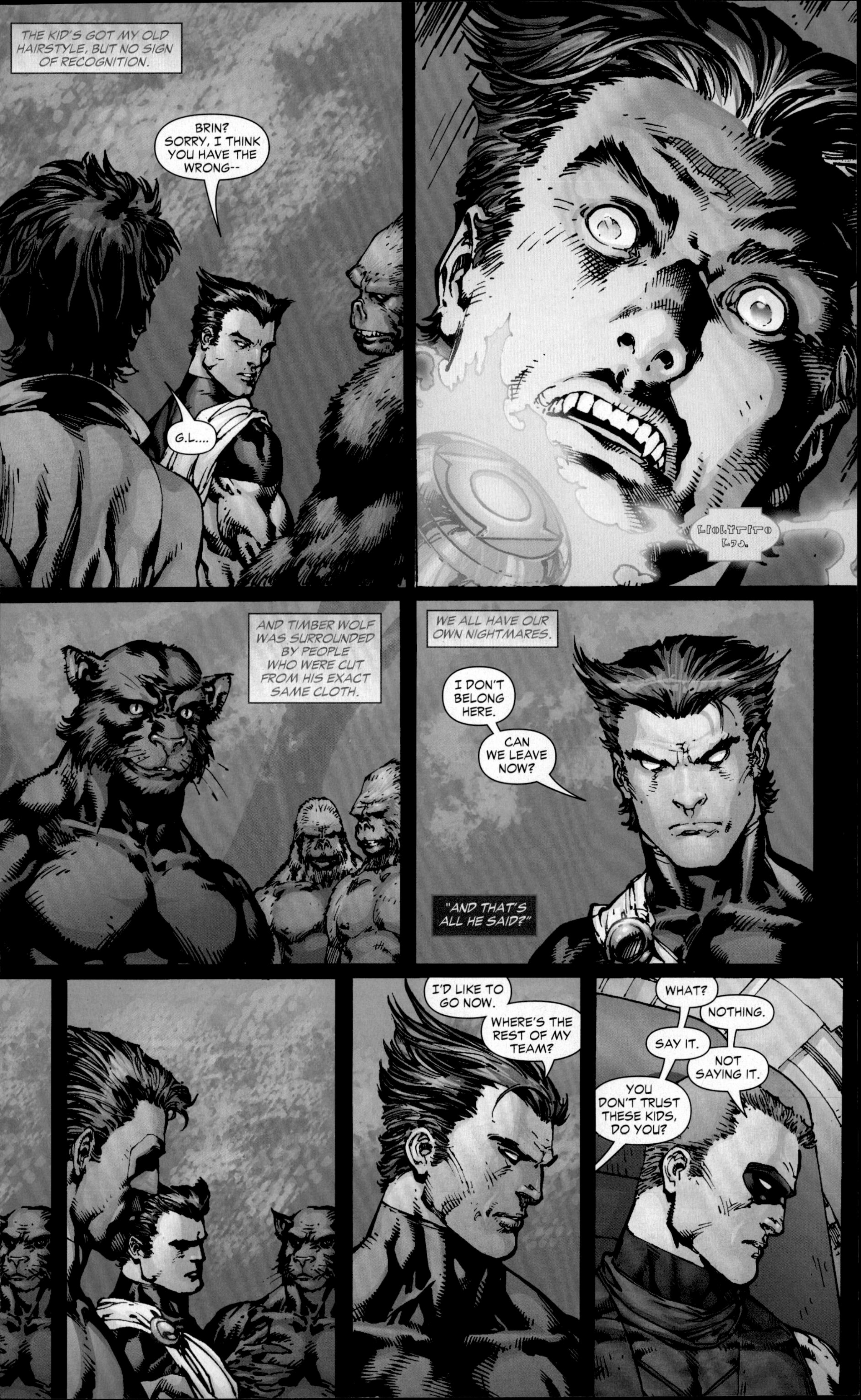
THE KID'S GOT MY OLD HAIRSTYLE, BUT NO SIGN OF RECOGNITION.
BRIN? SORRY, I THINK YOU HAVE THE WRONG--
G.L....
AND TIMBER WOLF WAS SURROUNDED BY PEOPLE WHO WERE CUT FROM HIS EXACT SAME CLOTH.
WE ALL HAVE OUR OWN NIGHTMARES.
I DON'T BELONG HERE.
CAN WE LEAVE NOW?
"AND THAT'S ALL HE SAID?"
I'D LIKE TO GO NOW.
WHERE'S THE REST OF MY TEAM?
WHAT?
NOTHING.
SAY IT.
NOT SAYING IT.
YOU DON'T TRUST THESE KIDS, DO YOU?

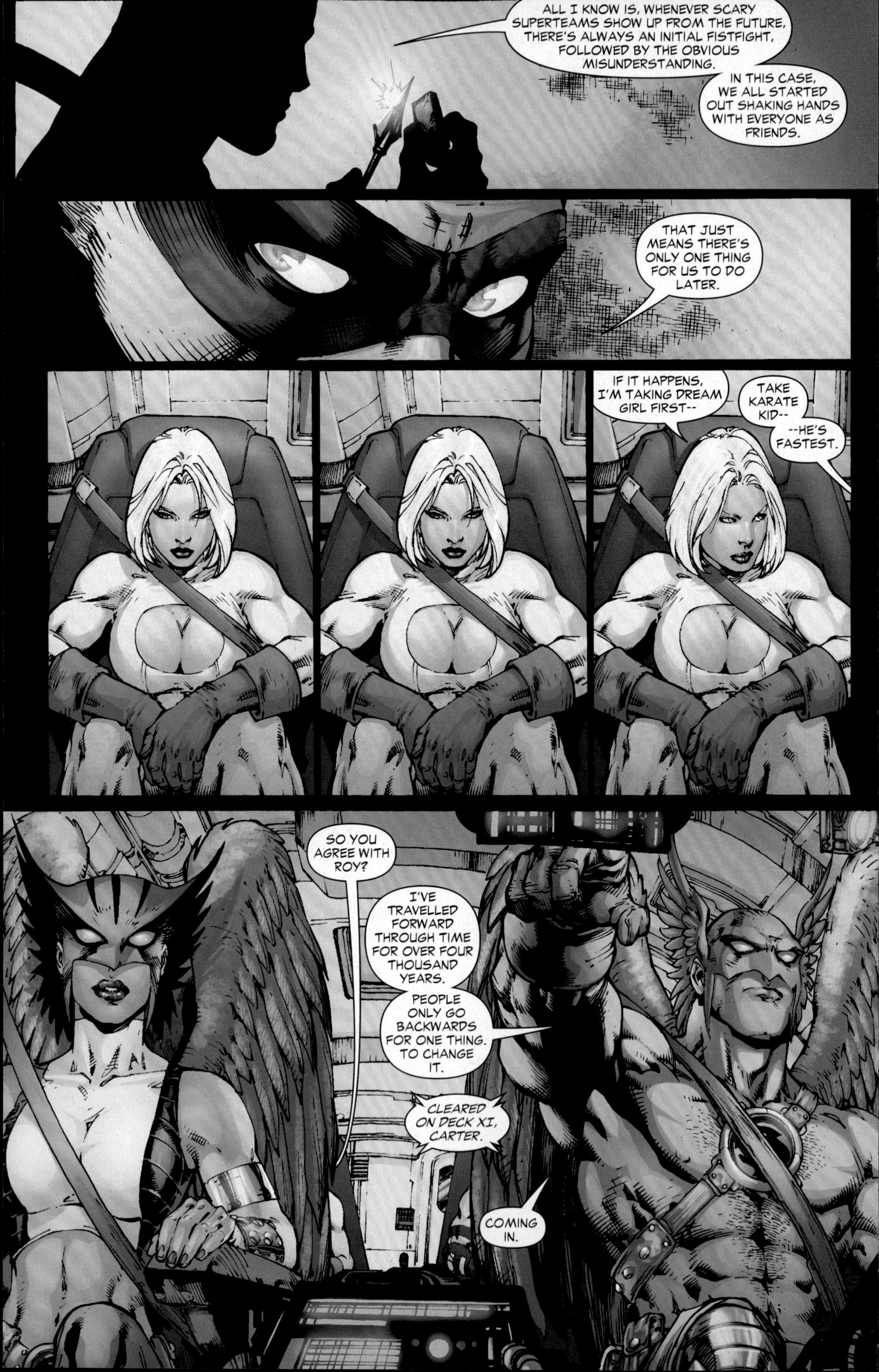
ALL I KNOW IS, WHENEVER SCARY SUPERTEAMS SHOW UP FROM THE FUTURE, THERE'S ALWAYS AN INITIAL FISTFIGHT, FOLLOWED BY THE OBVIOUS MISUNDERSTANDING.
IN THIS CASE, WE ALL STARTED OUT SHAKING HANDS WITH EVERYONE AS FRIENDS.
THAT JUST MEANS THERE'S ONLY ONE THING FOR US TO DO LATER.
IF IT HAPPENS, I'M TAKING DREAM GIRL FIRST--
TAKE KARATE KID--
--HE'S FASTEST.
SO YOU AGREE WITH ROY?
I'VE TRAVELLED FORWARD THROUGH TIME FOR OVER FOUR THOUSAND YEARS.
PEOPLE ONLY GO BACKWARDS FOR ONE THING. TO CHANGE IT.
CLEARED ON DECK XI, CARTER.
COMING IN.

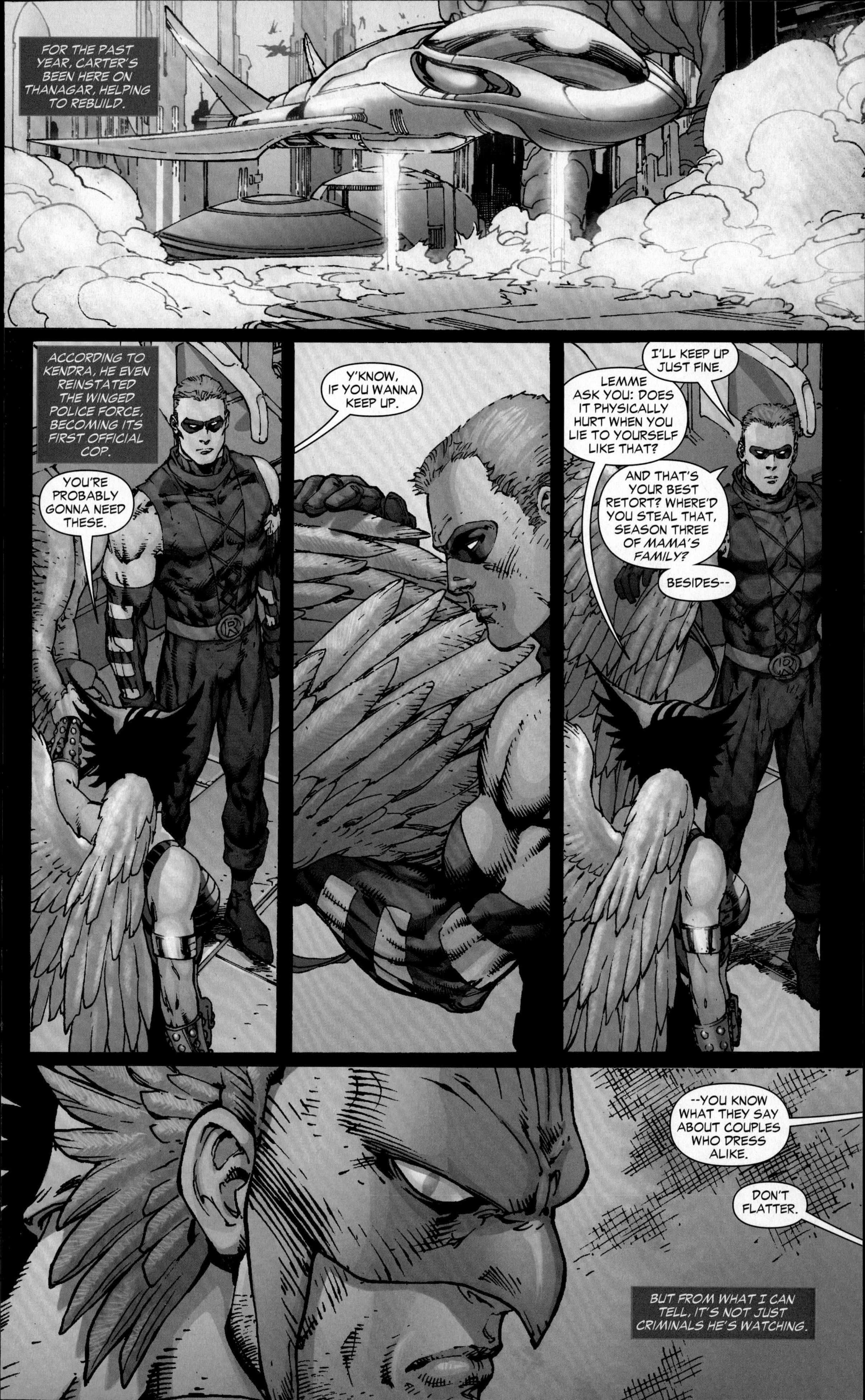
FOR THE PAST YEAR, CARTER'S BEEN HERE ON THANAGAR, HELPING TO REBUILD.
ACCORDING TO KENDRA, HE EVEN REINSTATED THE WINGED POLICE FORCE, BECOMING ITS FIRST OFFICIAL COP.
YOU'RE PROBABLY GONNA NEED THESE.
Y'KNOW, IF YOU WANNA KEEP UP.
I'LL KEEP UP JUST FINE.
LEMME ASK YOU: DOES IT PHYSICALLY HURT WHEN YOU LIE TO YOURSELF LIKE THAT?
AND THAT'S YOUR BEST RETORT? WHERE'D YOU STEAL THAT, SEASON THREE OF *MAMA'S FAMILY*?
BESIDES--
--YOU KNOW WHAT THEY SAY ABOUT COUPLES WHO DRESS ALIKE.
DON'T FLATTER.
BUT FROM WHAT I CAN TELL, IT'S NOT JUST CRIMINALS HE'S WATCHING.

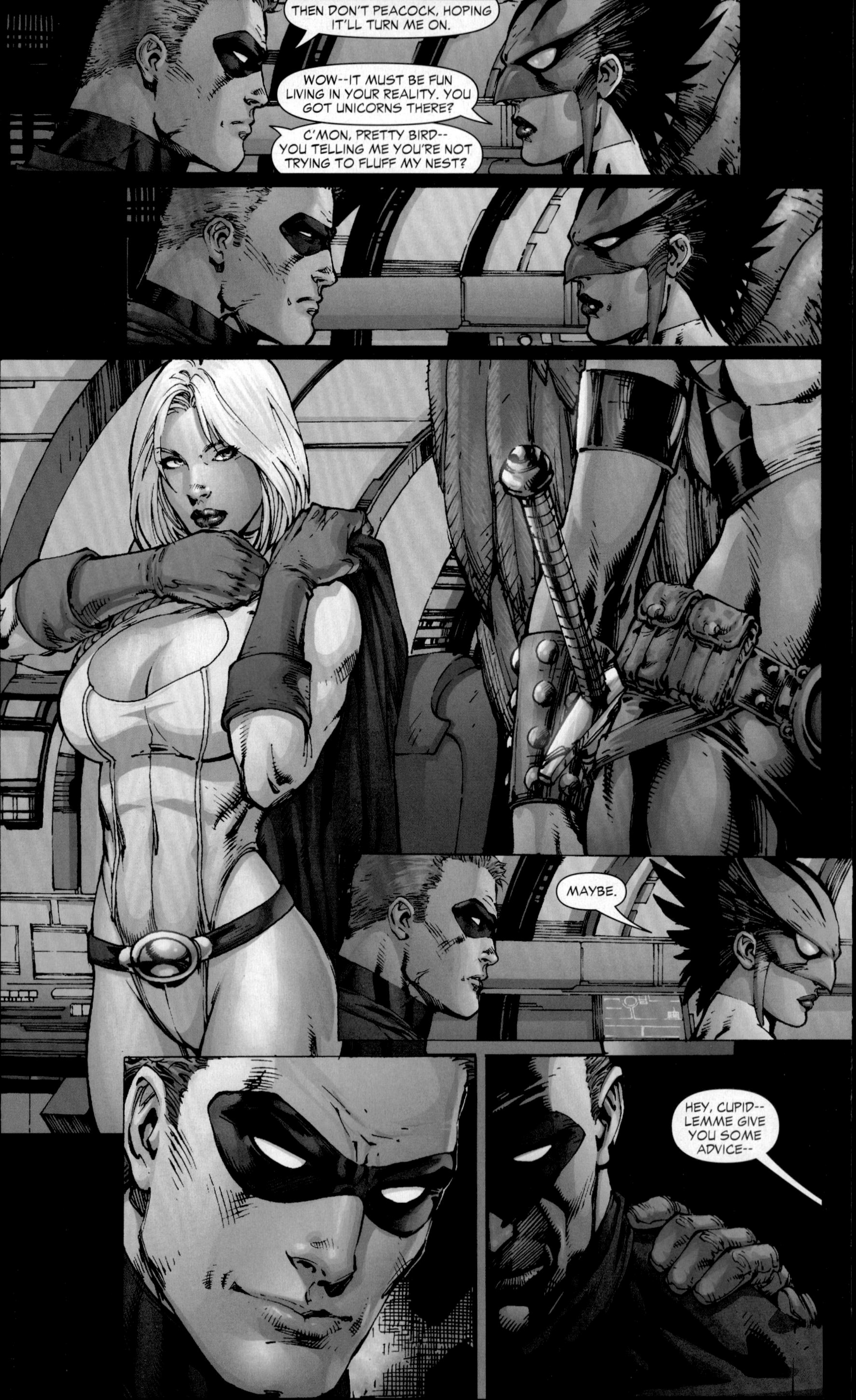
THEN DON'T PEACOCK, HOPING IT'LL TURN ME ON.
WOW--IT MUST BE FUN LIVING IN YOUR REALITY. YOU GOT UNICORNS THERE?
C'MON, PRETTY BIRD-- YOU TELLING ME YOU'RE NOT TRYING TO FLUFF MY NEST?
MAYBE.
HEY, CUPID-- LEMME GIVE YOU SOME ADVICE--

JUSTICE LEAGUE of AMERICA

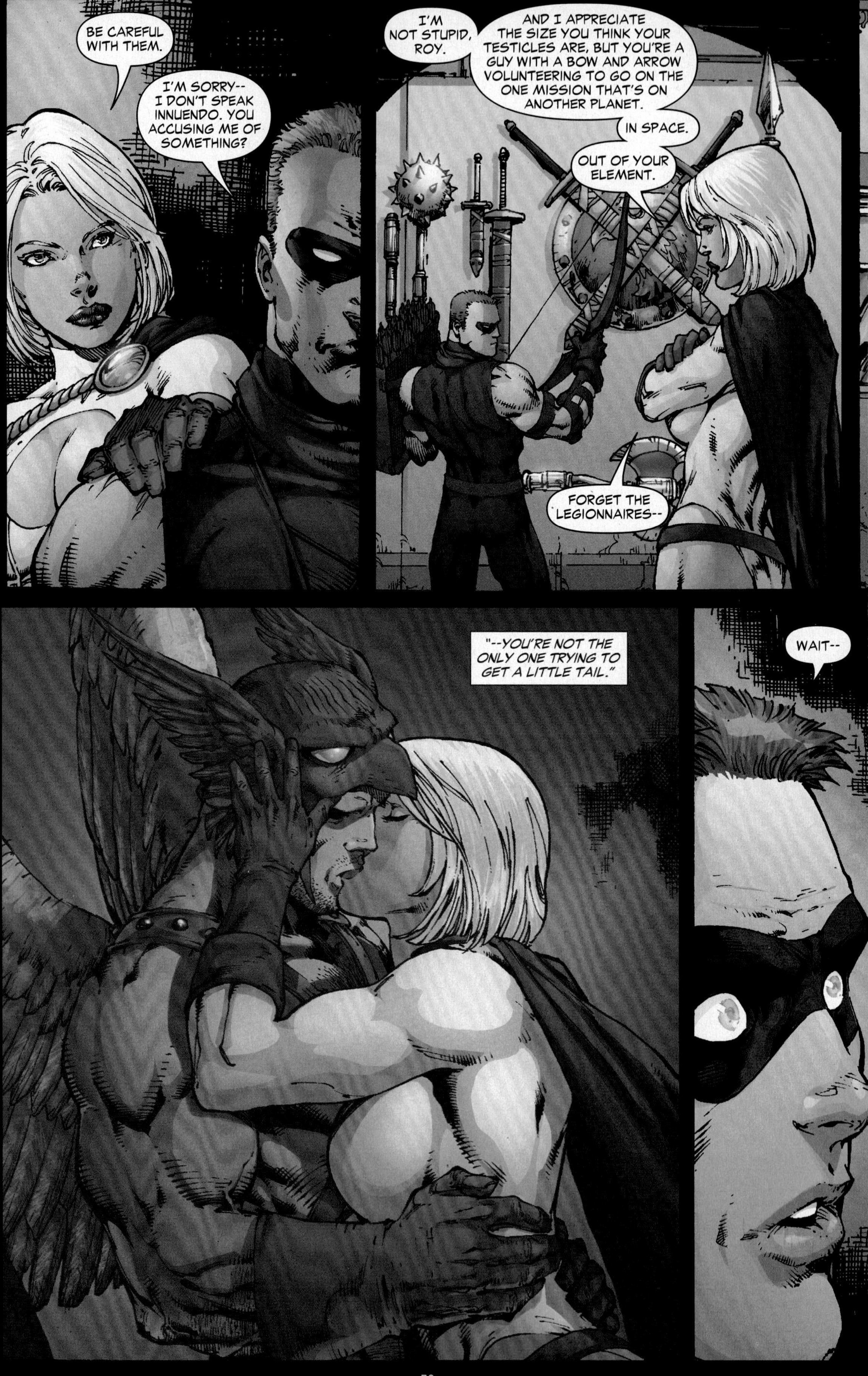
BE CAREFUL WITH THEM.
I'M SORRY-- I DON'T SPEAK INNUENDO. YOU ACCUSING ME OF SOMETHING?
I'M NOT STUPID, ROY.
AND I APPRECIATE THE SIZE YOU THINK YOUR TESTICLES ARE, BUT YOU'RE A GUY WITH A BOW AND ARROW VOLUNTEERING TO GO ON THE ONE MISSION THAT'S ON ANOTHER PLANET.
IN SPACE.
OUT OF YOUR ELEMENT.
FORGET THE LEGIONNAIRES--
"--YOU'RE NOT THE ONLY ONE TRYING TO GET A LITTLE TAIL."
WAIT--

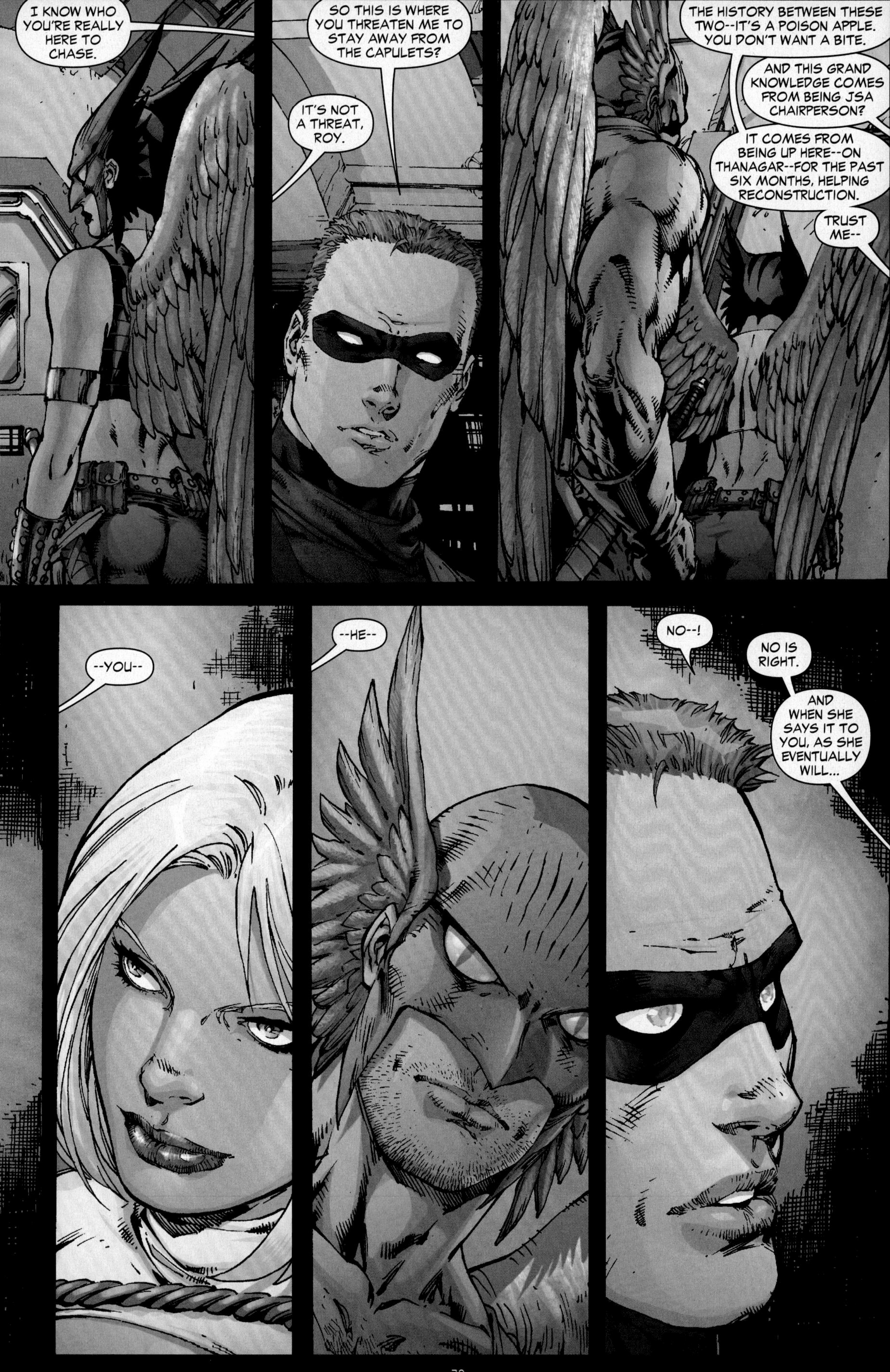
I KNOW WHO YOU'RE REALLY HERE TO CHASE.
SO THIS IS WHERE YOU THREATEN ME TO STAY AWAY FROM THE CAPULETS?
IT'S NOT A THREAT, ROY.
THE HISTORY BETWEEN THESE TWO--IT'S A POISON APPLE. YOU DON'T WANT A BITE.
AND THIS GRAND KNOWLEDGE COMES FROM BEING JSA CHAIRPERSON?
IT COMES FROM BEING UP HERE--ON THANAGAR--FOR THE PAST SIX MONTHS, HELPING RECONSTRUCTION.
TRUST ME--
--YOU--
--HE--
NO--!
NO IS RIGHT.
AND WHEN SHE SAYS IT TO YOU, AS SHE EVENTUALLY WILL...

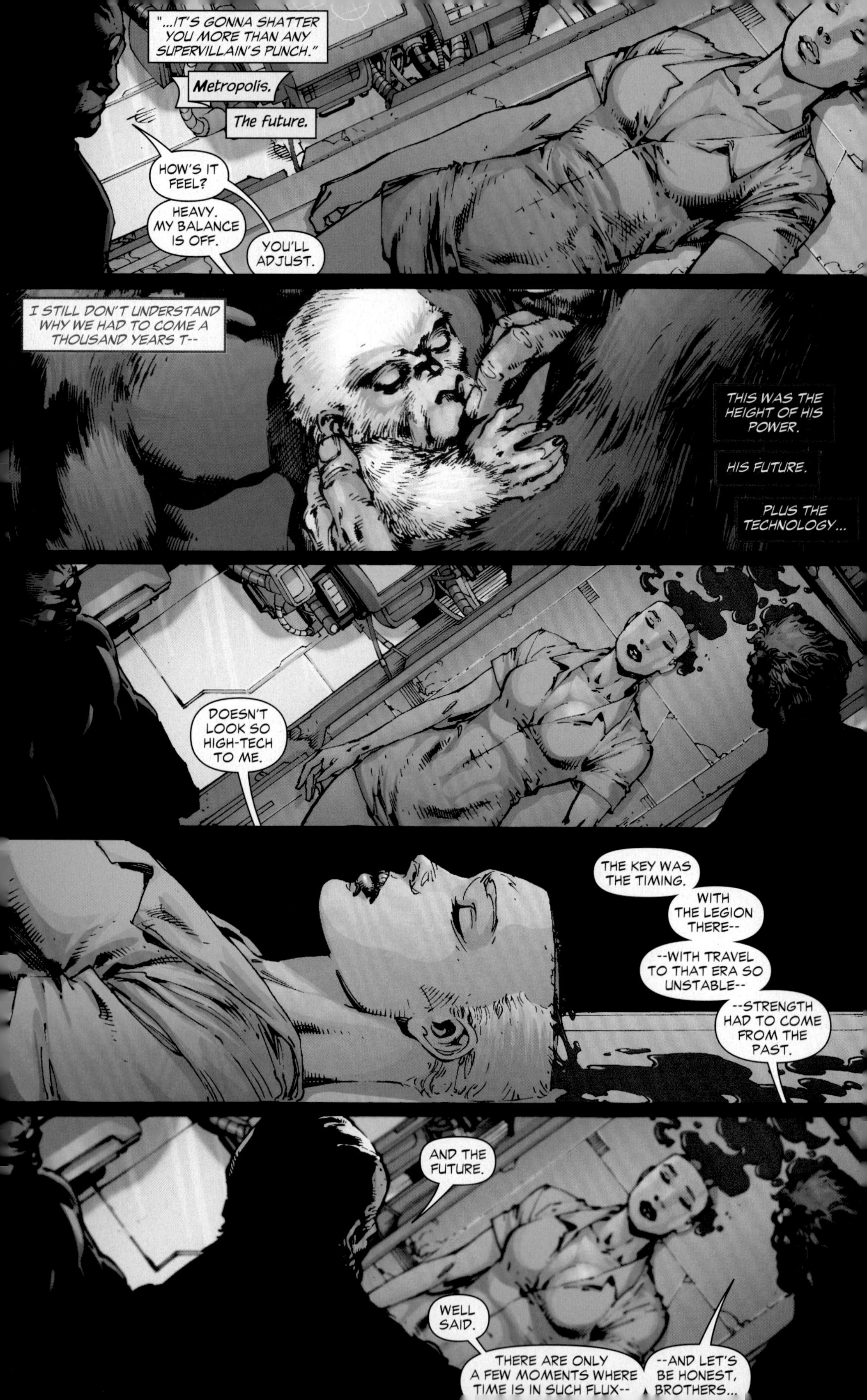

"...IT'S GONNA SHATTER YOU MORE THAN ANY SUPERVILLAIN'S PUNCH."
Metropolis.
The future.
HOW'S IT FEEL?
HEAVY. MY BALANCE IS OFF.
YOU'LL ADJUST.
I STILL DON'T UNDERSTAND WHY WE HAD TO COME A THOUSAND YEARS T--
THIS WAS THE HEIGHT OF HIS POWER.
HIS FUTURE.
PLUS THE TECHNOLOGY...
DOESN'T LOOK SO HIGH-TECH TO ME.
THE KEY WAS THE TIMING.
WITH THE LEGION THERE--
--WITH TRAVEL TO THAT ERA SO UNSTABLE--
--STRENGTH HAD TO COME FROM THE PAST.
AND THE FUTURE.
WELL SAID.
THERE ARE ONLY A FEW MOMENTS WHERE TIME IS IN SUCH FLUX--
--AND LET'S BE HONEST, BROTHERS...

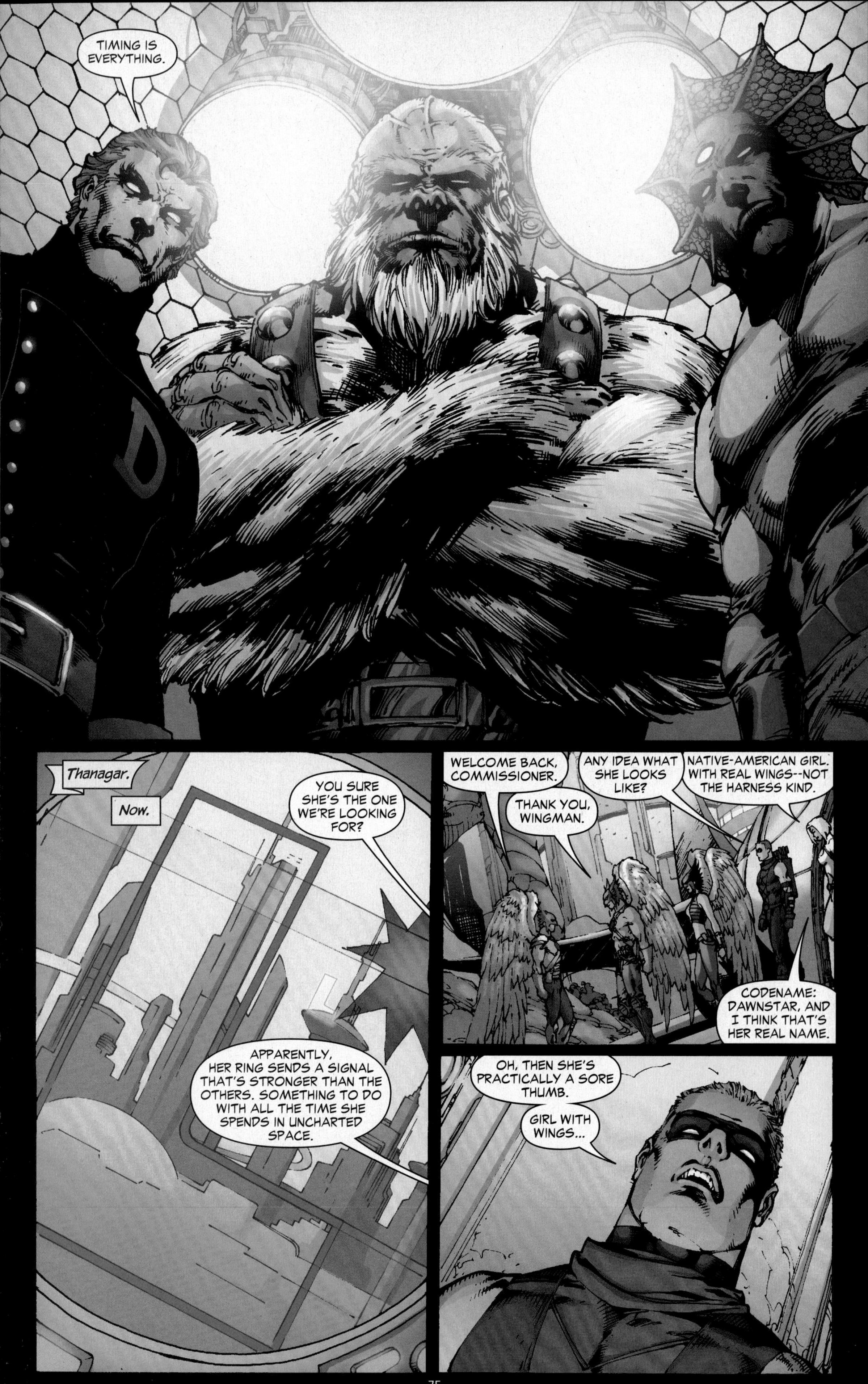
TIMING IS EVERYTHING.
Thanagar.
Now.
YOU SURE SHE'S THE ONE WE'RE LOOKING FOR?
APPARENTLY, HER RING SENDS A SIGNAL THAT'S STRONGER THAN THE OTHERS. SOMETHING TO DO WITH ALL THE TIME SHE SPENDS IN UNCHARTED SPACE.
WELCOME BACK, COMMISSIONER.
THANK YOU, WINGMAN.
ANY IDEA WHAT SHE LOOKS LIKE?
NATIVE-AMERICAN GIRL. WITH REAL WINGS--NOT THE HARNESS KIND.
CODENAME: DAWNSTAR, AND I THINK THAT'S HER REAL NAME.
OH, THEN SHE'S PRACTICALLY A SORE THUMB.
GIRL WITH WINGS...

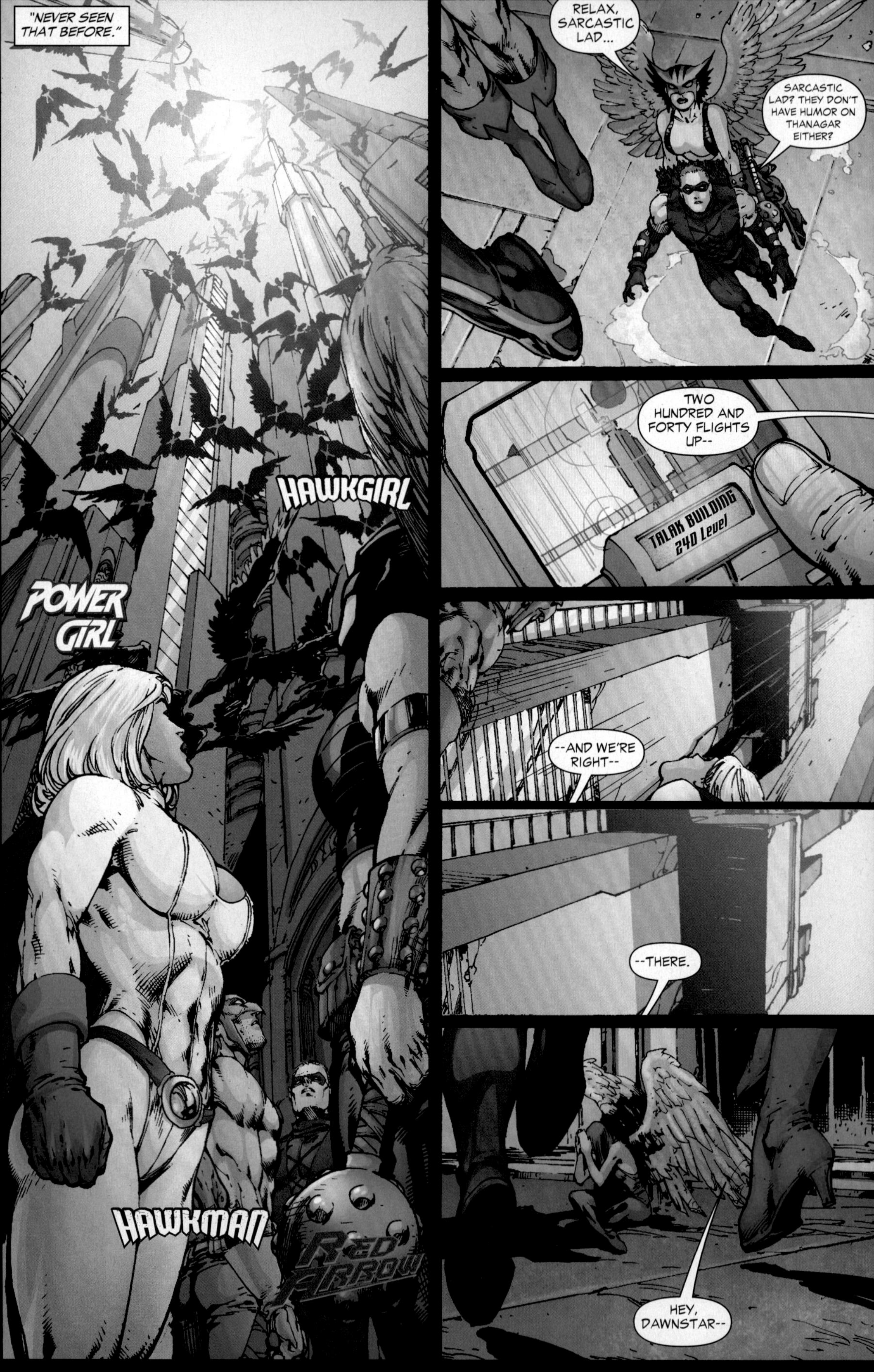
"NEVER SEEN THAT BEFORE."
HAWKGIRL
POWER GIRL
HAWKMAN
RED ARROW
RELAX, SARCASTIC LAD...
SARCASTIC LAD? THEY DON'T HAVE HUMOR ON THANAGAR EITHER?
TWO HUNDRED AND FORTY FLIGHTS UP--
TALAK BUILDING
240 Level
--AND WE'RE RIGHT--
--THERE.
HEY, DAWNSTAR--

LIOLYPITO LJU. I THINK YOU SAID IT WRONG.

LIOLYPITO LJU.

LIOLYPITO LJU.

MY APOLOGIES--

--CAN I HELP YOU WITH SOMETHING?

Aw, CRAP.

TO NO ONE'S SURPRISE, CARTER REFUSES TO BELIEVE IT.

NO-- WE READ IT WRONG.

YOUR WINGS AREN'T REAL.

Ah. YOU WANT NEELA.

YOU MEAN DAWNSTAR.

YOU'RE THE ONES SHE FELT, THEN? LIKE A BREEZE, SHE SAID--

--SHE COULDN'T SEE IT, COULDN'T TOUCH IT, BUT SHE COULD FEEL YOU THERE.

IT'S THE ONE LESSON HE'LL NEVER LEARN.

WHETHER IT'S THROUGH TIME OR SPACE--

--FINDING SOMEONE YOU TRULY LOVE DOESN'T MEAN YOU CAN'T FIND ANOTHER.

HER PROMISE THAT SHE WOULD COME BACK TO ME.

SHE AND I--

SHE SAID SHE'D COME BACK.

BUT HER RING...

BUT SHE'S NOT, IS SHE?

FOR HER TO FEEL HER FRIENDS FROM THIS FAR AWAY--

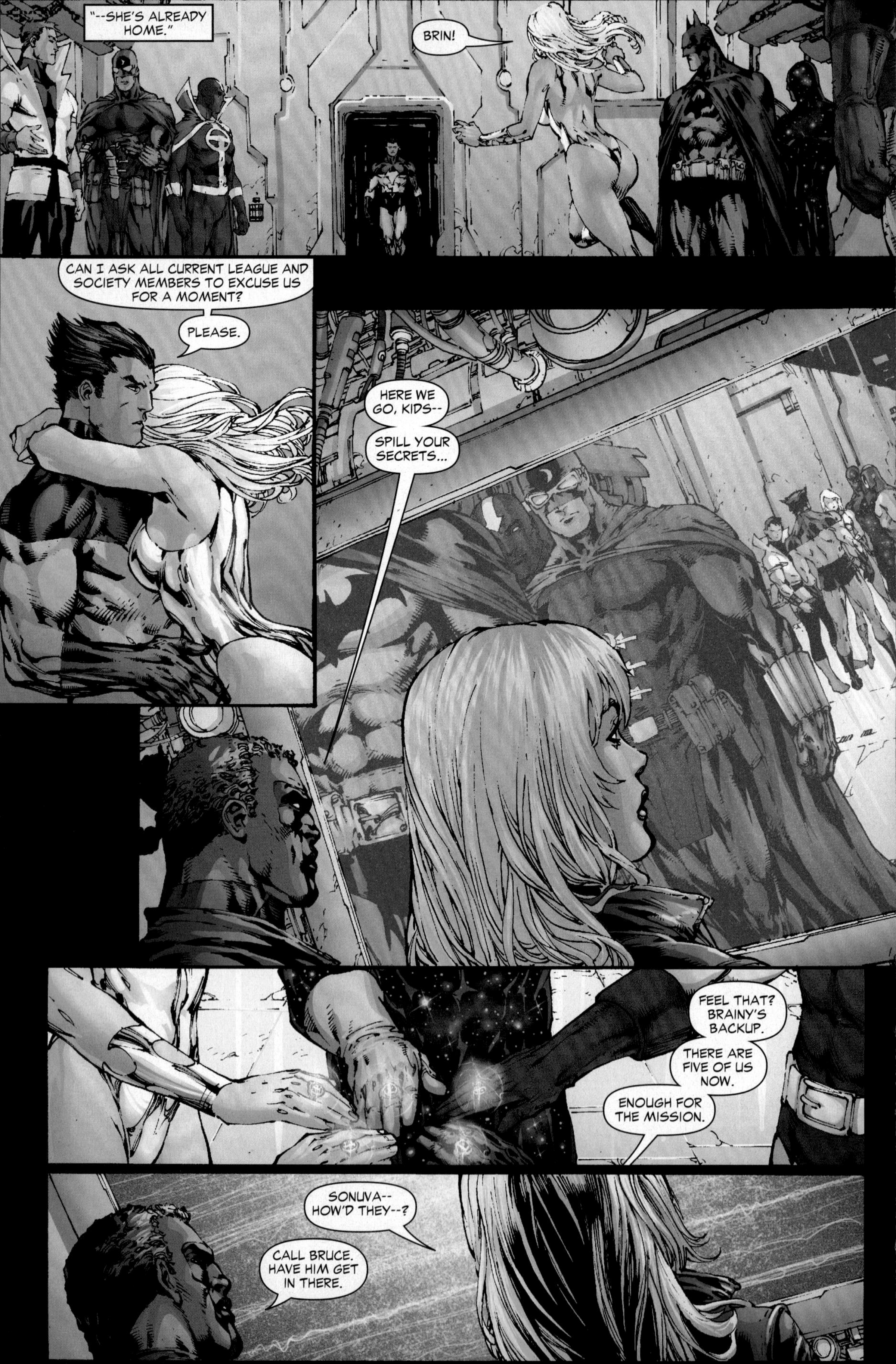
"--SHE'S ALREADY HOME."
BRIN!
CAN I ASK ALL CURRENT LEAGUE AND SOCIETY MEMBERS TO EXCUSE US FOR A MOMENT?
PLEASE.
HERE WE GO, KIDS--
SPILL YOUR SECRETS...
FEEL THAT? BRAINY'S BACKUP.
THERE ARE FIVE OF US NOW.
ENOUGH FOR THE MISSION.
SONUVA-- HOW'D THEY--?
CALL BRUCE. HAVE HIM GET IN THERE.

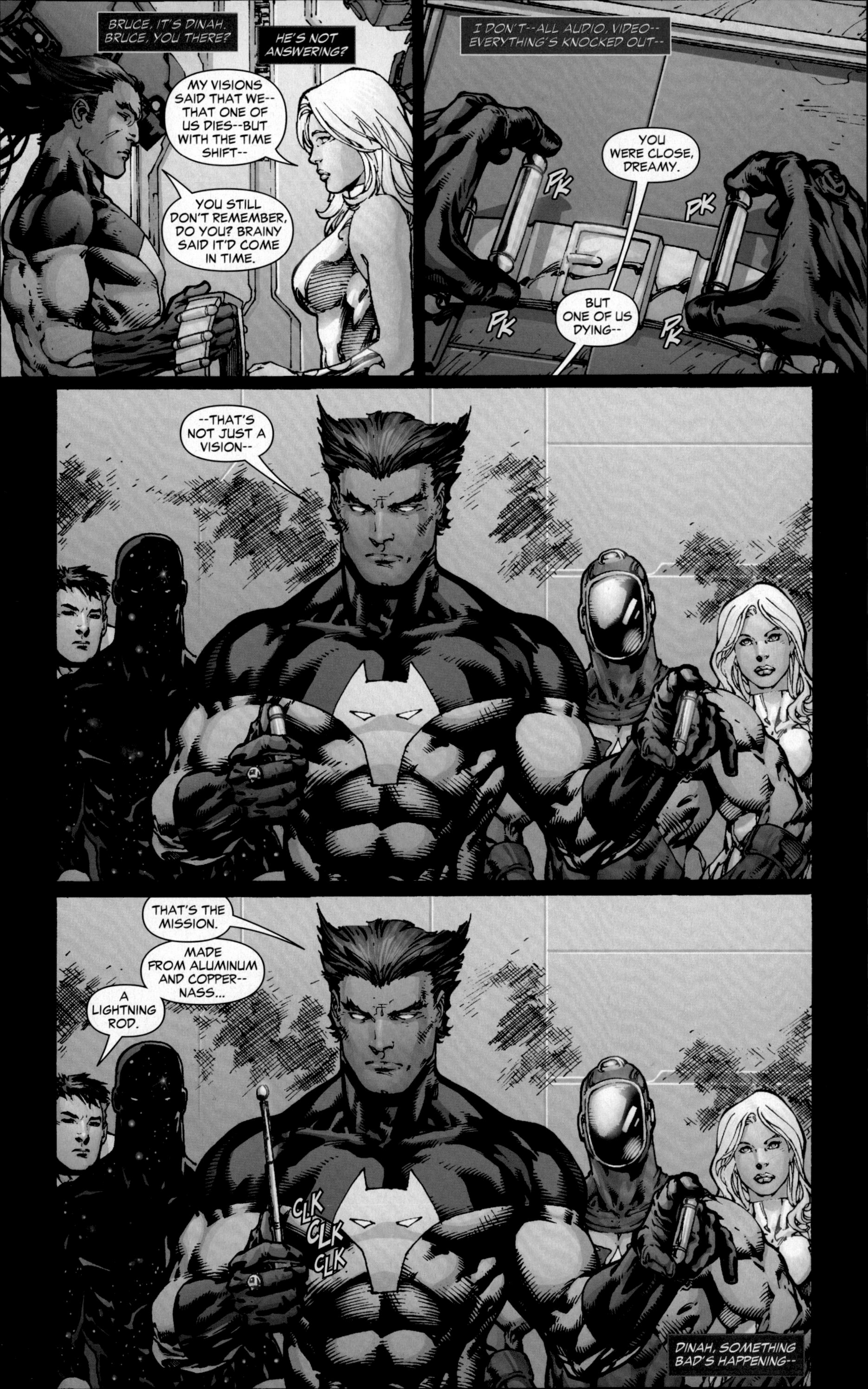
BRUCE, IT'S DINAH. BRUCE, YOU THERE?
HE'S NOT ANSWERING?
MY VISIONS SAID THAT WE--THAT ONE OF US DIES--BUT WITH THE TIME SHIFT--
YOU STILL DON'T REMEMBER, DO YOU? BRAINY SAID IT'D COME IN TIME.
I DON'T--ALL AUDIO, VIDEO--EVERYTHING'S KNOCKED OUT--
PK
YOU WERE CLOSE, DREAMY.
PK
PK
BUT ONE OF US DYING--
PK
--THAT'S NOT JUST A VISION--
THAT'S THE MISSION.
MADE FROM ALUMINUM AND COPPER--NASS...
A LIGHTNING ROD.
CLK CLK CLK
DINAH, SOMETHING BAD'S HAPPENING--

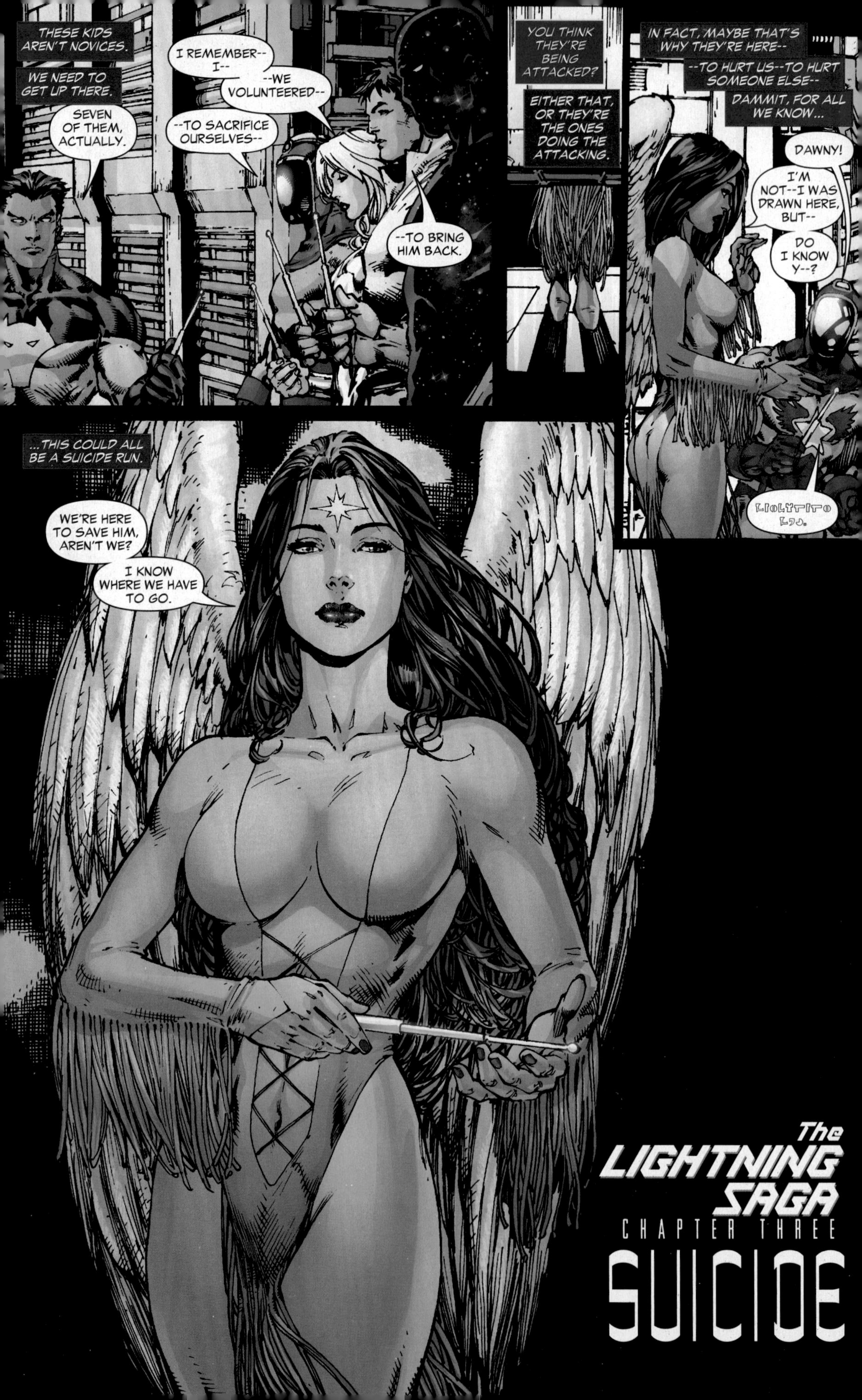
THESE KIDS AREN'T NOVICES.
WE NEED TO GET UP THERE.
SEVEN OF THEM, ACTUALLY.
I REMEMBER-- I--
--WE VOLUNTEERED--
--TO SACRIFICE OURSELVES--
--TO BRING HIM BACK.
YOU THINK THEY'RE BEING ATTACKED?
EITHER THAT, OR THEY'RE THE ONES DOING THE ATTACKING.
IN FACT, MAYBE THAT'S WHY THEY'RE HERE--
--TO HURT US--TO HURT SOMEONE ELSE--
DAMMIT, FOR ALL WE KNOW...
DAWNY!
I'M NOT--I WAS DRAWN HERE, BUT--
DO I KNOW Y--?
...THIS COULD ALL BE A SUICIDE RUN.
WE'RE HERE TO SAVE HIM, AREN'T WE?
I KNOW WHERE WE HAVE TO GO.
The LIGHTNING SAGA
CHAPTER THREE
SUICIDE

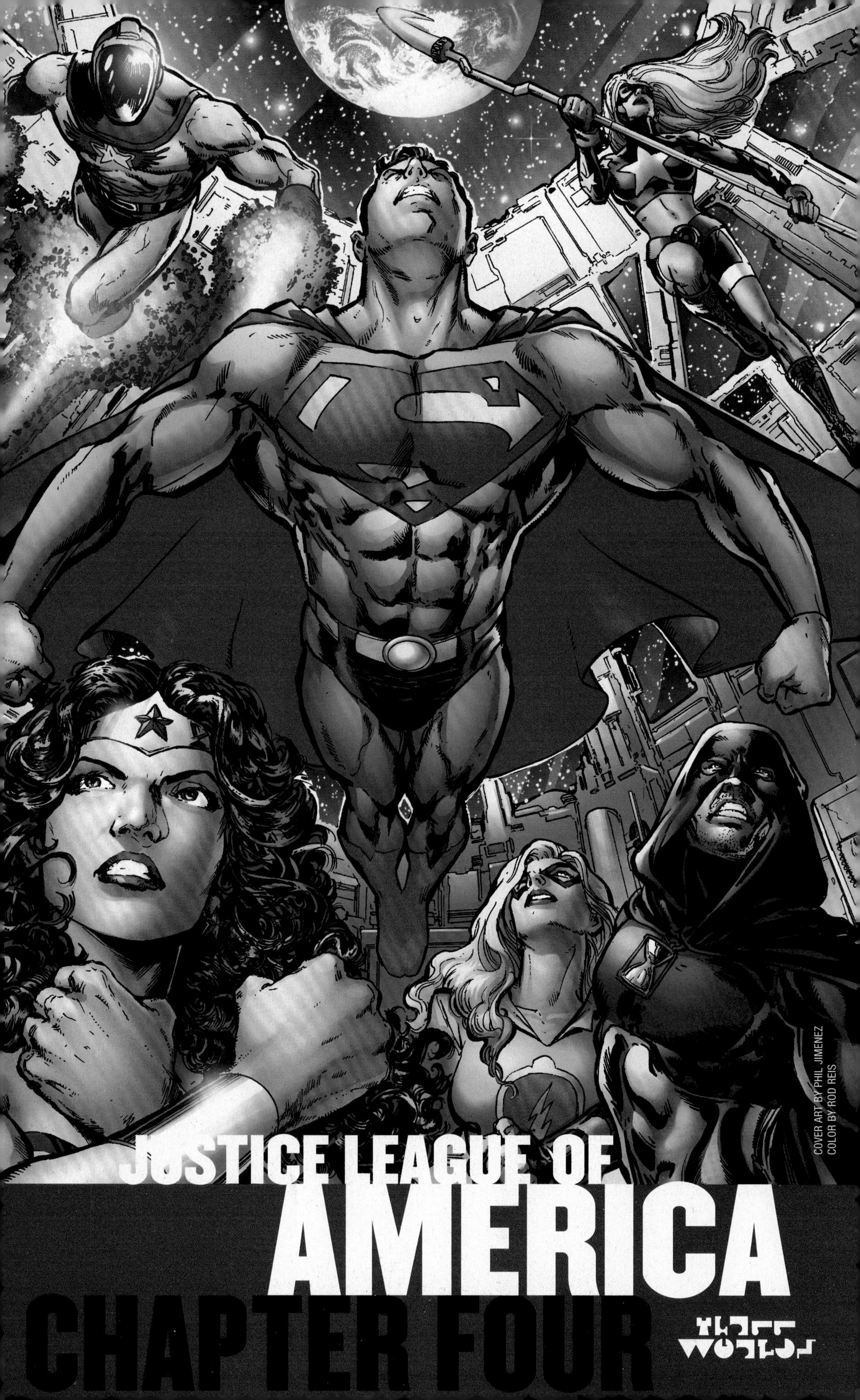
COVER ART BY PHIL JIMENEZ
COLOR BY ROD REIS

JUSTICE LEAGUE OF AMERICA
CHAPTER FOUR

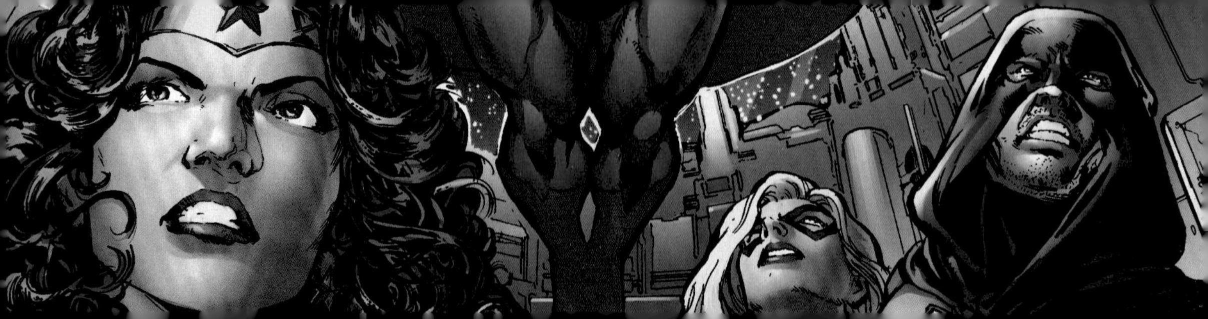

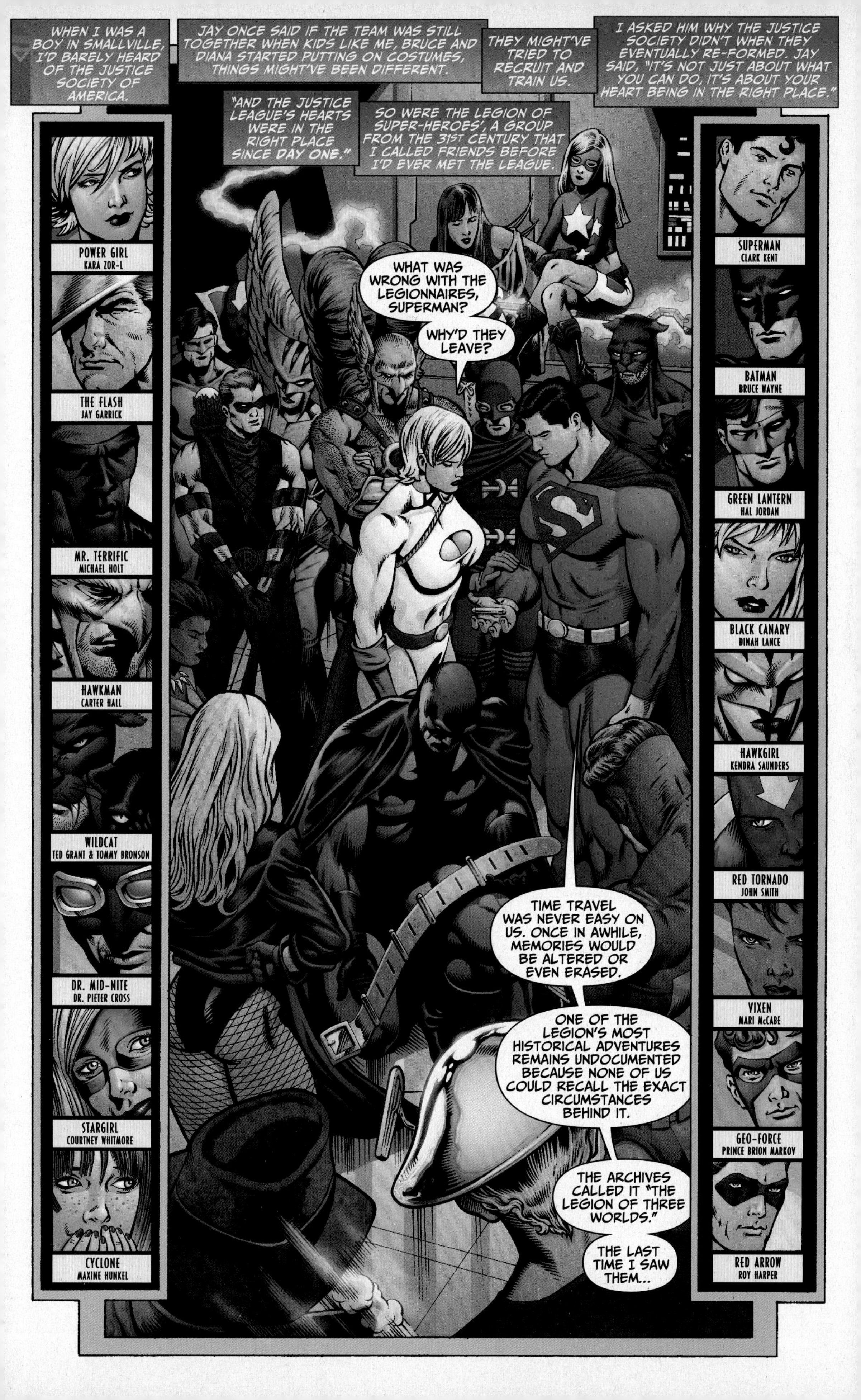
WHEN I WAS A BOY IN SMALLVILLE, I'D BARELY HEARD OF THE JUSTICE SOCIETY OF AMERICA.
JAY ONCE SAID IF THE TEAM WAS STILL TOGETHER WHEN KIDS LIKE ME, BRUCE AND DIANA STARTED PUTTING ON COSTUMES, THINGS MIGHT'VE BEEN DIFFERENT.
THEY MIGHT'VE TRIED TO RECRUIT AND TRAIN US.
I ASKED HIM WHY THE JUSTICE SOCIETY DIDN'T WHEN THEY EVENTUALLY RE-FORMED. JAY SAID, "IT'S NOT JUST ABOUT WHAT YOU CAN DO, IT'S ABOUT YOUR HEART BEING IN THE RIGHT PLACE."
"AND THE JUSTICE LEAGUE'S HEARTS WERE IN THE RIGHT PLACE SINCE DAY ONE."
SO WERE THE LEGION OF SUPER-HEROES', A GROUP FROM THE 31ST CENTURY THAT I CALLED FRIENDS BEFORE I'D EVER MET THE LEAGUE.
WHAT WAS WRONG WITH THE LEGIONNAIRES, SUPERMAN?
WHY'D THEY LEAVE?
TIME TRAVEL WAS NEVER EASY ON US. ONCE IN AWHILE, MEMORIES WOULD BE ALTERED OR EVEN ERASED.
ONE OF THE LEGION'S MOST HISTORICAL ADVENTURES REMAINS UNDOCUMENTED BECAUSE NONE OF US COULD RECALL THE EXACT CIRCUMSTANCES BEHIND IT.
THE ARCHIVES CALLED IT "THE LEGION OF THREE WORLDS."
THE LAST TIME I SAW THEM...
POWER GIRL KARA ZOR-L
THE FLASH JAY GARRICK
MR. TERRIFIC MICHAEL HOLT
HAWKMAN CARTER HALL
WILDCAT TED GRANT & TOMMY BRONSON
DR. MID-NITE DR. PIETER CROSS
STARGIRL COURTNEY WHITMORE
CYCLONE MAXINE HUNKEL
SUPERMAN CLARK KENT
BATMAN BRUCE WAYNE
GREEN LANTERN HAL JORDAN
BLACK CANARY DINAH LANCE
HAWKGIRL KENDRA SAUNDERS
RED TORNADO JOHN SMITH
VIXEN MARI McCABE
GEO-FORCE PRINCE BRION MARKOV
RED ARROW ROY HARPER

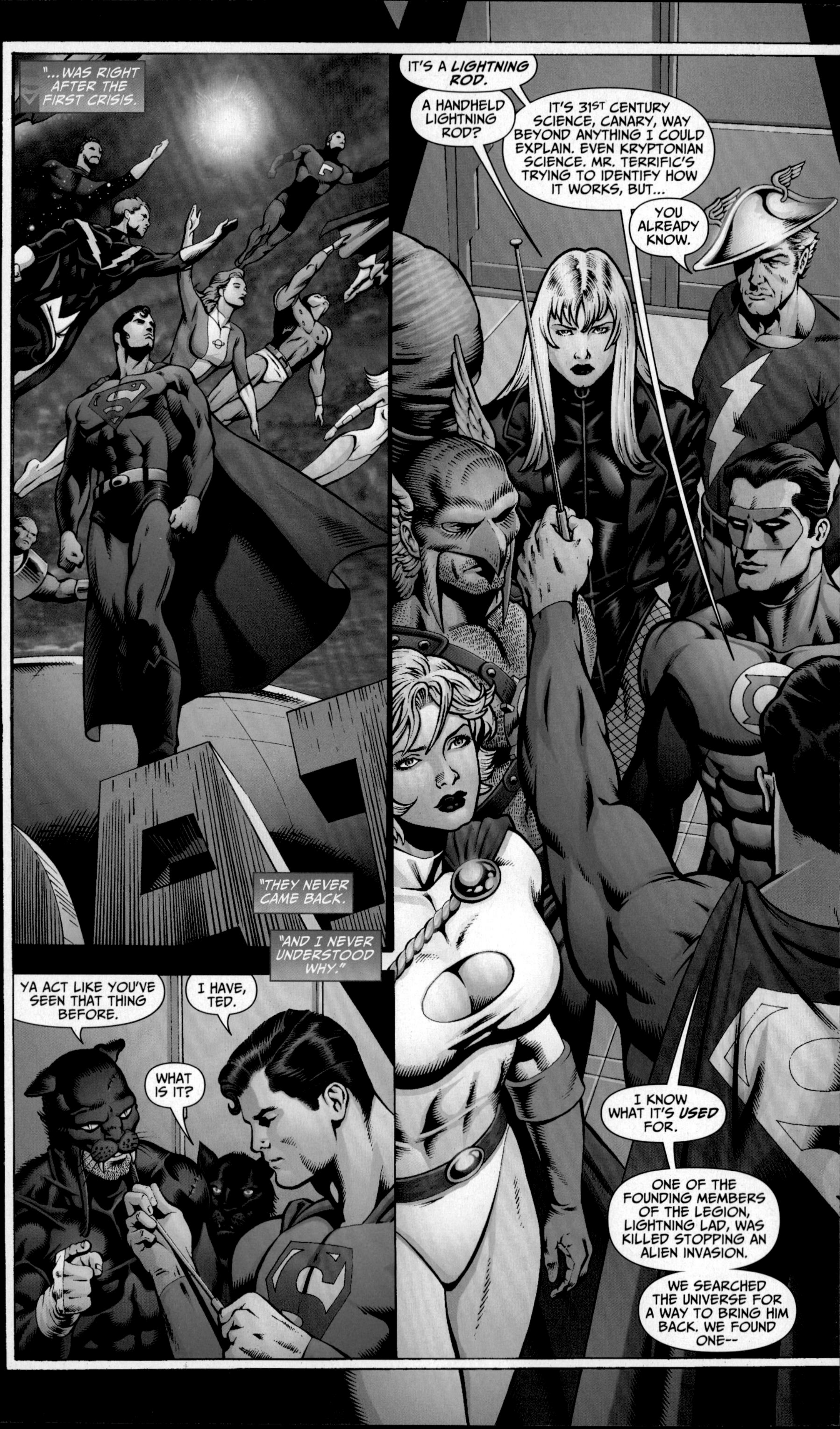
"...WAS RIGHT AFTER THE FIRST CRISIS.
"THEY NEVER CAME BACK.
"AND I NEVER UNDERSTOOD WHY."
IT'S A LIGHTNING ROD.
A HANDHELD LIGHTNING ROD?
IT'S 31ST CENTURY SCIENCE, CANARY, WAY BEYOND ANYTHING I COULD EXPLAIN. EVEN KRYPTONIAN SCIENCE. MR. TERRIFIC'S TRYING TO IDENTIFY HOW IT WORKS, BUT...
YOU ALREADY KNOW.
YA ACT LIKE YOU'VE SEEN THAT THING BEFORE.
I HAVE, TED.
WHAT IS IT?
I KNOW WHAT IT'S USED FOR.
ONE OF THE FOUNDING MEMBERS OF THE LEGION, LIGHTNING LAD, WAS KILLED STOPPING AN ALIEN INVASION.
WE SEARCHED THE UNIVERSE FOR A WAY TO BRING HIM BACK. WE FOUND ONE--

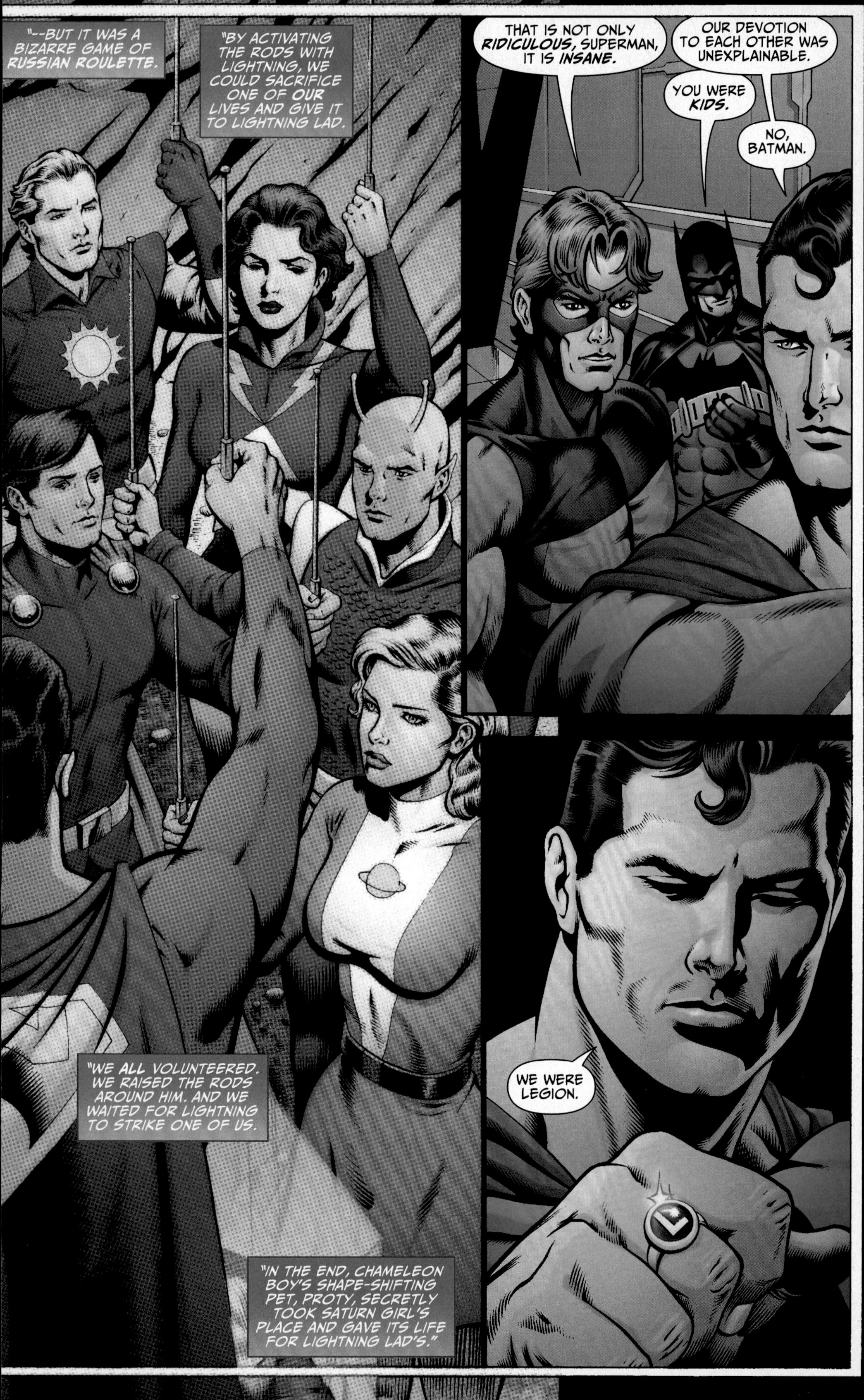
"--BUT IT WAS A BIZARRE GAME OF RUSSIAN ROULETTE.
"BY ACTIVATING THE RODS WITH LIGHTNING, WE COULD SACRIFICE ONE OF OUR LIVES AND GIVE IT TO LIGHTNING LAD.
"WE ALL VOLUNTEERED. WE RAISED THE RODS AROUND HIM. AND WE WAITED FOR LIGHTNING TO STRIKE ONE OF US.
"IN THE END, CHAMELEON BOY'S SHAPE-SHIFTING PET, PROTY, SECRETLY TOOK SATURN GIRL'S PLACE AND GAVE ITS LIFE FOR LIGHTNING LAD'S."
THAT IS NOT ONLY RIDICULOUS, SUPERMAN, IT IS INSANE.
OUR DEVOTION TO EACH OTHER WAS UNEXPLAINABLE.
YOU WERE KIDS.
NO, BATMAN.
WE WERE LEGION.

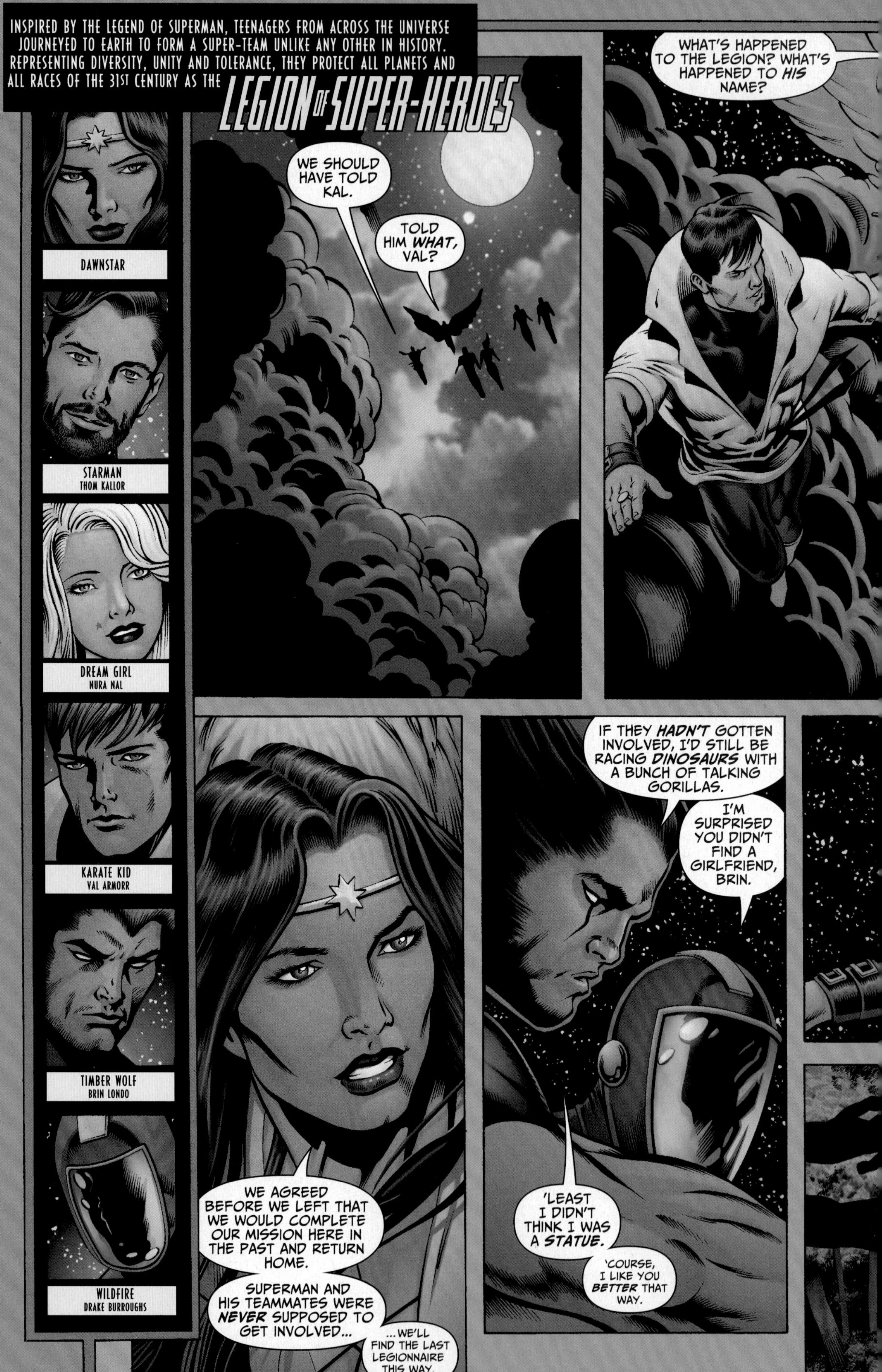

INSPIRED BY THE LEGEND OF SUPERMAN, TEENAGERS FROM ACROSS THE UNIVERSE JOURNEYED TO EARTH TO FORM A SUPER-TEAM UNLIKE ANY OTHER IN HISTORY. REPRESENTING DIVERSITY, UNITY AND TOLERANCE, THEY PROTECT ALL PLANETS AND ALL RACES OF THE 31ST CENTURY AS THE
LEGION OF SUPER-HEROES
DAWNSTAR
STARMAN
THOM KALLOR
DREAM GIRL
NURA NAL
KARATE KID
VAL ARMORR
TIMBER WOLF
BRIN LONDO
WILDFIRE
DRAKE BURROUGHS
WE SHOULD HAVE TOLD KAL.
TOLD HIM WHAT, VAL?
WHAT'S HAPPENED TO THE LEGION? WHAT'S HAPPENED TO HIS NAME?
WE AGREED BEFORE WE LEFT THAT WE WOULD COMPLETE OUR MISSION HERE IN THE PAST AND RETURN HOME.
SUPERMAN AND HIS TEAMMATES WERE NEVER SUPPOSED TO GET INVOLVED...
...WE'LL FIND THE LAST LEGIONNAIRE THIS WAY.
IF THEY HADN'T GOTTEN INVOLVED, I'D STILL BE RACING DINOSAURS WITH A BUNCH OF TALKING GORILLAS.
I'M SURPRISED YOU DIDN'T FIND A GIRLFRIEND, BRIN.
'LEAST I DIDN'T THINK I WAS A STATUE.
'COURSE, I LIKE YOU BETTER THAT WAY.

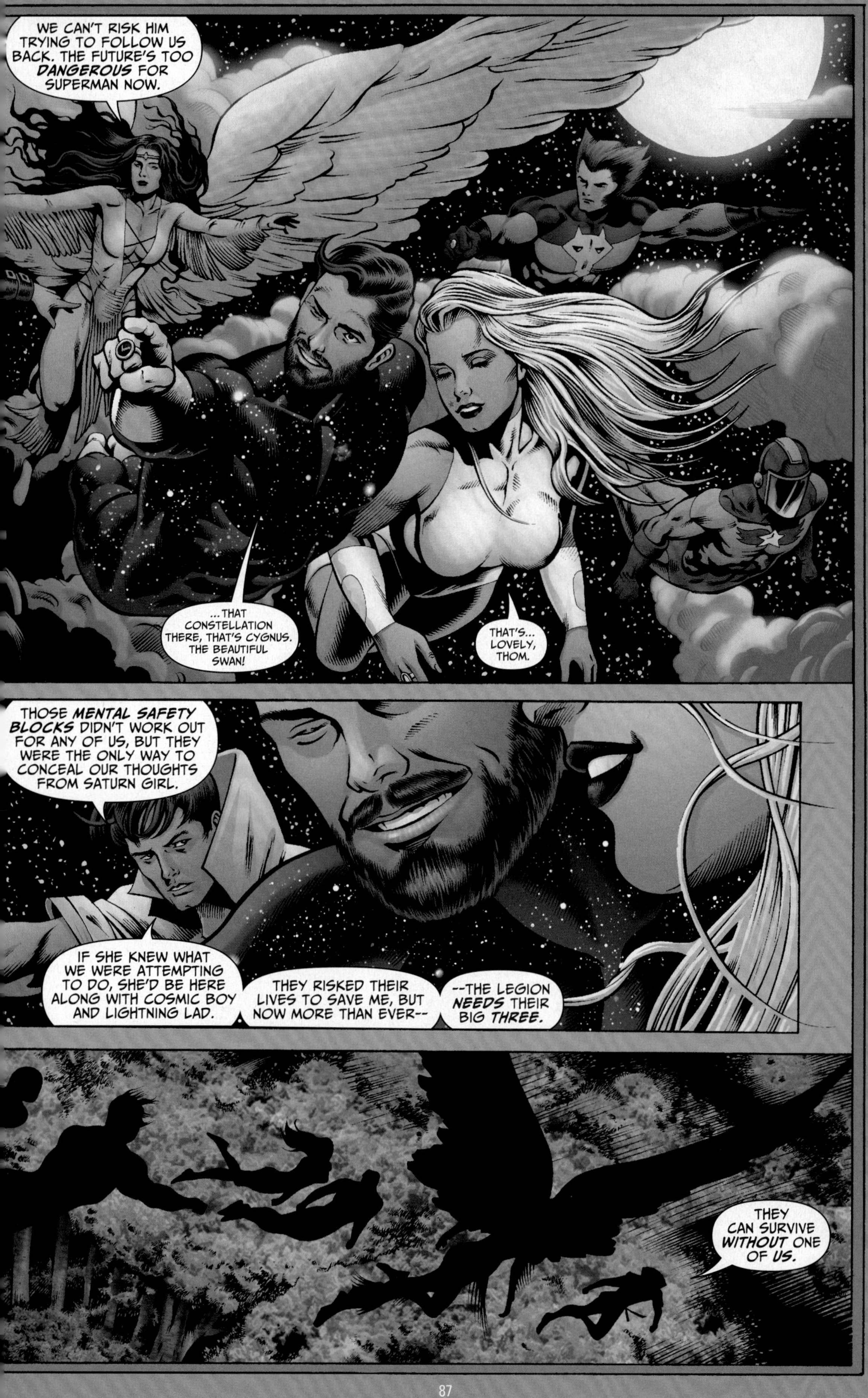
WE CAN'T RISK HIM TRYING TO FOLLOW US BACK. THE FUTURE'S TOO DANGEROUS FOR SUPERMAN NOW.
...THAT CONSTELLATION THERE, THAT'S CYGNUS. THE BEAUTIFUL SWAN!
THAT'S... LOVELY, THOM.
THOSE MENTAL SAFETY BLOCKS DIDN'T WORK OUT FOR ANY OF US, BUT THEY WERE THE ONLY WAY TO CONCEAL OUR THOUGHTS FROM SATURN GIRL.
IF SHE KNEW WHAT WE WERE ATTEMPTING TO DO, SHE'D BE HERE ALONG WITH COSMIC BOY AND LIGHTNING LAD.
THEY RISKED THEIR LIVES TO SAVE ME, BUT NOW MORE THAN EVER--
--THE LEGION NEEDS THEIR BIG THREE.
THEY CAN SURVIVE WITHOUT ONE OF US.

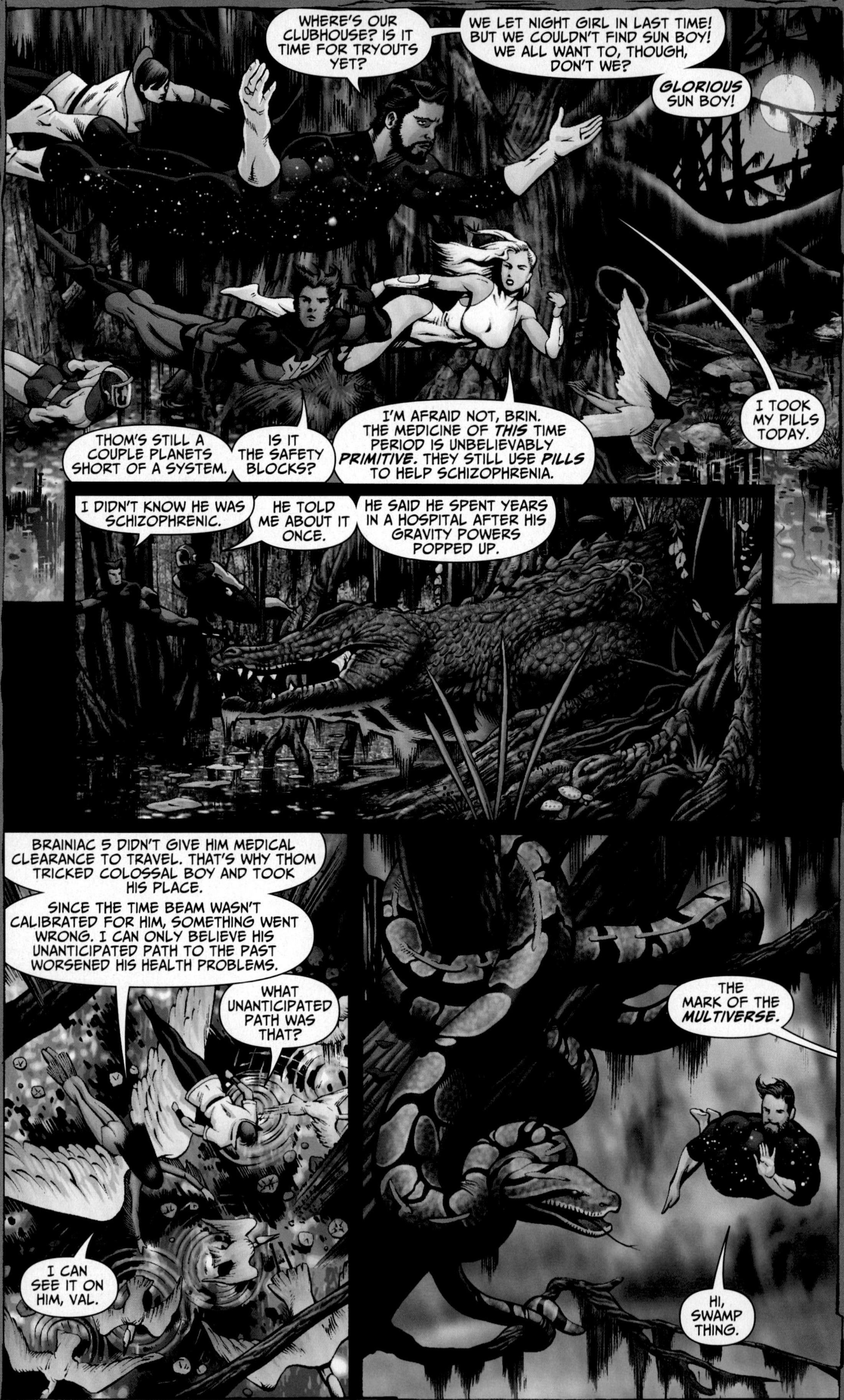
WHERE'S OUR CLUBHOUSE? IS IT TIME FOR TRYOUTS YET?
WE LET NIGHT GIRL IN LAST TIME! BUT WE COULDN'T FIND SUN BOY! WE ALL WANT TO, THOUGH, DON'T WE?
GLORIOUS SUN BOY!
THOM'S STILL A COUPLE PLANETS SHORT OF A SYSTEM.
IS IT THE SAFETY BLOCKS?
I'M AFRAID NOT, BRIN. THE MEDICINE OF THIS TIME PERIOD IS UNBELIEVABLY PRIMITIVE. THEY STILL USE PILLS TO HELP SCHIZOPHRENIA.
I TOOK MY PILLS TODAY.
I DIDN'T KNOW HE WAS SCHIZOPHRENIC.
HE TOLD ME ABOUT IT ONCE.
HE SAID HE SPENT YEARS IN A HOSPITAL AFTER HIS GRAVITY POWERS POPPED UP.
BRAINIAC 5 DIDN'T GIVE HIM MEDICAL CLEARANCE TO TRAVEL. THAT'S WHY THOM TRICKED COLOSSAL BOY AND TOOK HIS PLACE.
SINCE THE TIME BEAM WASN'T CALIBRATED FOR HIM, SOMETHING WENT WRONG. I CAN ONLY BELIEVE HIS UNANTICIPATED PATH TO THE PAST WORSENED HIS HEALTH PROBLEMS.
WHAT UNANTICIPATED PATH WAS THAT?
I CAN SEE IT ON HIM, VAL.
THE MARK OF THE MULTIVERSE.
HI, SWAMP THING.

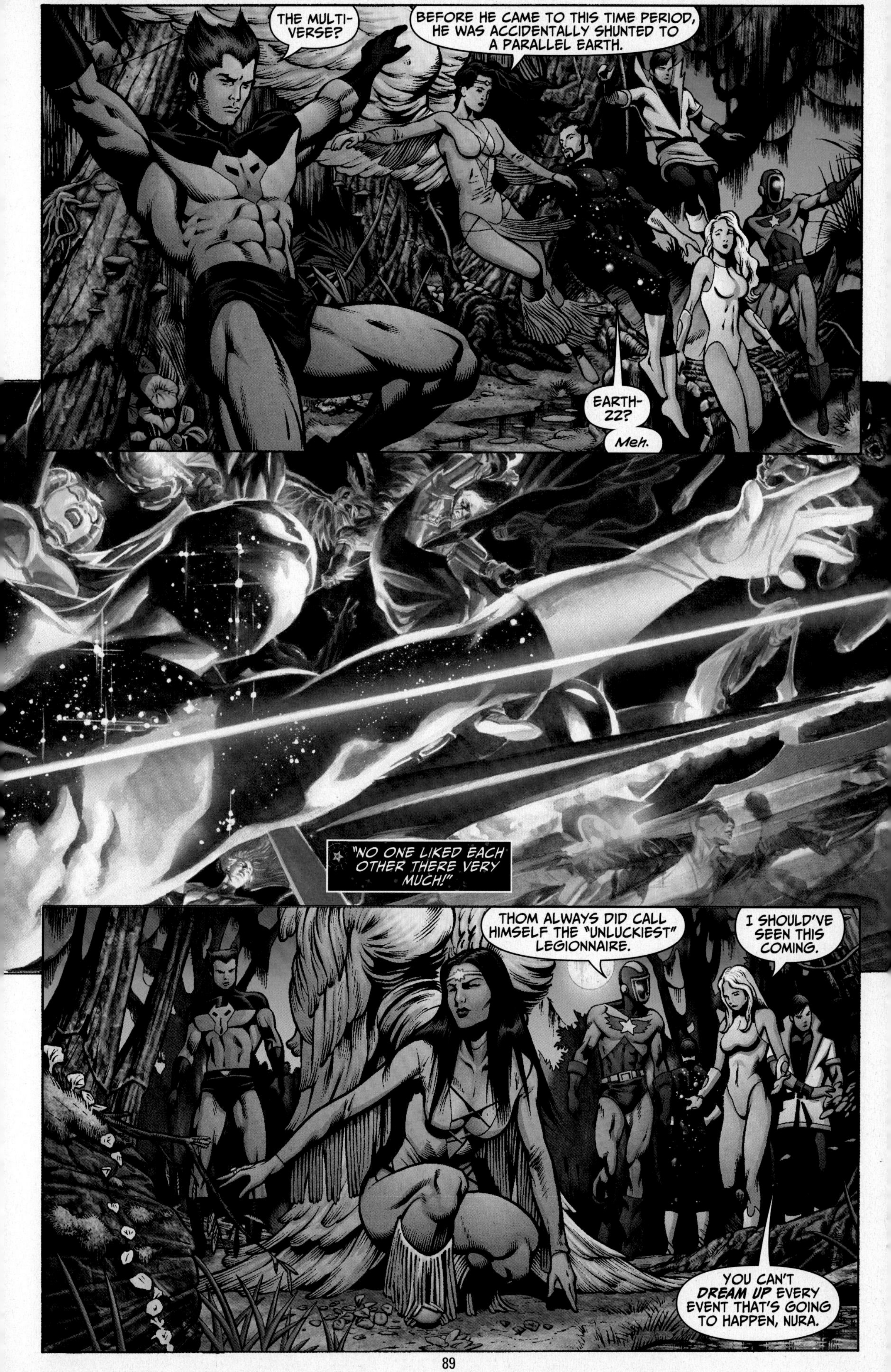
THE MULTI-VERSE?
BEFORE HE CAME TO THIS TIME PERIOD, HE WAS ACCIDENTALLY SHUNTED TO A PARALLEL EARTH.
EARTH-22?
Meh.
"NO ONE LIKED EACH OTHER THERE VERY MUCH!"
THOM ALWAYS DID CALL HIMSELF THE "UNLUCKIEST" LEGIONNAIRE.
I SHOULD'VE SEEN THIS COMING.
YOU CAN'T DREAM UP EVERY EVENT THAT'S GOING TO HAPPEN, NURA.

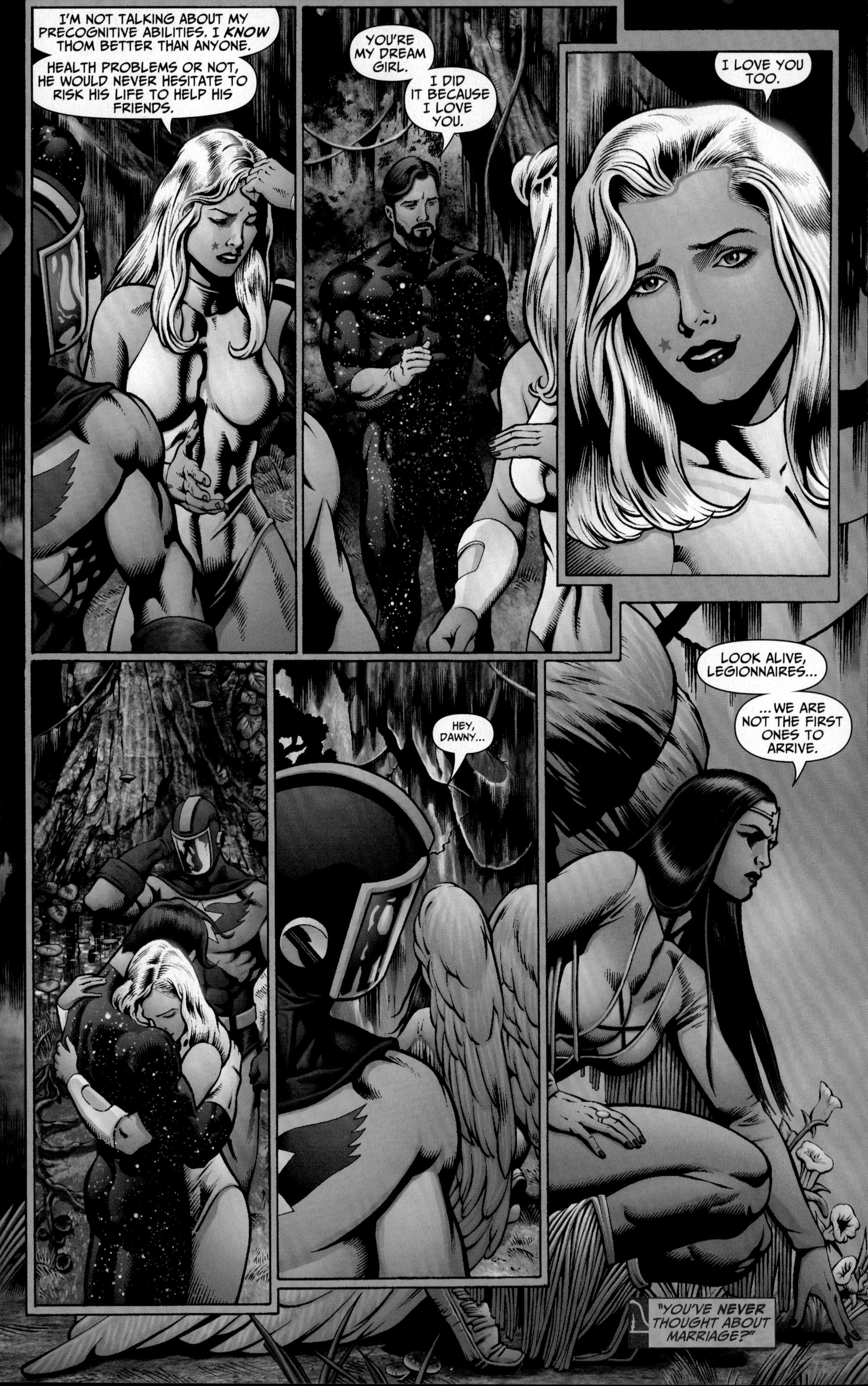
I'M NOT TALKING ABOUT MY PRECOGNITIVE ABILITIES. I *KNOW* THOM BETTER THAN ANYONE.
HEALTH PROBLEMS OR NOT, HE WOULD NEVER HESITATE TO RISK HIS LIFE TO HELP HIS FRIENDS.
YOU'RE MY DREAM GIRL.
I DID IT BECAUSE I LOVE YOU.
I LOVE YOU TOO.
HEY, DAWNY...
LOOK ALIVE, LEGIONNAIRES...
...WE ARE NOT THE FIRST ONES TO ARRIVE.
"YOU'VE *NEVER* THOUGHT ABOUT MARRIAGE?"

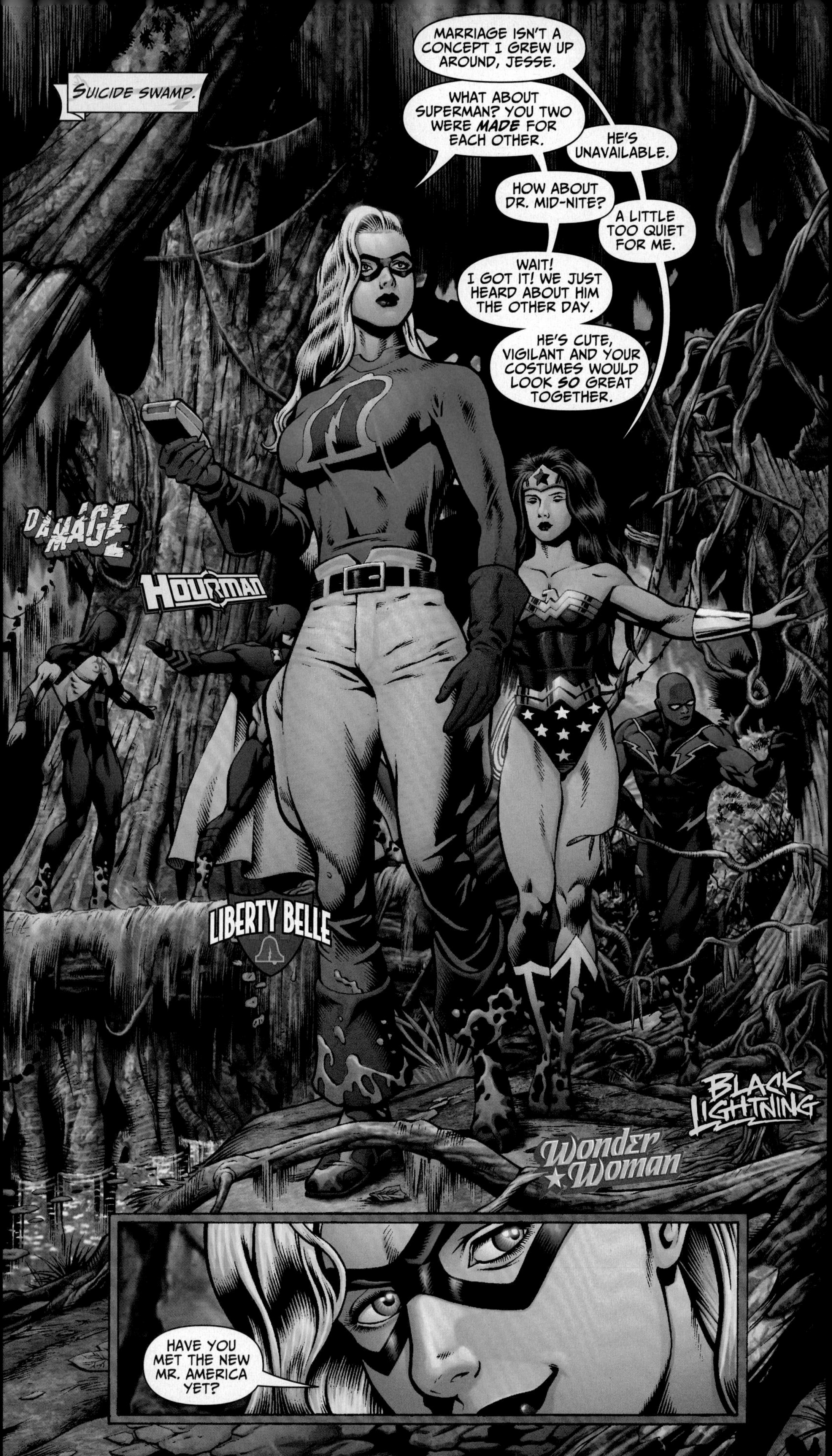
SUICIDE SWAMP.
MARRIAGE ISN'T A CONCEPT I GREW UP AROUND, JESSE.
WHAT ABOUT SUPERMAN? YOU TWO WERE MADE FOR EACH OTHER.
HE'S UNAVAILABLE.
HOW ABOUT DR. MID-NITE?
A LITTLE TOO QUIET FOR ME.
WAIT! I GOT IT! WE JUST HEARD ABOUT HIM THE OTHER DAY.
HE'S CUTE, VIGILANT AND YOUR COSTUMES WOULD LOOK SO GREAT TOGETHER.
DAMAGE
HOURMAN
LIBERTY BELLE
BLACK LIGHTNING
Wonder Woman
HAVE YOU MET THE NEW MR. AMERICA YET?

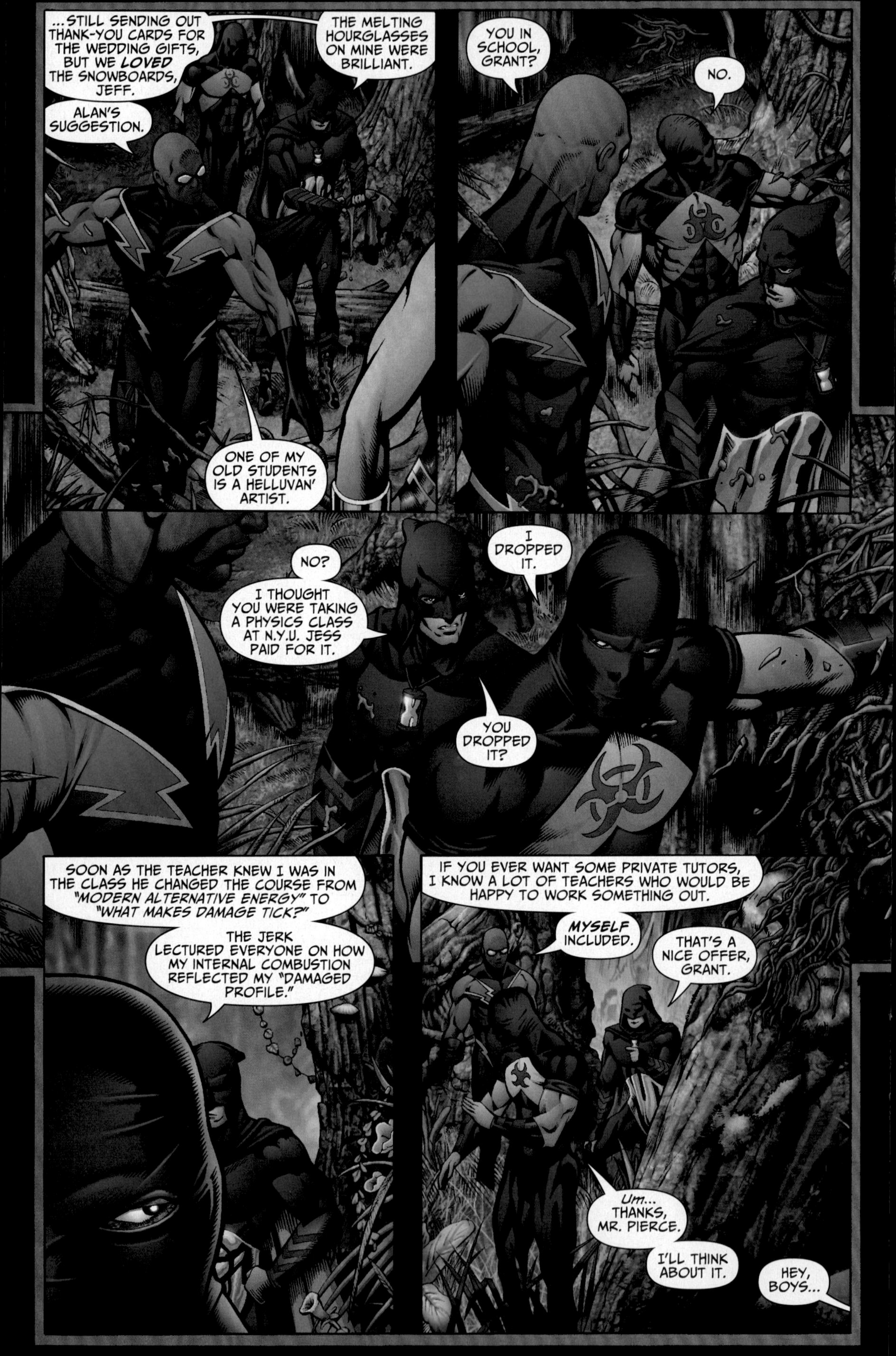
...STILL SENDING OUT THANK-YOU CARDS FOR THE WEDDING GIFTS, BUT WE *LOVED* THE SNOWBOARDS, JEFF.
THE MELTING HOURGLASSES ON MINE WERE BRILLIANT.
ALAN'S SUGGESTION.
ONE OF MY OLD STUDENTS IS A HELLUVAN' ARTIST.
YOU IN SCHOOL, GRANT?
NO.
NO?
I THOUGHT YOU WERE TAKING A PHYSICS CLASS AT N.Y.U. JESS PAID FOR IT.
I DROPPED IT.
YOU DROPPED IT?
SOON AS THE TEACHER KNEW I WAS IN THE CLASS HE CHANGED THE COURSE FROM *"MODERN ALTERNATIVE ENERGY"* TO *"WHAT MAKES DAMAGE TICK?"*
THE JERK LECTURED EVERYONE ON HOW MY INTERNAL COMBUSTION REFLECTED MY "DAMAGED PROFILE."
IF YOU EVER WANT SOME PRIVATE TUTORS, I KNOW A LOT OF TEACHERS WHO WOULD BE HAPPY TO WORK SOMETHING OUT.
MYSELF INCLUDED.
THAT'S A NICE OFFER, GRANT.
Um... THANKS, MR. PIERCE.
I'LL THINK ABOUT IT.
HEY, BOYS...

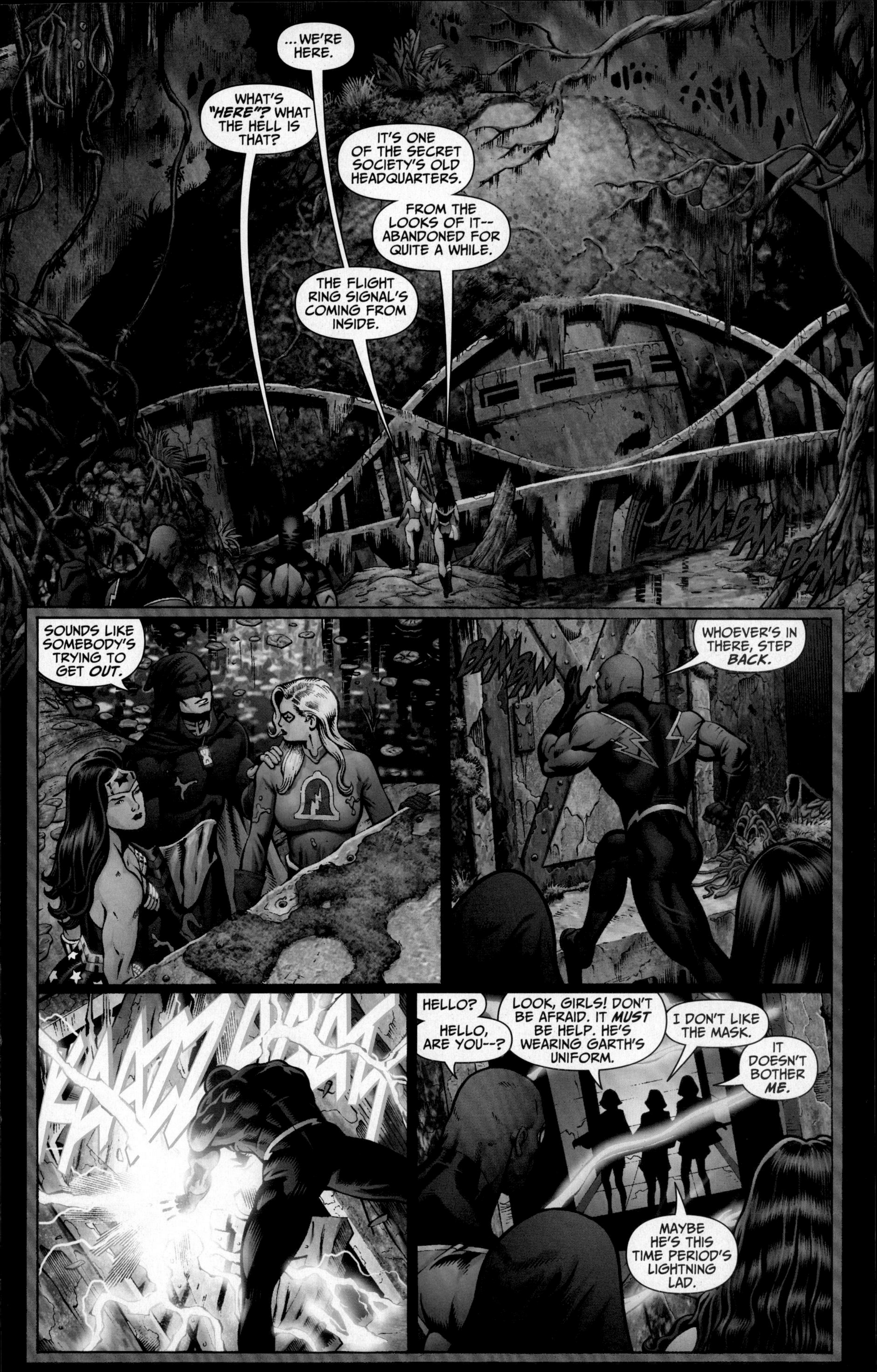
...WE'RE HERE.
WHAT'S "HERE"? WHAT THE HELL IS THAT?
IT'S ONE OF THE SECRET SOCIETY'S OLD HEADQUARTERS.
FROM THE LOOKS OF IT-- ABANDONED FOR QUITE A WHILE.
THE FLIGHT RING SIGNAL'S COMING FROM INSIDE.
BAM BAM BAM
SOUNDS LIKE SOMEBODY'S TRYING TO GET OUT.
BAM BAM
WHOEVER'S IN THERE, STEP BACK.
HELLO?
HELLO, ARE YOU--?
LOOK, GIRLS! DON'T BE AFRAID. IT MUST BE HELP. HE'S WEARING GARTH'S UNIFORM.
I DON'T LIKE THE MASK.
IT DOESN'T BOTHER ME.
MAYBE HE'S THIS TIME PERIOD'S LIGHTNING LAD.

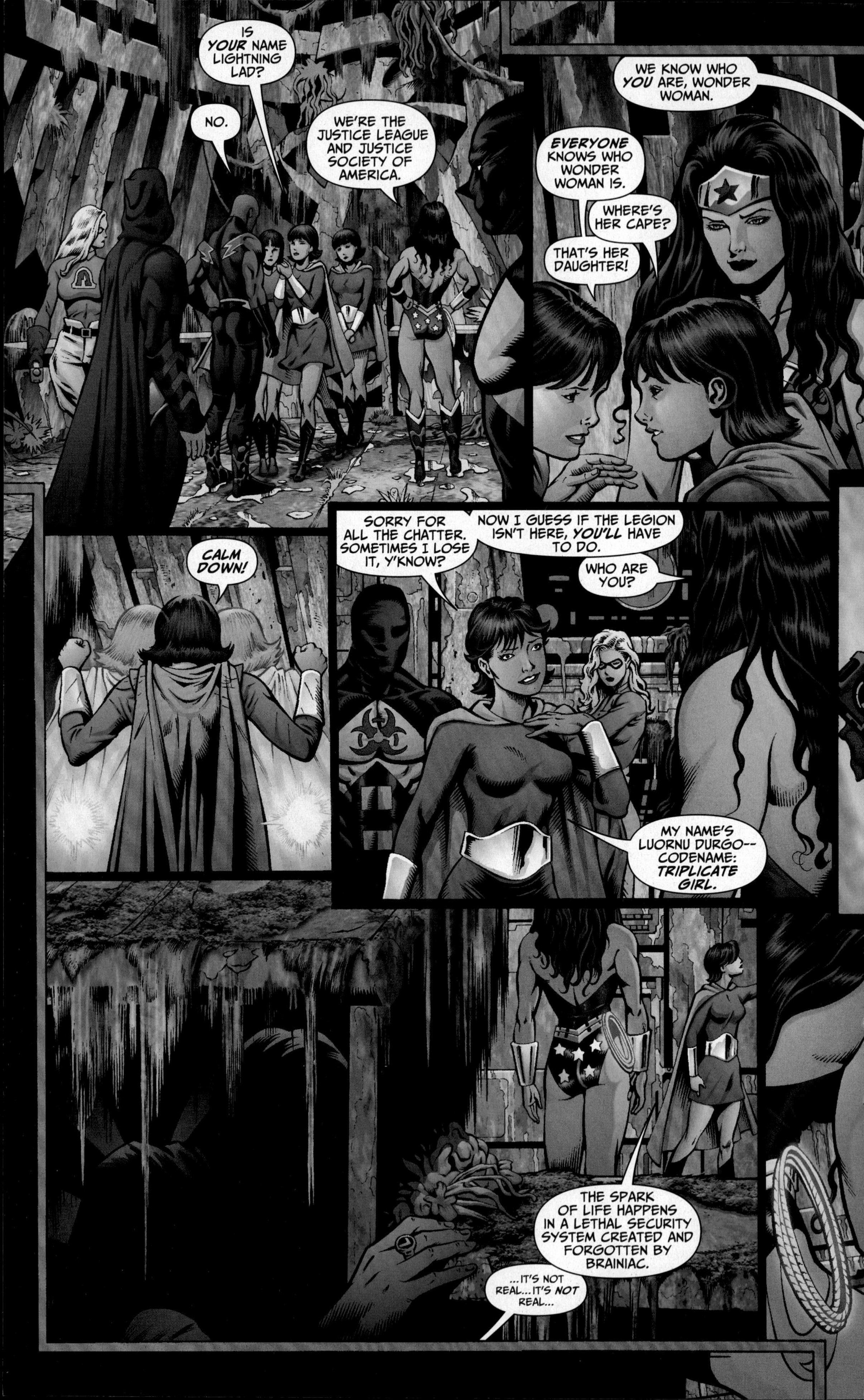

IS *YOUR* NAME LIGHTNING LAD?
NO.
WE'RE THE JUSTICE LEAGUE AND JUSTICE SOCIETY OF AMERICA.
WE KNOW WHO *YOU* ARE, WONDER WOMAN.
EVERYONE KNOWS WHO WONDER WOMAN IS.
WHERE'S HER CAPE?
THAT'S HER DAUGHTER!
CALM DOWN!
SORRY FOR ALL THE CHATTER. SOMETIMES I LOSE IT, Y'KNOW?
NOW I GUESS IF THE LEGION ISN'T HERE, *YOU'LL* HAVE TO DO.
WHO ARE YOU?
MY NAME'S LUORNU DURGO-- CODENAME: *TRIPLICATE GIRL.*
THE SPARK OF LIFE HAPPENS IN A LETHAL SECURITY SYSTEM CREATED AND FORGOTTEN BY BRAINIAC.
...IT'S NOT REAL...IT'S *NOT* REAL...

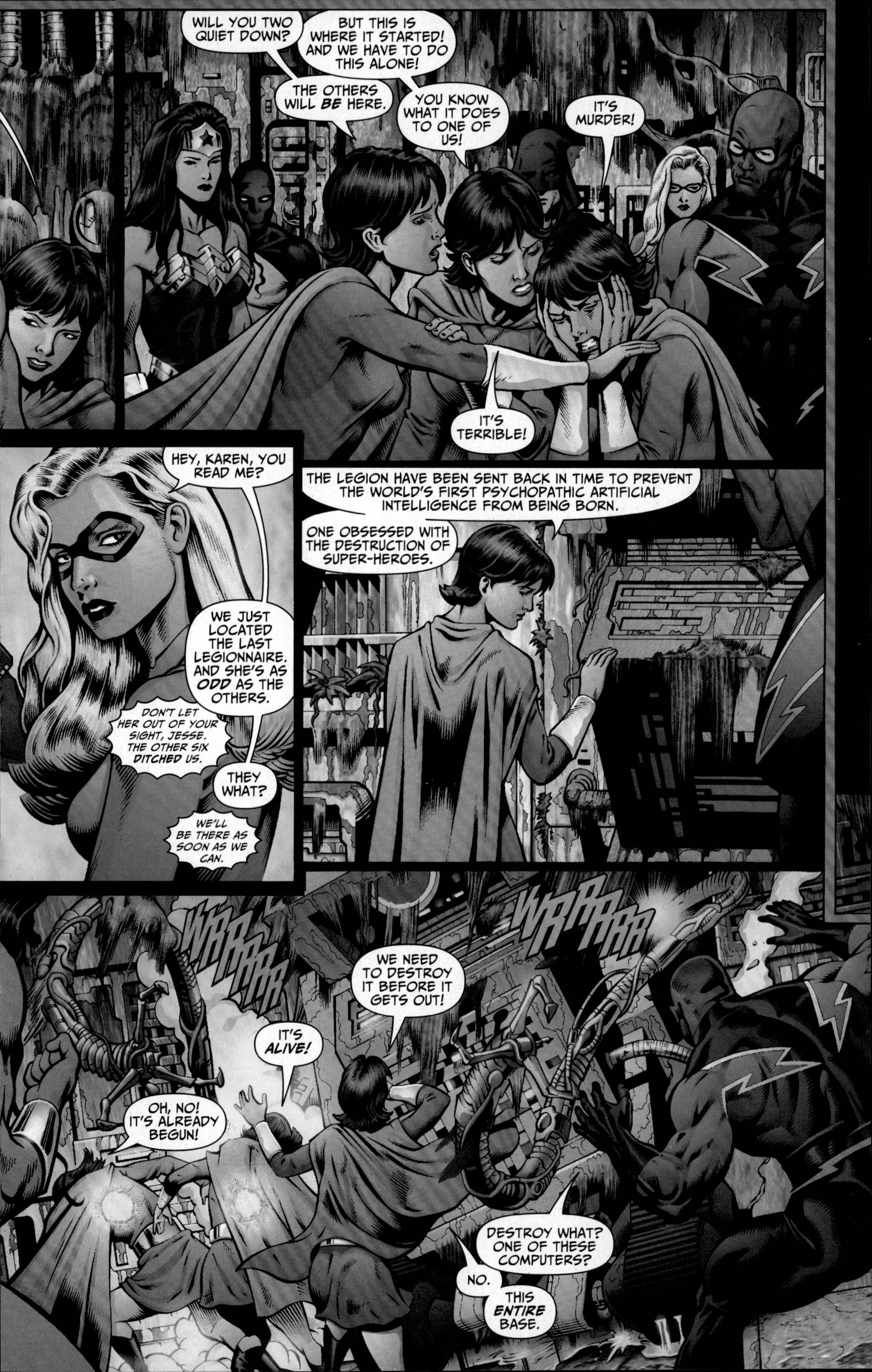
WILL YOU TWO QUIET DOWN?
BUT THIS IS WHERE IT STARTED! AND WE HAVE TO DO THIS ALONE!
THE OTHERS WILL BE HERE.
YOU KNOW WHAT IT DOES TO ONE OF US!
IT'S MURDER!
IT'S TERRIBLE!
HEY, KAREN, YOU READ ME?
WE JUST LOCATED THE LAST LEGIONNAIRE. AND SHE'S AS ODD AS THE OTHERS.
DON'T LET HER OUT OF YOUR SIGHT, JESSE. THE OTHER SIX DITCHED US.
THEY WHAT?
WE'LL BE THERE AS SOON AS WE CAN.
THE LEGION HAVE BEEN SENT BACK IN TIME TO PREVENT THE WORLD'S FIRST PSYCHOPATHIC ARTIFICIAL INTELLIGENCE FROM BEING BORN.
ONE OBSESSED WITH THE DESTRUCTION OF SUPER-HEROES.
WRRRR
WRRRRR
WE NEED TO DESTROY IT BEFORE IT GETS OUT!
IT'S ALIVE!
OH, NO! IT'S ALREADY BEGUN!
DESTROY WHAT? ONE OF THESE COMPUTERS?
NO.
THIS ENTIRE BASE.

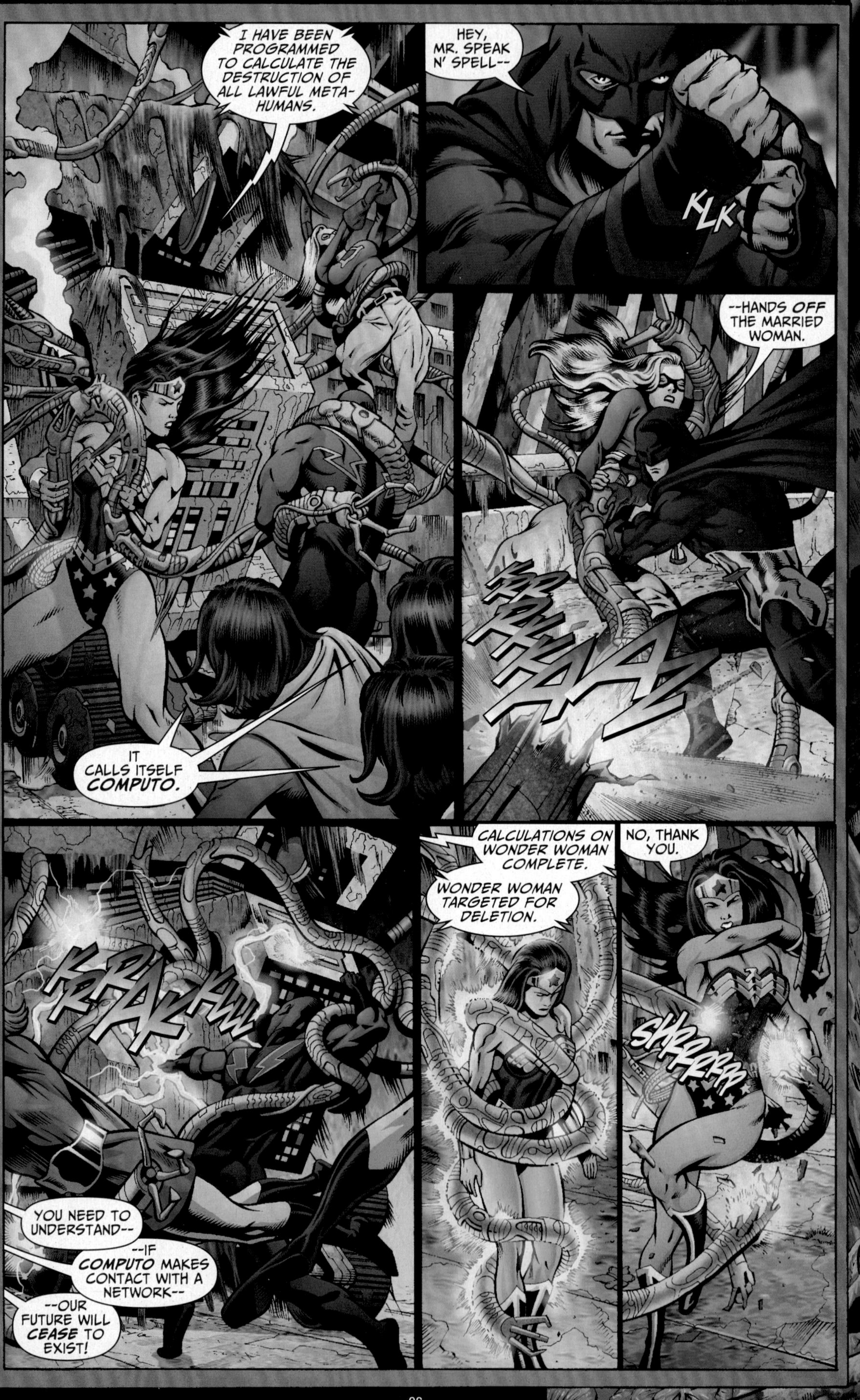
I HAVE BEEN PROGRAMMED TO CALCULATE THE DESTRUCTION OF ALL LAWFUL META-HUMANS.
HEY, MR. SPEAK N' SPELL--
KLK
--HANDS OFF THE MARRIED WOMAN.
IT CALLS ITSELF COMPUTO.
KRAKKHAAZ
KRAKAKAKHW
YOU NEED TO UNDERSTAND--
--IF COMPUTO MAKES CONTACT WITH A NETWORK--
--OUR FUTURE WILL CEASE TO EXIST!
CALCULATIONS ON WONDER WOMAN COMPLETE.
WONDER WOMAN TARGETED FOR DELETION.
NO, THANK YOU.
SHRRRRRR

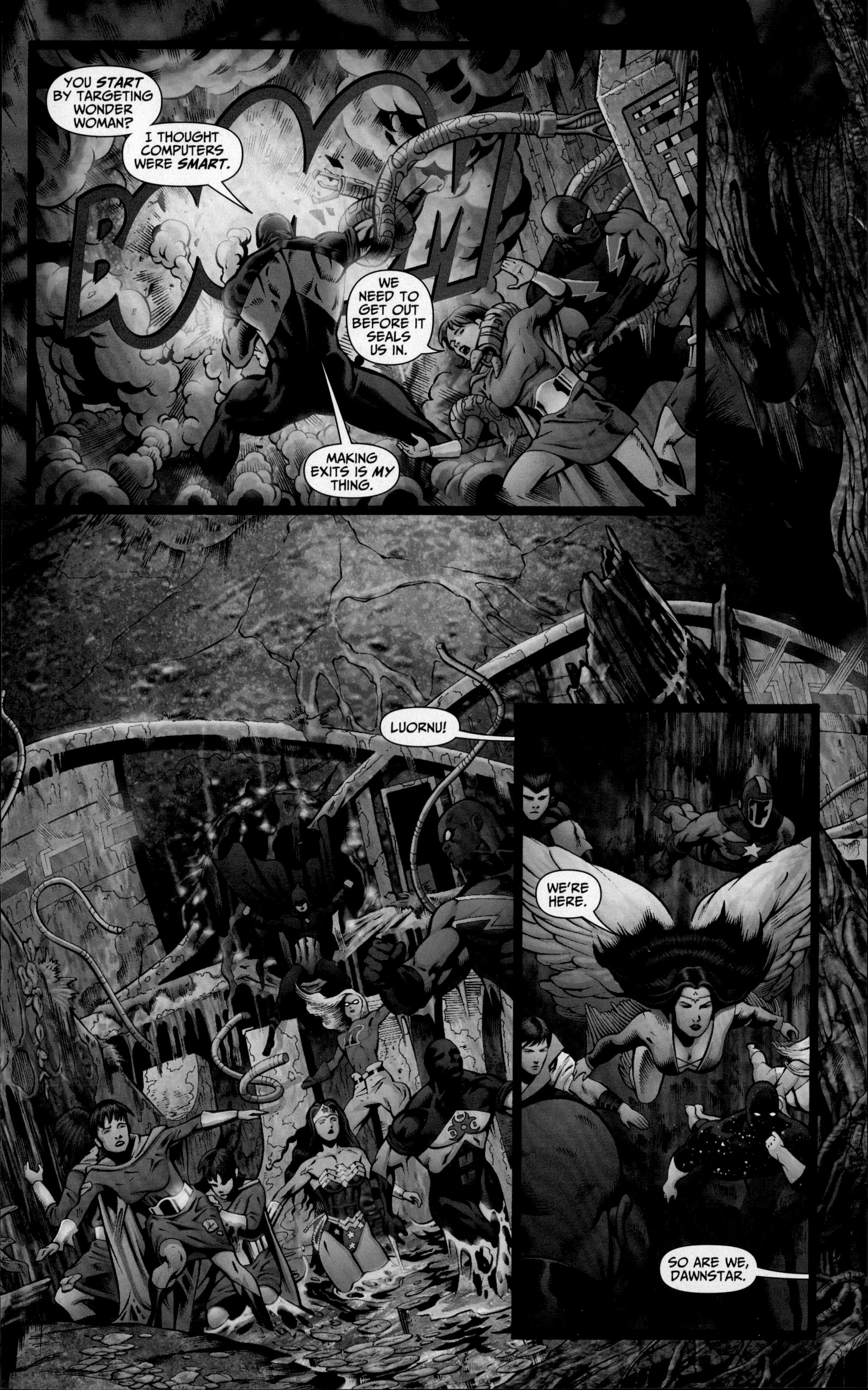
YOU START BY TARGETING WONDER WOMAN?
I THOUGHT COMPUTERS WERE SMART.
BOOM
WE NEED TO GET OUT BEFORE IT SEALS US IN.
MAKING EXITS IS MY THING.
LUORNU!
WE'RE HERE.
SO ARE WE, DAWNSTAR.

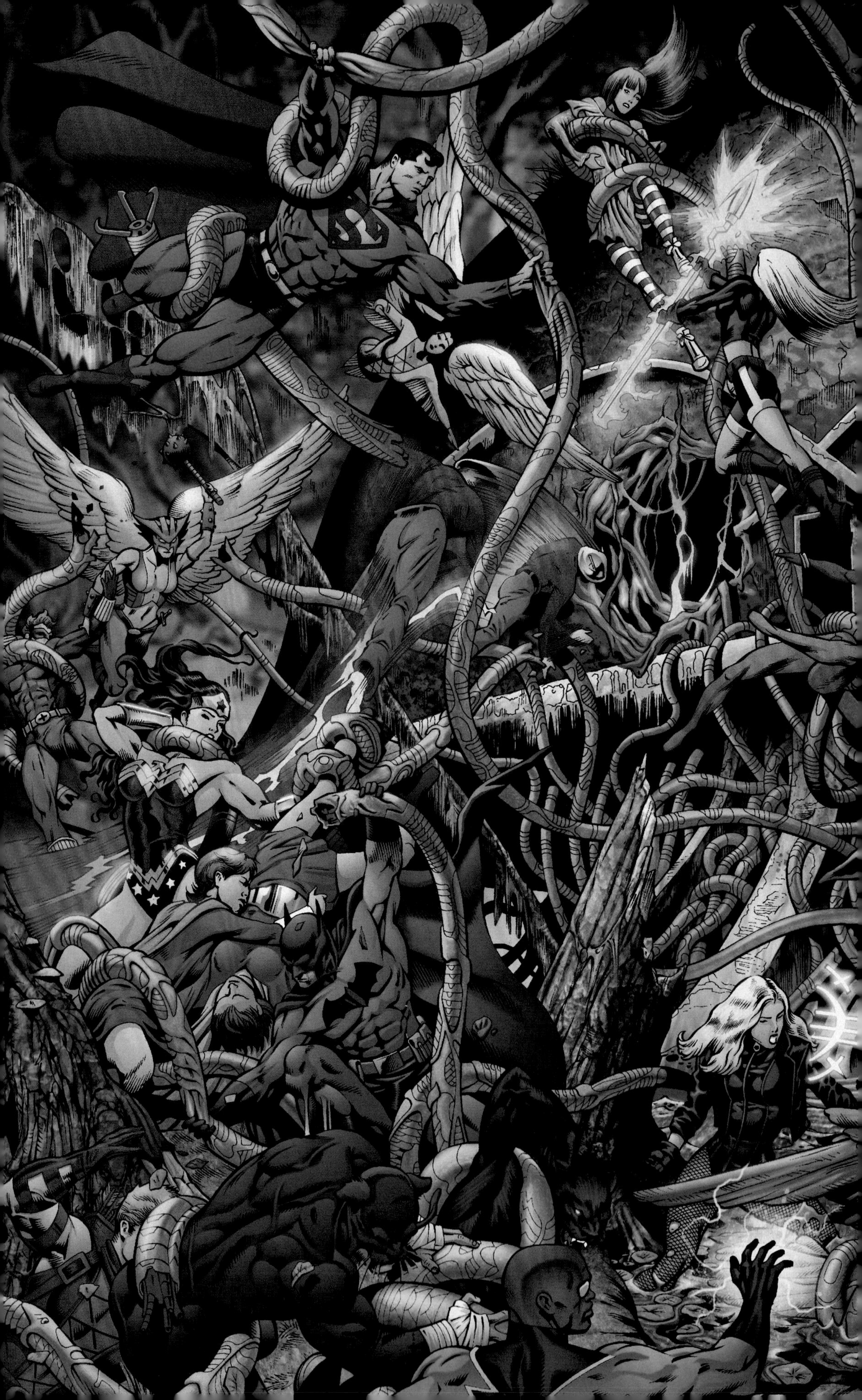

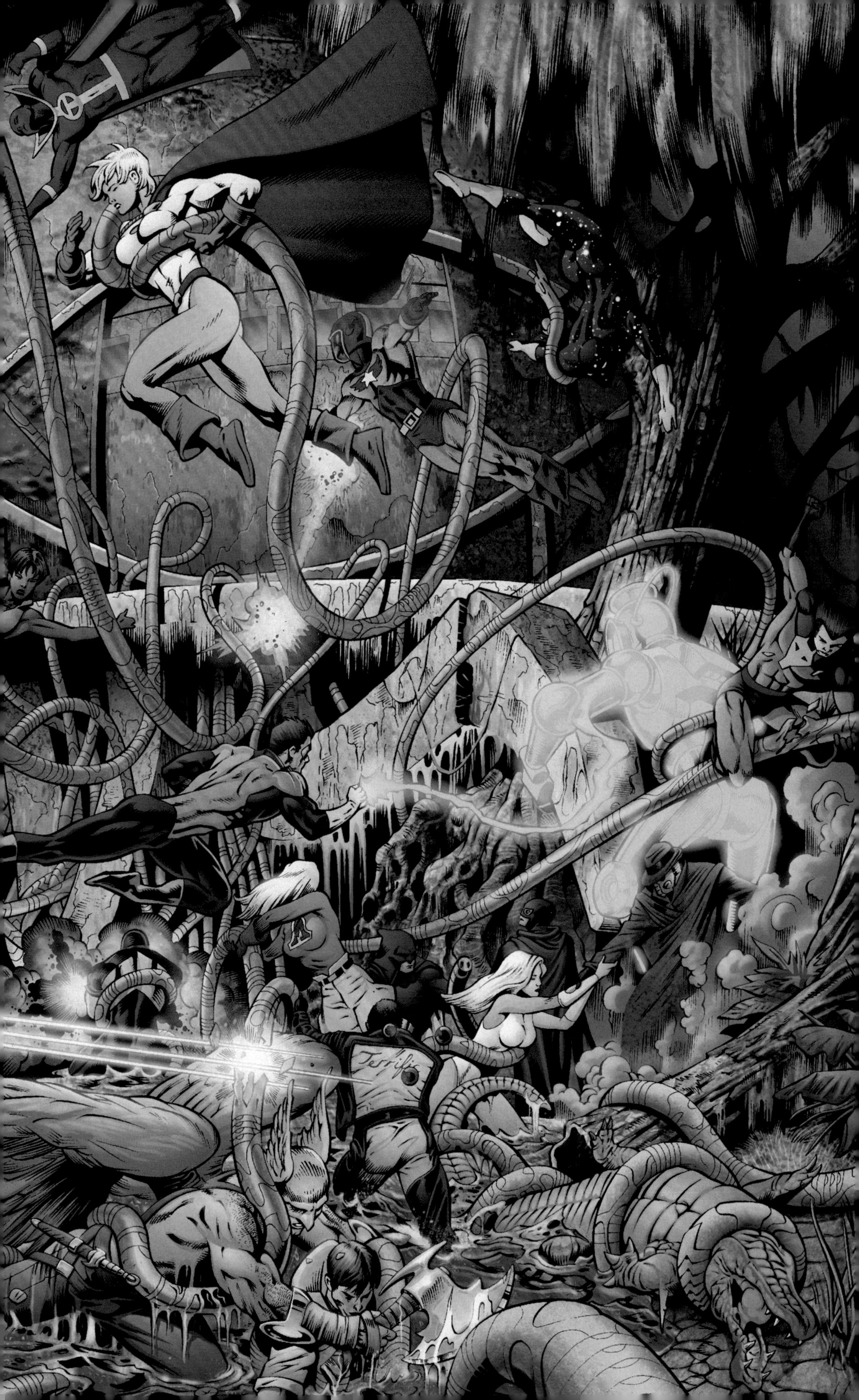
Terrifi

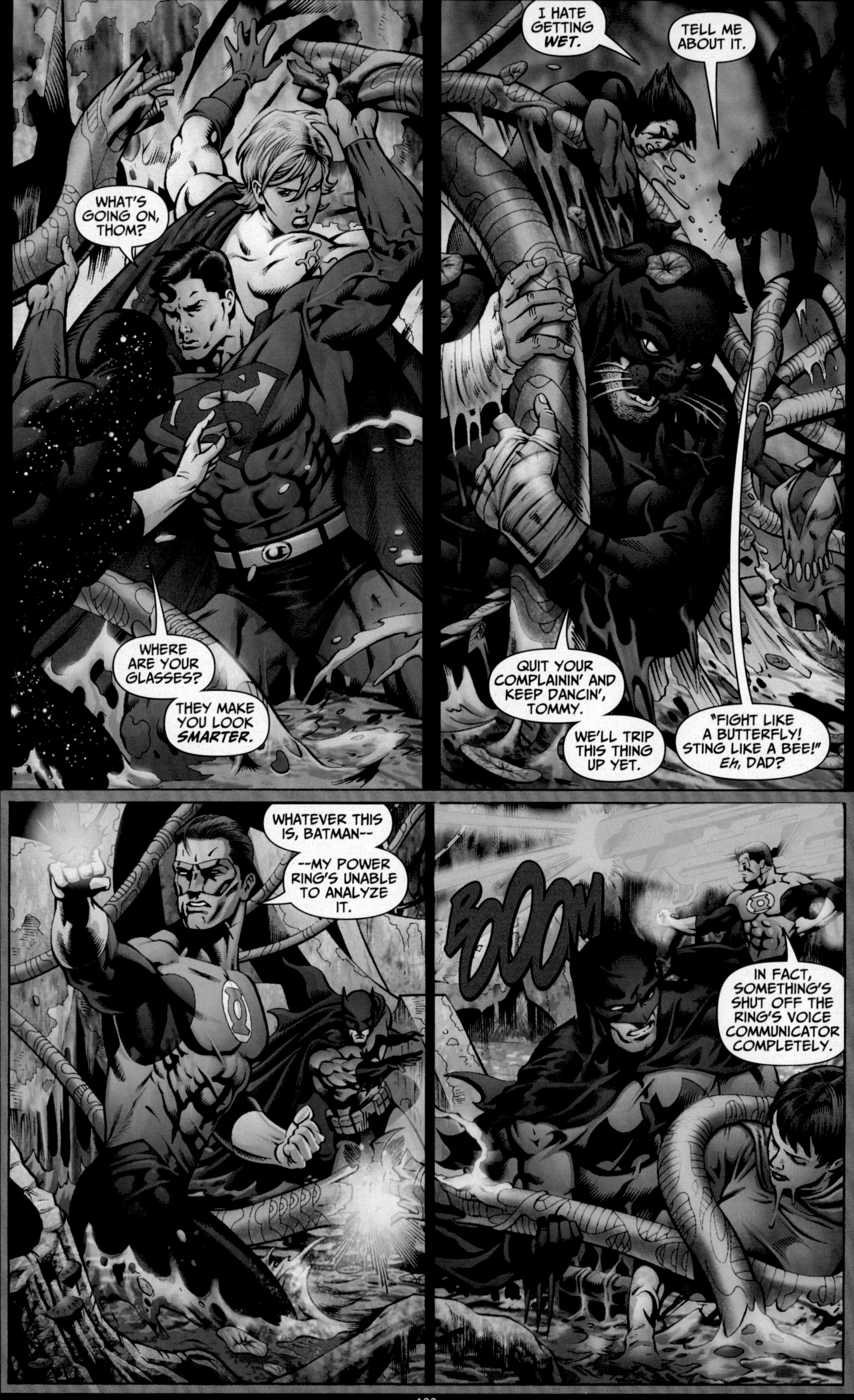
WHAT'S GOING ON, THOM?
WHERE ARE YOUR GLASSES?
THEY MAKE YOU LOOK SMARTER.
I HATE GETTING WET.
TELL ME ABOUT IT.
QUIT YOUR COMPLAININ' AND KEEP DANCIN', TOMMY.
WE'LL TRIP THIS THING UP YET.
"FIGHT LIKE A BUTTERFLY! STING LIKE A BEE!" Eh, DAD?
WHATEVER THIS IS, BATMAN--
--MY POWER RING'S UNABLE TO ANALYZE IT.
BOOOM
IN FACT, SOMETHING'S SHUT OFF THE RING'S VOICE COMMUNICATOR COMPLETELY.

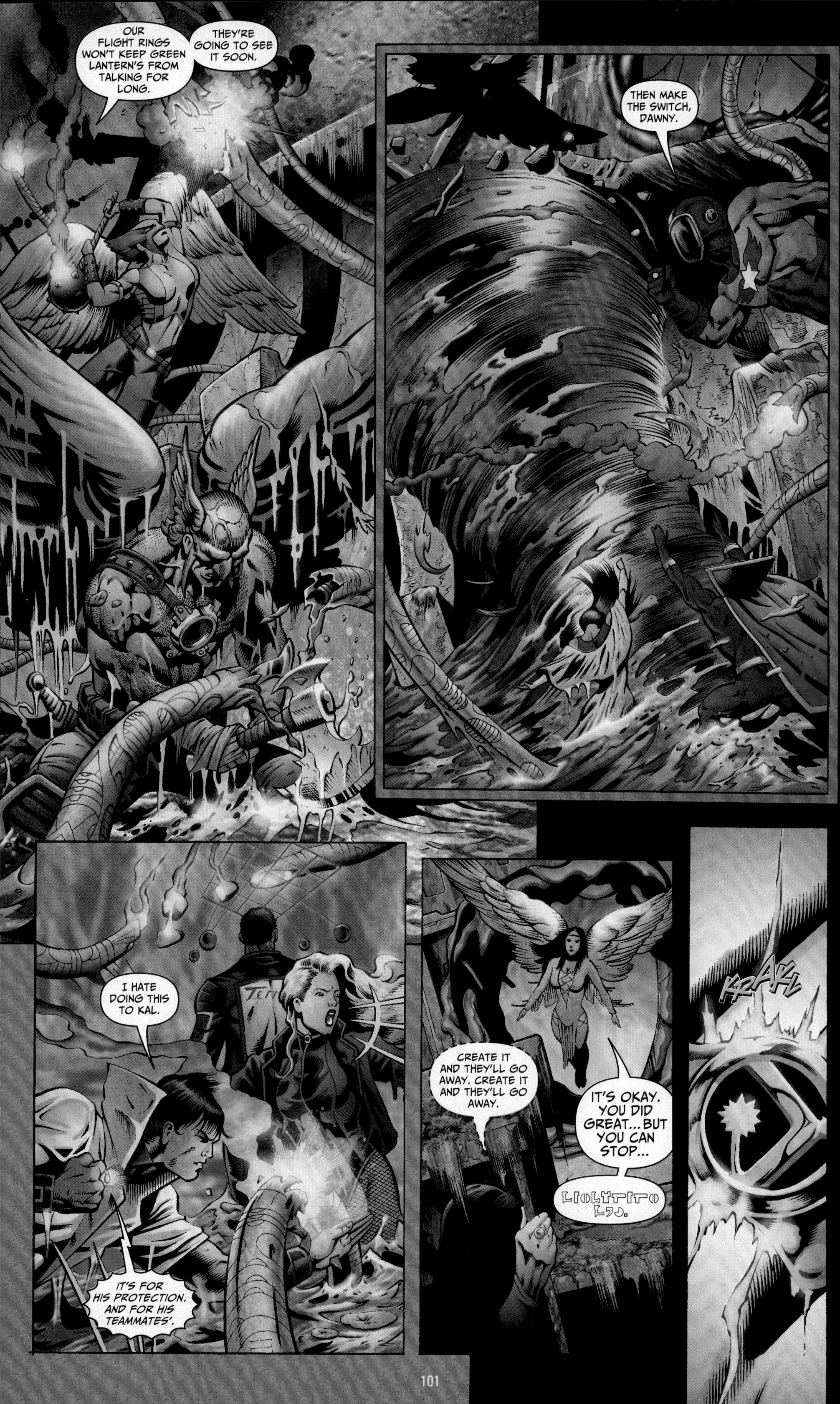
OUR FLIGHT RINGS WON'T KEEP GREEN LANTERN'S FROM TALKING FOR LONG.
THEY'RE GOING TO SEE IT SOON.
THEN MAKE THE SWITCH, DAWNY.
I HATE DOING THIS TO KAL.
IT'S FOR HIS PROTECTION. AND FOR HIS TEAMMATES'.
CREATE IT AND THEY'LL GO AWAY. CREATE IT AND THEY'LL GO AWAY.
IT'S OKAY. YOU DID GREAT... BUT YOU CAN STOP...
KRAKK

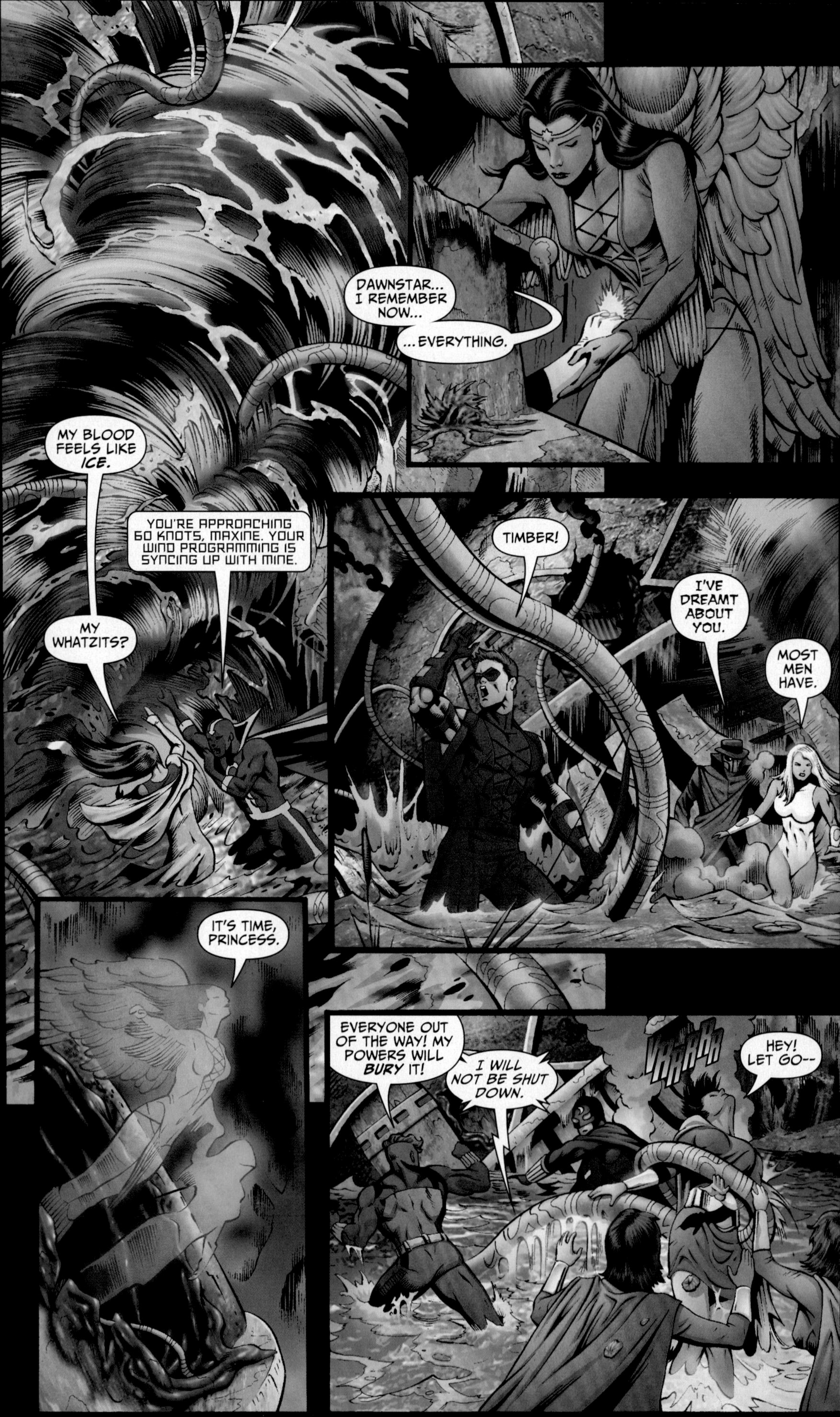
DAWNSTAR... I REMEMBER NOW...
...EVERYTHING.
MY BLOOD FEELS LIKE ICE.
YOU'RE APPROACHING 60 KNOTS, MAXINE. YOUR WIND PROGRAMMING IS SYNCING UP WITH MINE.
MY WHATZITS?
TIMBER!
I'VE DREAMT ABOUT YOU.
MOST MEN HAVE.
IT'S TIME, PRINCESS.
EVERYONE OUT OF THE WAY! MY POWERS WILL BURY IT!
I WILL NOT BE SHUT DOWN.
HEY! LET GO--

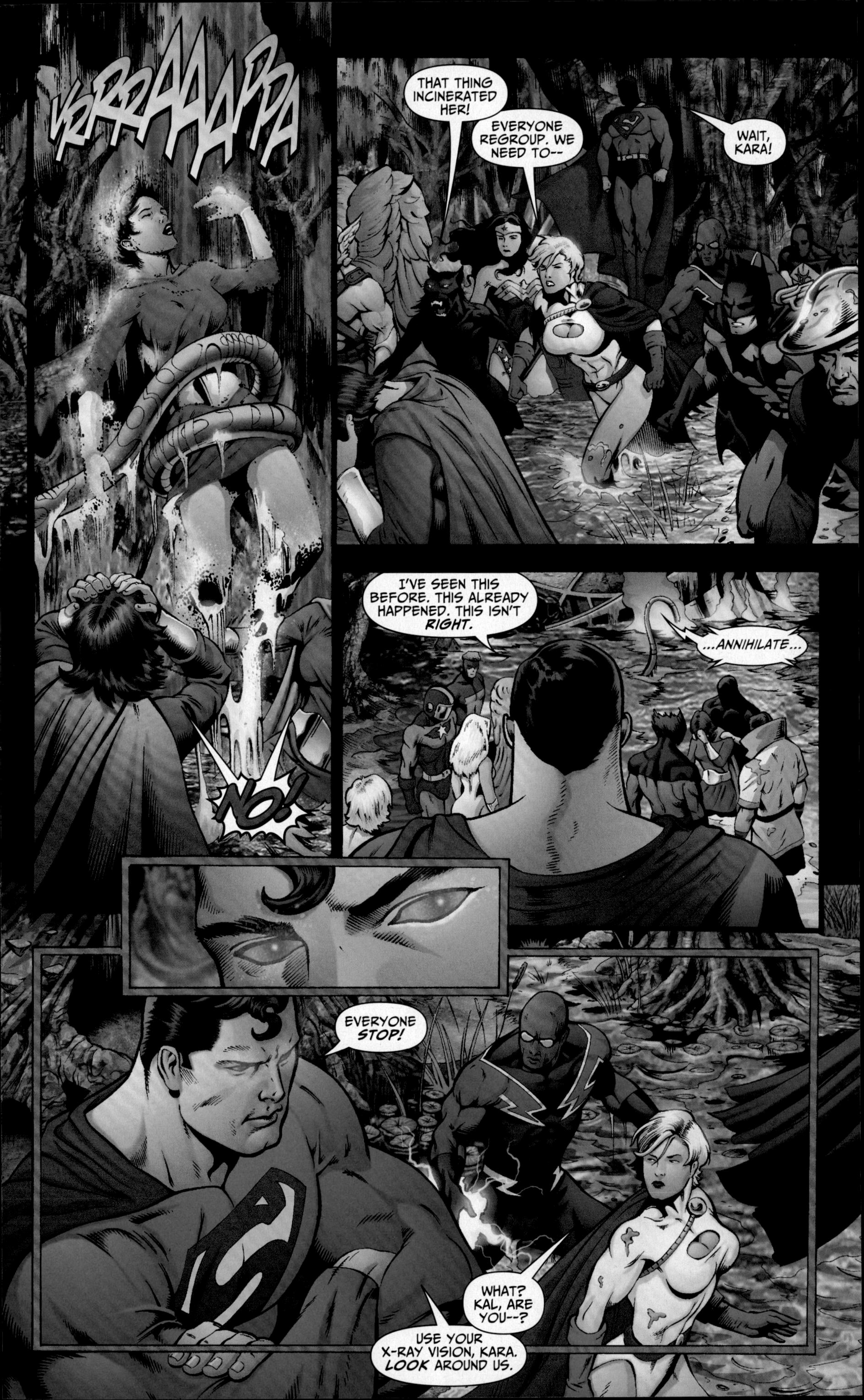
VRRAAAPPA
THAT THING INCINERATED HER!
EVERYONE REGROUP. WE NEED TO--
WAIT, KARA!
NO!
I'VE SEEN THIS BEFORE. THIS ALREADY HAPPENED. THIS ISN'T RIGHT.
...ANNIHILATE...
EVERYONE STOP!
WHAT? KAL, ARE YOU--?
USE YOUR X-RAY VISION, KARA. LOOK AROUND US.

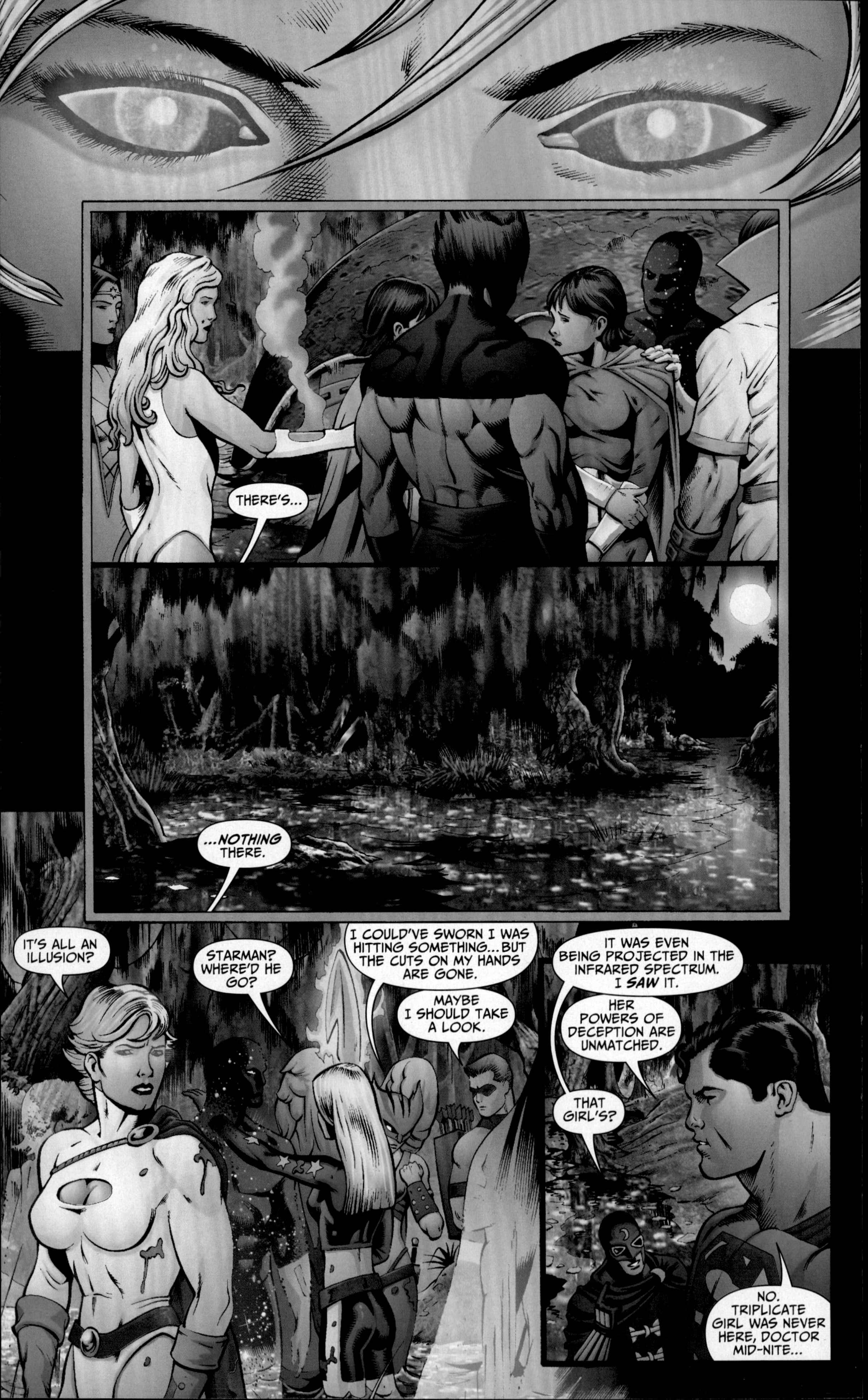

THERE'S...
...NOTHING THERE.
IT'S ALL AN ILLUSION?
STARMAN? WHERE'D HE GO?
I COULD'VE SWORN I WAS HITTING SOMETHING... BUT THE CUTS ON MY HANDS ARE GONE.
MAYBE I SHOULD TAKE A LOOK.
IT WAS EVEN BEING PROJECTED IN THE INFRARED SPECTRUM. I SAW IT.
HER POWERS OF DECEPTION ARE UNMATCHED.
THAT GIRL'S?
NO. TRIPLICATE GIRL WAS NEVER HERE, DOCTOR MID-NITE...

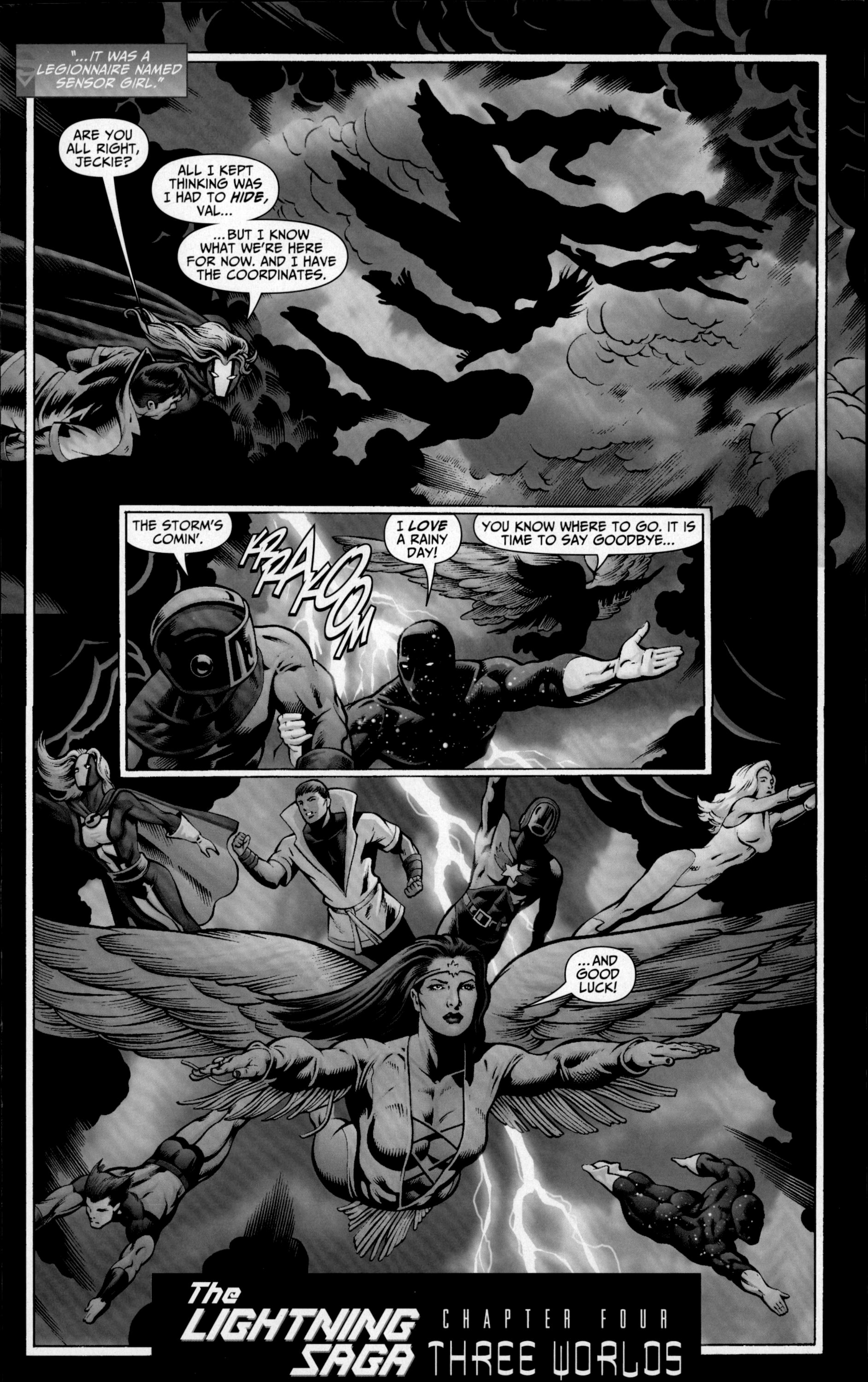
"...IT WAS A LEGIONNAIRE NAMED SENSOR GIRL."
ARE YOU ALL RIGHT, JECKIE?
ALL I KEPT THINKING WAS I HAD TO HIDE, VAL...
...BUT I KNOW WHAT WE'RE HERE FOR NOW. AND I HAVE THE COORDINATES.
THE STORM'S COMIN'.
KRAKOOM
I LOVE A RAINY DAY!
YOU KNOW WHERE TO GO. IT IS TIME TO SAY GOODBYE...
...AND GOOD LUCK!
The LIGHTNING SAGA
CHAPTER FOUR
THREE WORLDS

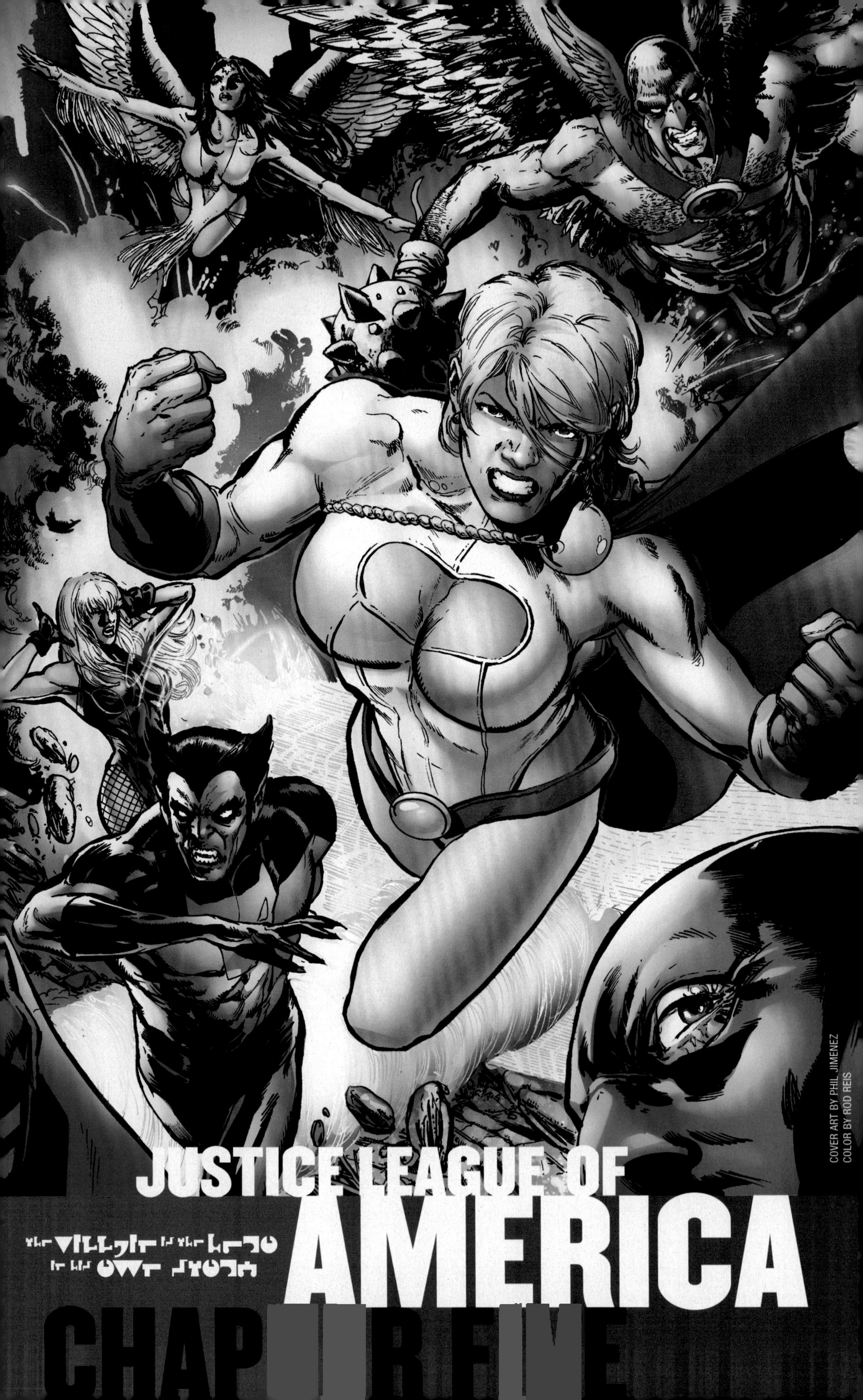
COVER ART BY PHIL JIMENEZ
COLOR BY ROD REIS
JUSTICE LEAGUE OF
AMERICA

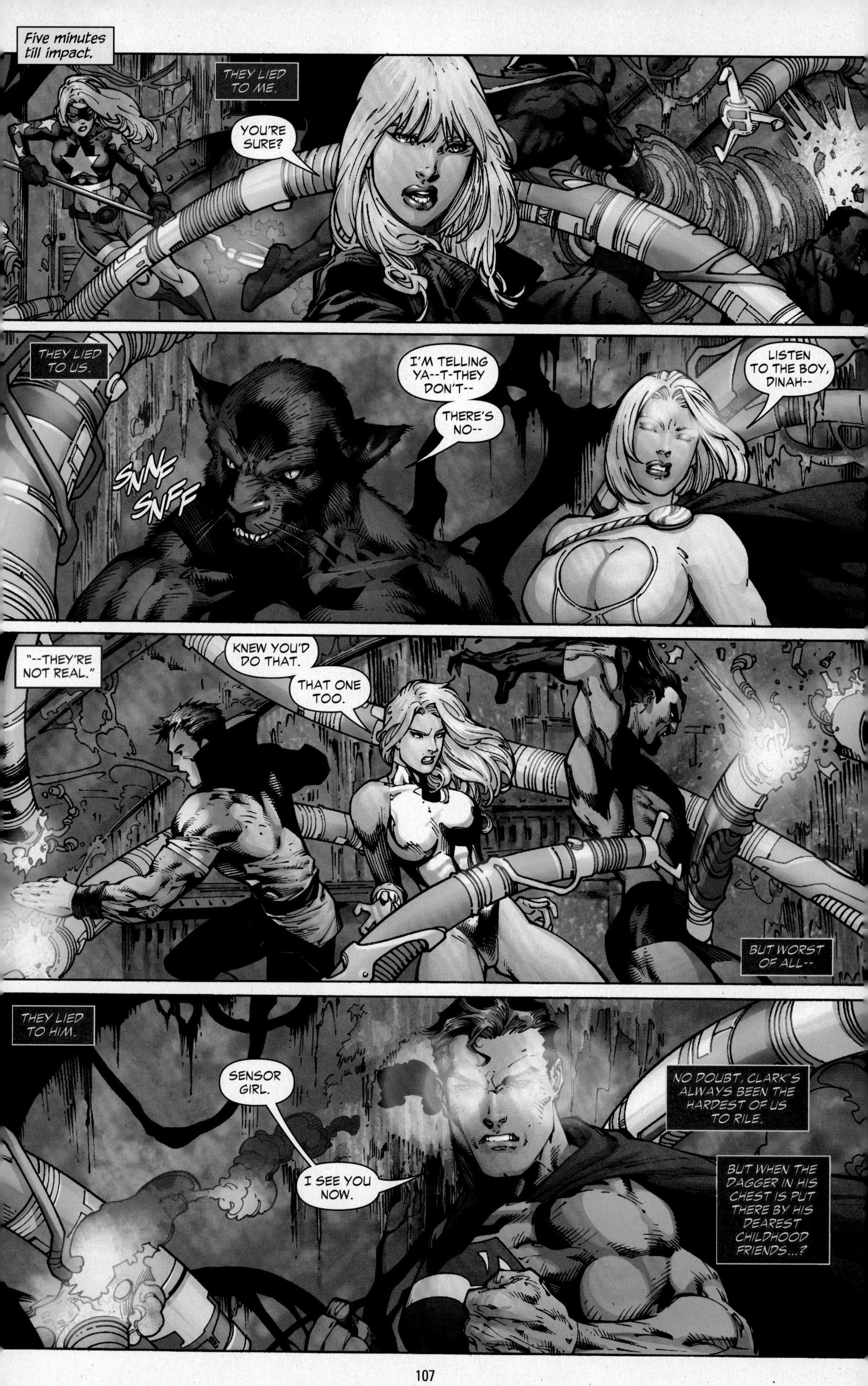
Five minutes till impact.
THEY LIED TO ME.
YOU'RE SURE?
THEY LIED TO US.
I'M TELLING YA--T-THEY DON'T--
THERE'S NO--
LISTEN TO THE BOY, DINAH--
SNFF SNFF
"--THEY'RE NOT REAL."
KNEW YOU'D DO THAT.
THAT ONE TOO.
BUT WORST OF ALL--
THEY LIED TO HIM.
SENSOR GIRL.
I SEE YOU NOW.
NO DOUBT, CLARK'S ALWAYS BEEN THE HARDEST OF US TO RILE.
BUT WHEN THE DAGGER IN HIS CHEST IS PUT THERE BY HIS DEAREST CHILDHOOD FRIENDS...?

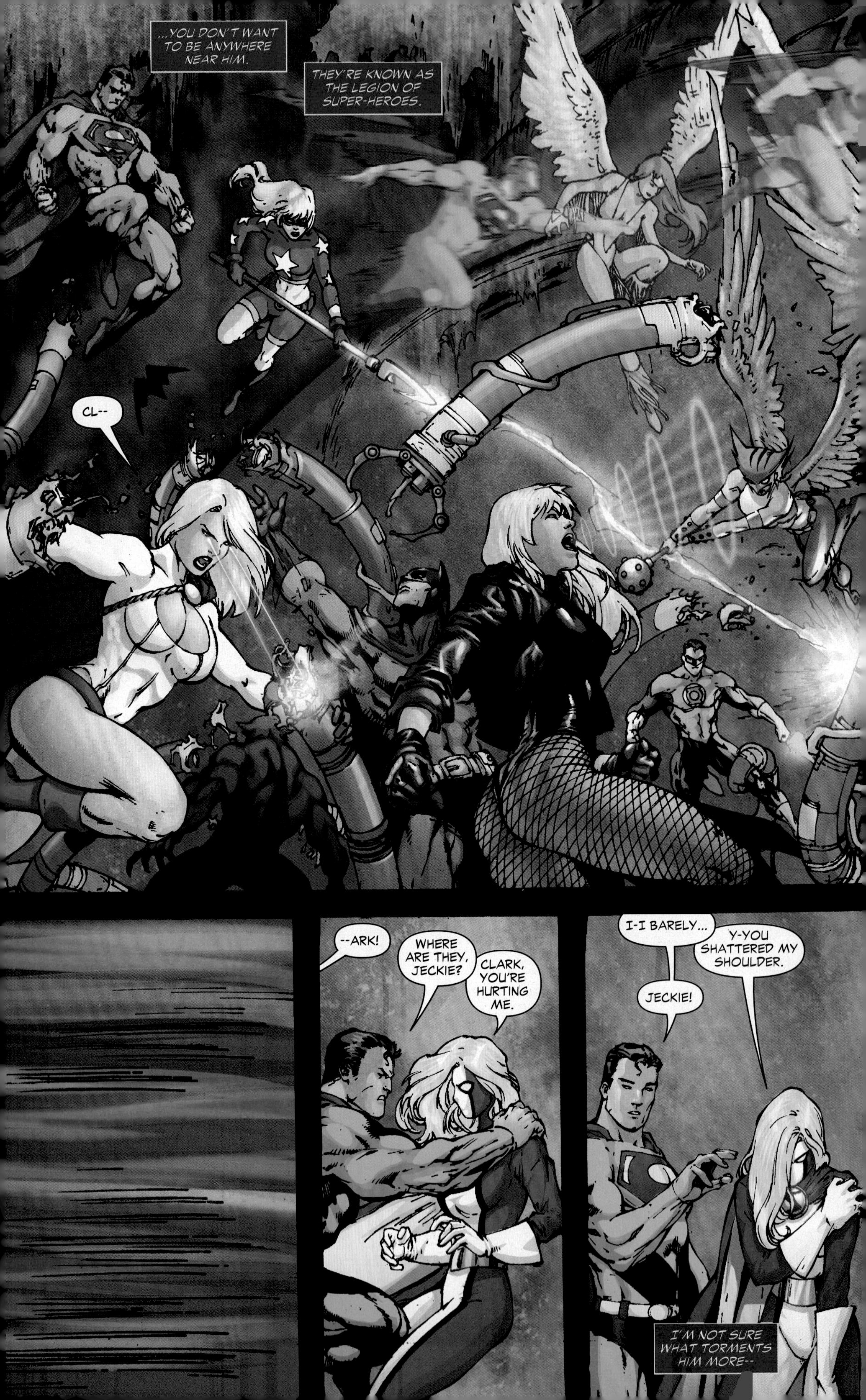
...YOU DON'T WANT TO BE ANYWHERE NEAR HIM.
THEY'RE KNOWN AS THE LEGION OF SUPER-HEROES.
CL--
--ARK!
WHERE ARE THEY, JECKIE?
CLARK, YOU'RE HURTING ME.
I-I BARELY...
Y-YOU SHATTERED MY SHOULDER.
JECKIE!
I'M NOT SURE WHAT TORMENTS HIM MORE--

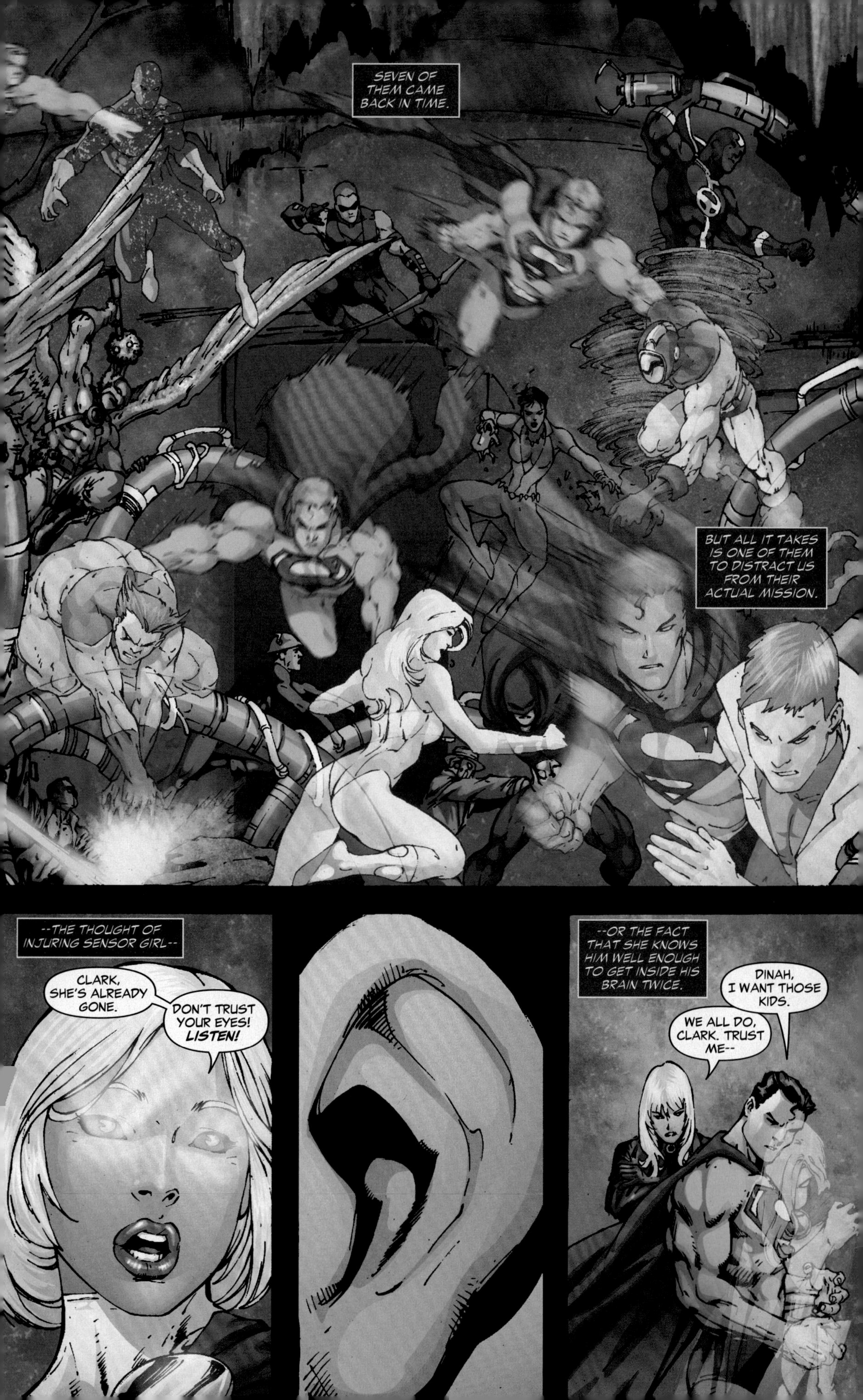
SEVEN OF THEM CAME BACK IN TIME.
BUT ALL IT TAKES IS ONE OF THEM TO DISTRACT US FROM THEIR ACTUAL MISSION.
--THE THOUGHT OF INJURING SENSOR GIRL--
CLARK, SHE'S ALREADY GONE.
DON'T TRUST YOUR EYES! LISTEN!
--OR THE FACT THAT SHE KNOWS HIM WELL ENOUGH TO GET INSIDE HIS BRAIN TWICE.
DINAH, I WANT THOSE KIDS.
WE ALL DO, CLARK. TRUST ME--

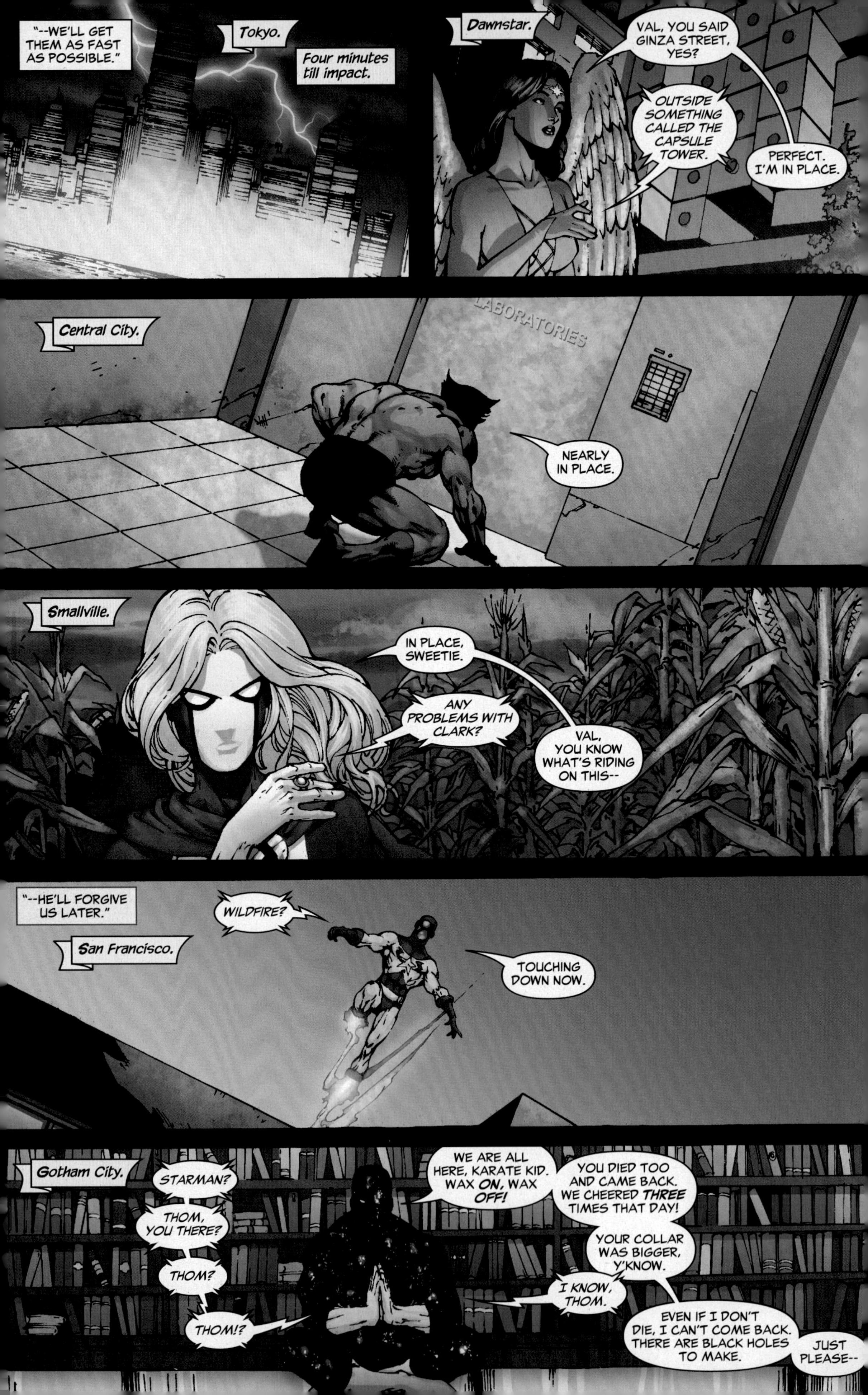
"--WE'LL GET THEM AS FAST AS POSSIBLE."
Tokyo.
Four minutes till impact.
Dawnstar.
VAL, YOU SAID GINZA STREET, YES?
OUTSIDE SOMETHING CALLED THE CAPSULE TOWER.
PERFECT. I'M IN PLACE.
Central City.
LABORATORIES
NEARLY IN PLACE.
Smallville.
IN PLACE, SWEETIE.
ANY PROBLEMS WITH CLARK?
VAL, YOU KNOW WHAT'S RIDING ON THIS--
"--HE'LL FORGIVE US LATER."
San Francisco.
WILDFIRE?
TOUCHING DOWN NOW.
Gotham City.
STARMAN?
THOM, YOU THERE?
THOM?
THOM!?
WE ARE ALL HERE, KARATE KID. WAX ON, WAX OFF!
YOU DIED TOO AND CAME BACK. WE CHEERED THREE TIMES THAT DAY!
YOUR COLLAR WAS BIGGER, Y'KNOW.
I KNOW, THOM.
EVEN IF I DON'T DIE, I CAN'T COME BACK. THERE ARE BLACK HOLES TO MAKE.
JUST PLEASE--

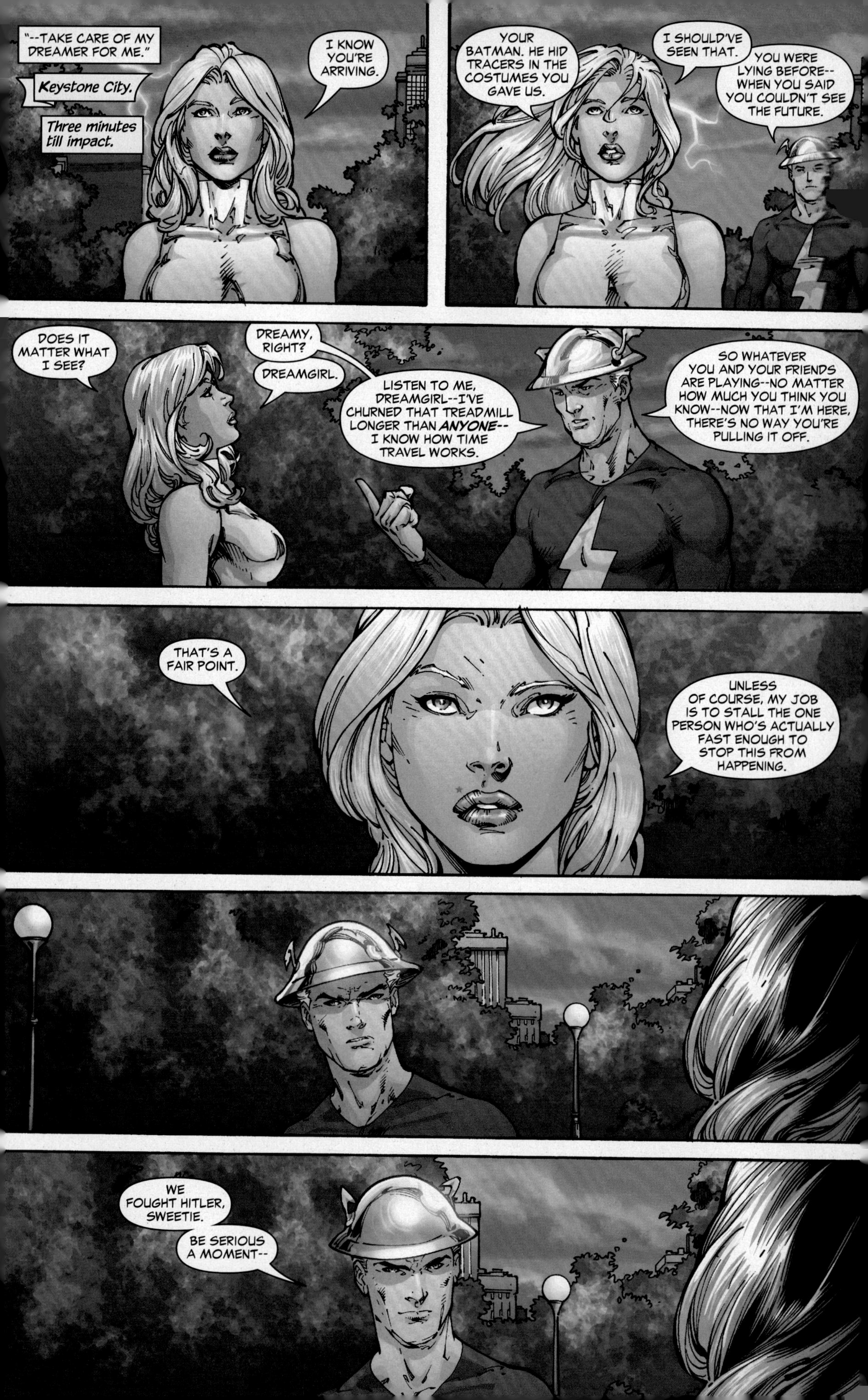
"--TAKE CARE OF MY DREAMER FOR ME."
Keystone City.
Three minutes till impact.
I KNOW YOU'RE ARRIVING.
YOUR BATMAN. HE HID TRACERS IN THE COSTUMES YOU GAVE US.
I SHOULD'VE SEEN THAT.
YOU WERE LYING BEFORE--WHEN YOU SAID YOU COULDN'T SEE THE FUTURE.
DOES IT MATTER WHAT I SEE?
DREAMY, RIGHT?
DREAMGIRL.
LISTEN TO ME, DREAMGIRL--I'VE CHURNED THAT TREADMILL LONGER THAN ANYONE--I KNOW HOW TIME TRAVEL WORKS.
SO WHATEVER YOU AND YOUR FRIENDS ARE PLAYING--NO MATTER HOW MUCH YOU THINK YOU KNOW--NOW THAT I'M HERE, THERE'S NO WAY YOU'RE PULLING IT OFF.
THAT'S A FAIR POINT.
UNLESS OF COURSE, MY JOB IS TO STALL THE ONE PERSON WHO'S ACTUALLY FAST ENOUGH TO STOP THIS FROM HAPPENING.
WE FOUGHT HITLER, SWEETIE.
BE SERIOUS A MOMENT--

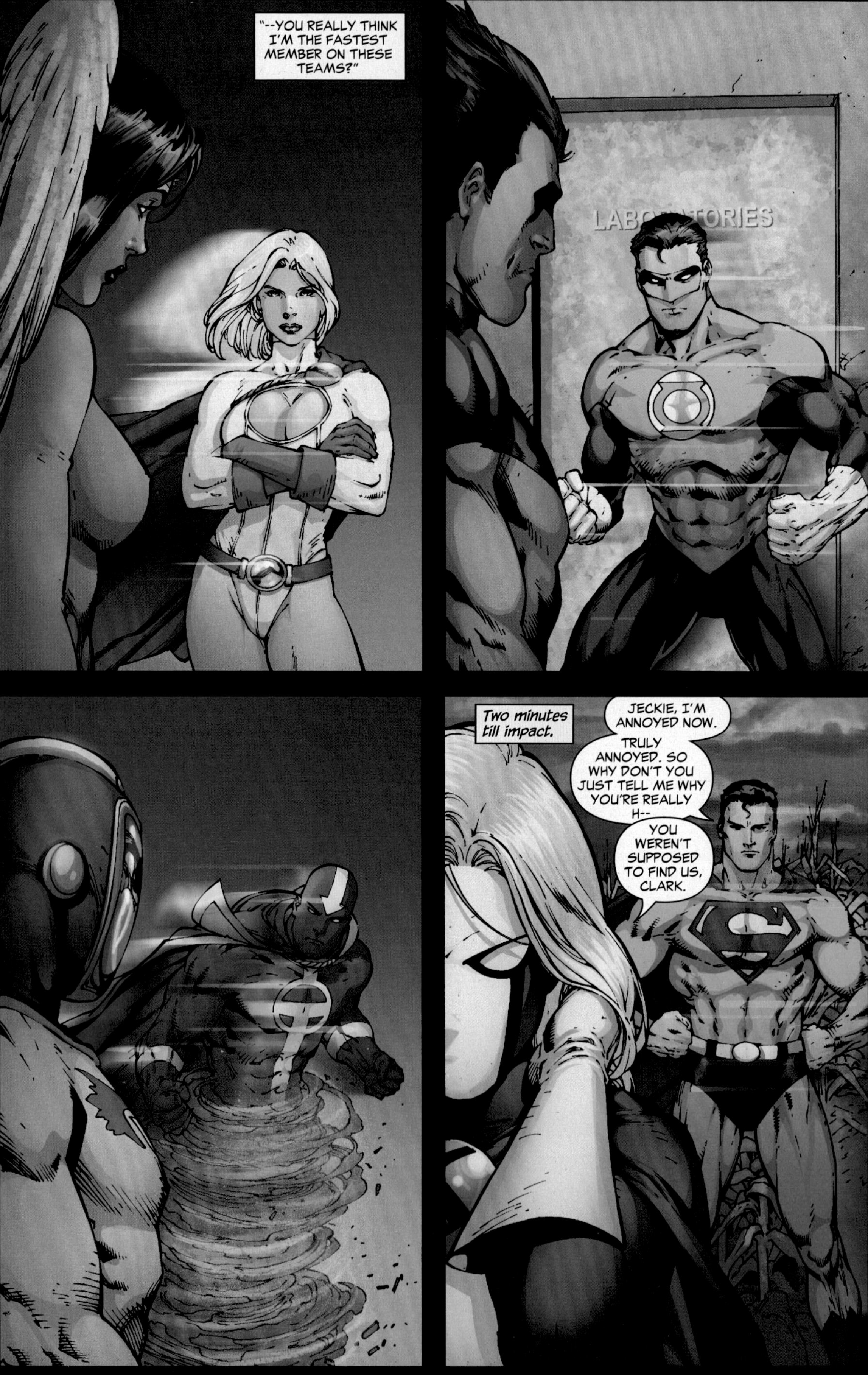
"--YOU REALLY THINK I'M THE FASTEST MEMBER ON THESE TEAMS?"
Two minutes till impact.
JECKIE, I'M ANNOYED NOW.
TRULY ANNOYED. SO WHY DON'T YOU JUST TELL ME WHY YOU'RE REALLY H--
YOU WEREN'T SUPPOSED TO FIND US, CLARK.

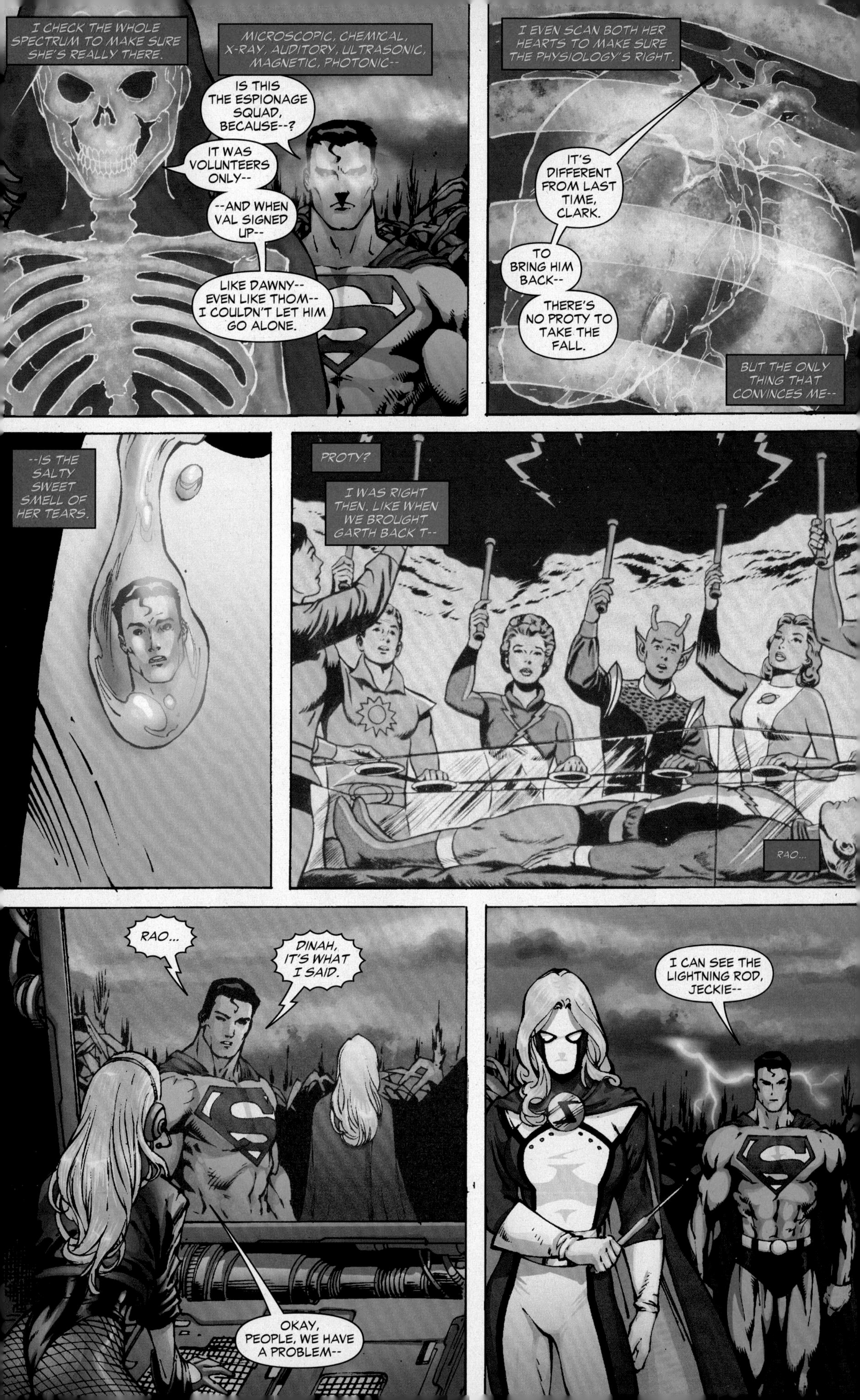
I CHECK THE WHOLE SPECTRUM TO MAKE SURE SHE'S REALLY THERE.
MICROSCOPIC, CHEMICAL, X-RAY, AUDITORY, ULTRASONIC, MAGNETIC, PHOTONIC--
IS THIS THE ESPIONAGE SQUAD, BECAUSE--?
IT WAS VOLUNTEERS ONLY--
--AND WHEN VAL SIGNED UP--
LIKE DAWNY-- EVEN LIKE THOM-- I COULDN'T LET HIM GO ALONE.
I EVEN SCAN BOTH HER HEARTS TO MAKE SURE THE PHYSIOLOGY'S RIGHT.
IT'S DIFFERENT FROM LAST TIME, CLARK.
TO BRING HIM BACK--
THERE'S NO PROTY TO TAKE THE FALL.
BUT THE ONLY THING THAT CONVINCES ME--
--IS THE SALTY SWEET SMELL OF HER TEARS.
PROTY?
I WAS RIGHT THEN. LIKE WHEN WE BROUGHT GARTH BACK T--
RAO...
RAO...
DINAH, IT'S WHAT I SAID.
OKAY, PEOPLE, WE HAVE A PROBLEM--
I CAN SEE THE LIGHTNING ROD, JECKIE--

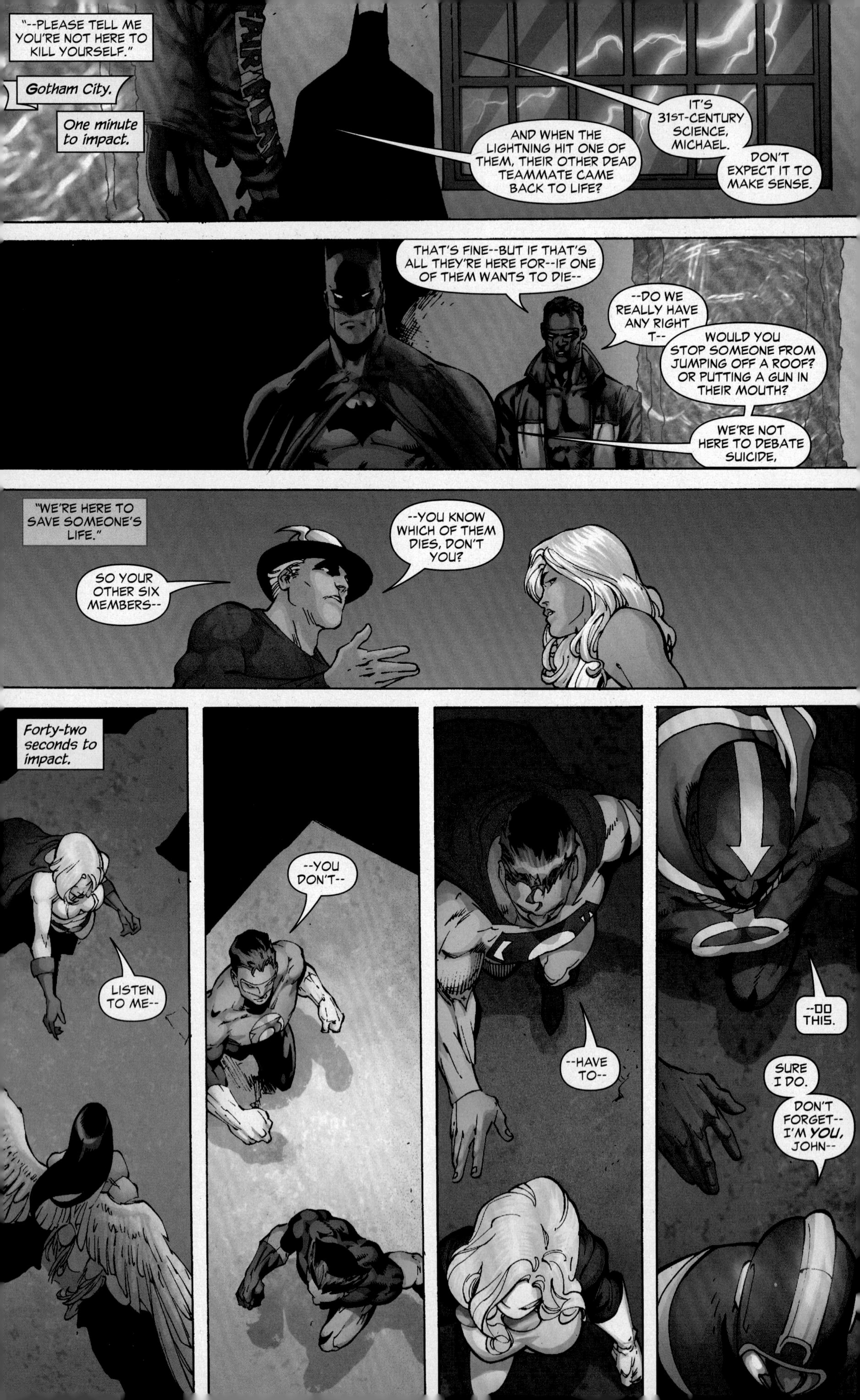
"--PLEASE TELL ME YOU'RE NOT HERE TO KILL YOURSELF."
Gotham City.
One minute to impact.
AND WHEN THE LIGHTNING HIT ONE OF THEM, THEIR OTHER DEAD TEAMMATE CAME BACK TO LIFE?
IT'S 31ST-CENTURY SCIENCE, MICHAEL.
DON'T EXPECT IT TO MAKE SENSE.
THAT'S FINE--BUT IF THAT'S ALL THEY'RE HERE FOR--IF ONE OF THEM WANTS TO DIE--
--DO WE REALLY HAVE ANY RIGHT T--
WOULD YOU STOP SOMEONE FROM JUMPING OFF A ROOF? OR PUTTING A GUN IN THEIR MOUTH?
WE'RE NOT HERE TO DEBATE SUICIDE,
"WE'RE HERE TO SAVE SOMEONE'S LIFE."
SO YOUR OTHER SIX MEMBERS--
--YOU KNOW WHICH OF THEM DIES, DON'T YOU?
Forty-two seconds to impact.
LISTEN TO ME--
--YOU DON'T--
--HAVE TO--
--DO THIS.
SURE I DO.
DON'T FORGET--I'M YOU, JOHN--

"--I *KNOW* HOW THIS ONE ENDS."

TWO LEGIONNAIRES UNACCOUNTED FOR.

RADIO TAGS SAY THEY'RE *BOTH*--

"--UPSTAIRS."

MY NEW TEAM IS GOING TO BE ANGRY.

AND STARMAN'S PAL-- *SUPERMAN!*

POOR LONELY KAL-L. HIS FRIENDS ARE ALWAYS LEAVING.

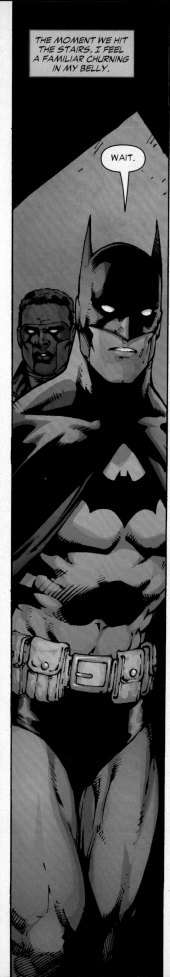

THE MOMENT WE HIT THE STAIRS, I FEEL A FAMILIAR CHURNING IN MY BELLY.

WAIT.

SO BUSY TRACKING HIM, I DIDN'T EVEN NOTICE.

WAIT.

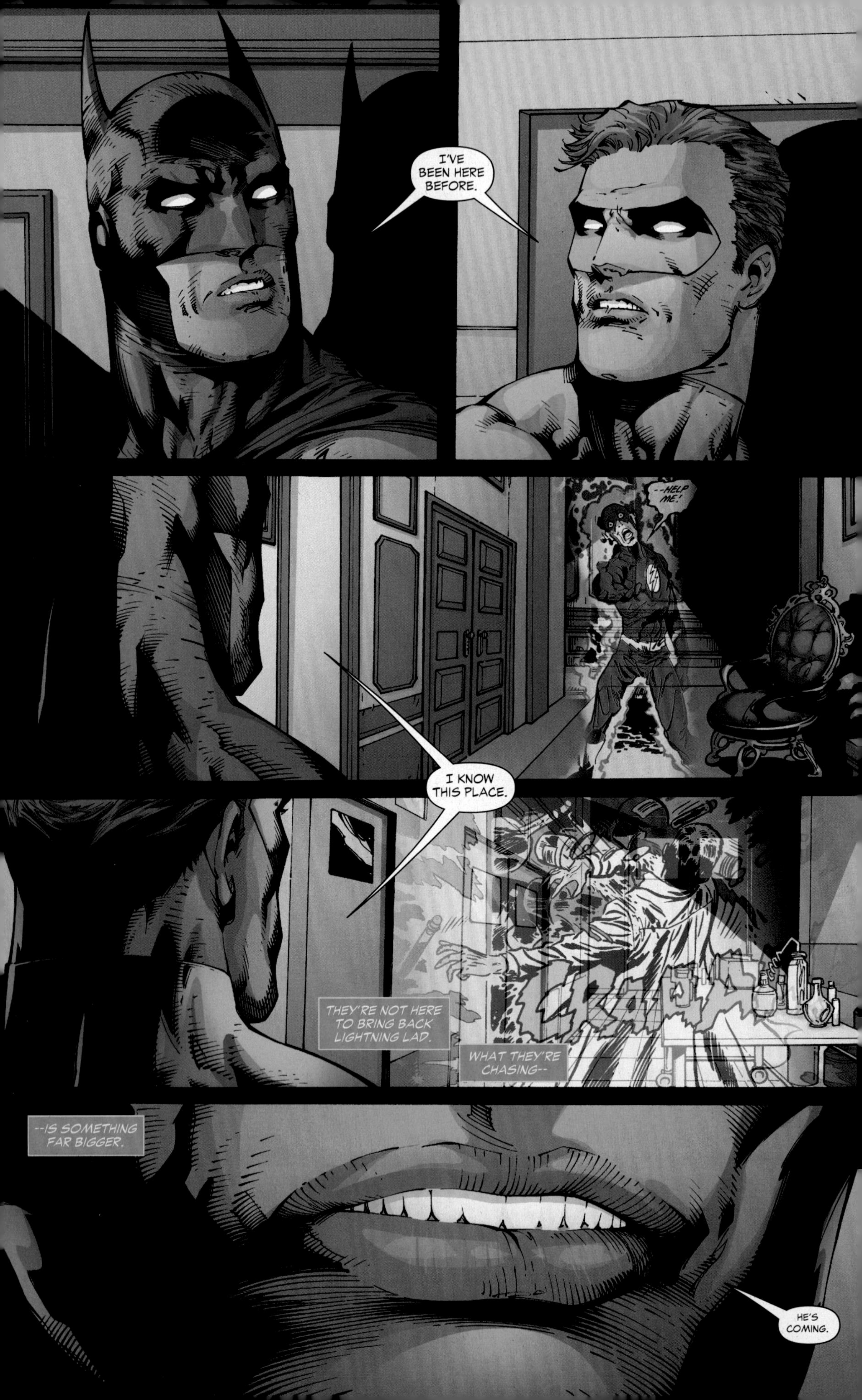
I'VE BEEN HERE BEFORE.
--HELP ME!
I KNOW THIS PLACE.
THEY'RE NOT HERE TO BRING BACK LIGHTNING LAD.
WHAT THEY'RE CHASING--
--IS SOMETHING FAR BIGGER.
HE'S COMING.

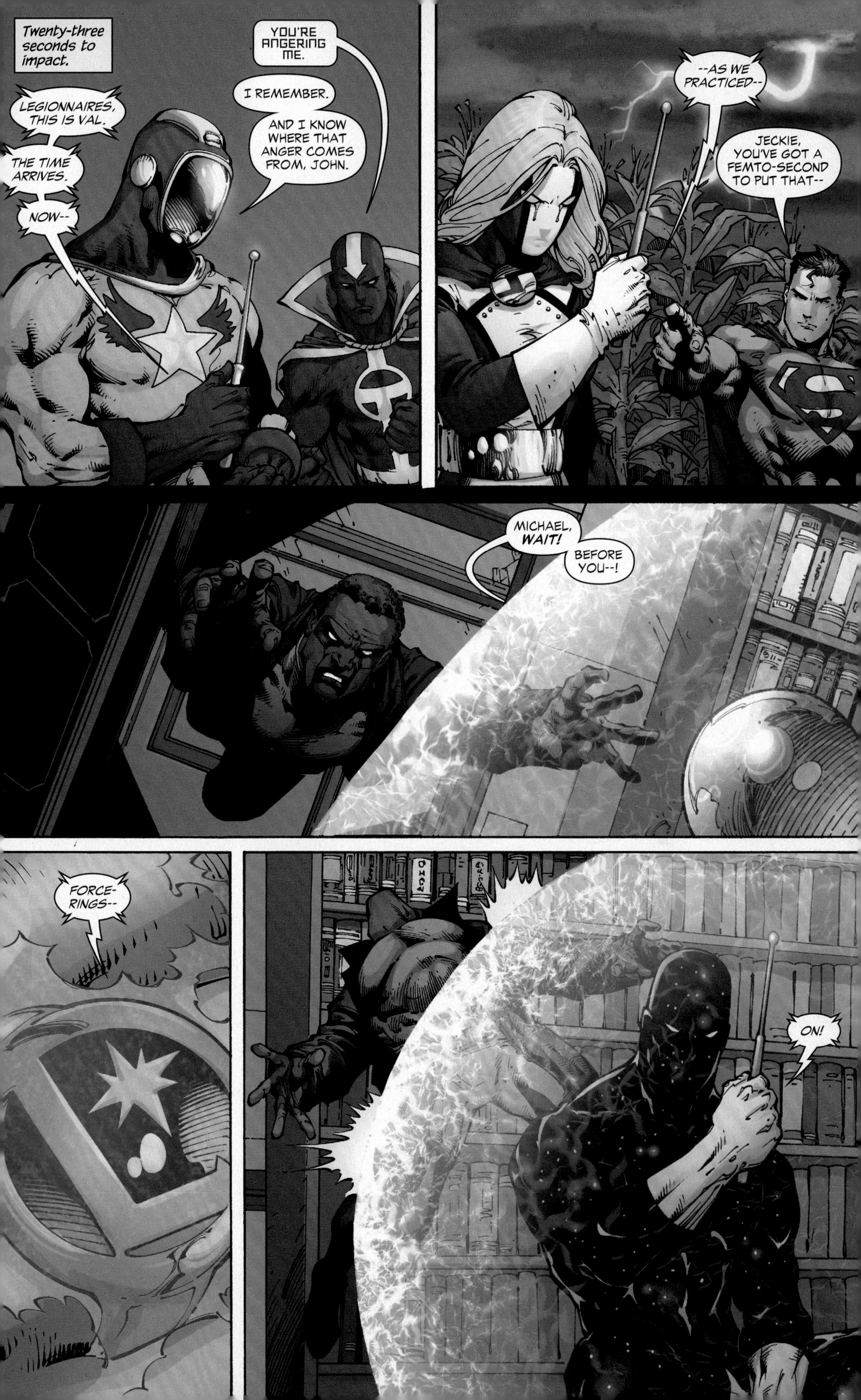
Twenty-three seconds to impact.
LEGIONNAIRES, THIS IS VAL.
THE TIME ARRIVES.
NOW--
YOU'RE ANGERING ME.
I REMEMBER.
AND I KNOW WHERE THAT ANGER COMES FROM, JOHN.
--AS WE PRACTICED--
JECKIE, YOU'VE GOT A FEMTO-SECOND TO PUT THAT--
MICHAEL, WAIT!
BEFORE YOU--!
FORCE-RINGS--
ON!

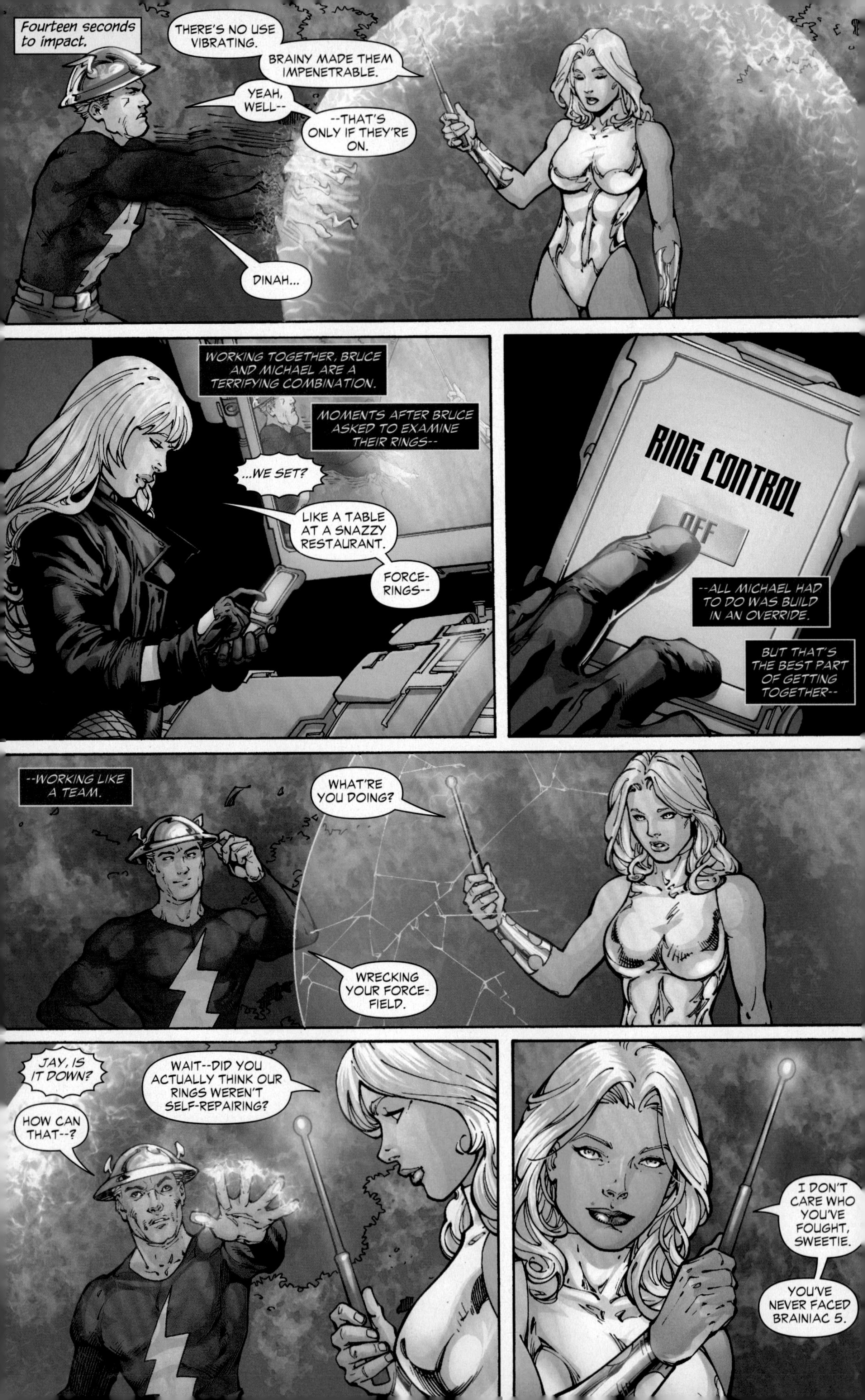
Fourteen seconds to impact.
THERE'S NO USE VIBRATING.
BRAINY MADE THEM IMPENETRABLE.
YEAH, WELL--
--THAT'S ONLY IF THEY'RE ON.
DINAH...
WORKING TOGETHER, BRUCE AND MICHAEL ARE A TERRIFYING COMBINATION.
MOMENTS AFTER BRUCE ASKED TO EXAMINE THEIR RINGS--
...WE SET?
LIKE A TABLE AT A SNAZZY RESTAURANT.
FORCE-RINGS--
RING CONTROL
OFF
--ALL MICHAEL HAD TO DO WAS BUILD IN AN OVERRIDE.
BUT THAT'S THE BEST PART OF GETTING TOGETHER--
--WORKING LIKE A TEAM.
WHAT'RE YOU DOING?
WRECKING YOUR FORCE-FIELD.
JAY, IS IT DOWN?
HOW CAN THAT--?
WAIT--DID YOU ACTUALLY THINK OUR RINGS WEREN'T SELF-REPAIRING?
I DON'T CARE WHO YOU'VE FOUGHT, SWEETIE.
YOU'VE NEVER FACED BRAINIAC 5.

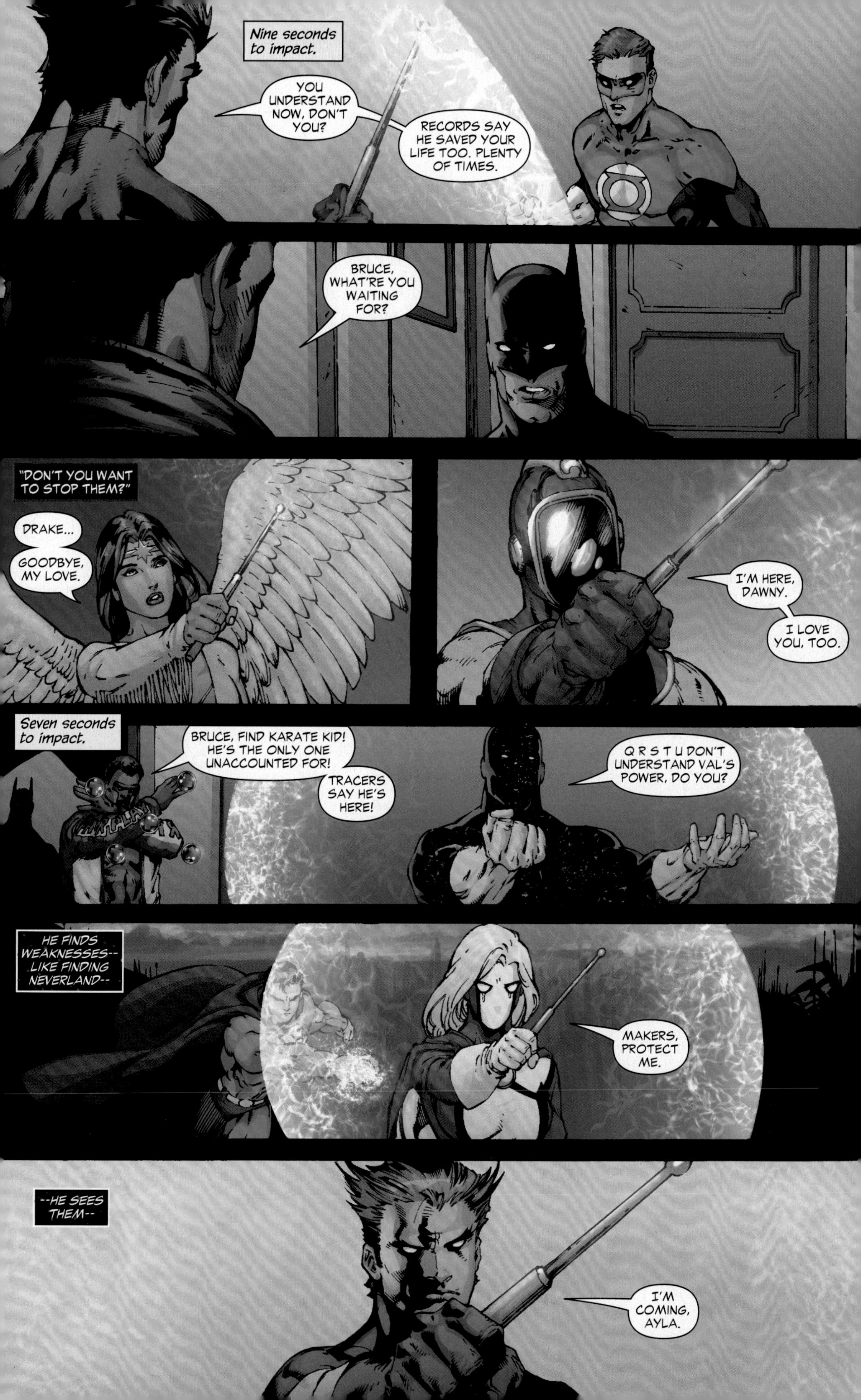
Nine seconds to impact.
YOU UNDERSTAND NOW, DON'T YOU?
RECORDS SAY HE SAVED YOUR LIFE TOO. PLENTY OF TIMES.
BRUCE, WHAT'RE YOU WAITING FOR?
"DON'T YOU WANT TO STOP THEM?"
DRAKE...
GOODBYE, MY LOVE.
I'M HERE, DAWNY.
I LOVE YOU, TOO.
Seven seconds to impact.
BRUCE, FIND KARATE KID! HE'S THE ONLY ONE UNACCOUNTED FOR!
TRACERS SAY HE'S HERE!
Q R S T U DON'T UNDERSTAND VAL'S POWER, DO YOU?
HE FINDS WEAKNESSES--LIKE FINDING NEVERLAND--
MAKERS, PROTECT ME.
--HE SEES THEM--
I'M COMING, AYLA.

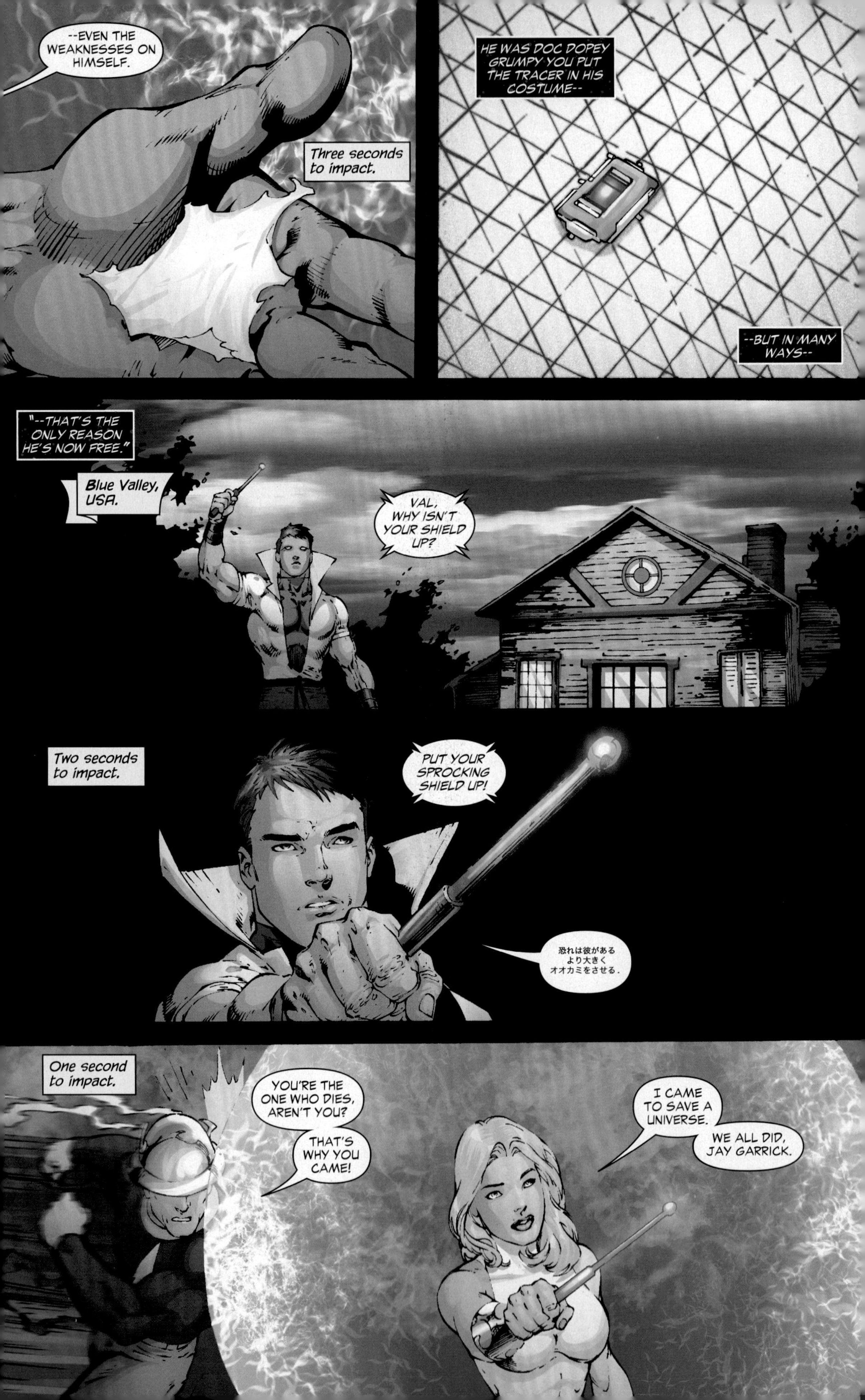
--EVEN THE WEAKNESSES ON HIMSELF.
Three seconds to impact.
HE WAS DOC DOPEY GRUMPY YOU PUT THE TRACER IN HIS COSTUME--
--BUT IN MANY WAYS--
"--THAT'S THE ONLY REASON HE'S NOW FREE."
Blue Valley, USA.
VAL, WHY ISN'T YOUR SHIELD UP?
Two seconds to impact.
PUT YOUR SPROCKING SHIELD UP!
恐れは彼がある より大きく オオカミをさせる.
One second to impact.
YOU'RE THE ONE WHO DIES, AREN'T YOU?
THAT'S WHY YOU CAME!
I CAME TO SAVE A UNIVERSE.
WE ALL DID, JAY GARRICK.

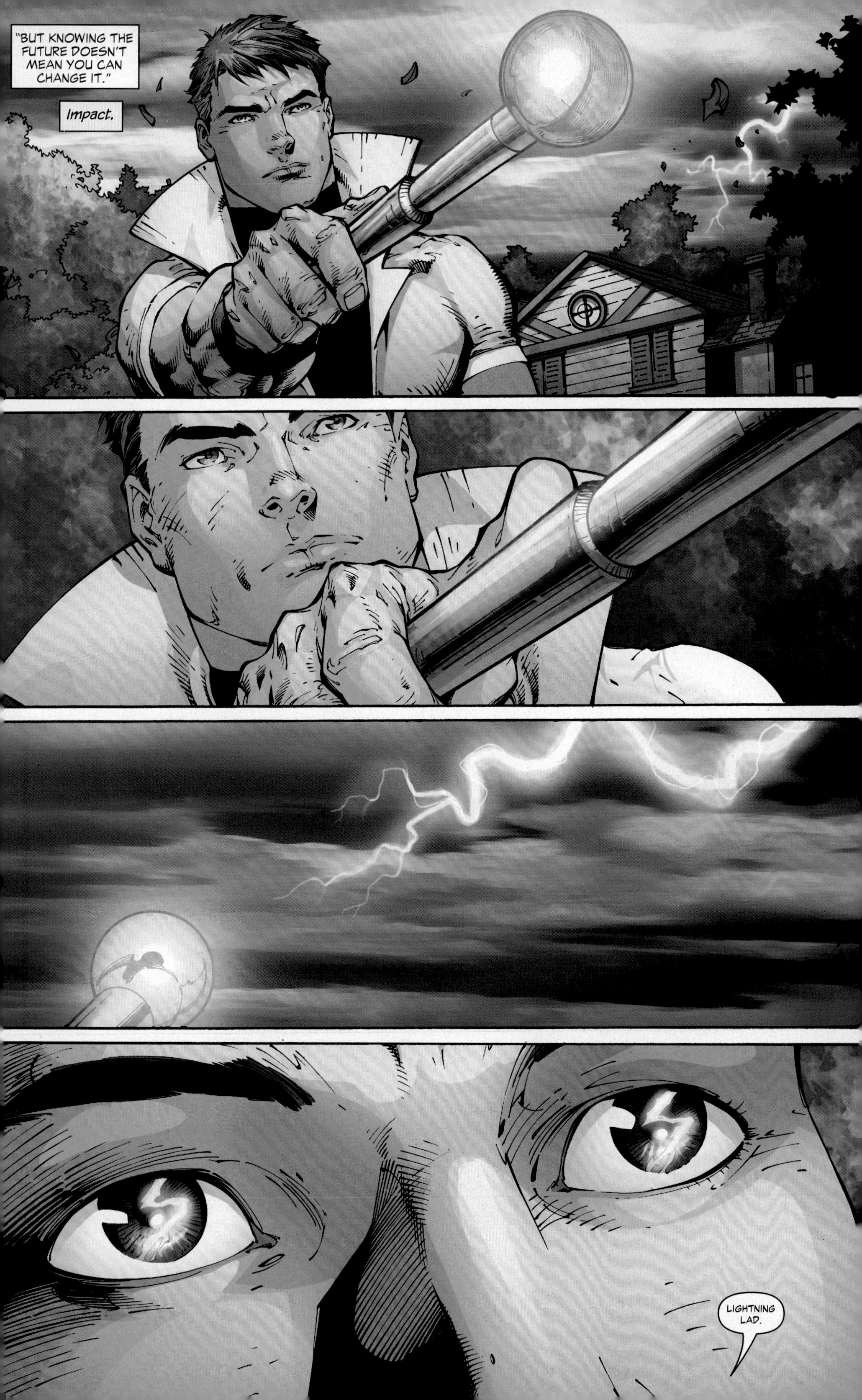
"BUT KNOWING THE FUTURE DOESN'T MEAN YOU CAN CHANGE IT."
Impact.
LIGHTNING LAD.

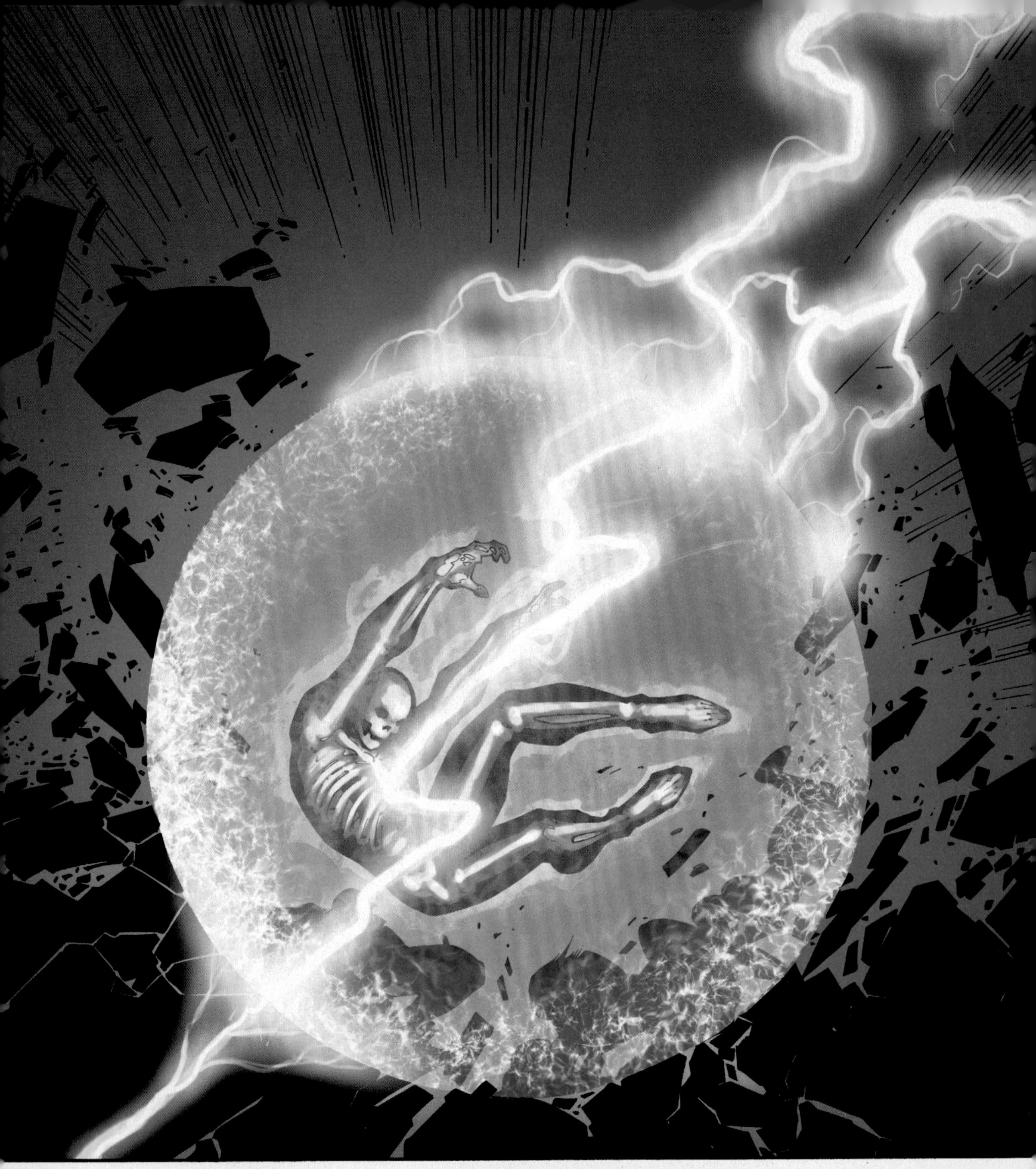

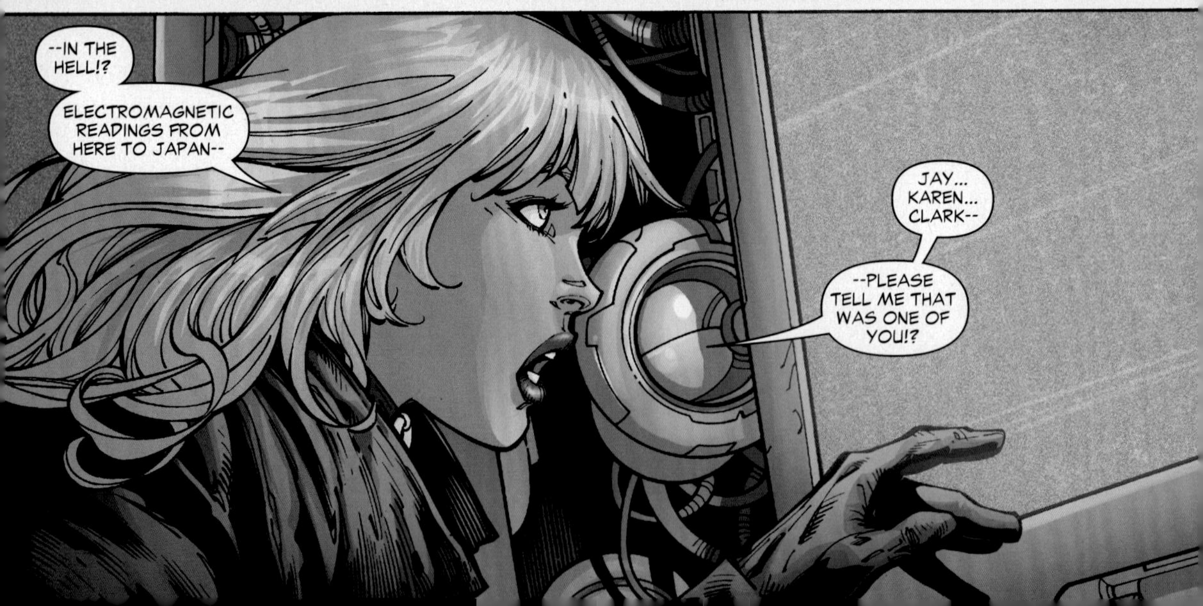
--IN THE HELL!?
ELECTROMAGNETIC READINGS FROM HERE TO JAPAN--
JAY... KAREN... CLARK--
--PLEASE TELL ME THAT WAS ONE OF YOU!?

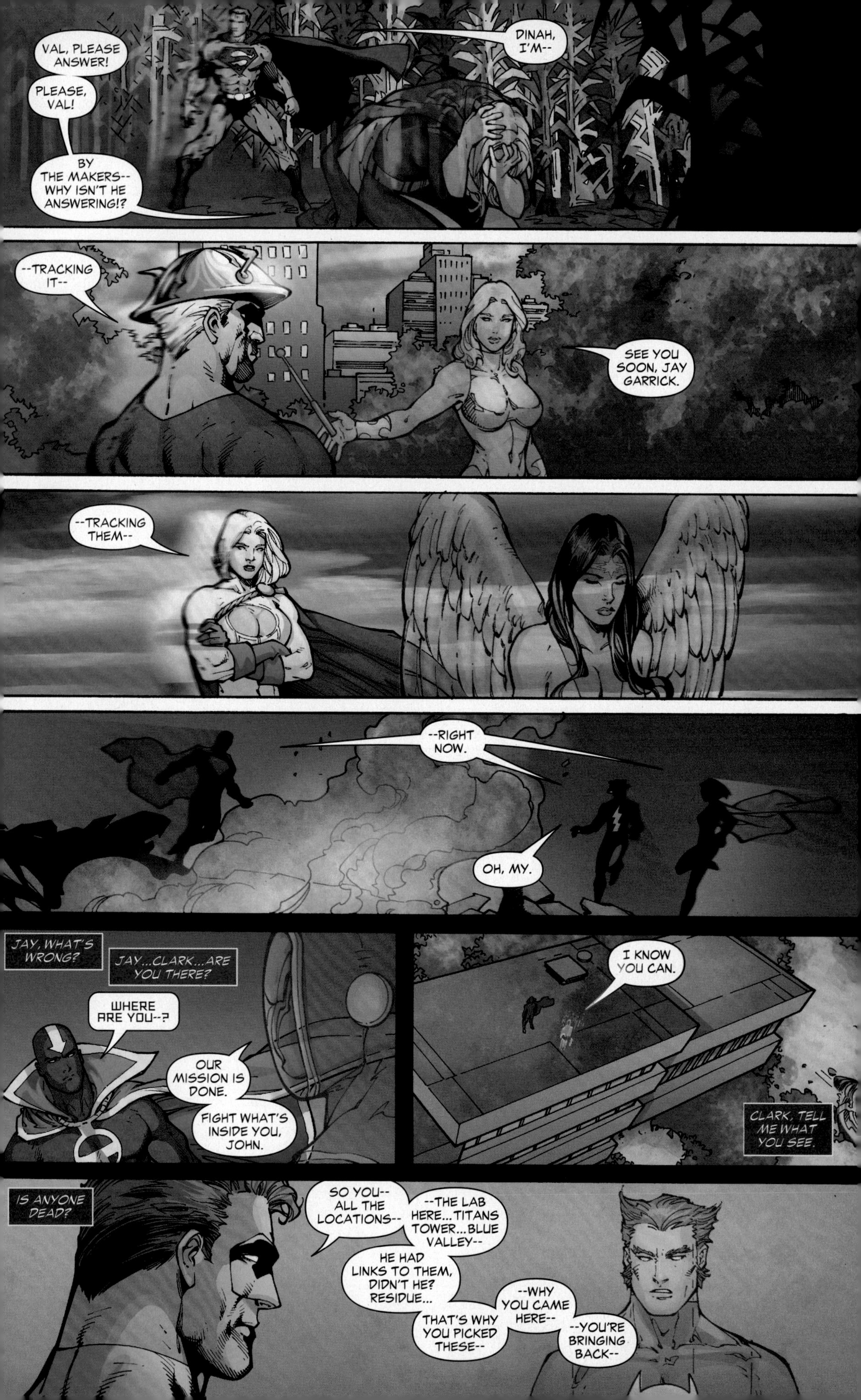
VAL, PLEASE ANSWER!
PLEASE, VAL!
BY THE MAKERS-- WHY ISN'T HE ANSWERING!?
DINAH, I'M--
--TRACKING IT--
SEE YOU SOON, JAY GARRICK.
--TRACKING THEM--
--RIGHT NOW.
OH, MY.
JAY, WHAT'S WRONG?
JAY...CLARK...ARE YOU THERE?
WHERE ARE YOU--?
OUR MISSION IS DONE.
FIGHT WHAT'S INSIDE YOU, JOHN.
I KNOW YOU CAN.
CLARK, TELL ME WHAT YOU SEE.
IS ANYONE DEAD?
SO YOU-- ALL THE LOCATIONS--
--THE LAB HERE...TITANS TOWER...BLUE VALLEY--
HE HAD LINKS TO THEM, DIDN'T HE? RESIDUE...
THAT'S WHY YOU PICKED THESE--
--WHY YOU CAME HERE--
--YOU'RE BRINGING BACK--

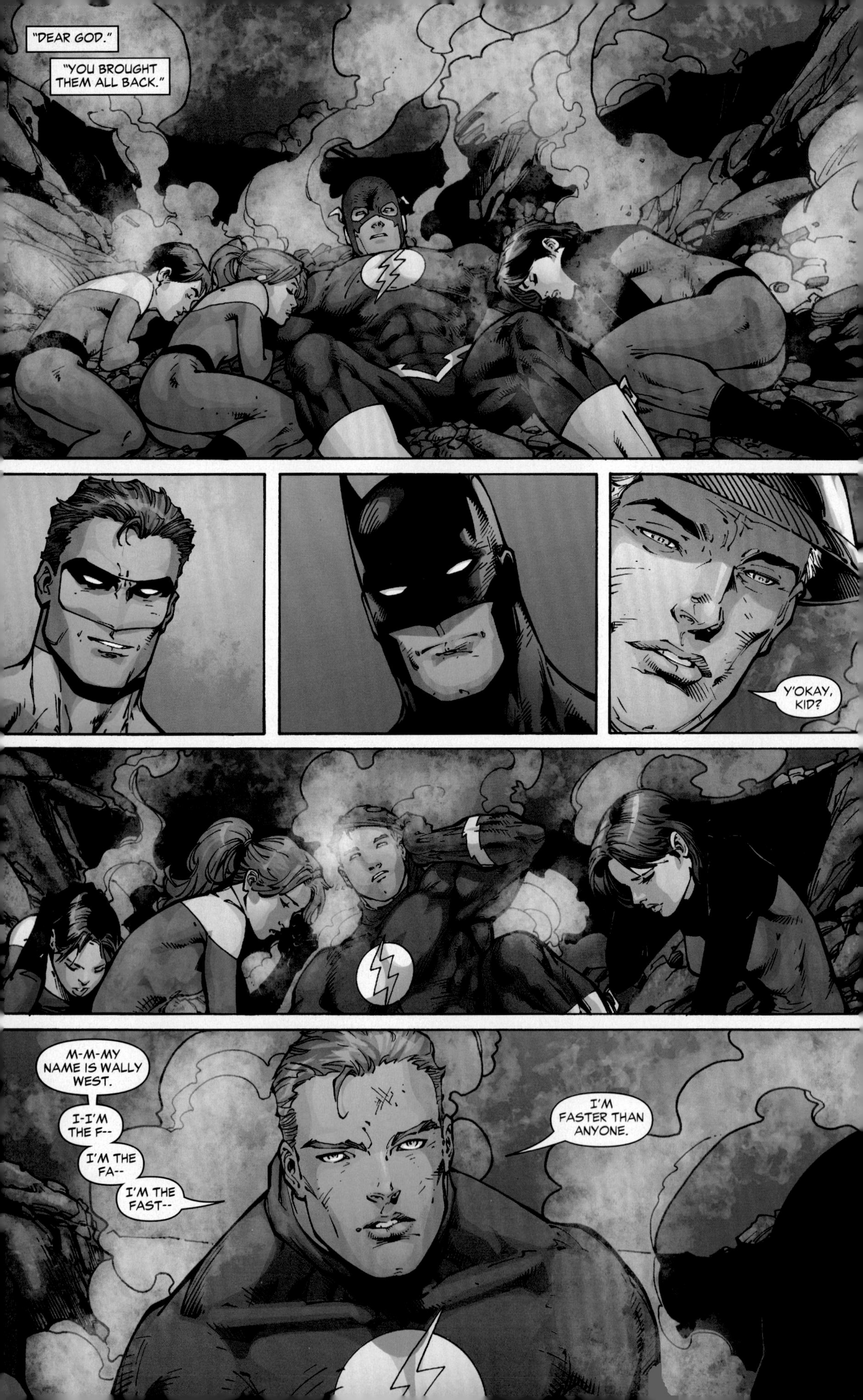
"DEAR GOD."
"YOU BROUGHT THEM ALL BACK."
Y'OKAY, KID?
M-M-MY NAME IS WALLY WEST.
I-I'M THE F--
I'M THE FA--
I'M THE FAST--
I'M FASTER THAN ANYONE.

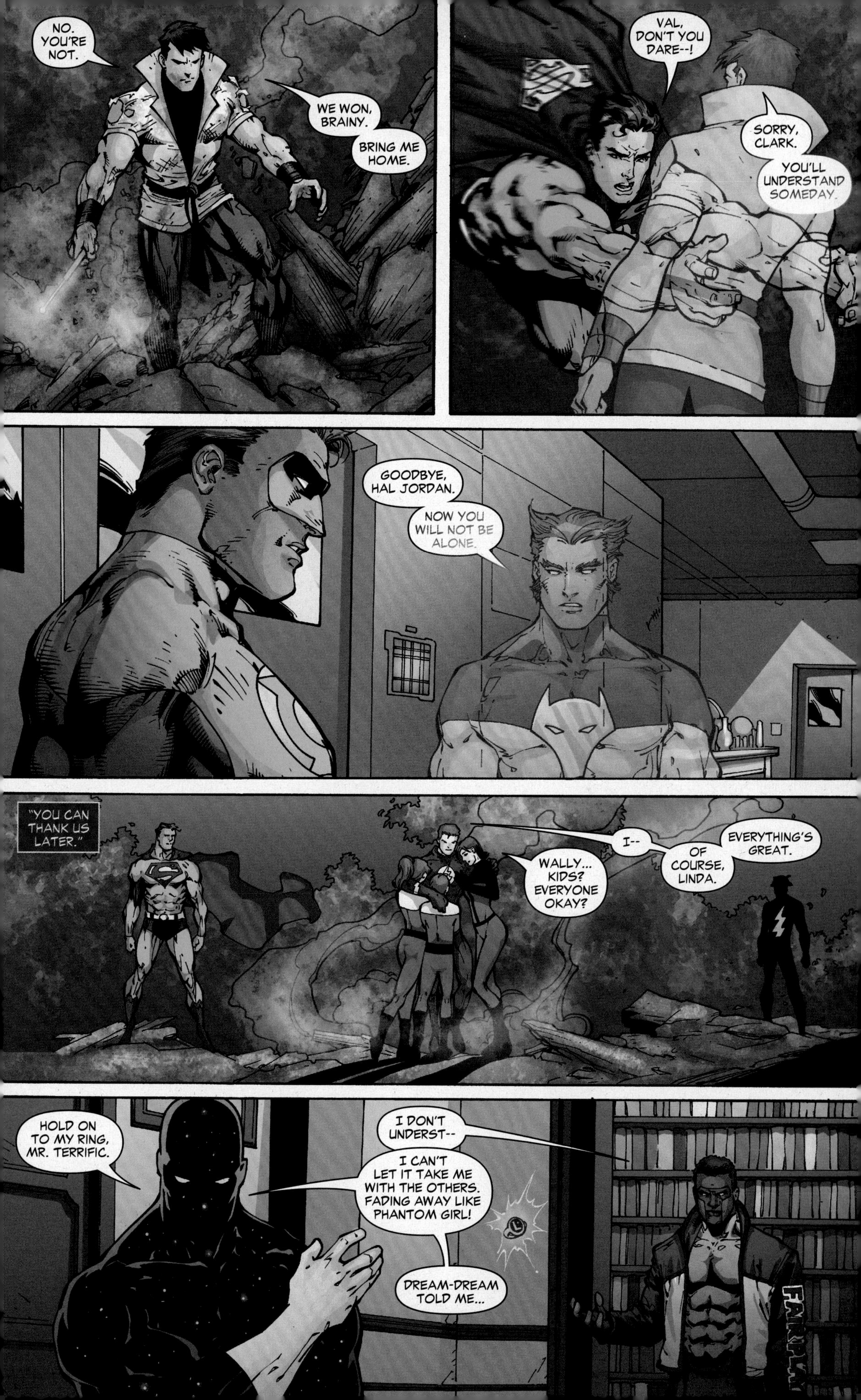
NO. YOU'RE NOT.
WE WON, BRAINY.
BRING ME HOME.
VAL, DON'T YOU DARE--!
SORRY, CLARK.
YOU'LL UNDERSTAND SOMEDAY.
GOODBYE, HAL JORDAN.
NOW YOU WILL NOT BE ALONE.
"YOU CAN THANK US LATER."
WALLY... KIDS? EVERYONE OKAY?
I--
OF COURSE, LINDA.
EVERYTHING'S GREAT.
HOLD ON TO MY RING, MR. TERRIFIC.
I DON'T UNDERST--
I CAN'T LET IT TAKE ME WITH THE OTHERS. FADING AWAY LIKE PHANTOM GIRL!
DREAM-DREAM TOLD ME...
FAIR PLAY

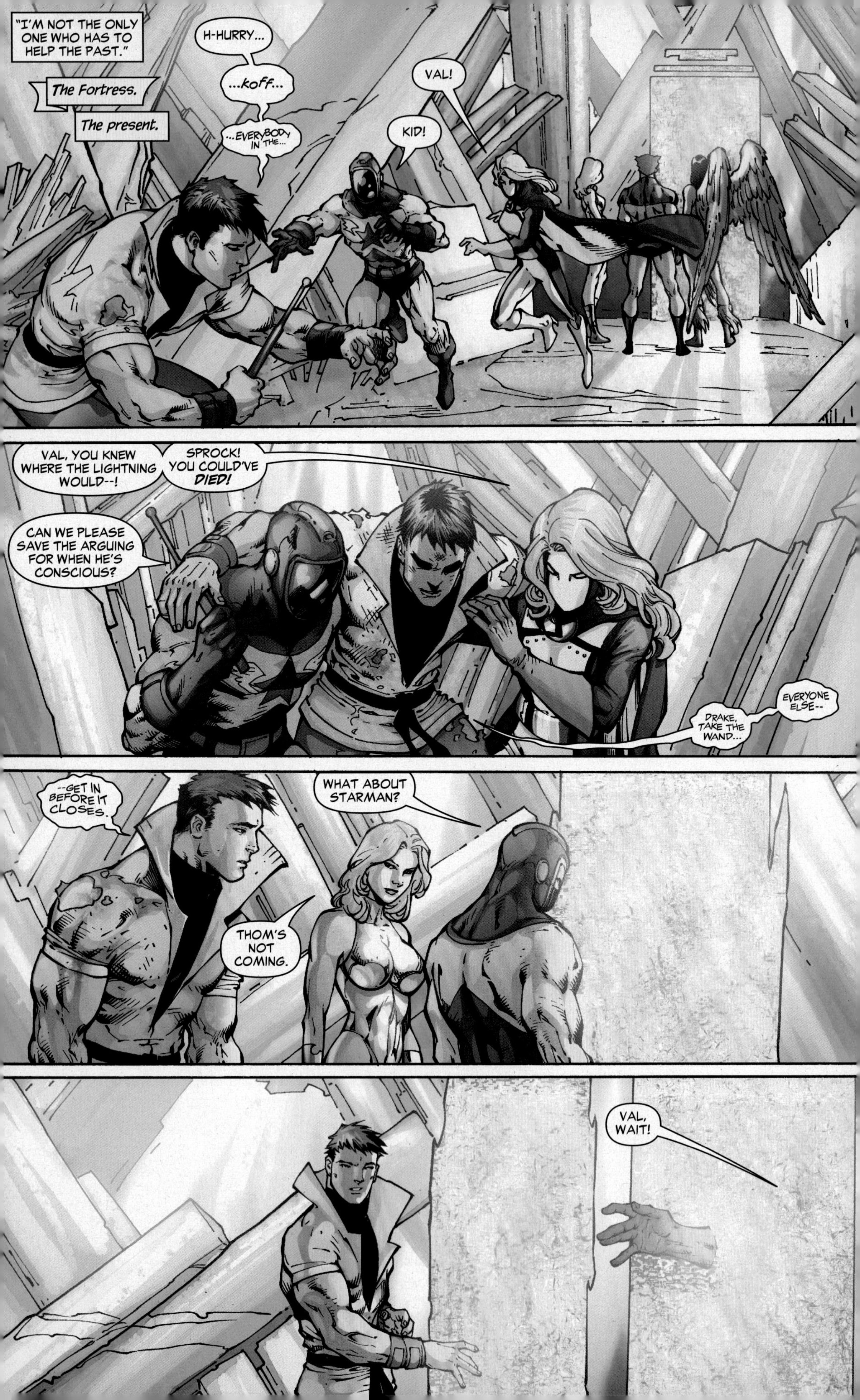
"I'M NOT THE ONLY ONE WHO HAS TO HELP THE PAST."
The Fortress.
The present.
H-HURRY...
...koff...
...EVERYBODY IN THE...
VAL!
KID!
VAL, YOU KNEW WHERE THE LIGHTNING WOULD--!
SPROCK! YOU COULD'VE DIED!
CAN WE PLEASE SAVE THE ARGUING FOR WHEN HE'S CONSCIOUS?
DRAKE, TAKE THE WAND...
EVERYONE ELSE--
--GET IN BEFORE IT CLOSES.
WHAT ABOUT STARMAN?
THOM'S NOT COMING.
VAL, WAIT!

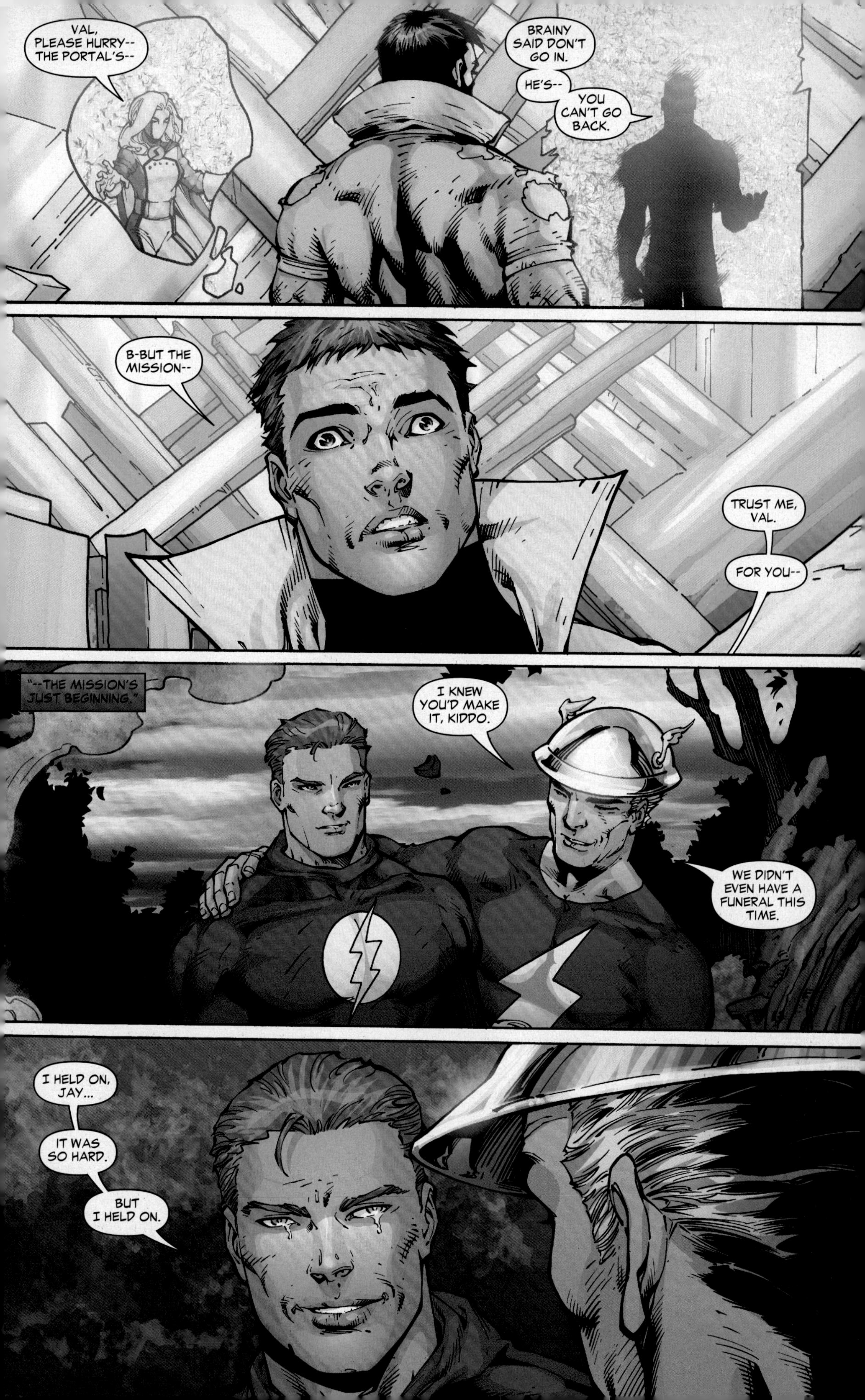
VAL, PLEASE HURRY-- THE PORTAL'S--
BRAINY SAID DON'T GO IN.
HE'S--
YOU CAN'T GO BACK.
B-BUT THE MISSION--
TRUST ME, VAL.
FOR YOU--
"--THE MISSION'S JUST BEGINNING."
I KNEW YOU'D MAKE IT, KIDDO.
WE DIDN'T EVEN HAVE A FUNERAL THIS TIME.
I HELD ON, JAY...
IT WAS SO HARD.
BUT I HELD ON.

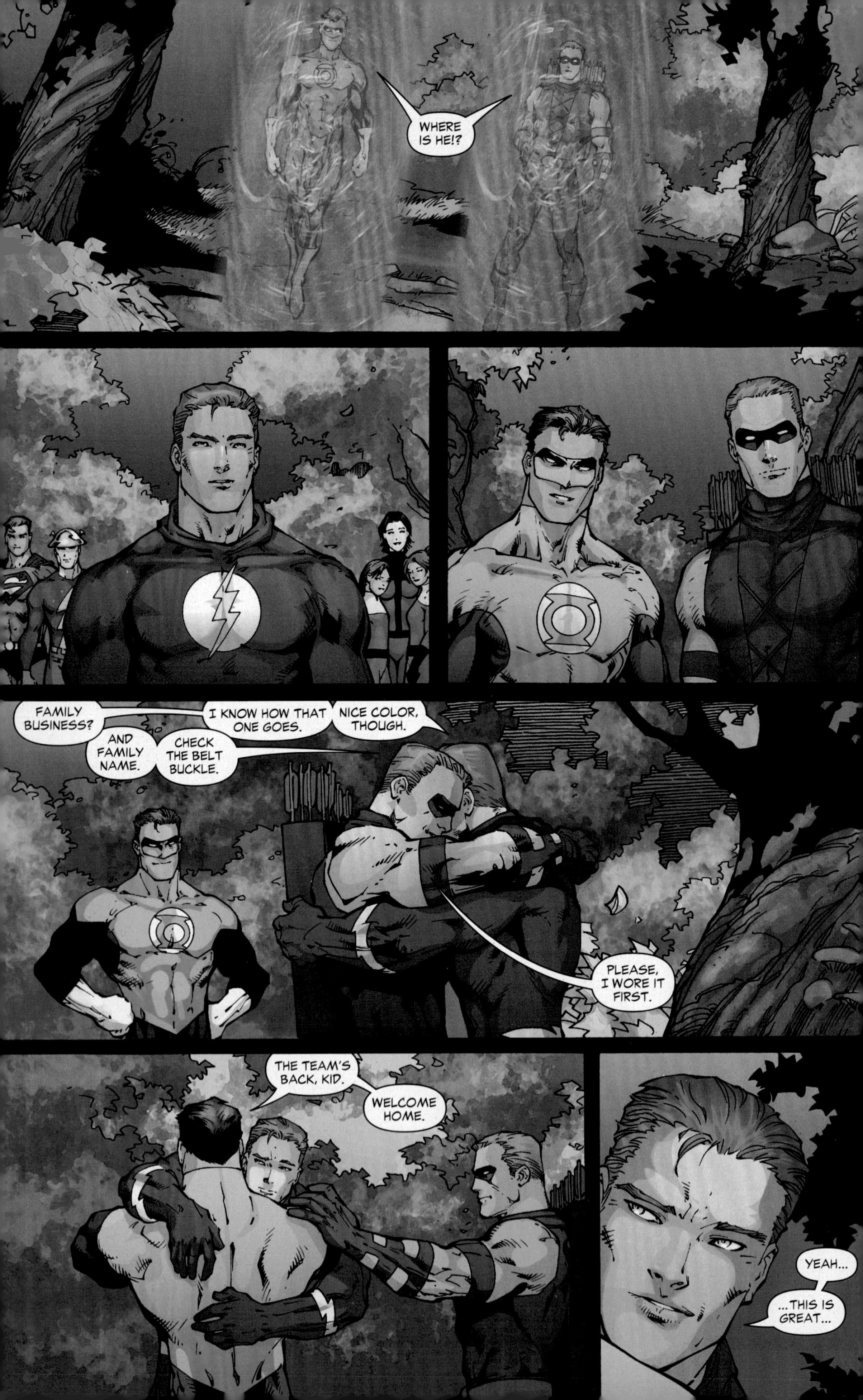
WHERE IS HE!?
FAMILY BUSINESS?
I KNOW HOW THAT ONE GOES.
NICE COLOR, THOUGH.
AND FAMILY NAME.
CHECK THE BELT BUCKLE.
PLEASE, I WORE IT FIRST.
THE TEAM'S BACK, KID.
WELCOME HOME.
YEAH...
...THIS IS GREAT...

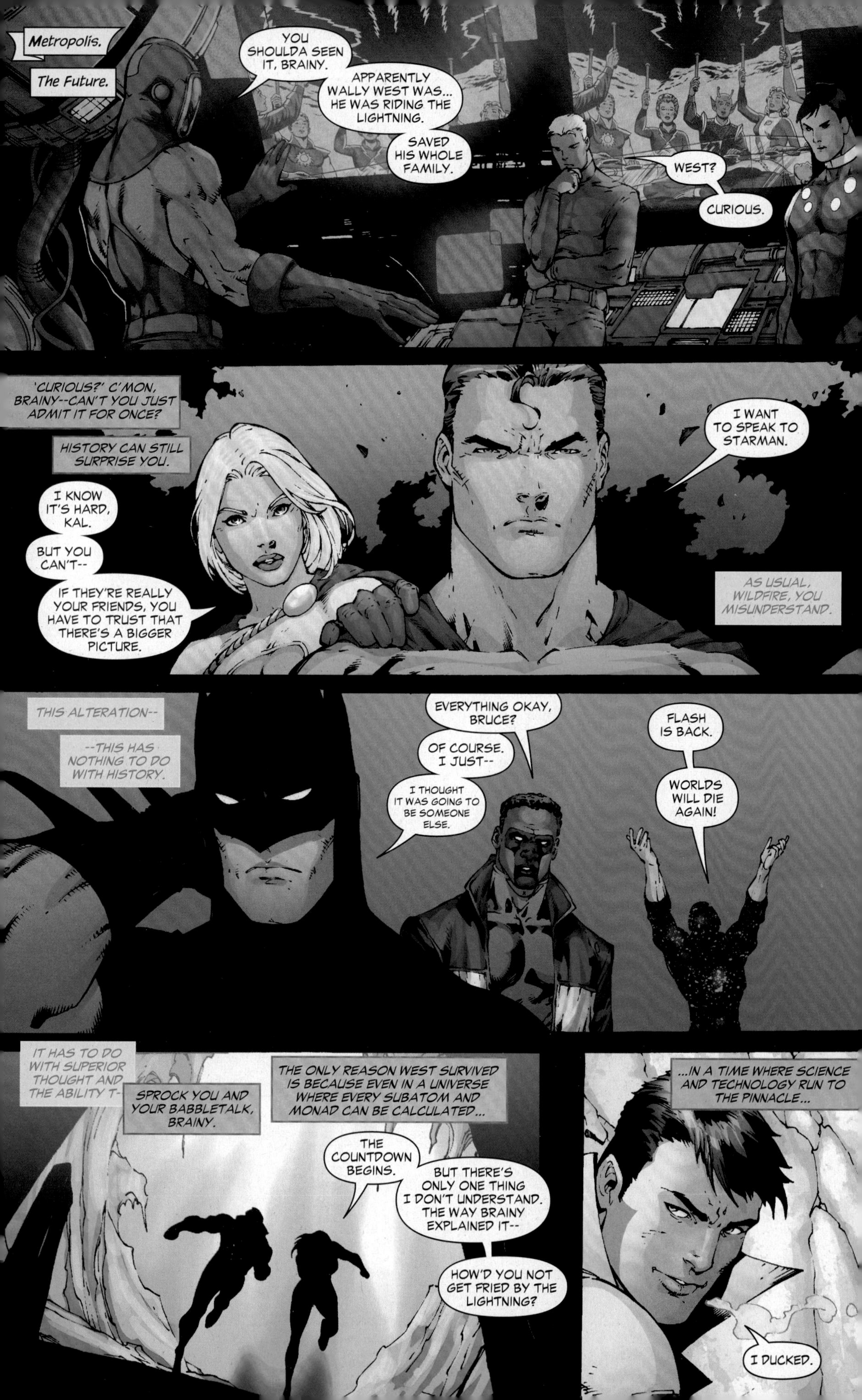

Metropolis.
The Future.
YOU SHOULDA SEEN IT, BRAINY.
APPARENTLY WALLY WEST WAS... HE WAS RIDING THE LIGHTNING.
SAVED HIS WHOLE FAMILY.
WEST?
CURIOUS.
'CURIOUS?' C'MON, BRAINY--CAN'T YOU JUST ADMIT IT FOR ONCE?
HISTORY CAN STILL SURPRISE YOU.
I KNOW IT'S HARD, KAL.
BUT YOU CAN'T--
IF THEY'RE REALLY YOUR FRIENDS, YOU HAVE TO TRUST THAT THERE'S A BIGGER PICTURE.
I WANT TO SPEAK TO STARMAN.
AS USUAL, WILDFIRE, YOU MISUNDERSTAND.
THIS ALTERATION--
--THIS HAS NOTHING TO DO WITH HISTORY.
EVERYTHING OKAY, BRUCE?
OF COURSE. I JUST--
I THOUGHT IT WAS GOING TO BE SOMEONE ELSE.
FLASH IS BACK.
WORLDS WILL DIE AGAIN!
IT HAS TO DO WITH SUPERIOR THOUGHT AND THE ABILITY T-
SPROCK YOU AND YOUR BABBLETALK, BRAINY.
THE ONLY REASON WEST SURVIVED IS BECAUSE EVEN IN A UNIVERSE WHERE EVERY SUBATOM AND MONAD CAN BE CALCULATED...
THE COUNTDOWN BEGINS.
BUT THERE'S ONLY ONE THING I DON'T UNDERSTAND. THE WAY BRAINY EXPLAINED IT--
HOW'D YOU NOT GET FRIED BY THE LIGHTNING?
...IN A TIME WHERE SCIENCE AND TECHNOLOGY RUN TO THE PINNACLE...
I DUCKED.

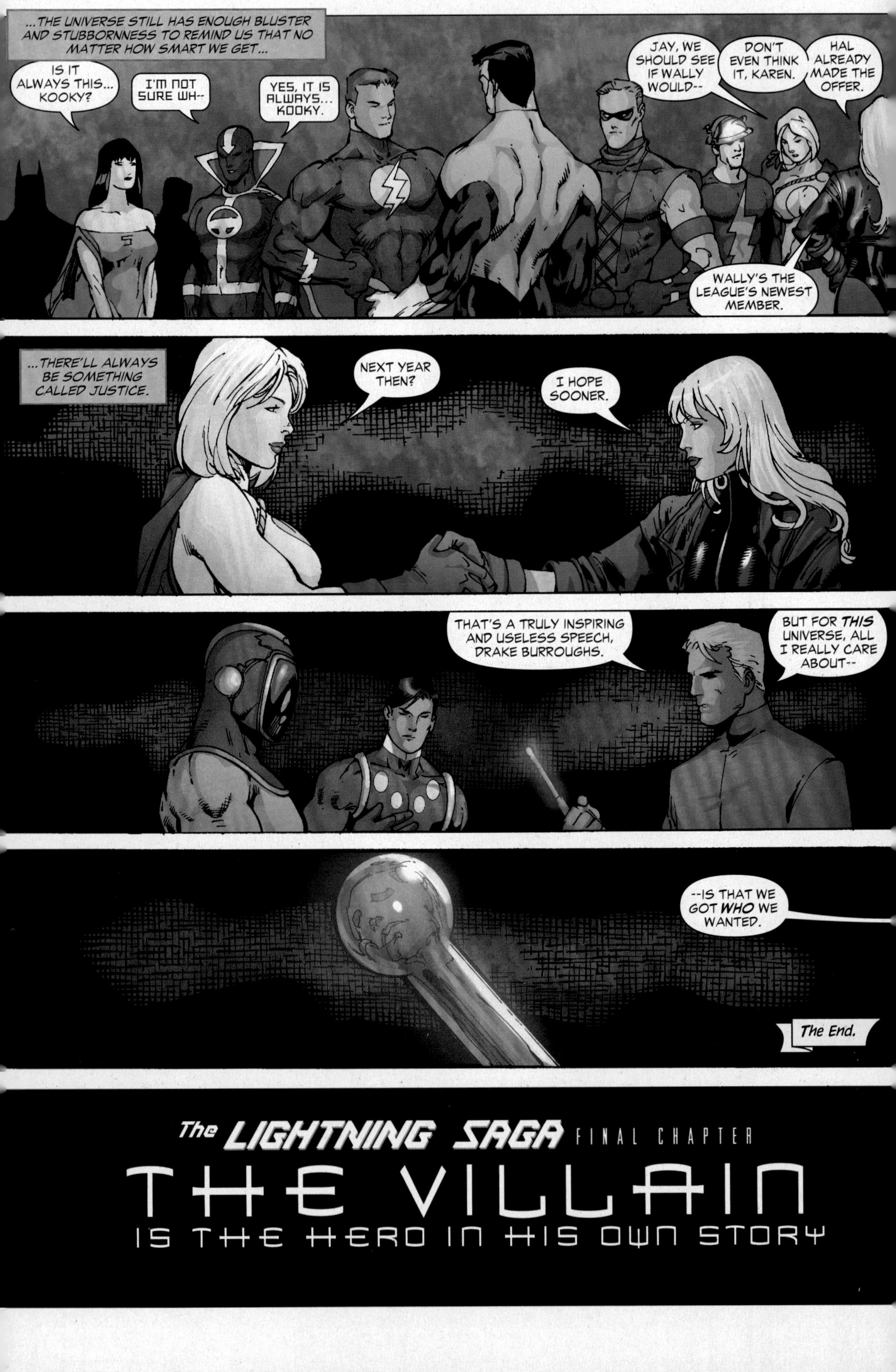
...THE UNIVERSE STILL HAS ENOUGH BLUSTER AND STUBBORNNESS TO REMIND US THAT NO MATTER HOW SMART WE GET...
IS IT ALWAYS THIS... KOOKY?
I'M NOT SURE WH--
YES, IT IS ALWAYS... KOOKY.
JAY, WE SHOULD SEE IF WALLY WOULD--
DON'T EVEN THINK IT, KAREN.
HAL ALREADY MADE THE OFFER.
WALLY'S THE LEAGUE'S NEWEST MEMBER.
...THERE'LL ALWAYS BE SOMETHING CALLED JUSTICE.
NEXT YEAR THEN?
I HOPE SOONER.
THAT'S A TRULY INSPIRING AND USELESS SPEECH, DRAKE BURROUGHS.
BUT FOR THIS UNIVERSE, ALL I REALLY CARE ABOUT--
--IS THAT WE GOT WHO WE WANTED.
The End.
The LIGHTNING SAGA FINAL CHAPTER
THE VILLAIN
IS THE HERO IN HIS OWN STORY

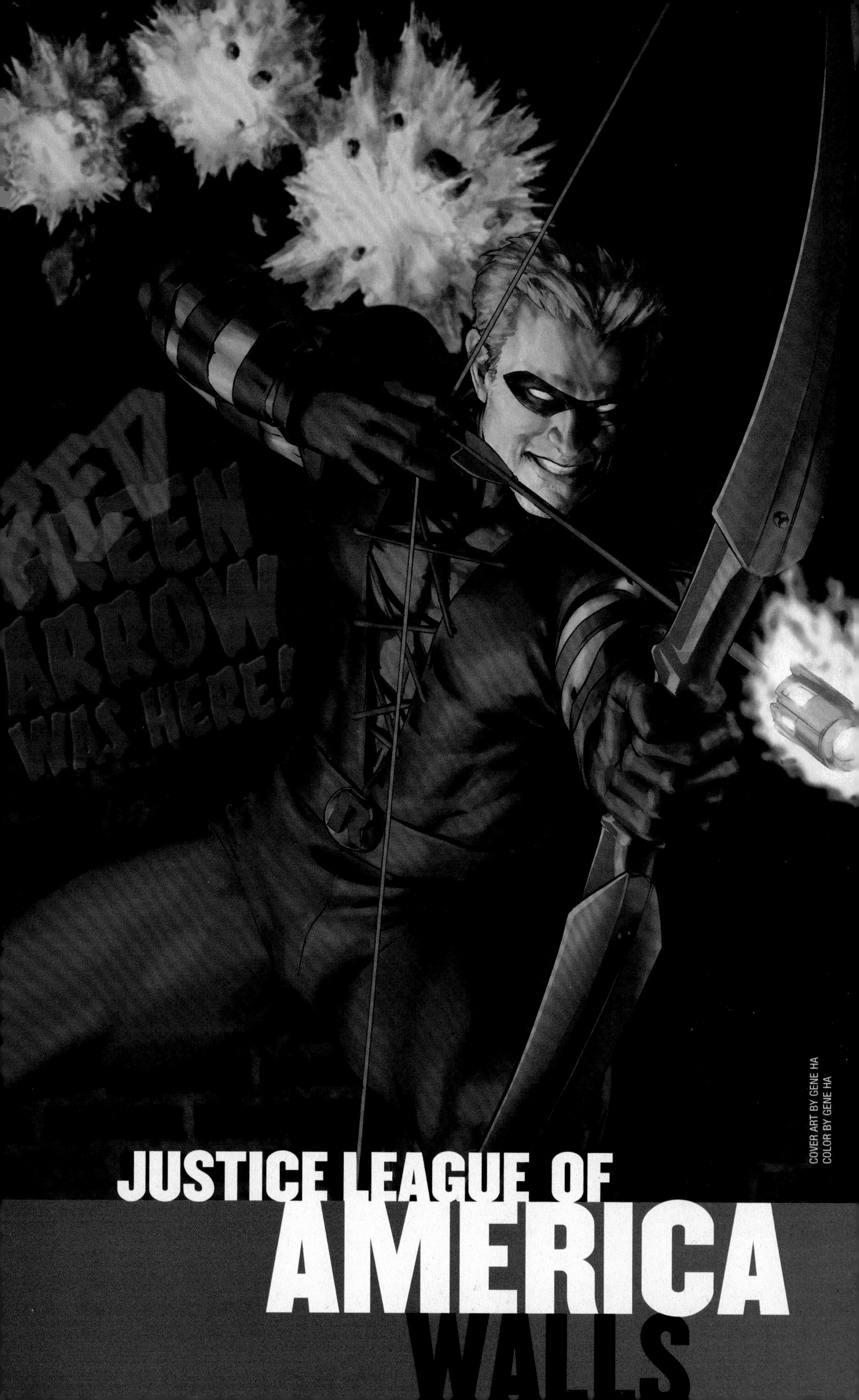
GREEN
ARROW
WAS HERE!

COVER ART BY GENE HA
COLOR BY GENE HA

JUSTICE LEAGUE OF AMERICA
WALLS

"We all fight for different things."

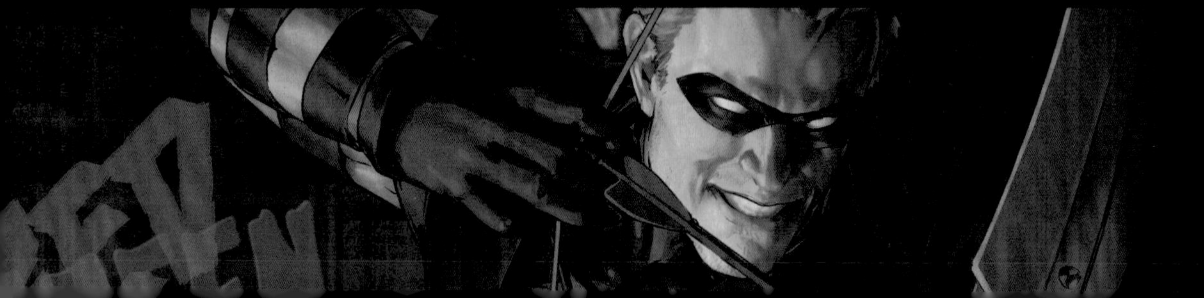

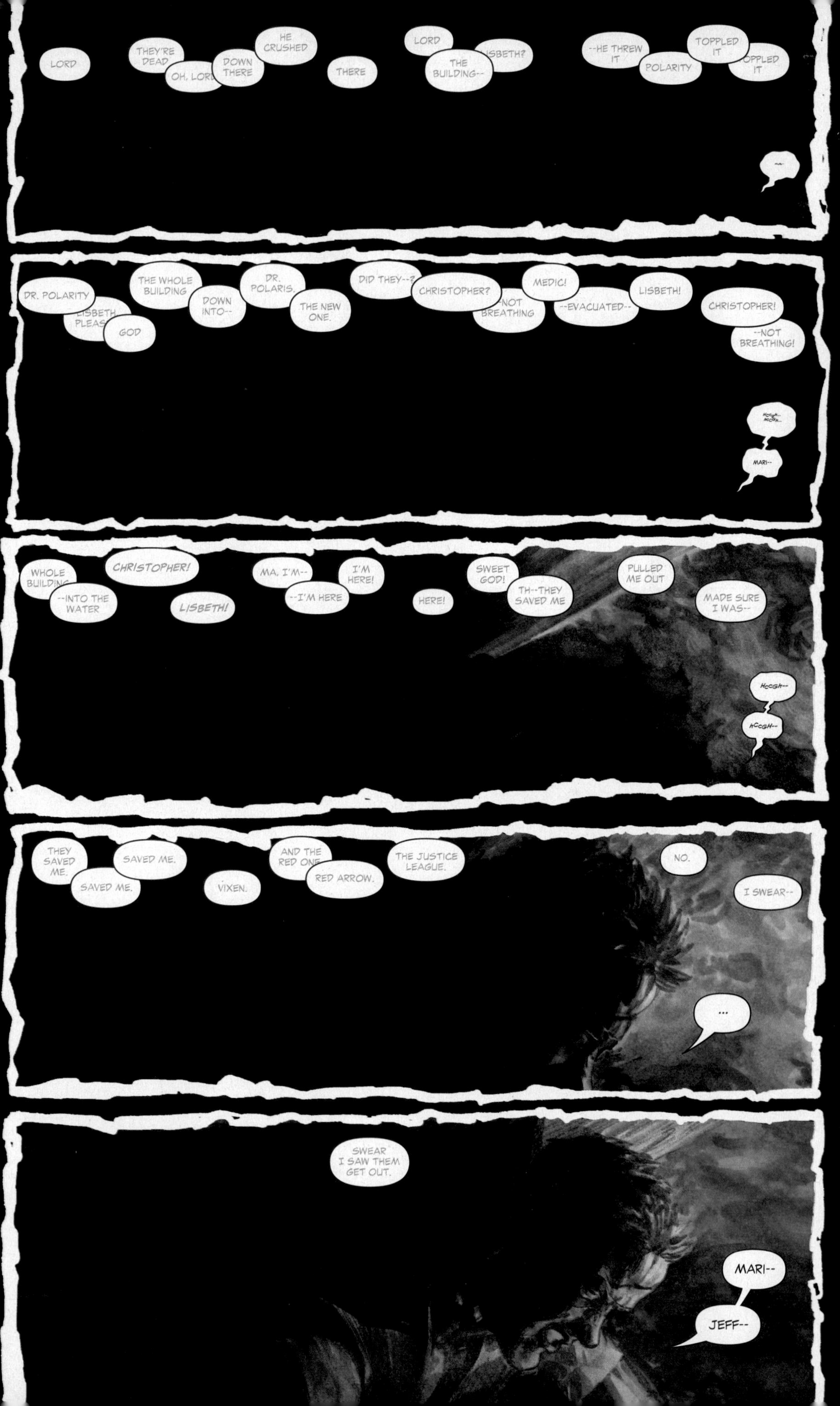
LORD
THEY'RE DEAD
OH, LOR
DOWN THERE
HE CRUSHED
THERE
LORD
THE BUILDING--
ISBETH?
--HE THREW IT
POLARITY
TOPPLED IT
OPPLED IT
DR. POLARITY
LISBETH PLEAS
GOD
THE WHOLE BUILDING
DOWN INTO--
DR. POLARIS.
THE NEW ONE.
DID THEY--?
CHRISTOPHER?
-NOT BREATHING
MEDIC!
--EVACUATED--
LISBETH!
CHRISTOPHER!
--NOT BREATHING!
HCCGH... HCCGH...
MARI--
WHOLE BUILDIN
--INTO THE WATER
CHRISTOPHER!
LISBETH!
MA, I'M--
--I'M HERE
I'M HERE!
HERE!
SWEET GOD!
TH--THEY SAVED ME
PULLED ME OUT
MADE SURE I WAS--
HCCGH--
HCCGH--
THEY SAVED ME.
SAVED ME.
SAVED ME.
VIXEN.
AND THE RED ONE
RED ARROW.
THE JUSTICE LEAGUE.
NO.
I SWEAR--
...
SWEAR I SAW THEM GET OUT.
MARI--
JEFF--

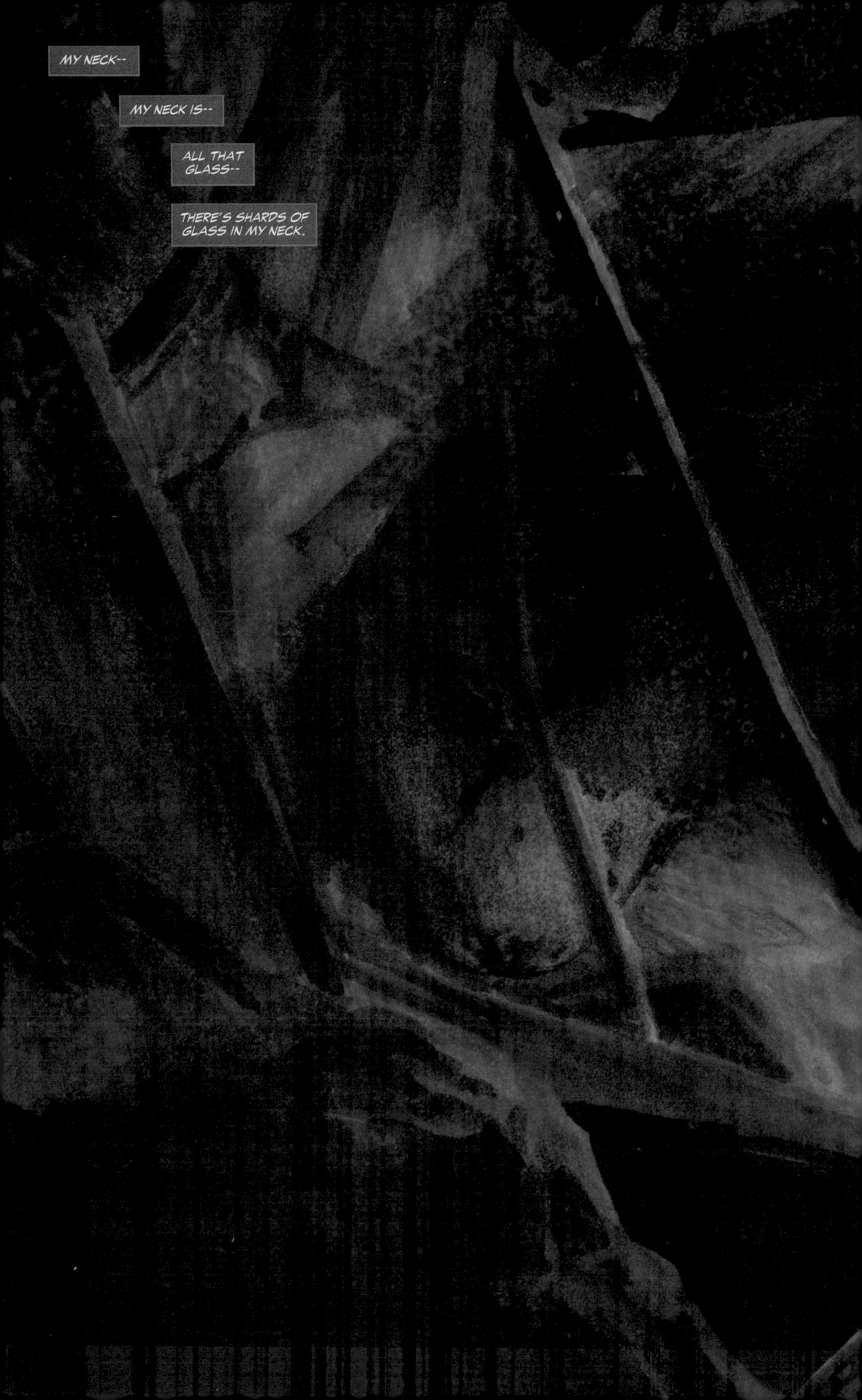
MY NECK--
MY NECK IS--
ALL THAT GLASS--
THERE'S SHARDS OF GLASS IN MY NECK.

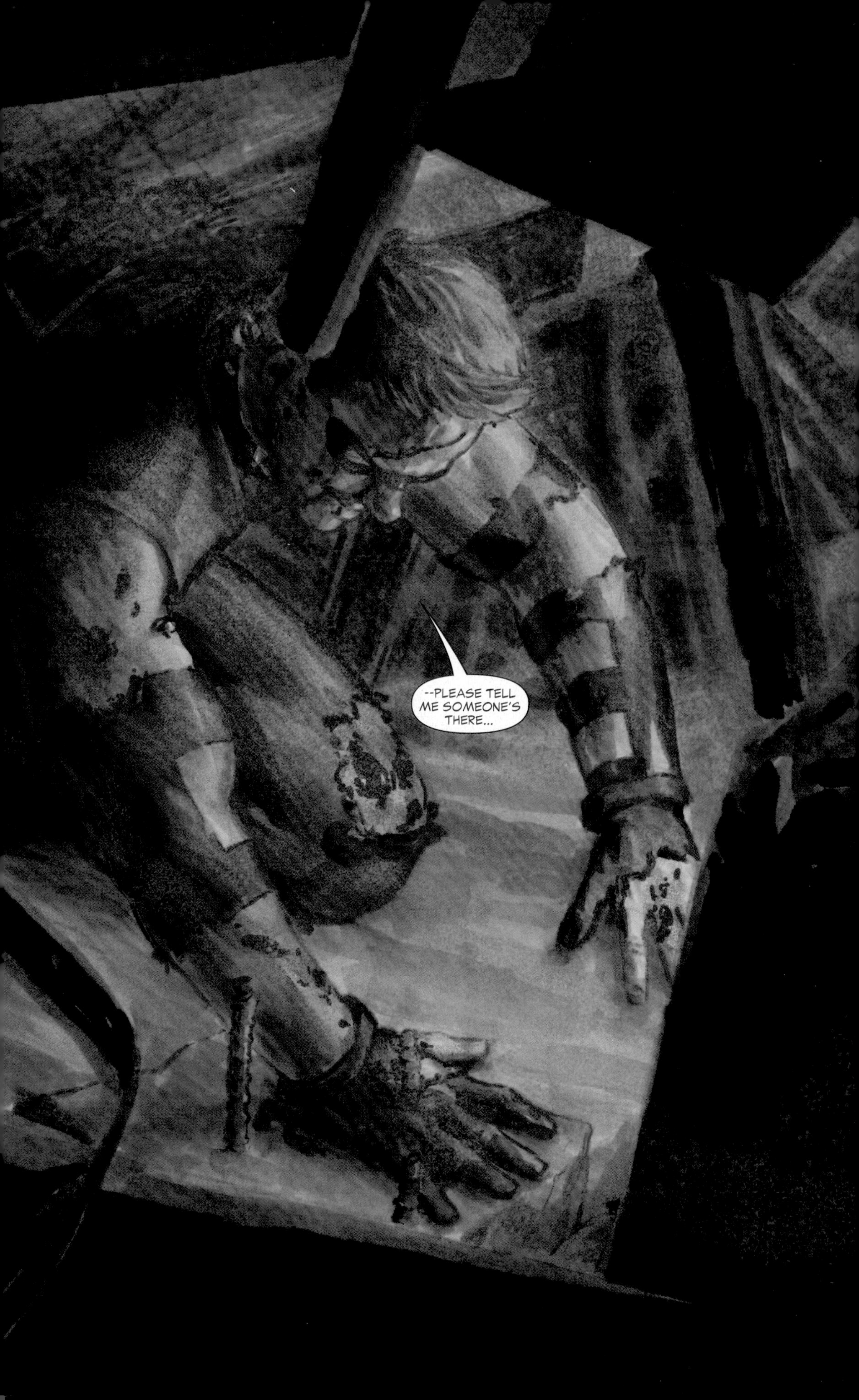
--PLEASE TELL ME SOMEONE'S THERE...

JEFF! MARI!

I'M GETTING CRUSHED DOWN HERE!

THE DARKNESS--

ALL THE SMOKE--

I CAN'T TELL WHICH WAY'S UP.

THE ROOF DRILLS MY HEAD.

THERE'S GLASS IN MY HEAD.

BODY ARMOR IN THE QUIVER SAVED MY SPINE, BUT THERE'S SHARDS IN MY NECK.

HEAD TOO.

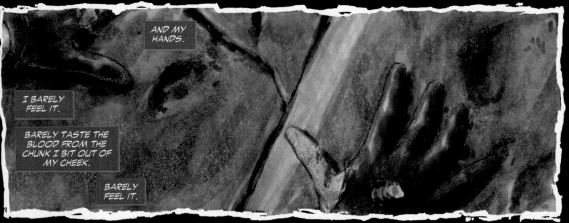

AND MY HANDS.

I BARELY FEEL IT.

BARELY TASTE THE BLOOD FROM THE CHUNK I BIT OUT OF MY CHEEK.

BARELY FEEL IT.

THE CEILING'S PUSHING DOWN--

THERE'S A TICKLE IN MY THROAT AND I REALIZE I'VE SWALLOWED MY BACK MOLAR. FINE.

TOOTH'S FAKE ANYWAY.

HAD IT KNOCKED OUT FOUR TIMES.

FIRST WAS SPARRING WITH OLLIE.

OLLIE.

FOCUS ON OLLIE.

FOCUS ON TRAINING.

BODY'S IN SHOCK.

ON BREATHING.

BREATHE.

ALWAYS BREATHING.

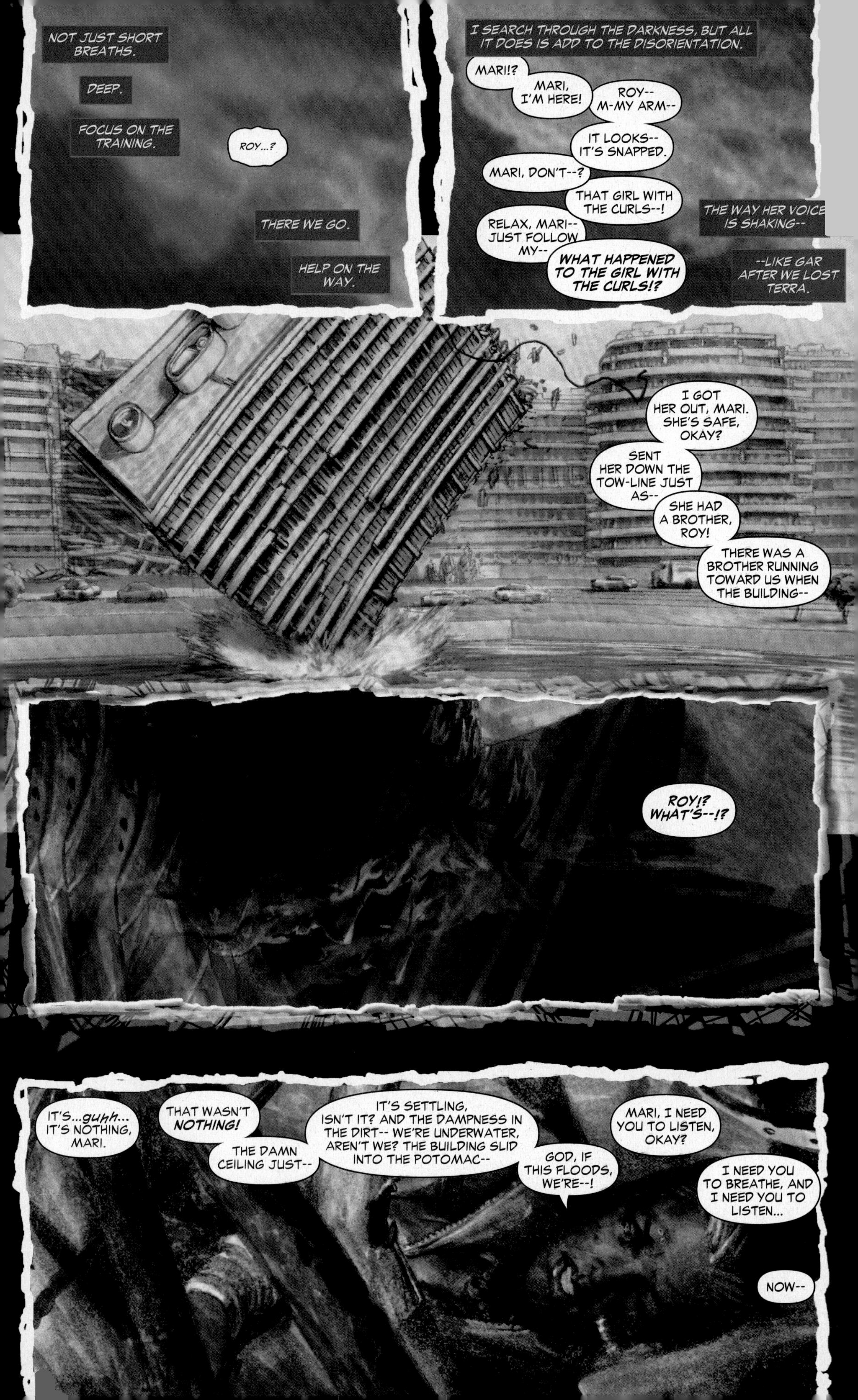
NOT JUST SHORT BREATHS.
DEEP.
FOCUS ON THE TRAINING.
ROY...?
THERE WE GO.
HELP ON THE WAY.
I SEARCH THROUGH THE DARKNESS, BUT ALL IT DOES IS ADD TO THE DISORIENTATION.
MARI!?
MARI, I'M HERE!
ROY-- M-MY ARM--
IT LOOKS-- IT'S SNAPPED.
MARI, DON'T--?
THAT GIRL WITH THE CURLS--!
RELAX, MARI-- JUST FOLLOW MY--
WHAT HAPPENED TO THE GIRL WITH THE CURLS!?
THE WAY HER VOICE IS SHAKING--
--LIKE GAR AFTER WE LOST TERRA.
I GOT HER OUT, MARI. SHE'S SAFE, OKAY?
SENT HER DOWN THE TOW-LINE JUST AS--
SHE HAD A BROTHER, ROY!
THERE WAS A BROTHER RUNNING TOWARD US WHEN THE BUILDING--
ROY!? WHAT'S--!?
IT'S...*guhh*... IT'S NOTHING, MARI.
THAT WASN'T *NOTHING!*
THE DAMN CEILING JUST--
IT'S SETTLING, ISN'T IT? AND THE DAMPNESS IN THE DIRT-- WE'RE UNDERWATER, AREN'T WE? THE BUILDING SLID INTO THE POTOMAC--
GOD, IF THIS FLOODS, WE'RE--!
MARI, I NEED YOU TO LISTEN, OKAY?
I NEED YOU TO BREATHE, AND I NEED YOU TO LISTEN...
NOW--

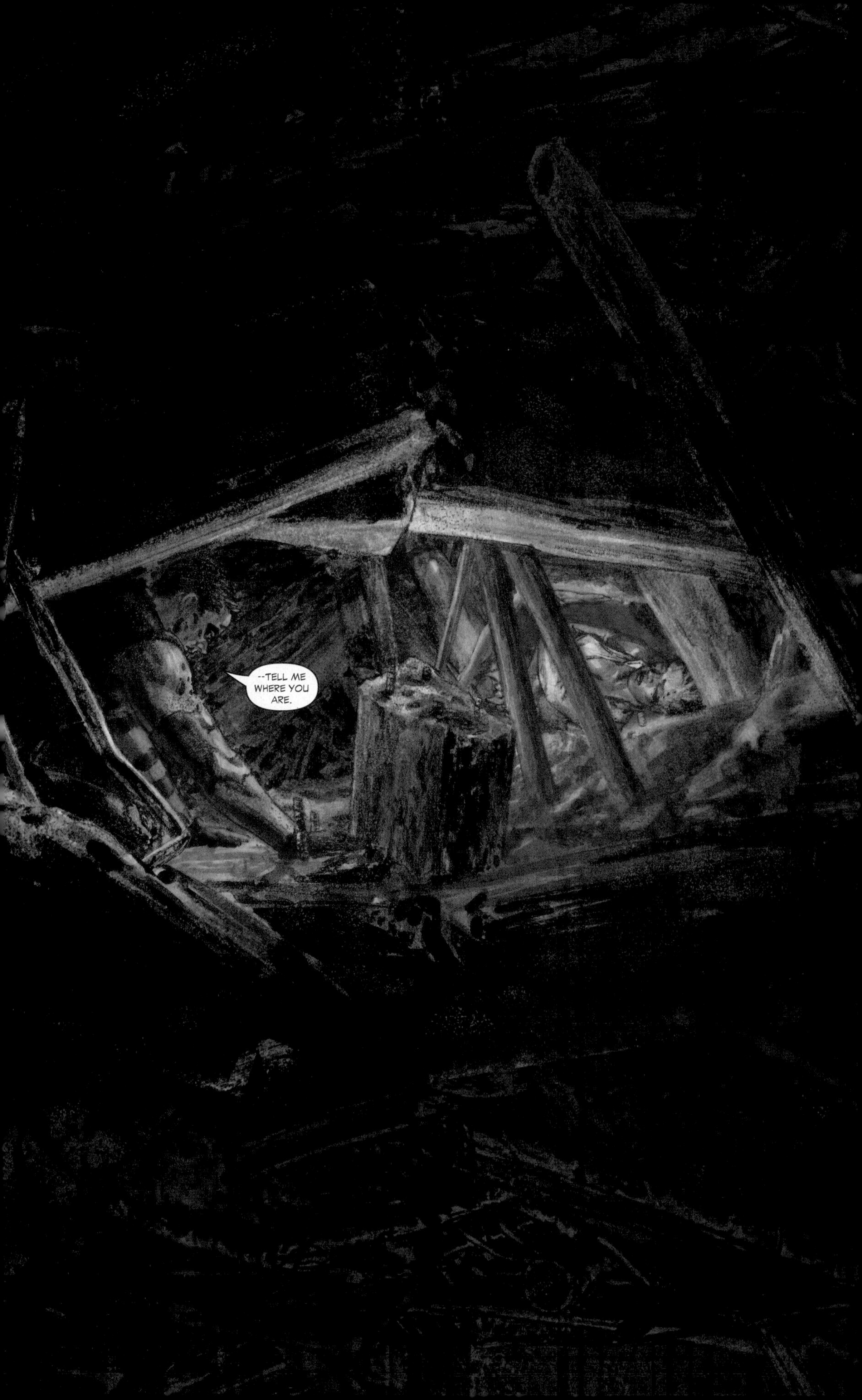
--TELL ME WHERE YOU ARE.

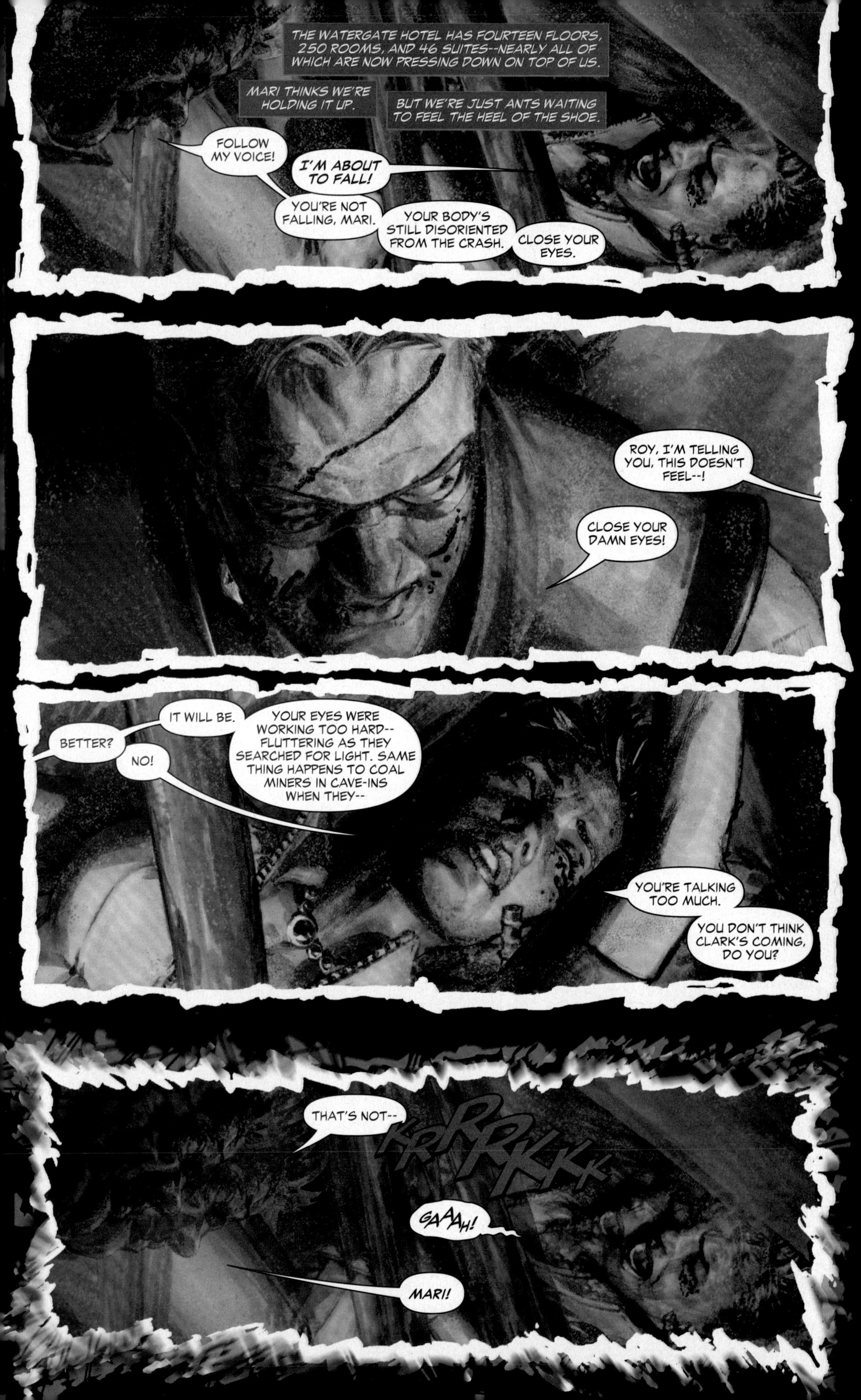
THE WATERGATE HOTEL HAS FOURTEEN FLOORS, 250 ROOMS, AND 46 SUITES--NEARLY ALL OF WHICH ARE NOW PRESSING DOWN ON TOP OF US.
MARI THINKS WE'RE HOLDING IT UP.
BUT WE'RE JUST ANTS WAITING TO FEEL THE HEEL OF THE SHOE.
FOLLOW MY VOICE!
I'M ABOUT TO FALL!
YOU'RE NOT FALLING, MARI.
YOUR BODY'S STILL DISORIENTED FROM THE CRASH.
CLOSE YOUR EYES.
ROY, I'M TELLING YOU, THIS DOESN'T FEEL--!
CLOSE YOUR DAMN EYES!
BETTER?
IT WILL BE.
NO!
YOUR EYES WERE WORKING TOO HARD--FLUTTERING AS THEY SEARCHED FOR LIGHT. SAME THING HAPPENS TO COAL MINERS IN CAVE-INS WHEN THEY--
YOU'RE TALKING TOO MUCH.
YOU DON'T THINK CLARK'S COMING, DO YOU?
THAT'S NOT--
KRRRKKK
GAAAH!
MARI!

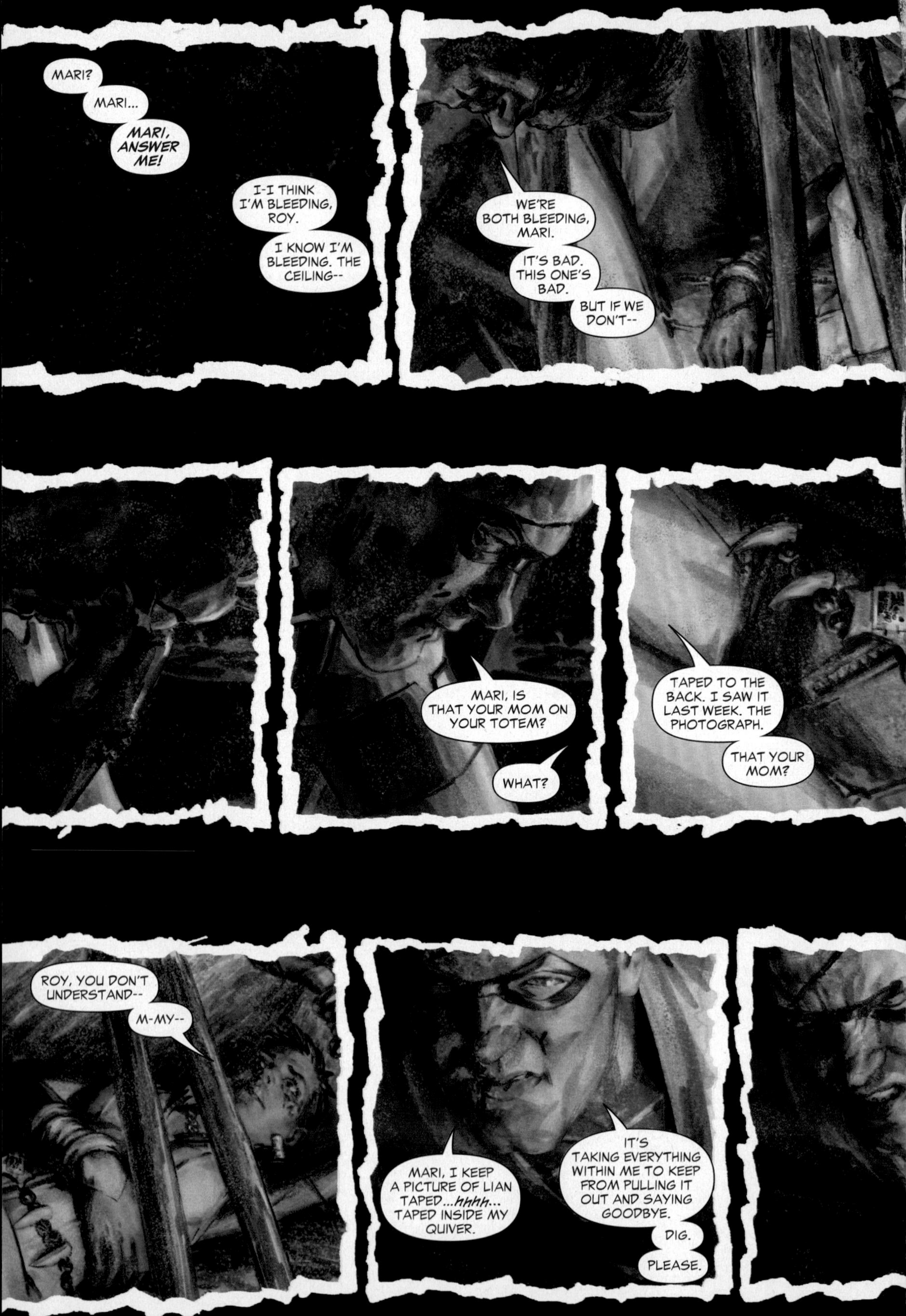
MARI?
MARI...
MARI, ANSWER ME!
I-I THINK I'M BLEEDING, ROY.
I KNOW I'M BLEEDING. THE CEILING--
WE'RE BOTH BLEEDING, MARI.
IT'S BAD. THIS ONE'S BAD.
BUT IF WE DON'T--
MARI, IS THAT YOUR MOM ON YOUR TOTEM?
WHAT?
TAPED TO THE BACK. I SAW IT LAST WEEK. THE PHOTOGRAPH.
THAT YOUR MOM?
ROY, YOU DON'T UNDERSTAND--
M-MY--
MARI, I KEEP A PICTURE OF LIAN TAPED...*hhhh*... TAPED INSIDE MY QUIVER.
IT'S TAKING EVERYTHING WITHIN ME TO KEEP FROM PULLING IT OUT AND SAYING GOODBYE.
DIG.
PLEASE.

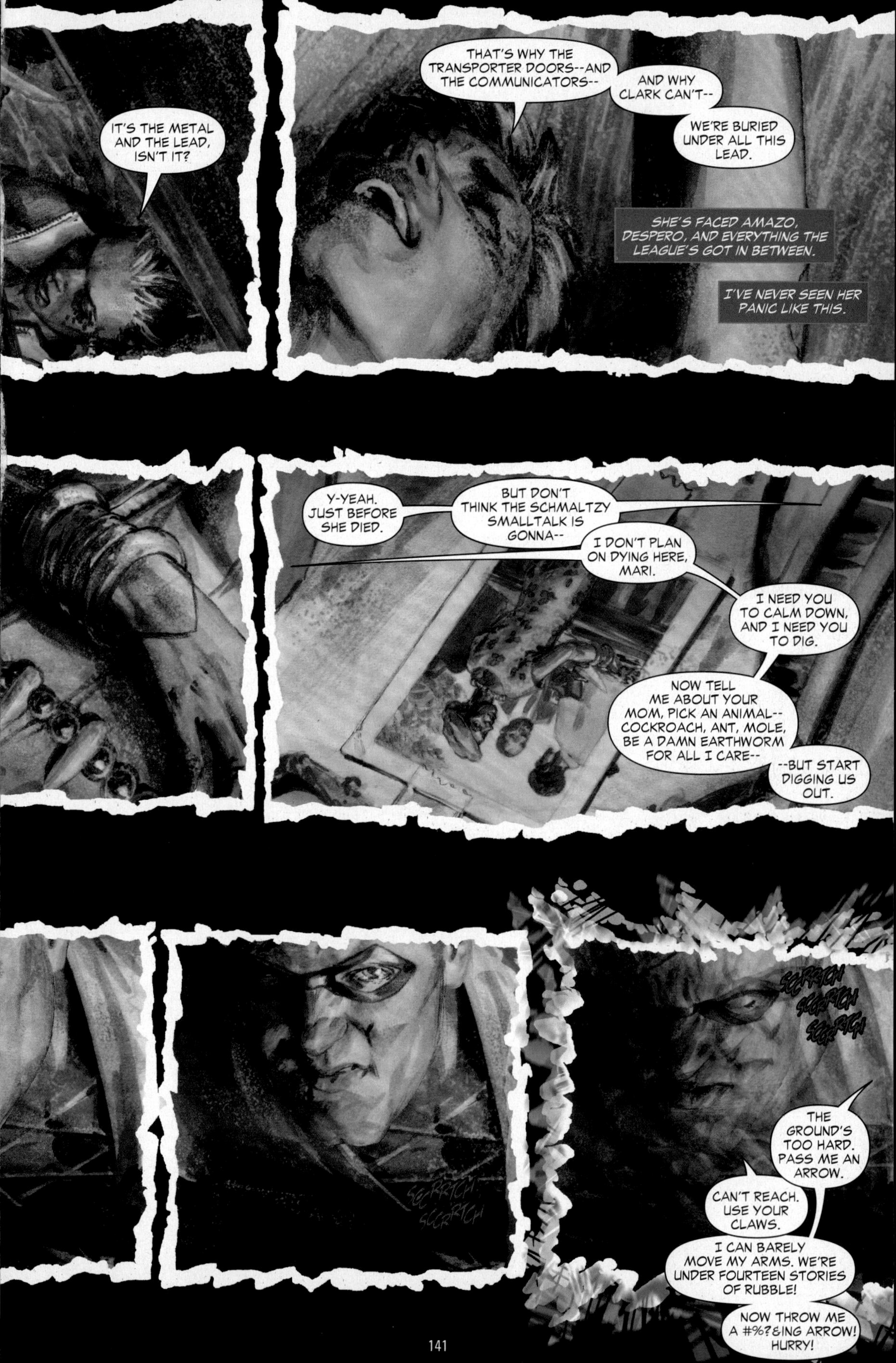

IT'S THE METAL AND THE LEAD, ISN'T IT?
THAT'S WHY THE TRANSPORTER DOORS--AND THE COMMUNICATORS--
AND WHY CLARK CAN'T--
WE'RE BURIED UNDER ALL THIS LEAD.
SHE'S FACED AMAZO, DESPERO, AND EVERYTHING THE LEAGUE'S GOT IN BETWEEN.
I'VE NEVER SEEN HER PANIC LIKE THIS.
Y-YEAH. JUST BEFORE SHE DIED.
BUT DON'T THINK THE SCHMALTZY SMALLTALK IS GONNA--
I DON'T PLAN ON DYING HERE, MARI.
I NEED YOU TO CALM DOWN, AND I NEED YOU TO DIG.
NOW TELL ME ABOUT YOUR MOM, PICK AN ANIMAL--COCKROACH, ANT, MOLE, BE A DAMN EARTHWORM FOR ALL I CARE--
--BUT START DIGGING US OUT.
SCCRRTCH SCCRRTCH
SCCRRTCH SCCRRTCH SCCRRTCH
THE GROUND'S TOO HARD. PASS ME AN ARROW.
CAN'T REACH. USE YOUR CLAWS.
I CAN BARELY MOVE MY ARMS. WE'RE UNDER FOURTEEN STORIES OF RUBBLE!
NOW THROW ME A #%?&ING ARROW! HURRY!

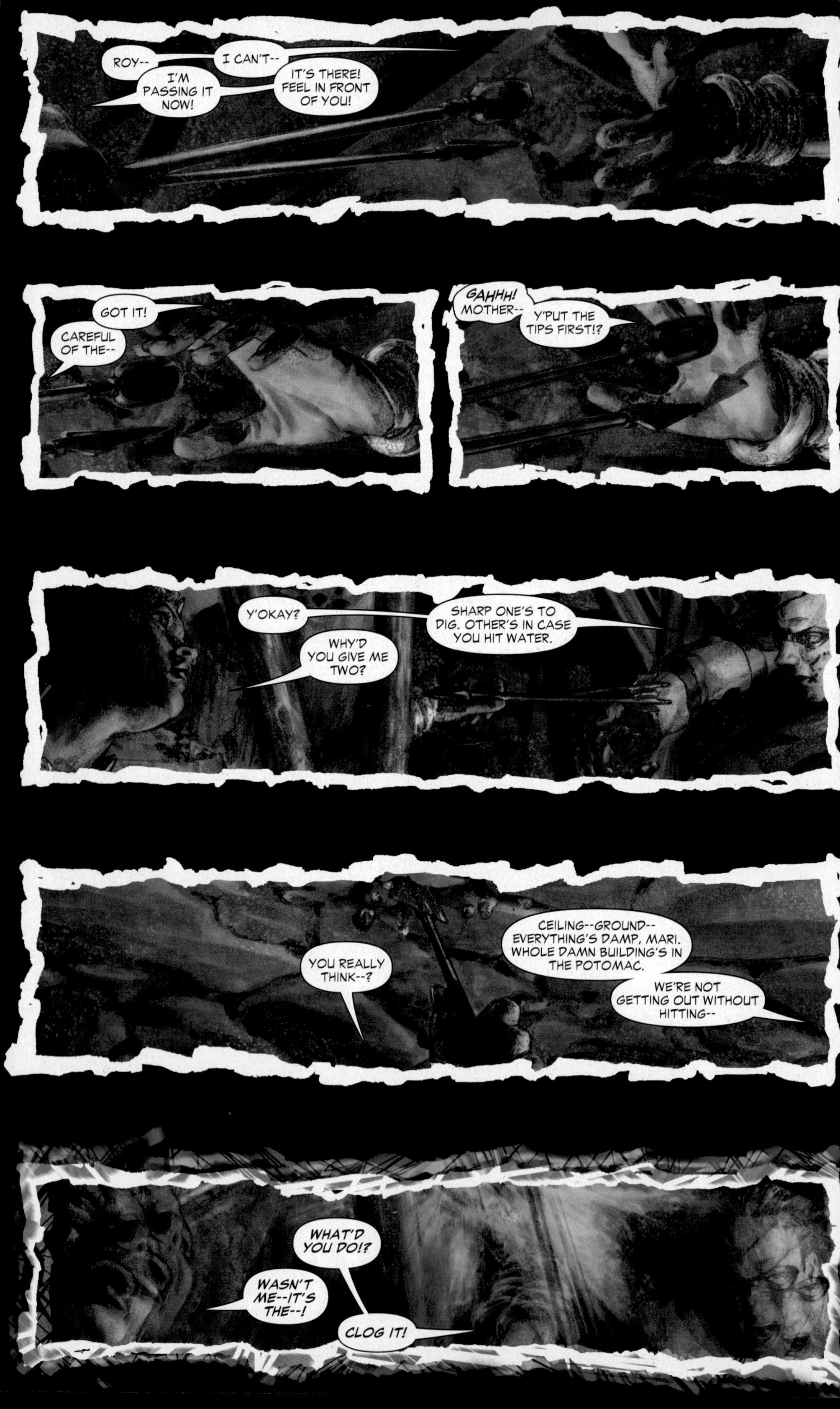
ROY--
I CAN'T--
I'M PASSING IT NOW!
IT'S THERE! FEEL IN FRONT OF YOU!
GOT IT!
CAREFUL OF THE--
GAHHH! MOTHER--
Y'PUT THE TIPS FIRST!?
Y'OKAY?
SHARP ONE'S TO DIG. OTHER'S IN CASE YOU HIT WATER.
WHY'D YOU GIVE ME TWO?
CEILING--GROUND--EVERYTHING'S DAMP, MARI. WHOLE DAMN BUILDING'S IN THE POTOMAC.
YOU REALLY THINK--?
WE'RE NOT GETTING OUT WITHOUT HITTING--
WHAT'D YOU DO!?
WASN'T ME--IT'S THE--!
CLOG IT!

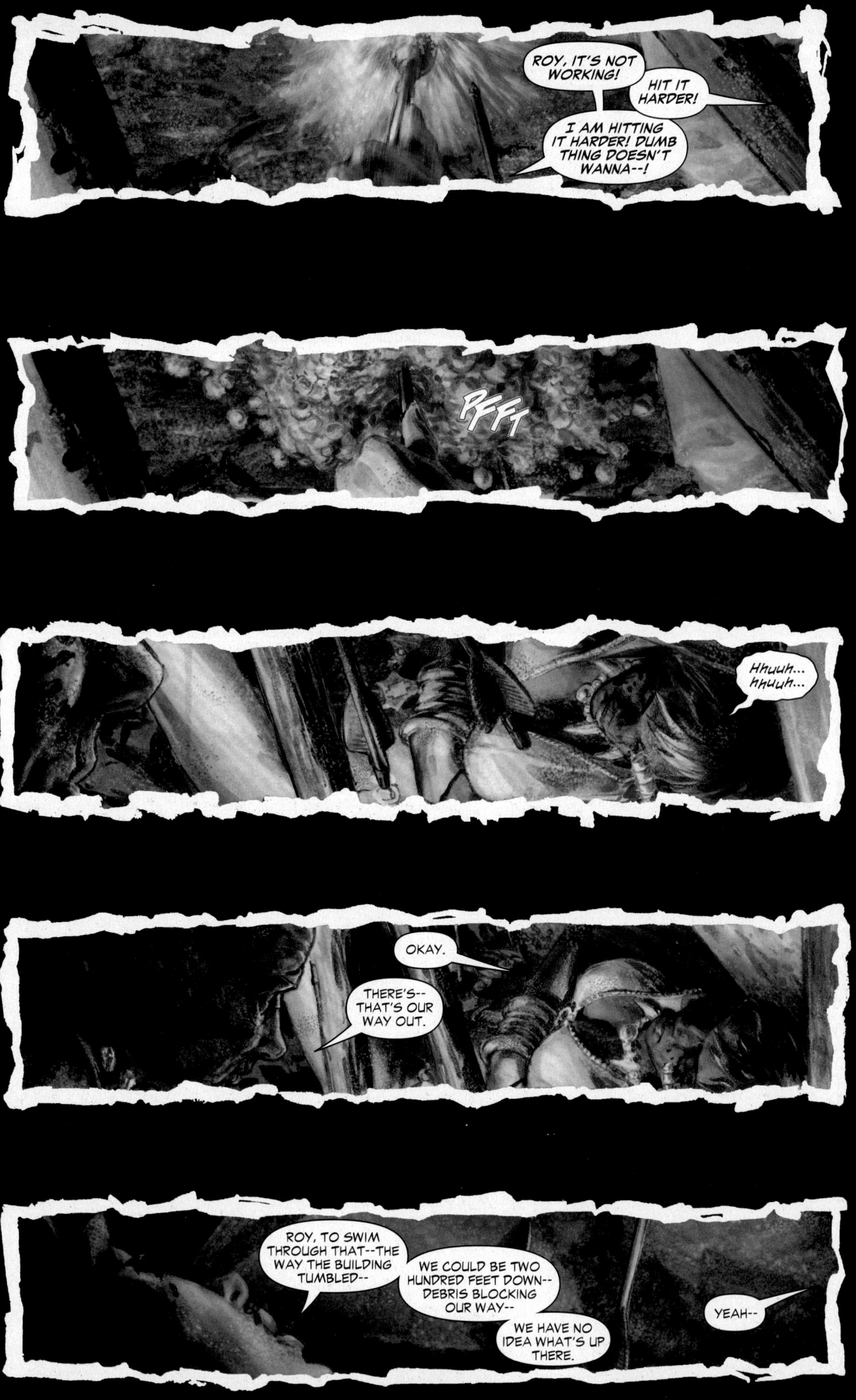
ROY, IT'S NOT WORKING!
HIT IT HARDER!
I AM HITTING IT HARDER! DUMB THING DOESN'T WANNA--!
PFFT
Hhuuh... hhuuh...
OKAY.
THERE'S-- THAT'S OUR WAY OUT.
ROY, TO SWIM THROUGH THAT--THE WAY THE BUILDING TUMBLED--
WE COULD BE TWO HUNDRED FEET DOWN-- DEBRIS BLOCKING OUR WAY--
WE HAVE NO IDEA WHAT'S UP THERE.
YEAH--

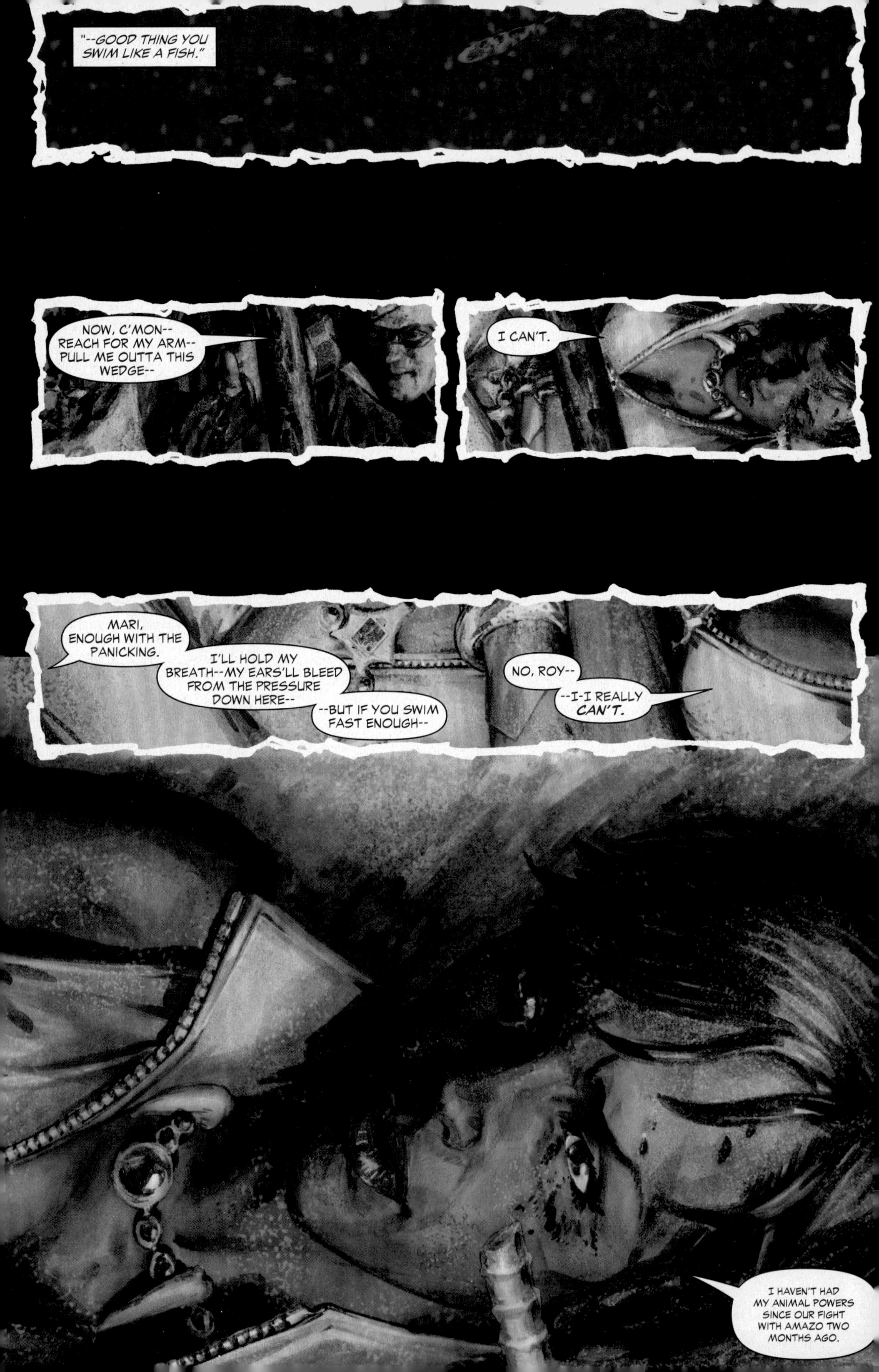
"--GOOD THING YOU SWIM LIKE A FISH."
NOW, C'MON-- REACH FOR MY ARM-- PULL ME OUTTA THIS WEDGE--
I CAN'T.
MARI, ENOUGH WITH THE PANICKING.
I'LL HOLD MY BREATH--MY EARS'LL BLEED FROM THE PRESSURE DOWN HERE--
--BUT IF YOU SWIM FAST ENOUGH--
NO, ROY--
--I-I REALLY *CAN'T.*
I HAVEN'T HAD MY ANIMAL POWERS SINCE OUR FIGHT WITH AMAZO TWO MONTHS AGO.

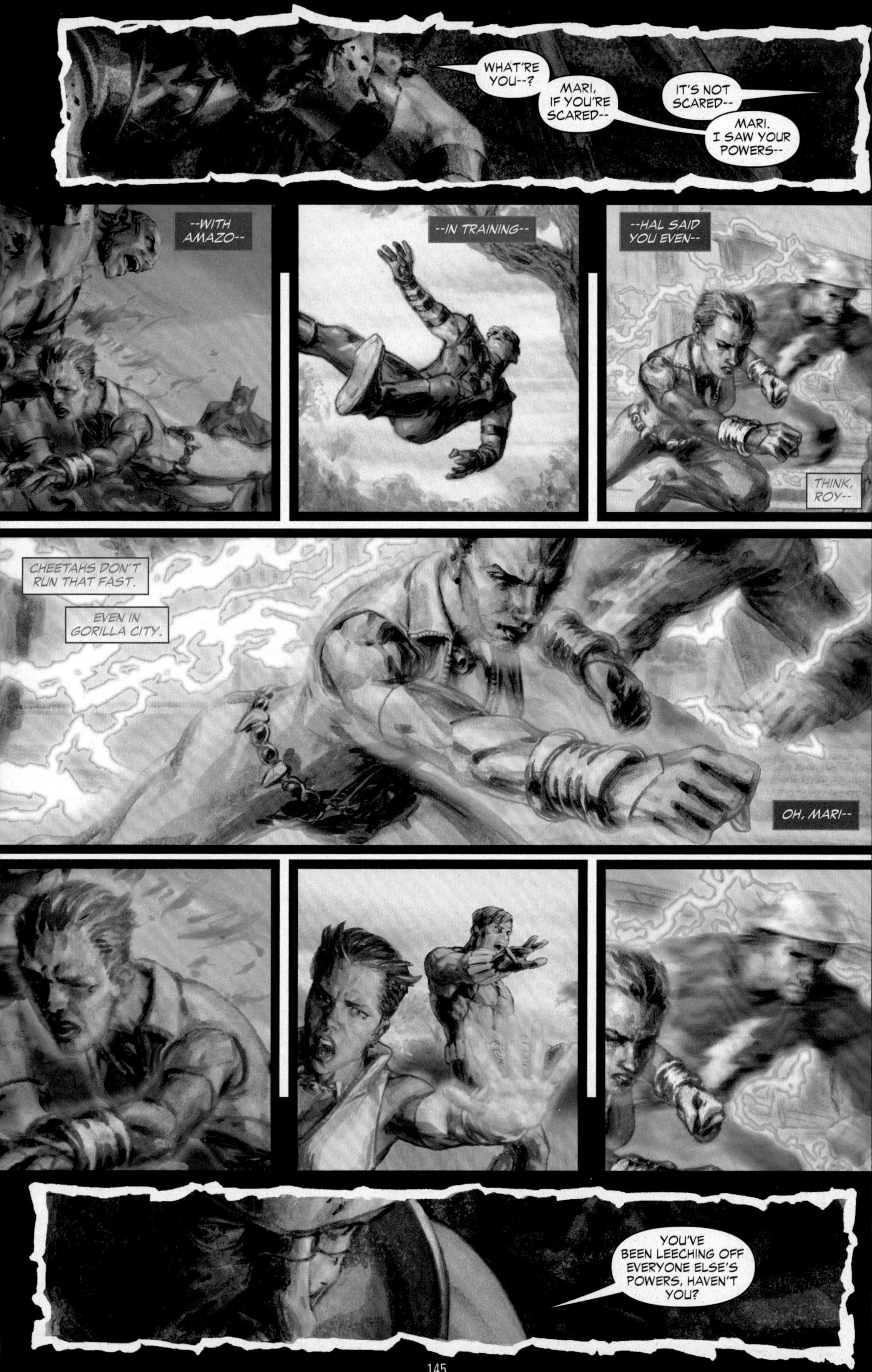
WHAT'RE YOU--?
MARI, IF YOU'RE SCARED--
IT'S NOT SCARED--
MARI. I SAW YOUR POWERS--
--WITH AMAZO--
--IN TRAINING--
--HAL SAID YOU EVEN--
THINK, ROY--
CHEETAHS DON'T RUN THAT FAST.
EVEN IN GORILLA CITY.
OH, MARI--
YOU'VE BEEN LEECHING OFF EVERYONE ELSE'S POWERS, HAVEN'T YOU?

IT WASN'T ON PURPOSE--

WHEN I LOST MYSELF--

--WITH THE BIRDS--

THE ONLY WAY BACK WAS ABSORBING THE HUMAN ANIMAL, AND THEN--

--THEN THAT'S ALL I COULD DO.

WHOSE POWERS DO YOU HAVE NOW?

JEFF'S.

THE LIGHTNING.

BUT IF I USE IT IN THE WATER--

--YOU'LL FRY US BOTH.

DAMMIT, WE'RE IN THE STUPID GARBAGE COMPACTOR SCENE AND YOU COULDN'T'VE STOLEN ANYTHING FROM CLARK?

LISTEN, I STILL NEED YOU TO SWIM--

ROY--

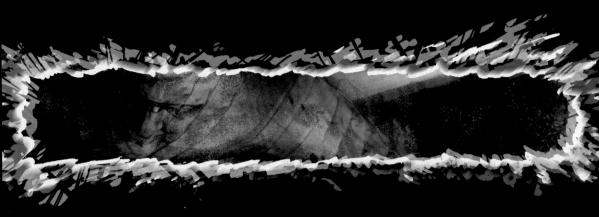

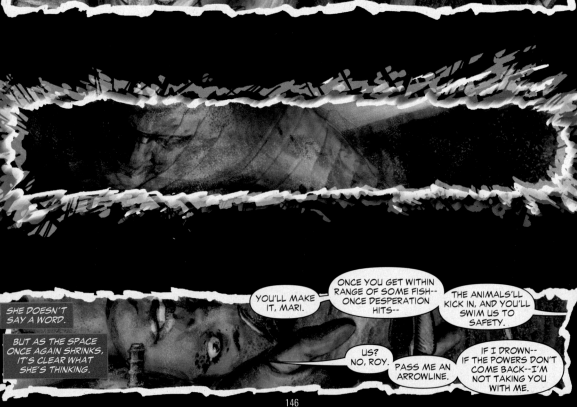

SHE DOESN'T SAY A WORD.

BUT AS THE SPACE ONCE AGAIN SHRINKS, IT'S CLEAR WHAT SHE'S THINKING.

YOU'LL MAKE IT, MARI.

ONCE YOU GET WITHIN RANGE OF SOME FISH-- ONCE DESPERATION HITS--

THE ANIMALS'LL KICK IN, AND YOU'LL SWIM US TO SAFETY.

US? NO, ROY.

PASS ME AN ARROWLINE.

IF I DROWN-- IF THE POWERS DON'T COME BACK--I'M NOT TAKING YOU WITH ME.

146

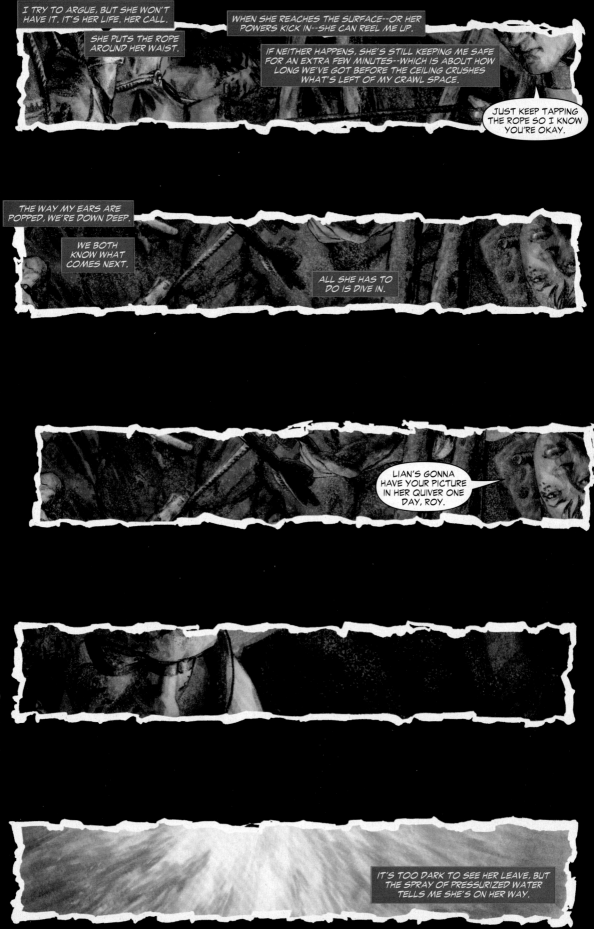

I TRY TO ARGUE, BUT SHE WON'T HAVE IT. IT'S HER LIFE. HER CALL.

SHE PUTS THE ROPE AROUND HER WAIST.

WHEN SHE REACHES THE SURFACE--OR HER POWERS KICK IN--SHE CAN REEL ME UP.

IF NEITHER HAPPENS, SHE'S STILL KEEPING ME SAFE FOR AN EXTRA FEW MINUTES--WHICH IS ABOUT HOW LONG WE'VE GOT BEFORE THE CEILING CRUSHES WHAT'S LEFT OF MY CRAWL SPACE.

JUST KEEP TAPPING THE ROPE SO I KNOW YOU'RE OKAY.

THE WAY MY EARS ARE POPPED, WE'RE DOWN DEEP.

WE BOTH KNOW WHAT COMES NEXT.

ALL SHE HAS TO DO IS DIVE IN.

LIAN'S GONNA HAVE YOUR PICTURE IN HER QUIVER ONE DAY, ROY.

IT'S TOO DARK TO SEE HER LEAVE, BUT THE SPRAY OF PRESSURIZED WATER TELLS ME SHE'S ON HER WAY.

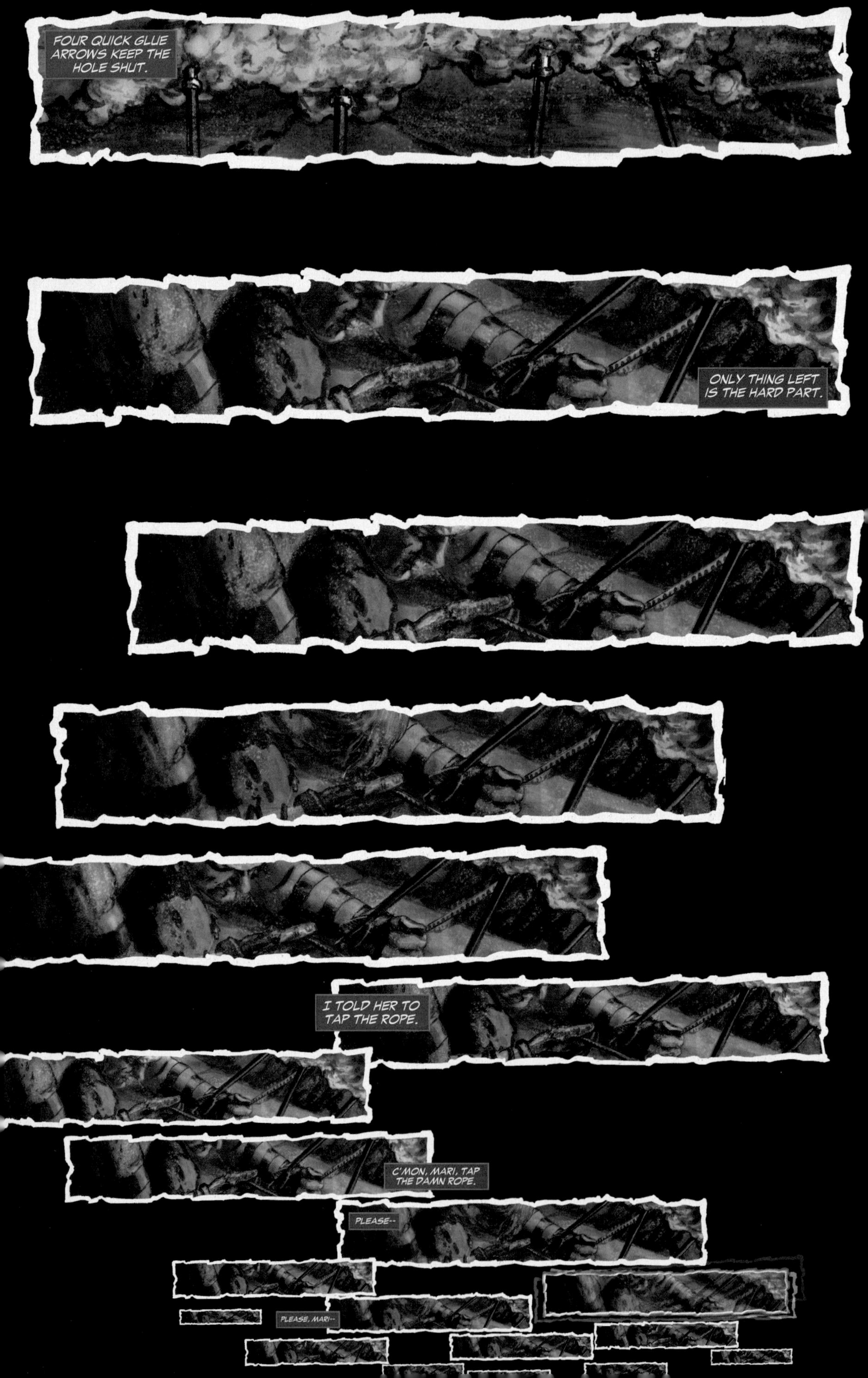

FOUR QUICK GLUE ARROWS KEEP THE HOLE SHUT.
ONLY THING LEFT IS THE HARD PART.
I TOLD HER TO TAP THE ROPE.
C'MON, MARI, TAP THE DAMN ROPE.
PLEASE--
PLEASE, MARI--

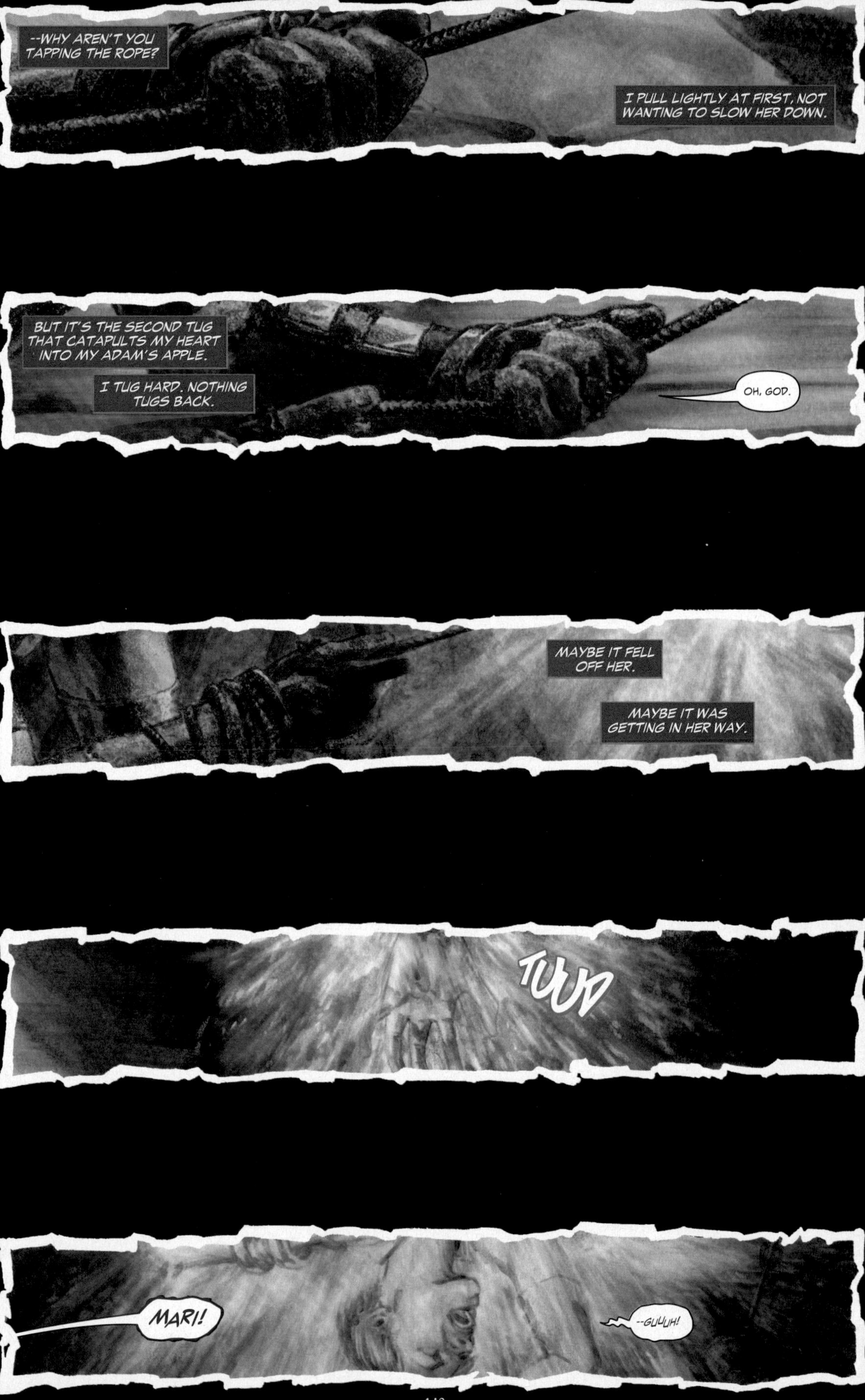
--WHY AREN'T YOU TAPPING THE ROPE?
I PULL LIGHTLY AT FIRST, NOT WANTING TO SLOW HER DOWN.
BUT IT'S THE SECOND TUG THAT CATAPULTS MY HEART INTO MY ADAM'S APPLE.
I TUG HARD. NOTHING TUGS BACK.
OH, GOD.
MAYBE IT FELL OFF HER.
MAYBE IT WAS GETTING IN HER WAY.
TUUD
MARI!
--GUUUH!

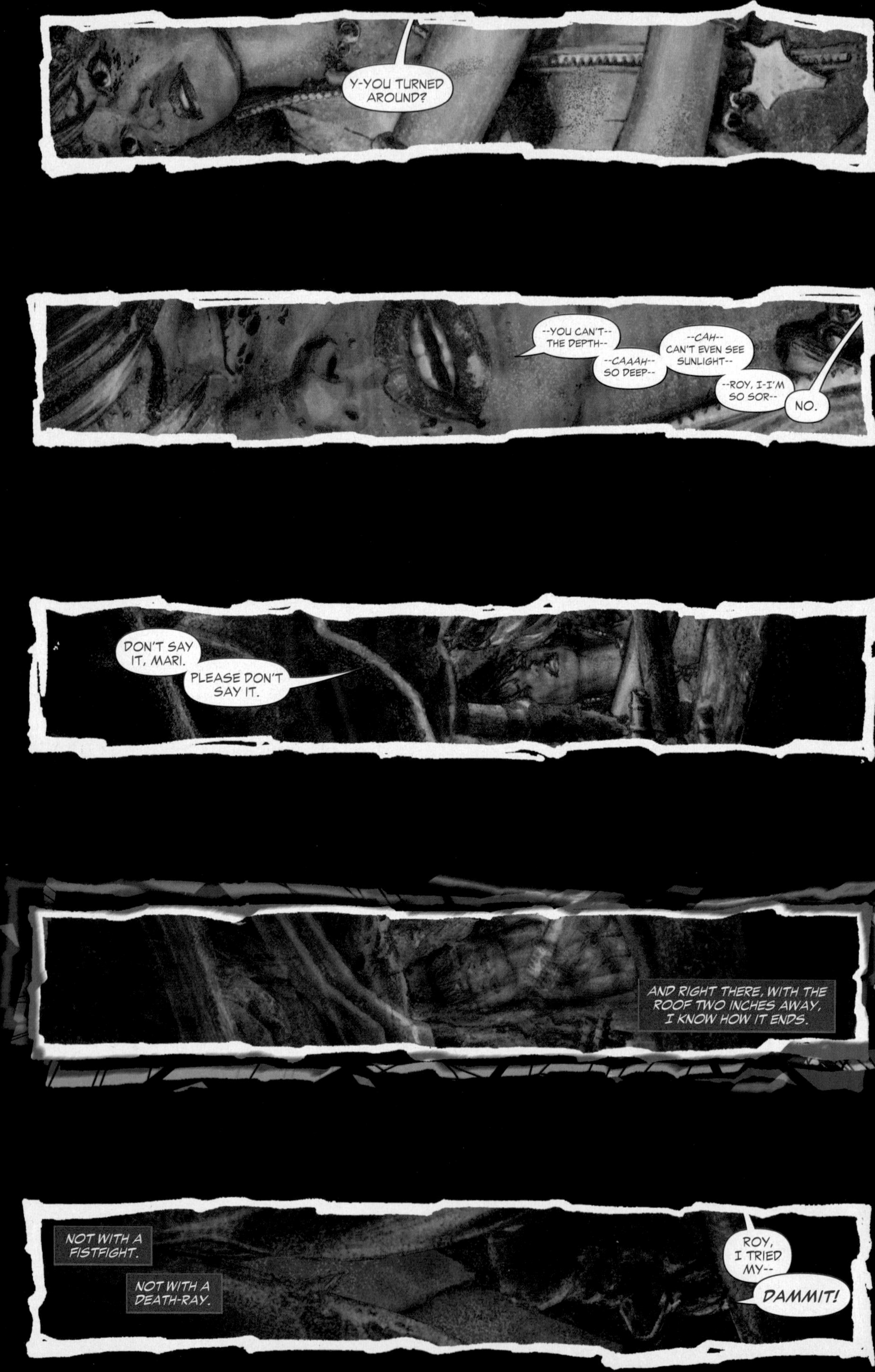
Y-YOU TURNED AROUND?
--YOU CAN'T-- THE DEPTH--
--CAAAH-- SO DEEP--
--CAH-- CAN'T EVEN SEE SUNLIGHT--
--ROY, I-I'M SO SOR--
NO.
DON'T SAY IT, MARI.
PLEASE DON'T SAY IT.
AND RIGHT THERE, WITH THE ROOF TWO INCHES AWAY, I KNOW HOW IT ENDS.
NOT WITH A FISTFIGHT.
NOT WITH A DEATH-RAY.
ROY, I TRIED MY--
DAMMIT!

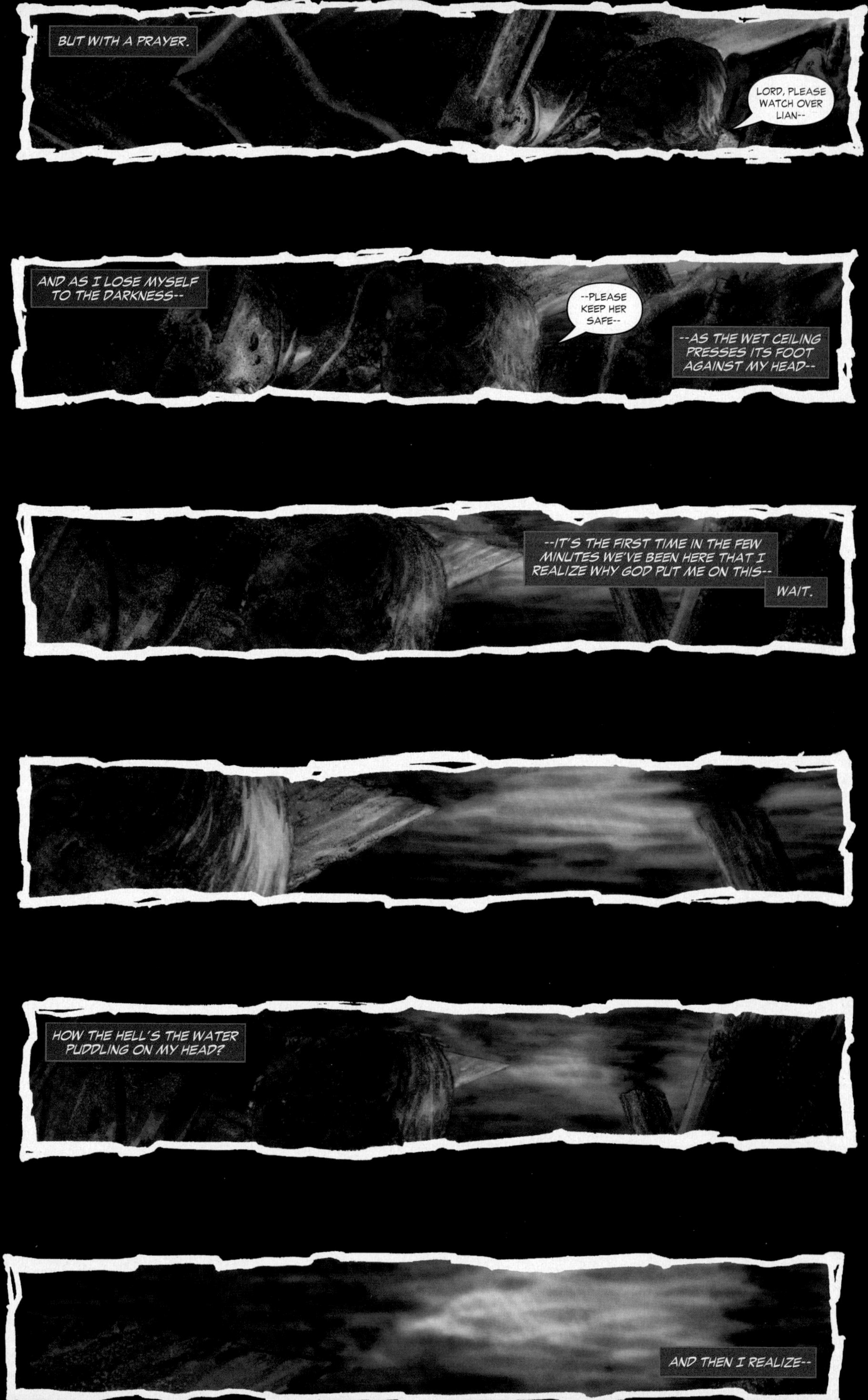
BUT WITH A PRAYER.
LORD, PLEASE WATCH OVER LIAN--
AND AS I LOSE MYSELF TO THE DARKNESS--
--PLEASE KEEP HER SAFE--
--AS THE WET CEILING PRESSES ITS FOOT AGAINST MY HEAD--
--IT'S THE FIRST TIME IN THE FEW MINUTES WE'VE BEEN HERE THAT I REALIZE WHY GOD PUT ME ON THIS--
WAIT.
HOW THE HELL'S THE WATER PUDDLING ON MY HEAD?
AND THEN I REALIZE--

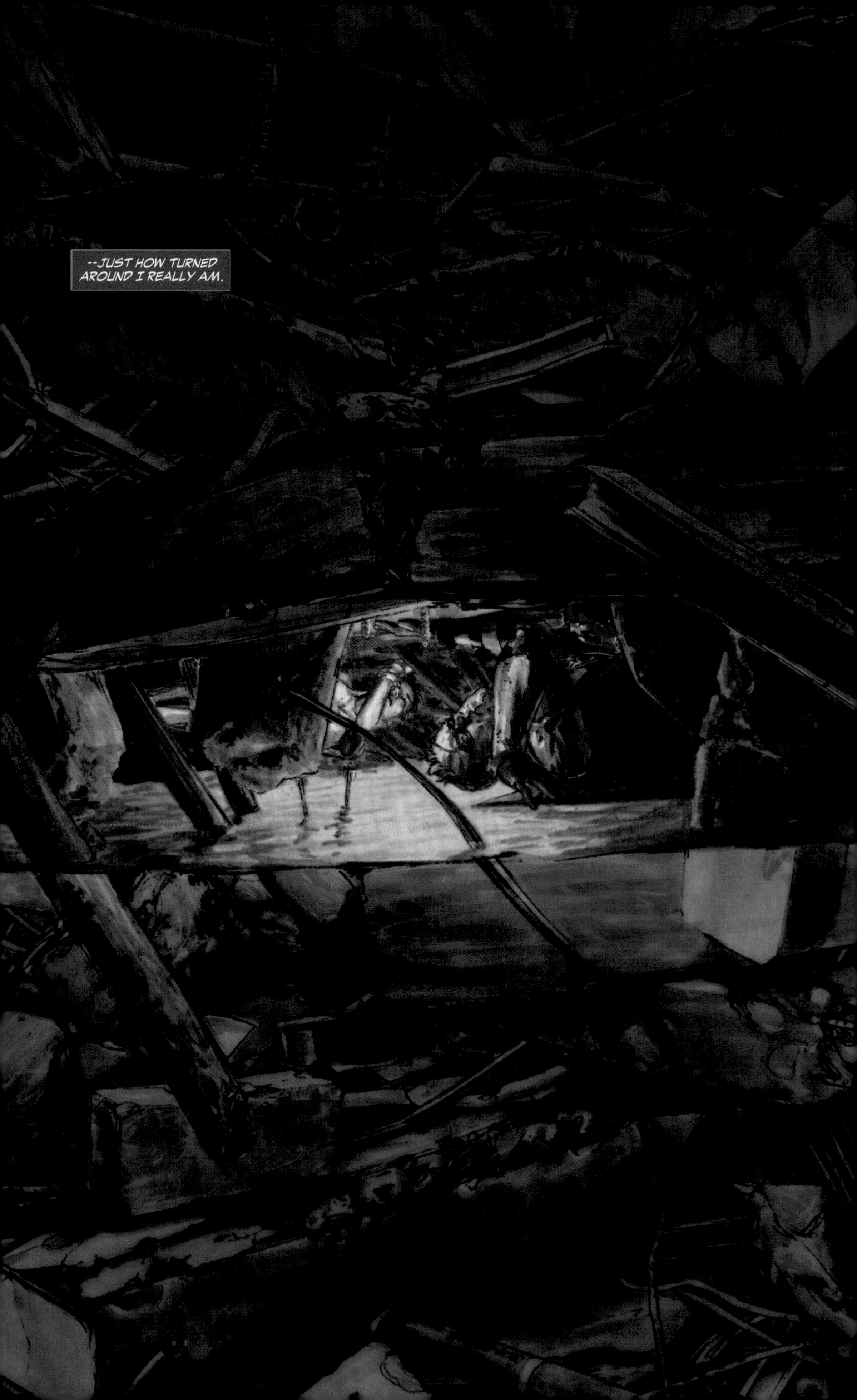
--JUST HOW TURNED AROUND I REALLY AM.

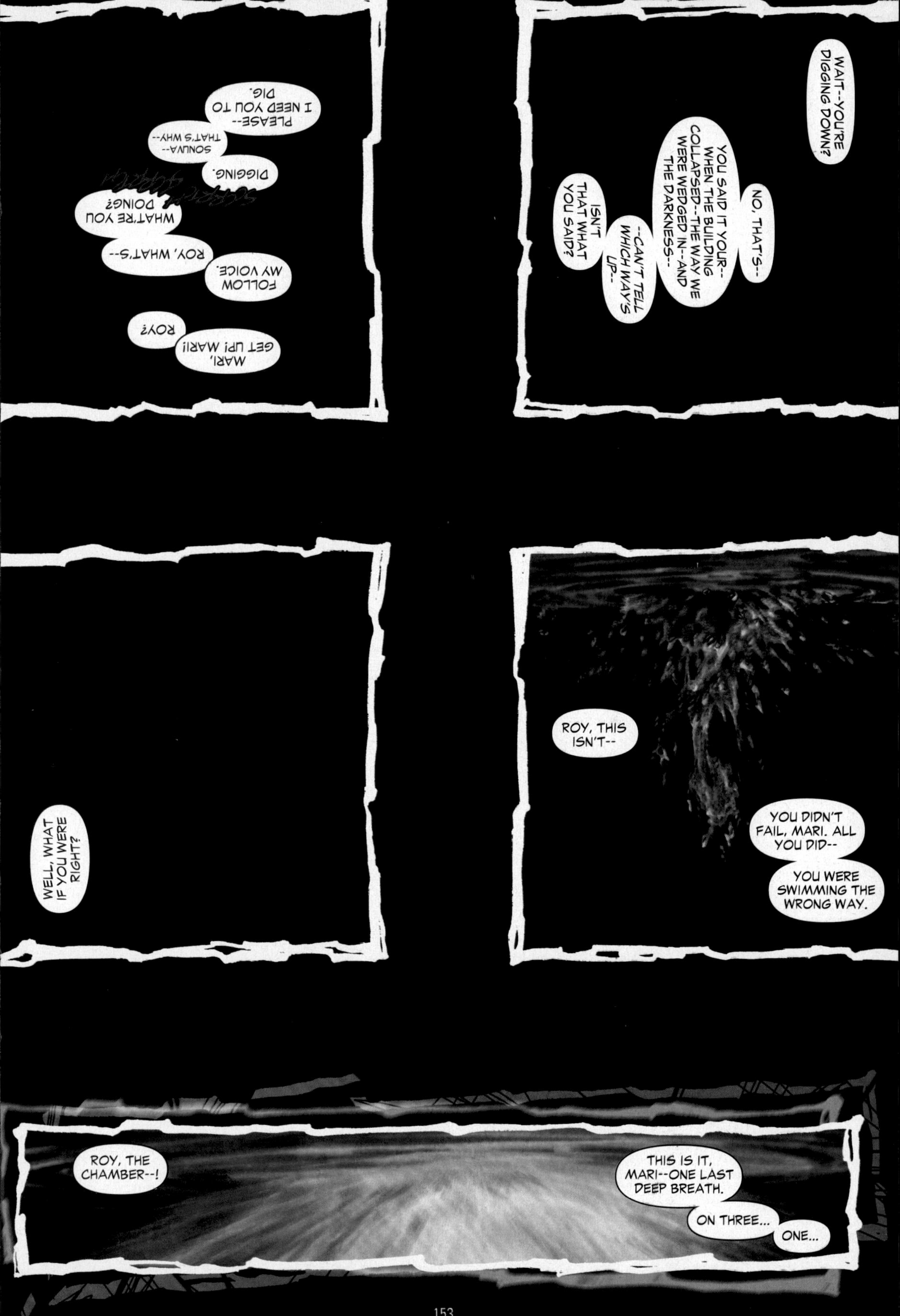

MARI, GET UP! MARI!
ROY?
FOLLOW MY VOICE.
ROY, WHAT'S--
WHAT'RE YOU DOING?
DIGGING.
SONUVA-- THAT'S WHY--
PLEASE-- I NEED YOU TO DIG.
WAIT--YOU'RE DIGGING DOWN?
NO, THAT'S--
YOU SAID IT YOUR-- WHEN THE BUILDING COLLAPSED--THE WAY WE WERE WEDGED IN--AND THE DARKNESS--
--CAN'T TELL WHICH WAY'S UP--
ISN'T THAT WHAT YOU SAID?
WELL, WHAT IF YOU WERE RIGHT?
ROY, THIS ISN'T--
YOU DIDN'T FAIL, MARI. ALL YOU DID--
YOU WERE SWIMMING THE WRONG WAY.
ROY, THE CHAMBER--!
THIS IS IT, MARI--ONE LAST DEEP BREATH.
ON THREE...
ONE...

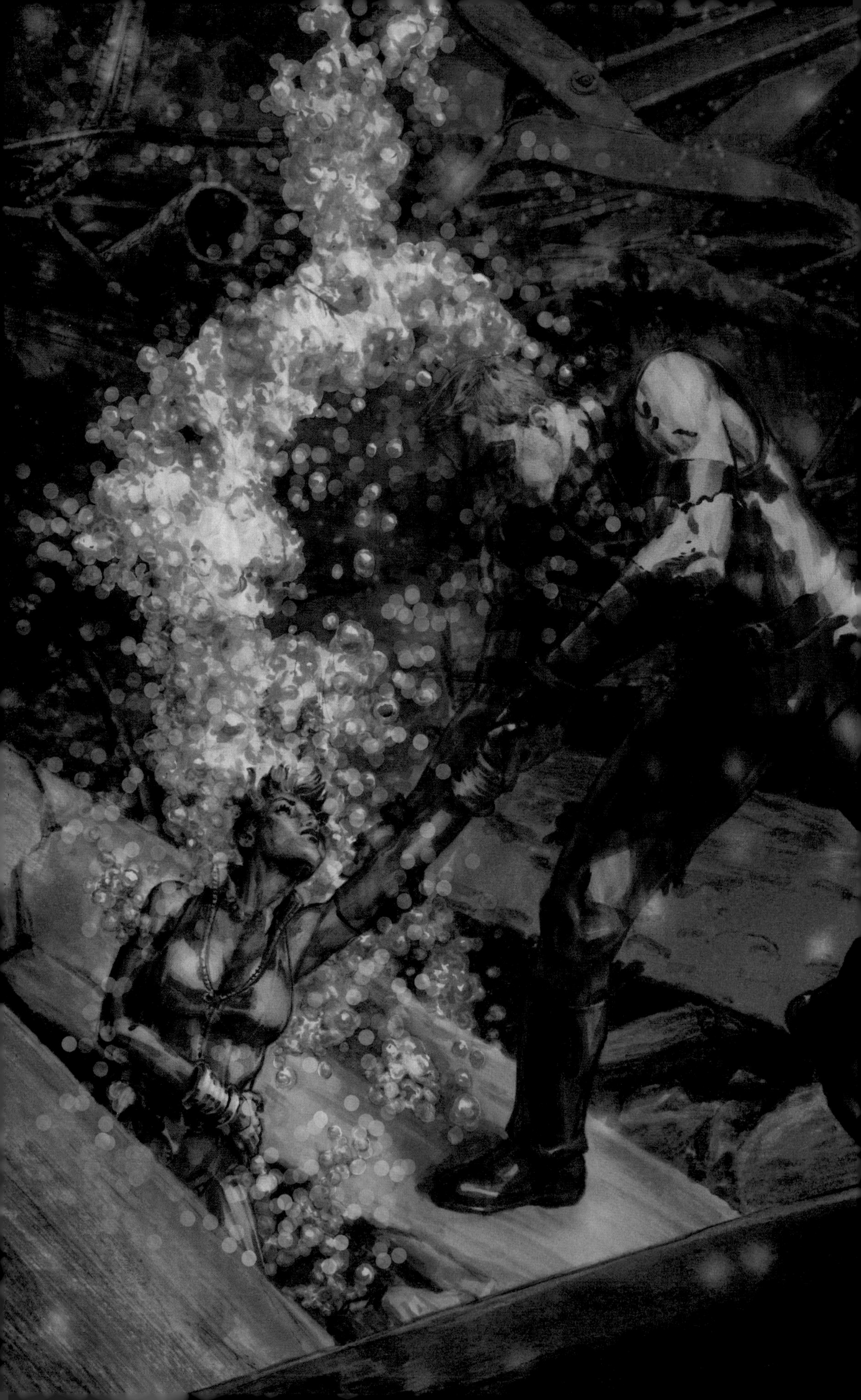

THE PRESSURE'S SO GREAT, I FEEL IT IN THE BAD VEIN DOWN MY FOREHEAD.

NEXT TO ME, MARI'S ALREADY SLOWING DOWN.

SHE THINKS IT'S BECAUSE SHE LOST CONTACT WITH THE TOTEM.

BUT SHE'S NOT ON THIS TEAM FOR THE TOTEM-- OR FOR HER ANIMAL POWERS-- OR EVEN FOR A BOW AND ARROW.

SHE'S ON THIS TEAM BECAUSE SHE'LL FIGHT.

LIKE BRUCE TAUGHT DICK.

LIKE DICK TAUGHT ME.

WE ALL FIGHT FOR DIFFERENT THINGS.

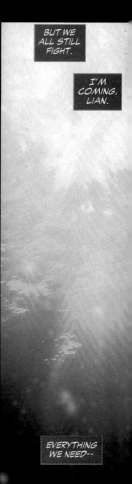

BUT WE ALL STILL FIGHT.

I'M COMING, LIAN.

EVERYTHING WE NEED--

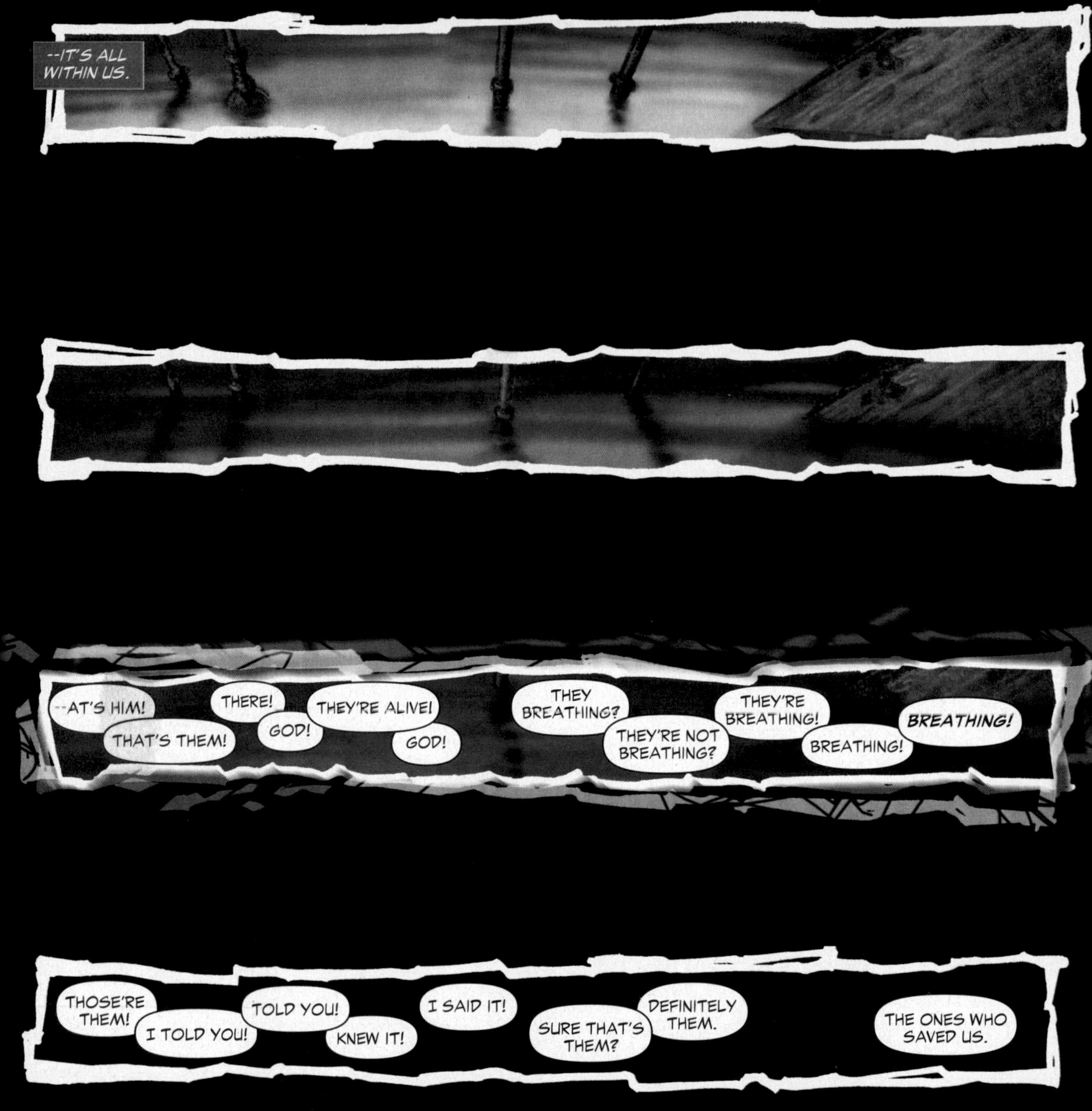
--IT'S ALL WITHIN US.
--AT'S HIM!
THAT'S THEM!
THERE!
GOD!
THEY'RE ALIVE!
GOD!
THEY BREATHING?
THEY'RE NOT BREATHING?
THEY'RE BREATHING!
BREATHING!
BREATHING!
THOSE'RE THEM!
I TOLD YOU!
TOLD YOU!
KNEW IT!
I SAID IT!
SURE THAT'S THEM?
DEFINITELY THEM.
THE ONES WHO SAVED US.

WALLS

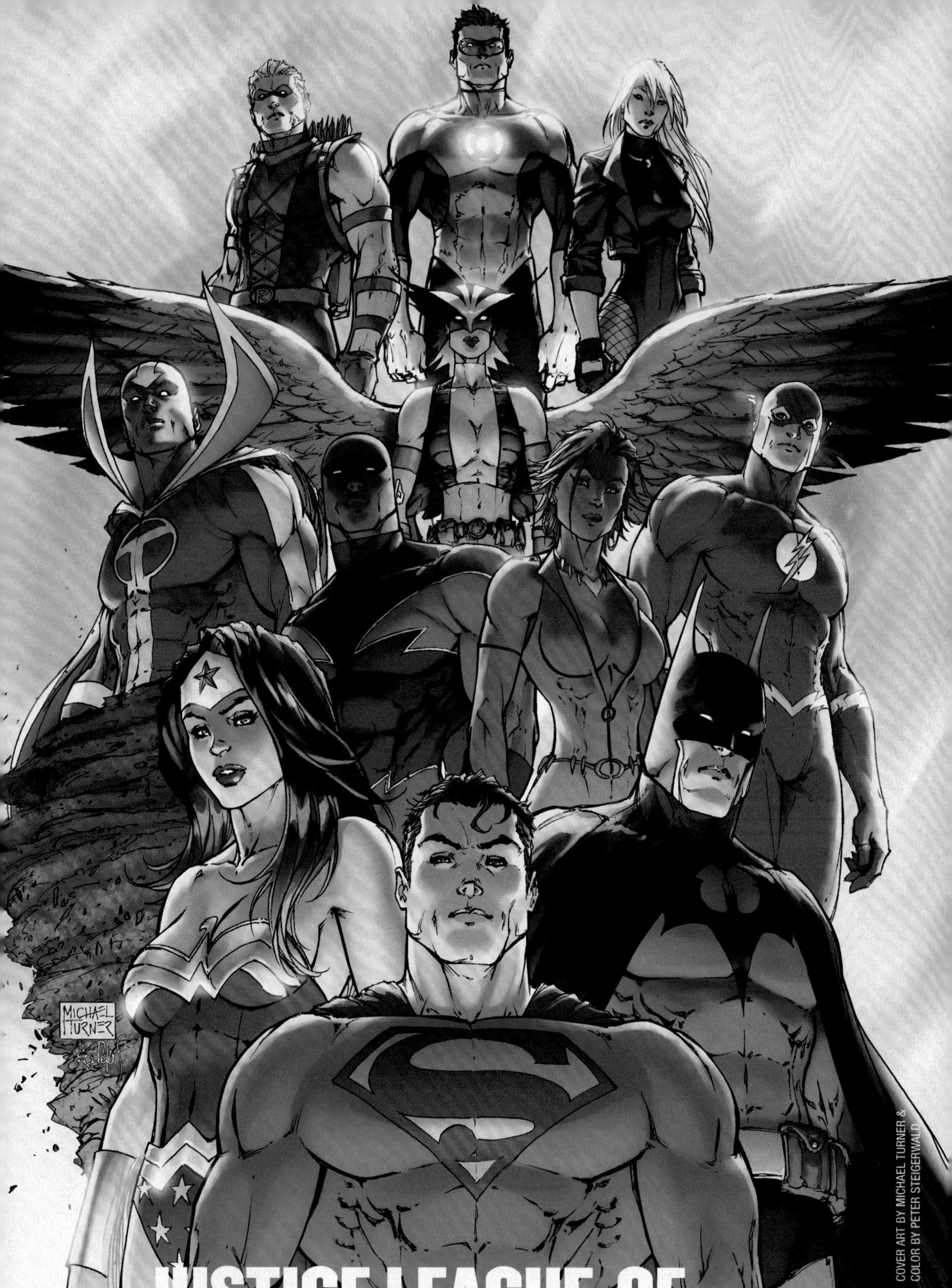
MICHAEL TURNER

COVER ART BY MICHAEL TURNER &
COLOR BY PETER STEIGERWALD

JUSTICE LEAGUE OF AMERICA

MONITOR DUTY

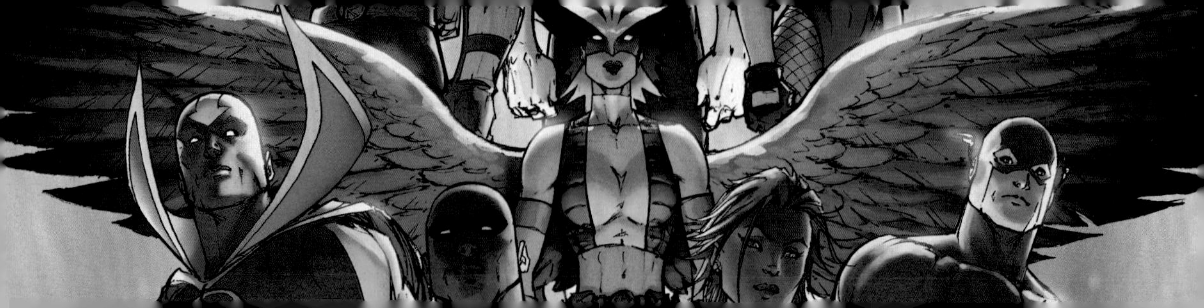

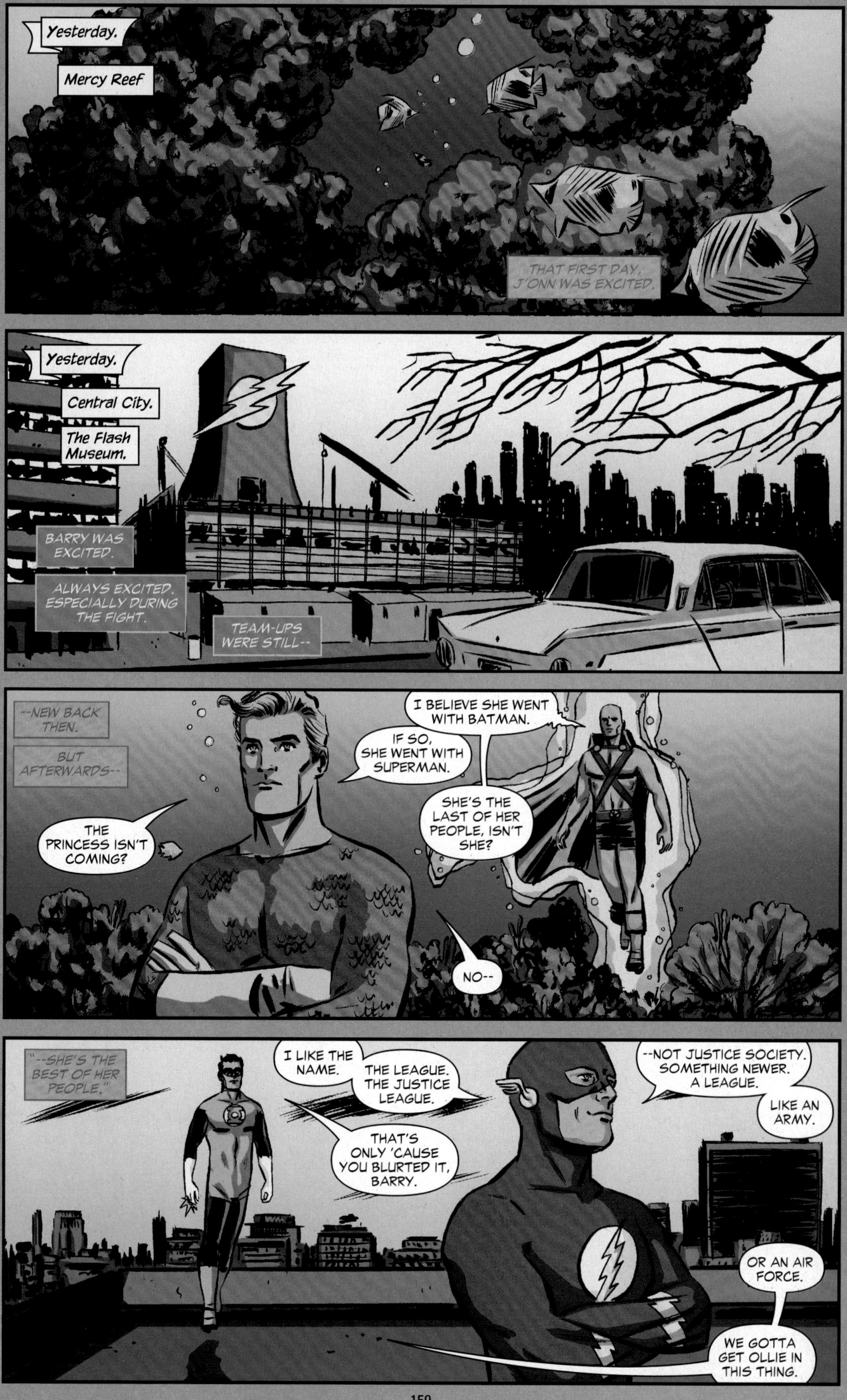

Yesterday.
Mercy Reef
THAT FIRST DAY, J'ONN WAS EXCITED.
Yesterday.
Central City.
The Flash Museum.
BARRY WAS EXCITED.
ALWAYS EXCITED. ESPECIALLY DURING THE FIGHT.
TEAM-UPS WERE STILL--
--NEW BACK THEN.
BUT AFTERWARDS--
THE PRINCESS ISN'T COMING?
I BELIEVE SHE WENT WITH BATMAN.
IF SO, SHE WENT WITH SUPERMAN.
SHE'S THE LAST OF HER PEOPLE, ISN'T SHE?
NO--
"--SHE'S THE BEST OF HER PEOPLE."
I LIKE THE NAME.
THE LEAGUE. THE JUSTICE LEAGUE.
--NOT JUSTICE SOCIETY. SOMETHING NEWER. A LEAGUE.
LIKE AN ARMY.
THAT'S ONLY 'CAUSE YOU BLURTED IT, BARRY.
OR AN AIR FORCE.
WE GOTTA GET OLLIE IN THIS THING.

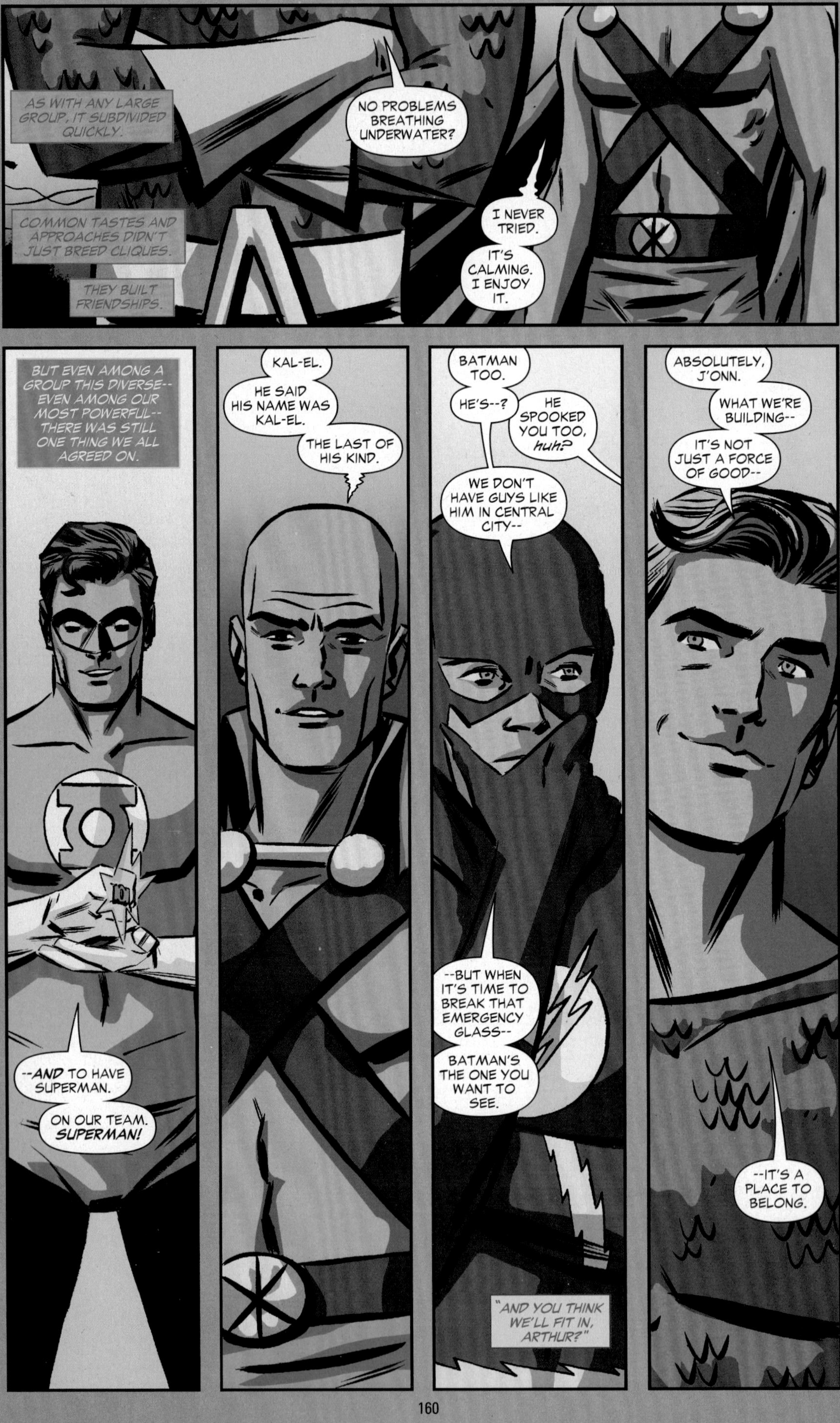
AS WITH ANY LARGE GROUP, IT SUBDIVIDED QUICKLY.
NO PROBLEMS BREATHING UNDERWATER?
COMMON TASTES AND APPROACHES DIDN'T JUST BREED CLIQUES.
THEY BUILT FRIENDSHIPS.
I NEVER TRIED.
IT'S CALMING. I ENJOY IT.
BUT EVEN AMONG A GROUP THIS DIVERSE-- EVEN AMONG OUR MOST POWERFUL-- THERE WAS STILL ONE THING WE ALL AGREED ON.
--AND TO HAVE SUPERMAN.
ON OUR TEAM. SUPERMAN!
KAL-EL.
HE SAID HIS NAME WAS KAL-EL.
THE LAST OF HIS KIND.
BATMAN TOO.
HE'S--?
HE SPOOKED YOU TOO, huh?
WE DON'T HAVE GUYS LIKE HIM IN CENTRAL CITY--
--BUT WHEN IT'S TIME TO BREAK THAT EMERGENCY GLASS--
BATMAN'S THE ONE YOU WANT TO SEE.
"AND YOU THINK WE'LL FIT IN, ARTHUR?"
ABSOLUTELY, J'ONN.
WHAT WE'RE BUILDING--
IT'S NOT JUST A FORCE OF GOOD--
--IT'S A PLACE TO BELONG.

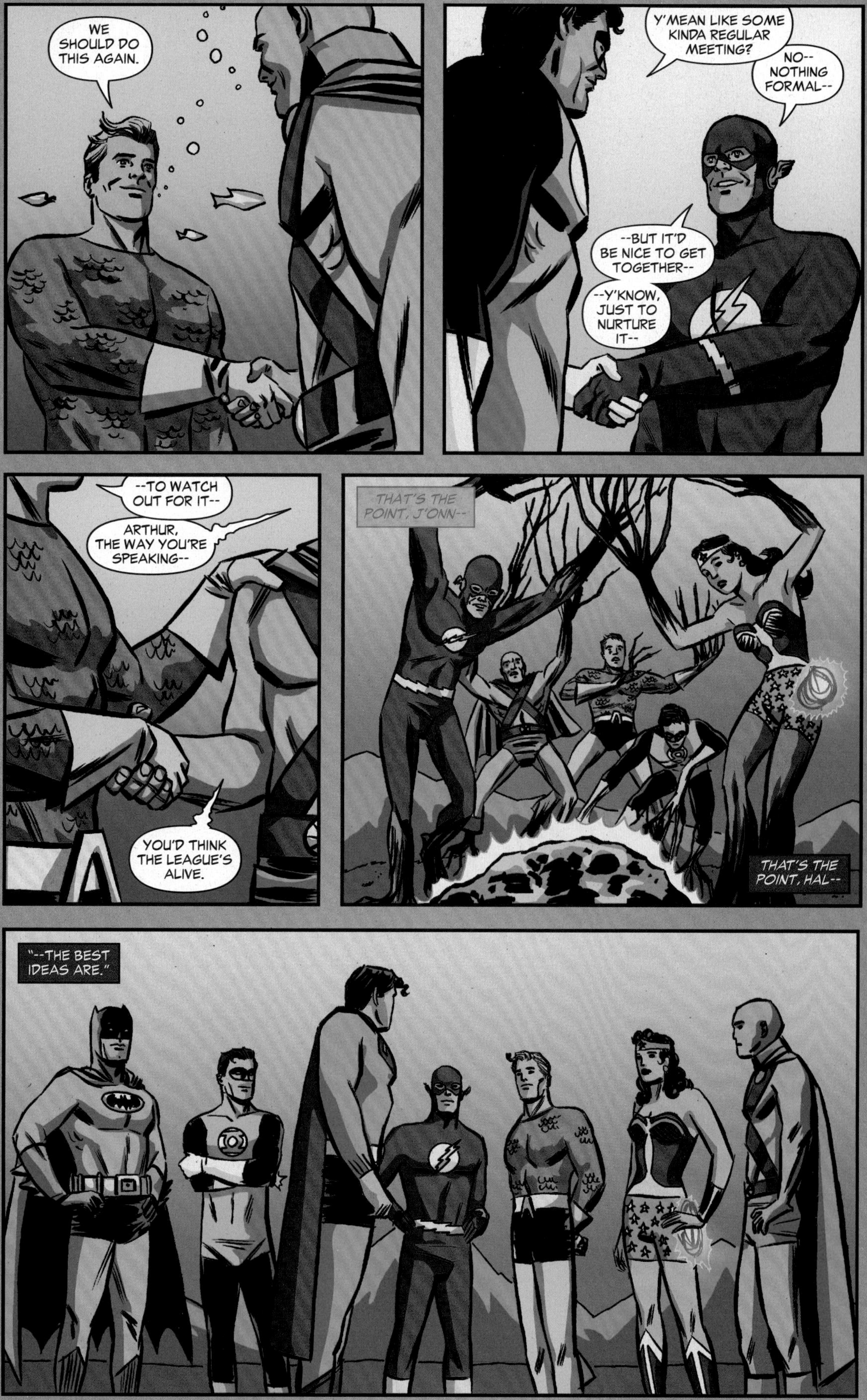
WE SHOULD DO THIS AGAIN.
Y'MEAN LIKE SOME KINDA REGULAR MEETING?
NO-- NOTHING FORMAL--
--BUT IT'D BE NICE TO GET TOGETHER--
--Y'KNOW, JUST TO NURTURE IT--
--TO WATCH OUT FOR IT--
ARTHUR, THE WAY YOU'RE SPEAKING--
YOU'D THINK THE LEAGUE'S ALIVE.
THAT'S THE POINT, J'ONN--
THAT'S THE POINT, HAL--
"--THE BEST IDEAS ARE."

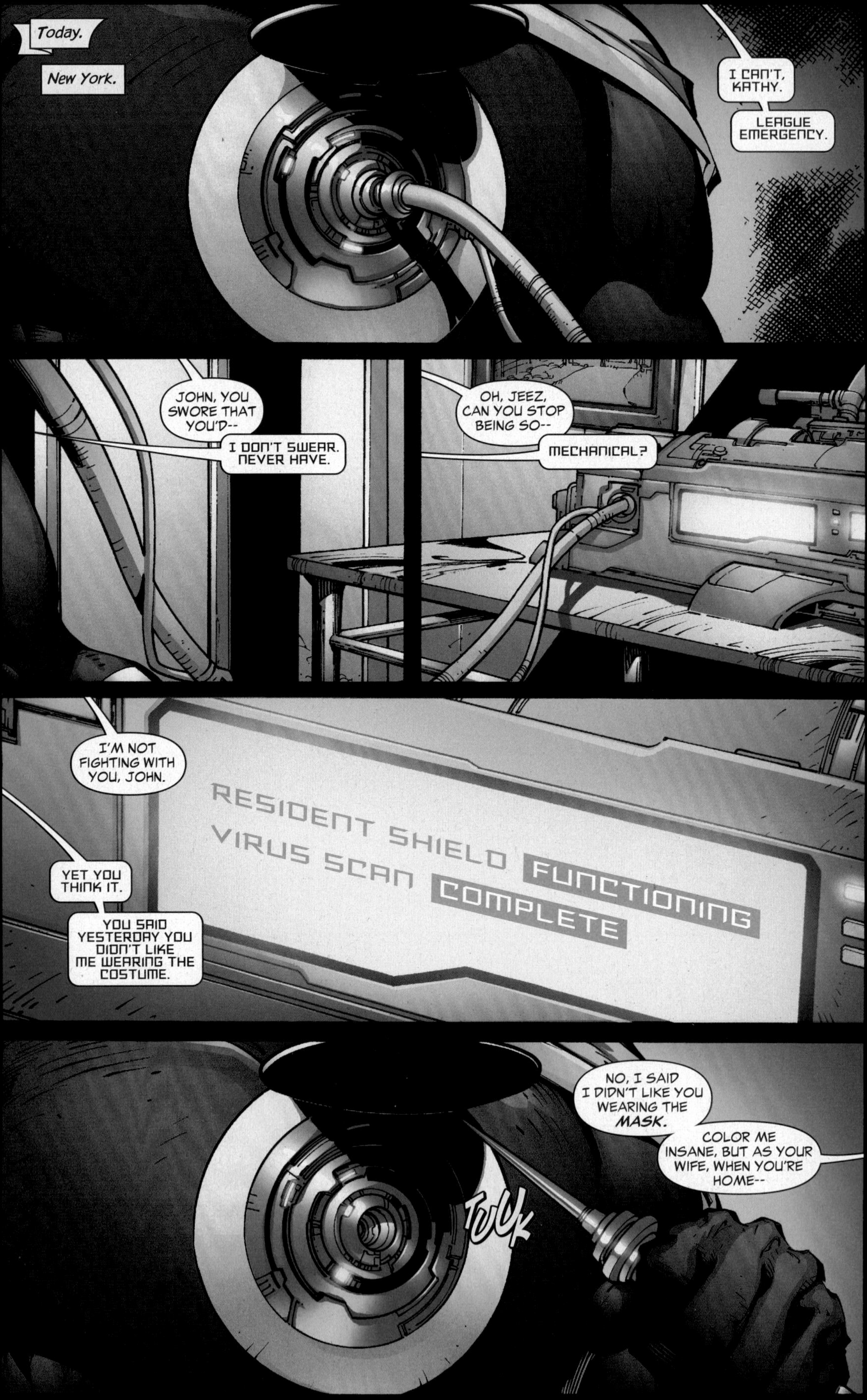
Today.
New York.
I CAN'T, KATHY.
LEAGUE EMERGENCY.
JOHN, YOU SWORE THAT YOU'D--
I DON'T SWEAR. NEVER HAVE.
OH, JEEZ, CAN YOU STOP BEING SO--
MECHANICAL?
I'M NOT FIGHTING WITH YOU, JOHN.
RESIDENT SHIELD FUNCTIONING
VIRUS SCAN COMPLETE
YET YOU THINK IT.
YOU SAID YESTERDAY YOU DIDN'T LIKE ME WEARING THE COSTUME.
NO, I SAID I DIDN'T LIKE YOU WEARING THE MASK.
COLOR ME INSANE, BUT AS YOUR WIFE, WHEN YOU'RE HOME--
TUCK

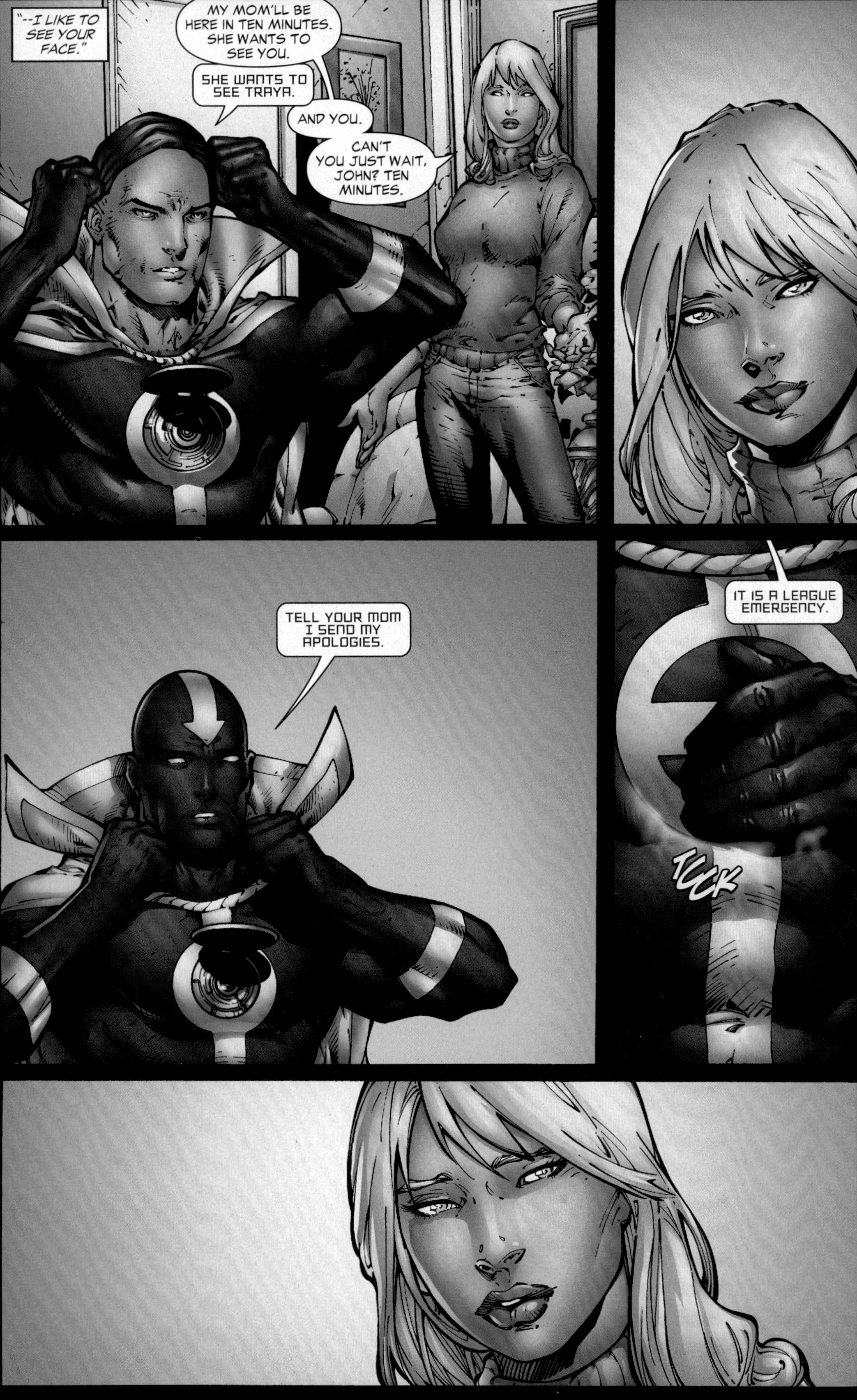
"--I LIKE TO SEE YOUR FACE."
MY MOM'LL BE HERE IN TEN MINUTES. SHE WANTS TO SEE YOU.
SHE WANTS TO SEE TRAYA.
AND YOU.
CAN'T YOU JUST WAIT, JOHN? TEN MINUTES.
TELL YOUR MOM I SEND MY APOLOGIES.
IT IS A LEAGUE EMERGENCY.
TUCK

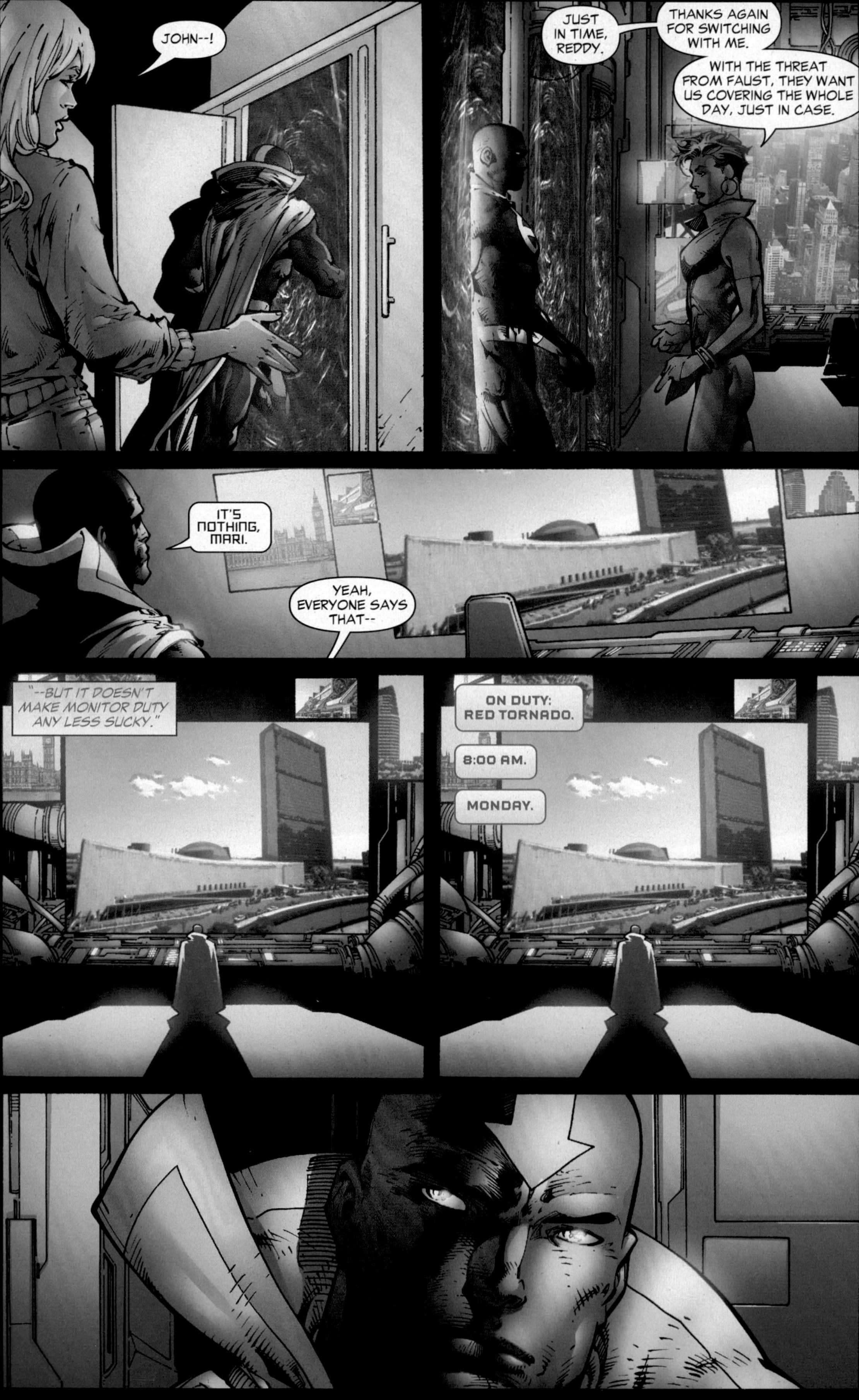
JOHN--!
JUST IN TIME, REDDY.
THANKS AGAIN FOR SWITCHING WITH ME.
WITH THE THREAT FROM FAUST, THEY WANT US COVERING THE WHOLE DAY, JUST IN CASE.
IT'S NOTHING, MARI.
YEAH, EVERYONE SAYS THAT--
"--BUT IT DOESN'T MAKE MONITOR DUTY ANY LESS SUCKY."
ON DUTY: RED TORNADO.
8:00 AM.
MONDAY.

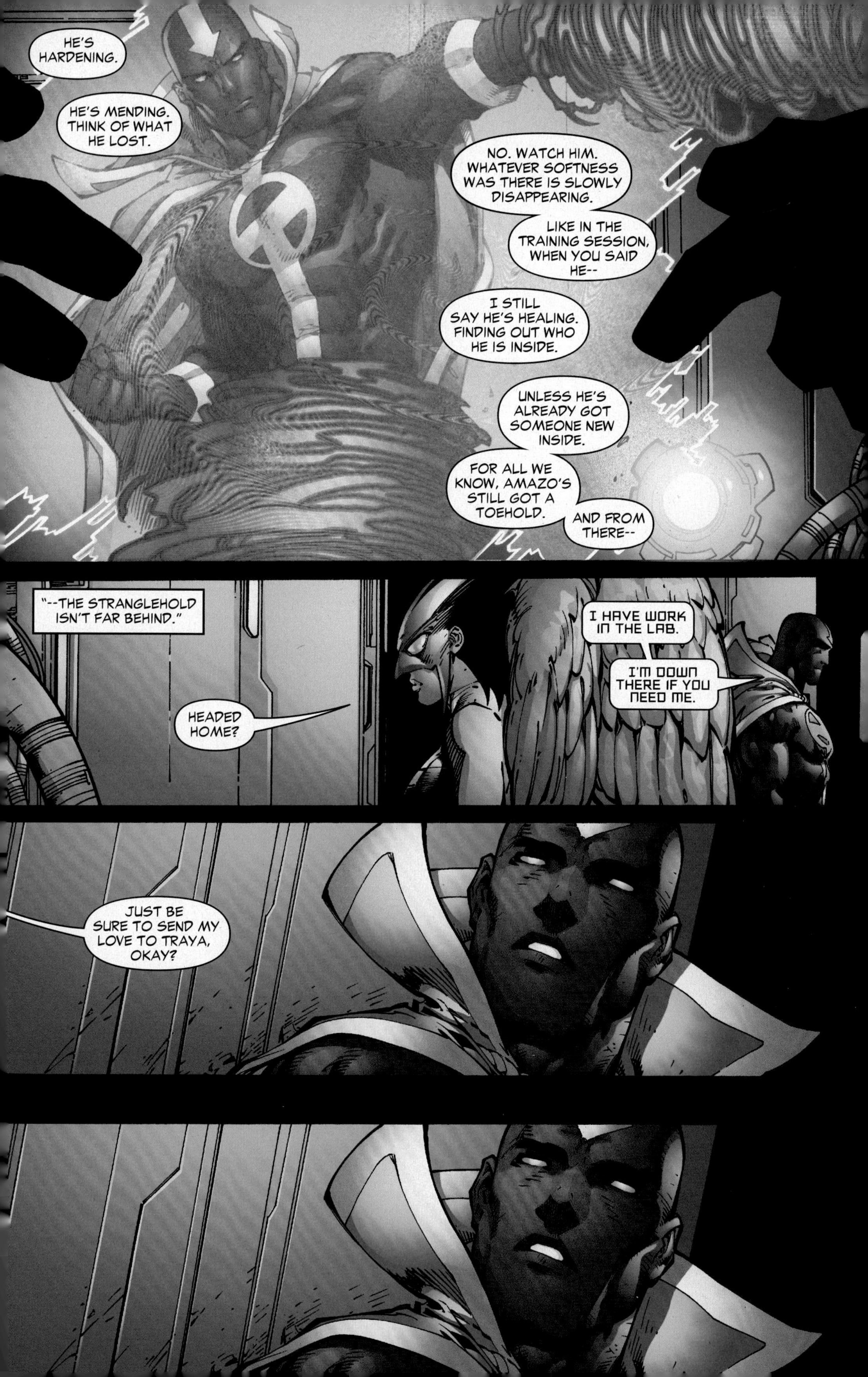
HE'S HARDENING.
HE'S MENDING. THINK OF WHAT HE LOST.
NO. WATCH HIM. WHATEVER SOFTNESS WAS THERE IS SLOWLY DISAPPEARING.
LIKE IN THE TRAINING SESSION, WHEN YOU SAID HE--
I STILL SAY HE'S HEALING. FINDING OUT WHO HE IS INSIDE.
UNLESS HE'S ALREADY GOT SOMEONE NEW INSIDE.
FOR ALL WE KNOW, AMAZO'S STILL GOT A TOEHOLD.
AND FROM THERE--
"--THE STRANGLEHOLD ISN'T FAR BEHIND."
HEADED HOME?
I HAVE WORK IN THE LAB.
I'M DOWN THERE IF YOU NEED ME.
JUST BE SURE TO SEND MY LOVE TO TRAYA, OKAY?

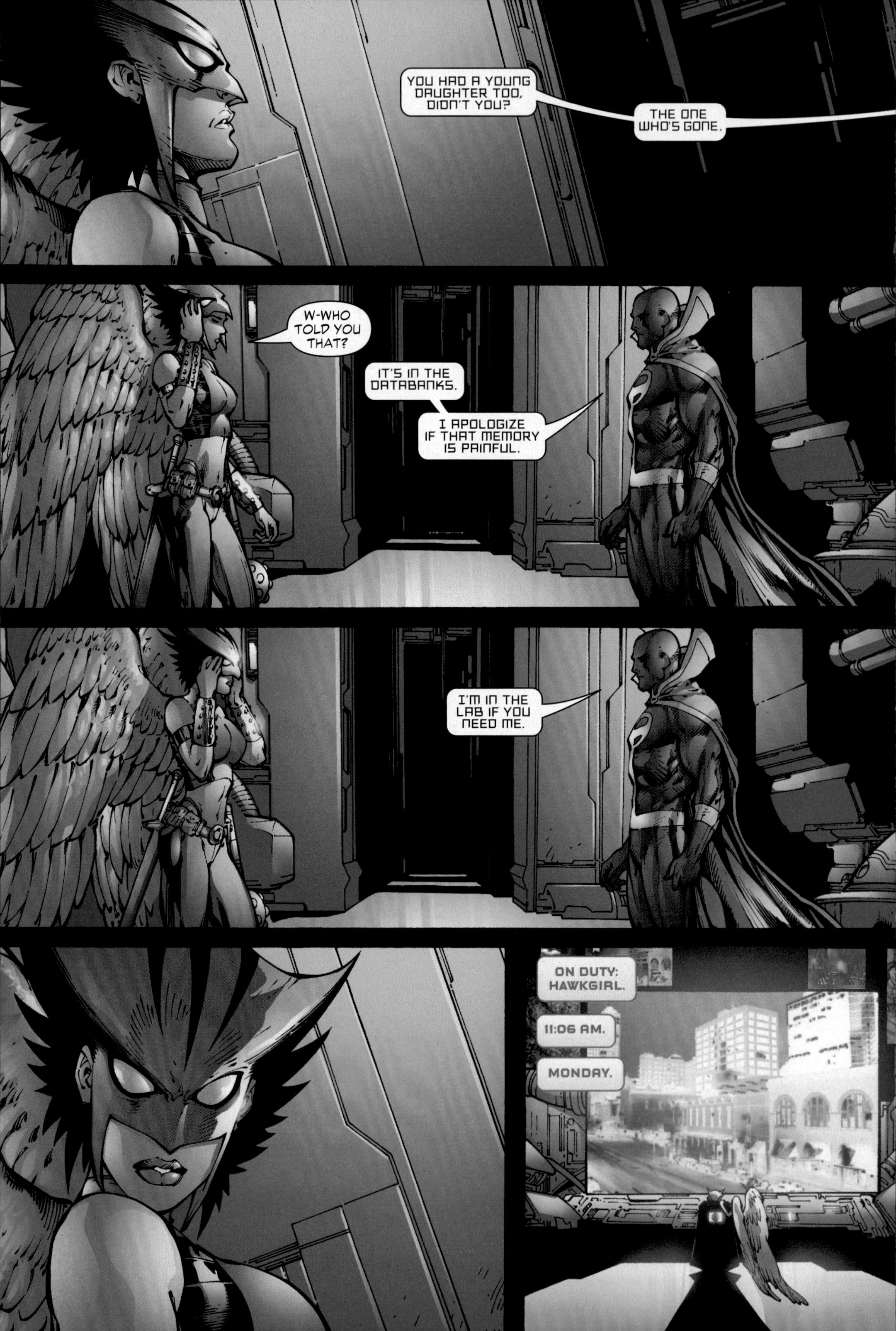
YOU HAD A YOUNG DAUGHTER TOO, DIDN'T YOU?
THE ONE WHO'S GONE.
W-WHO TOLD YOU THAT?
IT'S IN THE DATABANKS.
I APOLOGIZE IF THAT MEMORY IS PAINFUL.
I'M IN THE LAB IF YOU NEED ME.
ON DUTY: HAWKGIRL.
11:06 AM.
MONDAY.

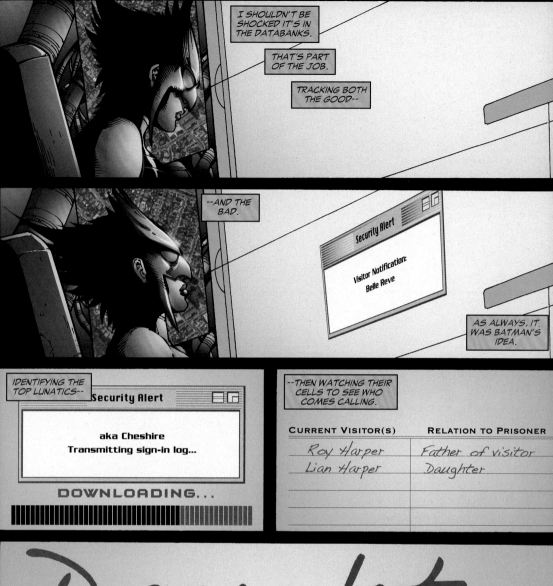

I SHOULDN'T BE SHOCKED IT'S IN THE DATABANKS.

THAT'S PART OF THE JOB.

TRACKING BOTH THE GOOD--

--AND THE BAD.

Security Alert

Visitor Notification: Belle Reve

AS ALWAYS, IT WAS BATMAN'S IDEA.

IDENTIFYING THE TOP LUNATICS--

Security Alert

aka Cheshire
Transmitting sign-in log...

DOWNLOADING...

--THEN WATCHING THEIR CELLS TO SEE WHO COMES CALLING.

CURRENT VISITOR(S)	RELATION TO PRISONER
Roy Harper	Father of visitor
Lian Harper	Daughter

Daughter

H-HE HAS A DAUGHTER?

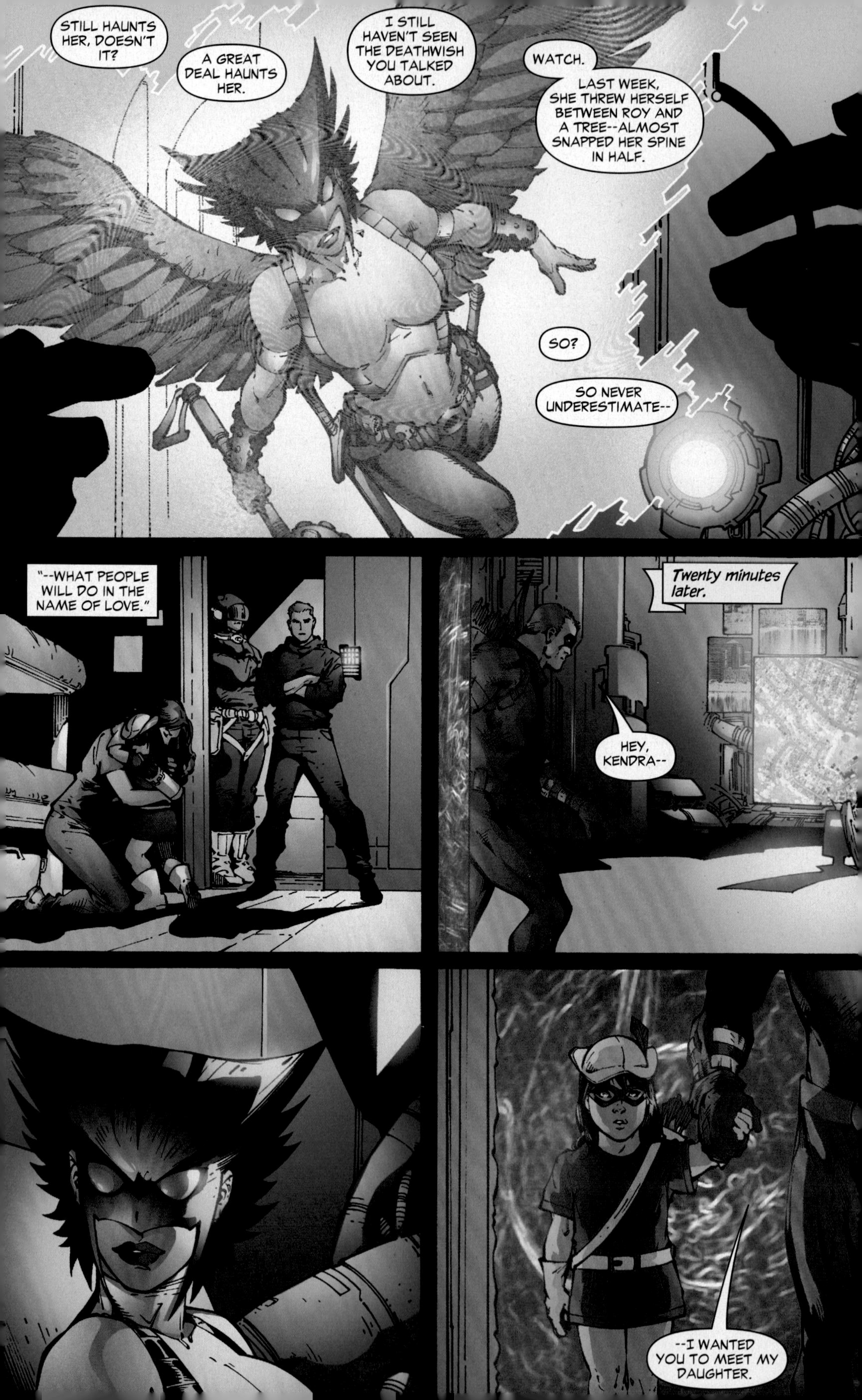
STILL HAUNTS HER, DOESN'T IT?
A GREAT DEAL HAUNTS HER.
I STILL HAVEN'T SEEN THE DEATHWISH YOU TALKED ABOUT.
WATCH.
LAST WEEK, SHE THREW HERSELF BETWEEN ROY AND A TREE--ALMOST SNAPPED HER SPINE IN HALF.
SO?
SO NEVER UNDERESTIMATE--
"--WHAT PEOPLE WILL DO IN THE NAME OF LOVE."
Twenty minutes later.
HEY, KENDRA--
--I WANTED YOU TO MEET MY DAUGHTER.

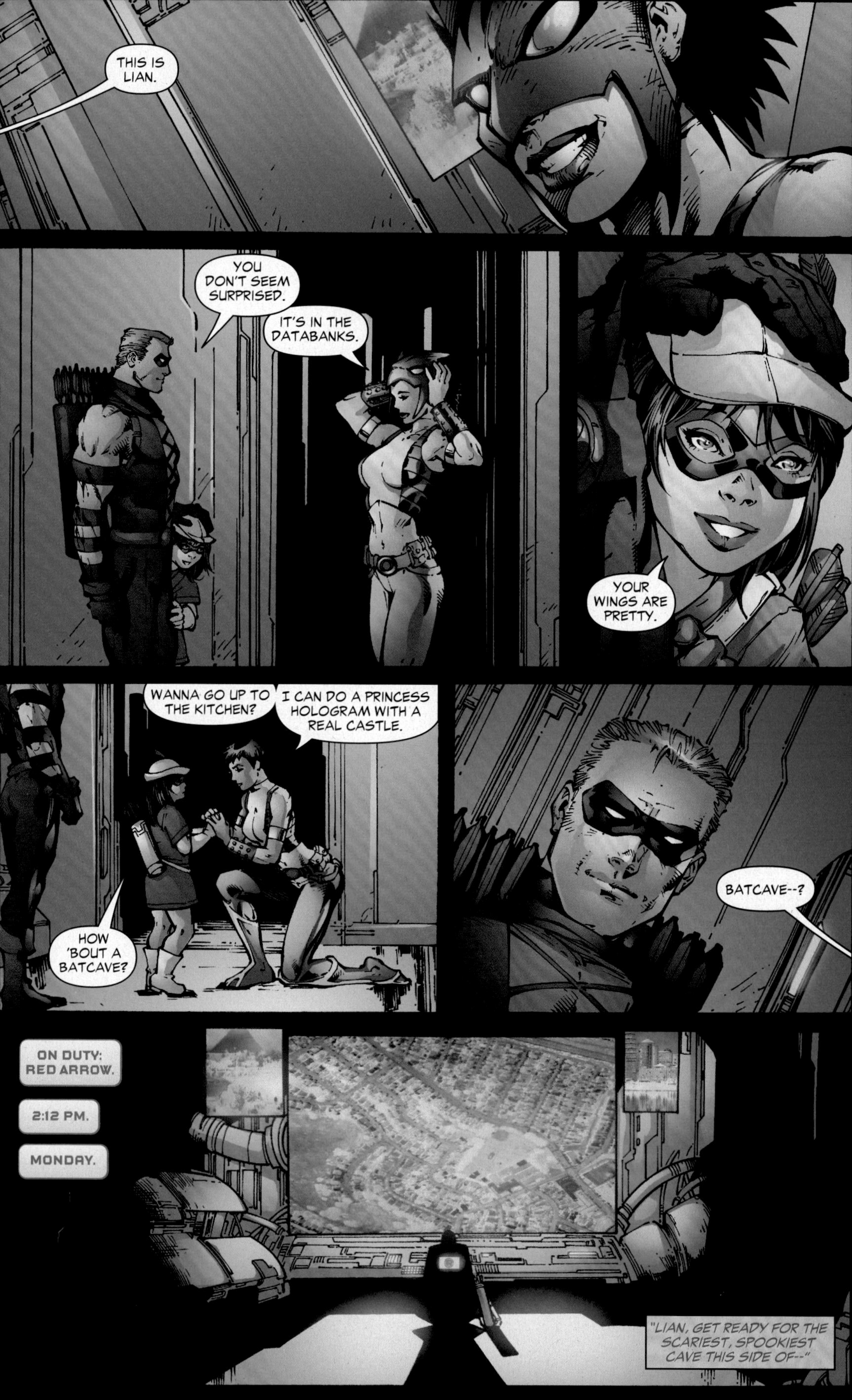
THIS IS LIAN.
YOU DON'T SEEM SURPRISED.
IT'S IN THE DATABANKS.
YOUR WINGS ARE PRETTY.
WANNA GO UP TO THE KITCHEN?
I CAN DO A PRINCESS HOLOGRAM WITH A REAL CASTLE.
HOW 'BOUT A BATCAVE?
BATCAVE--?
ON DUTY: RED ARROW.
2:12 PM.
MONDAY.
"LIAN, GET READY FOR THE SCARIEST, SPOOKIEST CAVE THIS SIDE OF--"

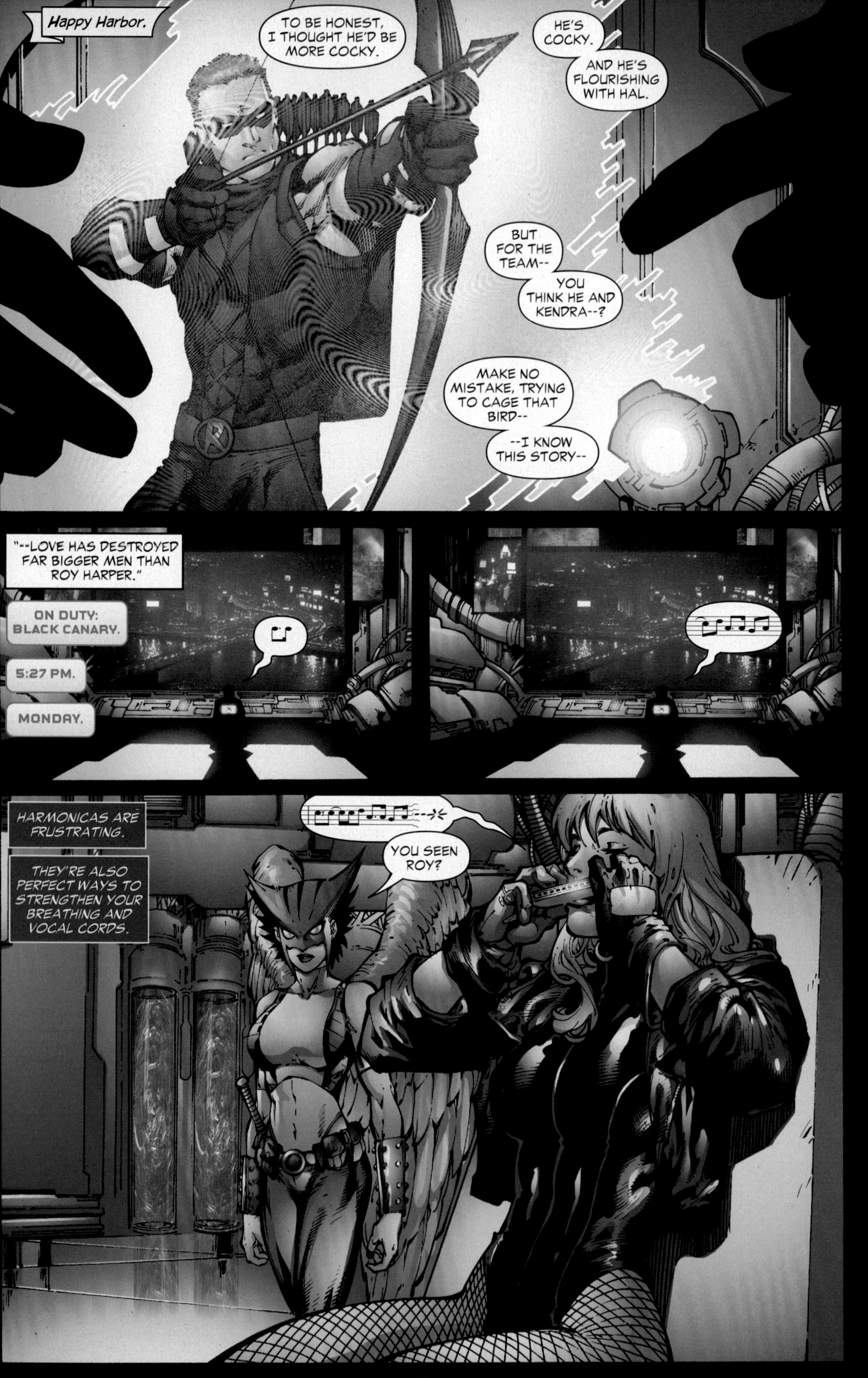
Happy Harbor.
TO BE HONEST, I THOUGHT HE'D BE MORE COCKY.
HE'S COCKY.
AND HE'S FLOURISHING WITH HAL.
BUT FOR THE TEAM--
YOU THINK HE AND KENDRA--?
MAKE NO MISTAKE, TRYING TO CAGE THAT BIRD--
--I KNOW THIS STORY--
"--LOVE HAS DESTROYED FAR BIGGER MEN THAN ROY HARPER."
ON DUTY: BLACK CANARY.
5:27 PM.
MONDAY.
HARMONICAS ARE FRUSTRATING.
THEY'RE ALSO PERFECT WAYS TO STRENGTHEN YOUR BREATHING AND VOCAL CORDS.
YOU SEEN ROY?

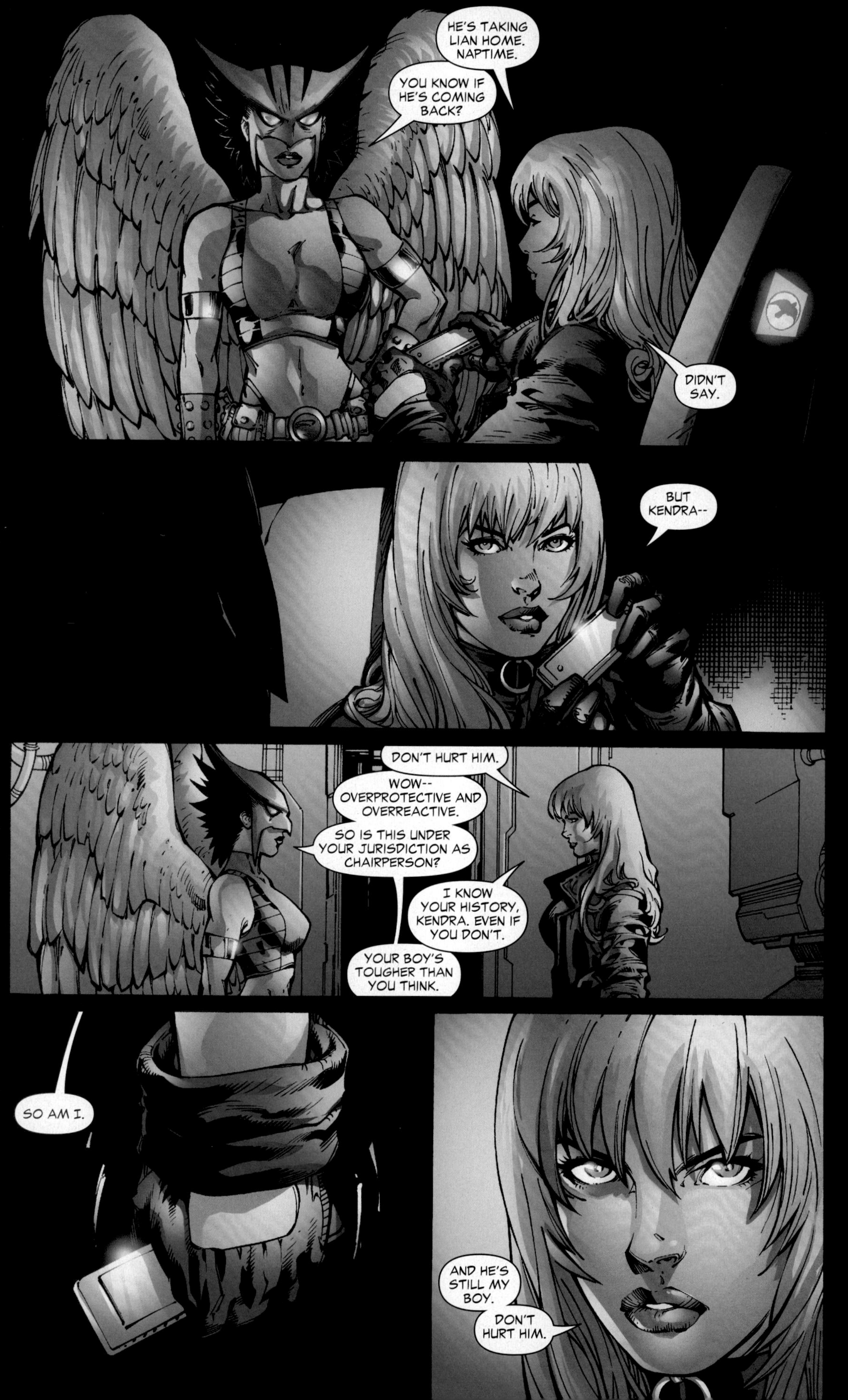
HE'S TAKING LIAN HOME. NAPTIME.
YOU KNOW IF HE'S COMING BACK?
DIDN'T SAY.
BUT KENDRA--
DON'T HURT HIM.
WOW-- OVERPROTECTIVE AND OVERREACTIVE.
SO IS THIS UNDER YOUR JURISDICTION AS CHAIRPERSON?
I KNOW YOUR HISTORY, KENDRA. EVEN IF YOU DON'T.
YOUR BOY'S TOUGHER THAN YOU THINK.
SO AM I.
AND HE'S STILL MY BOY.
DON'T HURT HIM.

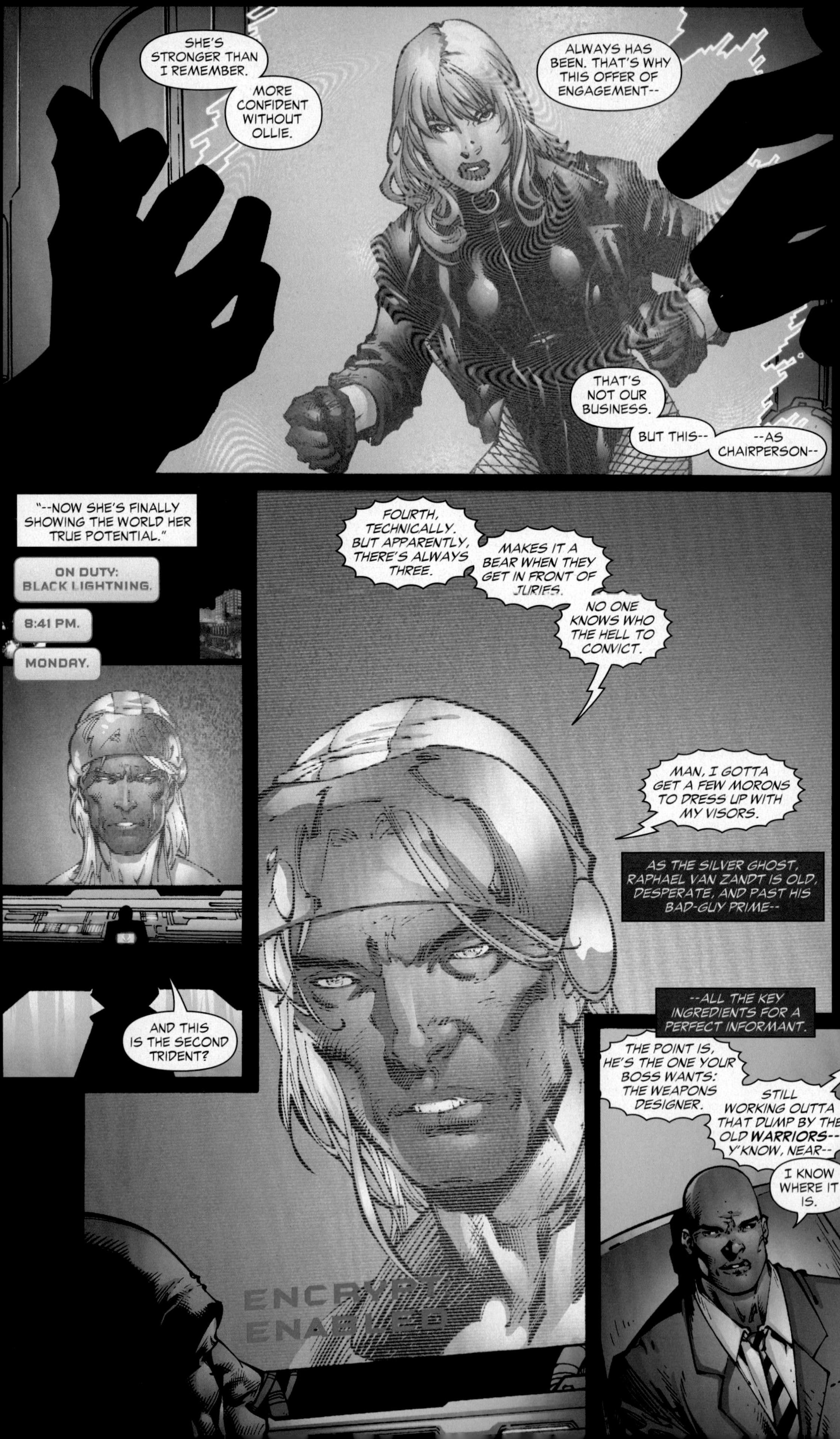
SHE'S STRONGER THAN I REMEMBER.
MORE CONFIDENT WITHOUT OLLIE.
ALWAYS HAS BEEN. THAT'S WHY THIS OFFER OF ENGAGEMENT--
THAT'S NOT OUR BUSINESS.
BUT THIS--
--AS CHAIRPERSON--
"--NOW SHE'S FINALLY SHOWING THE WORLD HER TRUE POTENTIAL."
ON DUTY: BLACK LIGHTNING.
8:41 PM.
MONDAY.
AND THIS IS THE SECOND TRIDENT?
FOURTH, TECHNICALLY. BUT APPARENTLY, THERE'S ALWAYS THREE.
MAKES IT A BEAR WHEN THEY GET IN FRONT OF JURIES.
NO ONE KNOWS WHO THE HELL TO CONVICT.
MAN, I GOTTA GET A FEW MORONS TO DRESS UP WITH MY VISORS.
AS THE SILVER GHOST, RAPHAEL VAN ZANDT IS OLD, DESPERATE, AND PAST HIS BAD-GUY PRIME--
--ALL THE KEY INGREDIENTS FOR A PERFECT INFORMANT.
THE POINT IS, HE'S THE ONE YOUR BOSS WANTS: THE WEAPONS DESIGNER.
STILL WORKING OUTTA THAT DUMP BY THE OLD WARRIORS-- Y'KNOW, NEAR--
I KNOW WHERE IT IS.
ENCRYPT ENABLED

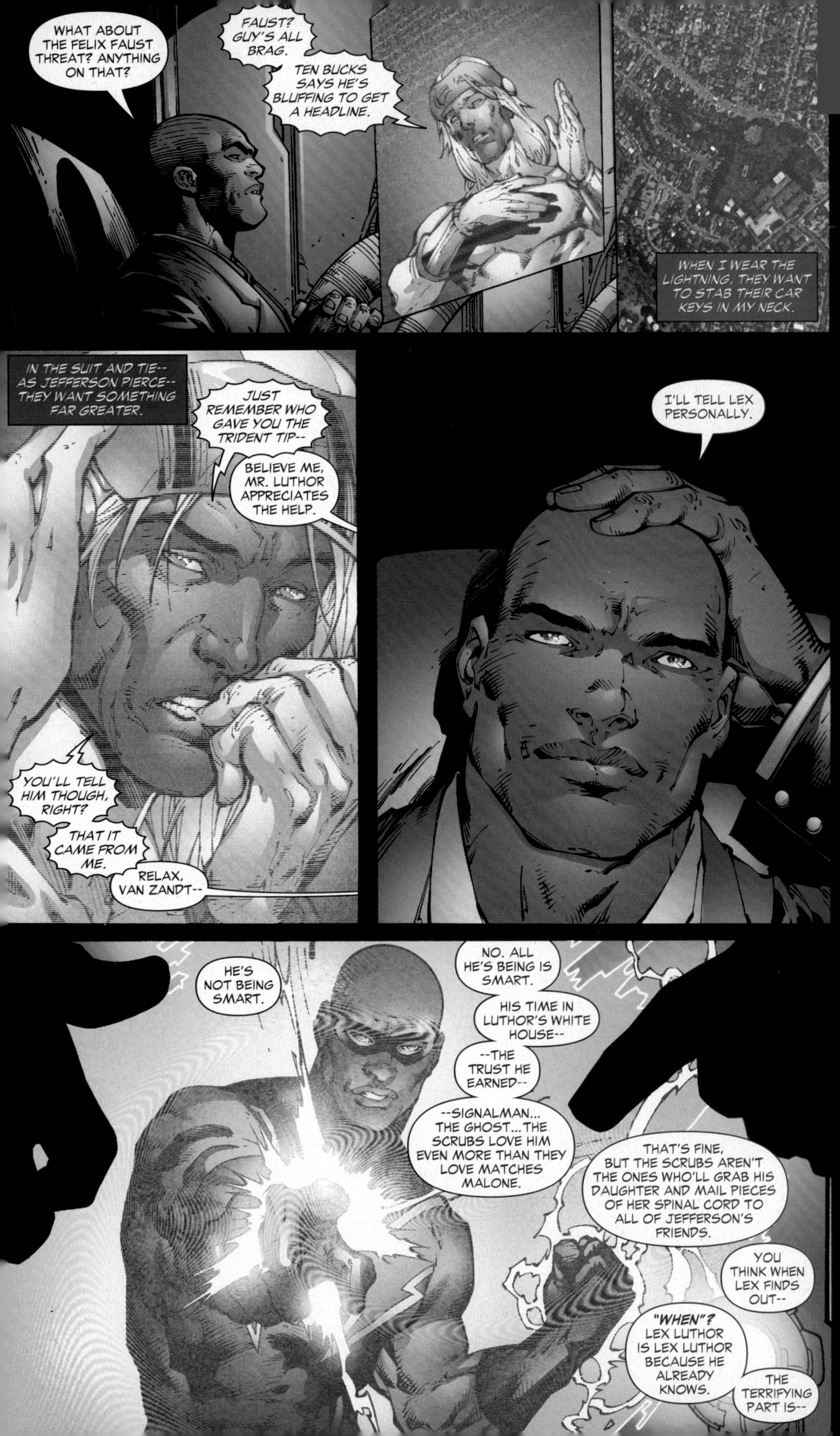
WHAT ABOUT THE FELIX FAUST THREAT? ANYTHING ON THAT?
FAUST? GUY'S ALL BRAG.
TEN BUCKS SAYS HE'S BLUFFING TO GET A HEADLINE.
WHEN I WEAR THE LIGHTNING, THEY WANT TO STAB THEIR CAR KEYS IN MY NECK.
IN THE SUIT AND TIE-- AS JEFFERSON PIERCE-- THEY WANT SOMETHING FAR GREATER.
JUST REMEMBER WHO GAVE YOU THE TRIDENT TIP--
BELIEVE ME, MR. LUTHOR APPRECIATES THE HELP.
YOU'LL TELL HIM THOUGH, RIGHT?
THAT IT CAME FROM ME.
RELAX, VAN ZANDT--
I'LL TELL LEX PERSONALLY.
HE'S NOT BEING SMART.
NO. ALL HE'S BEING IS SMART.
HIS TIME IN LUTHOR'S WHITE HOUSE--
--THE TRUST HE EARNED--
--SIGNALMAN... THE GHOST... THE SCRUBS LOVE HIM EVEN MORE THAN THEY LOVE MATCHES MALONE.
THAT'S FINE, BUT THE SCRUBS AREN'T THE ONES WHO'LL GRAB HIS DAUGHTER AND MAIL PIECES OF HER SPINAL CORD TO ALL OF JEFFERSON'S FRIENDS.
YOU THINK WHEN LEX FINDS OUT--
"WHEN"? LEX LUTHOR IS LEX LUTHOR BECAUSE HE ALREADY KNOWS.
THE TERRIFYING PART IS--

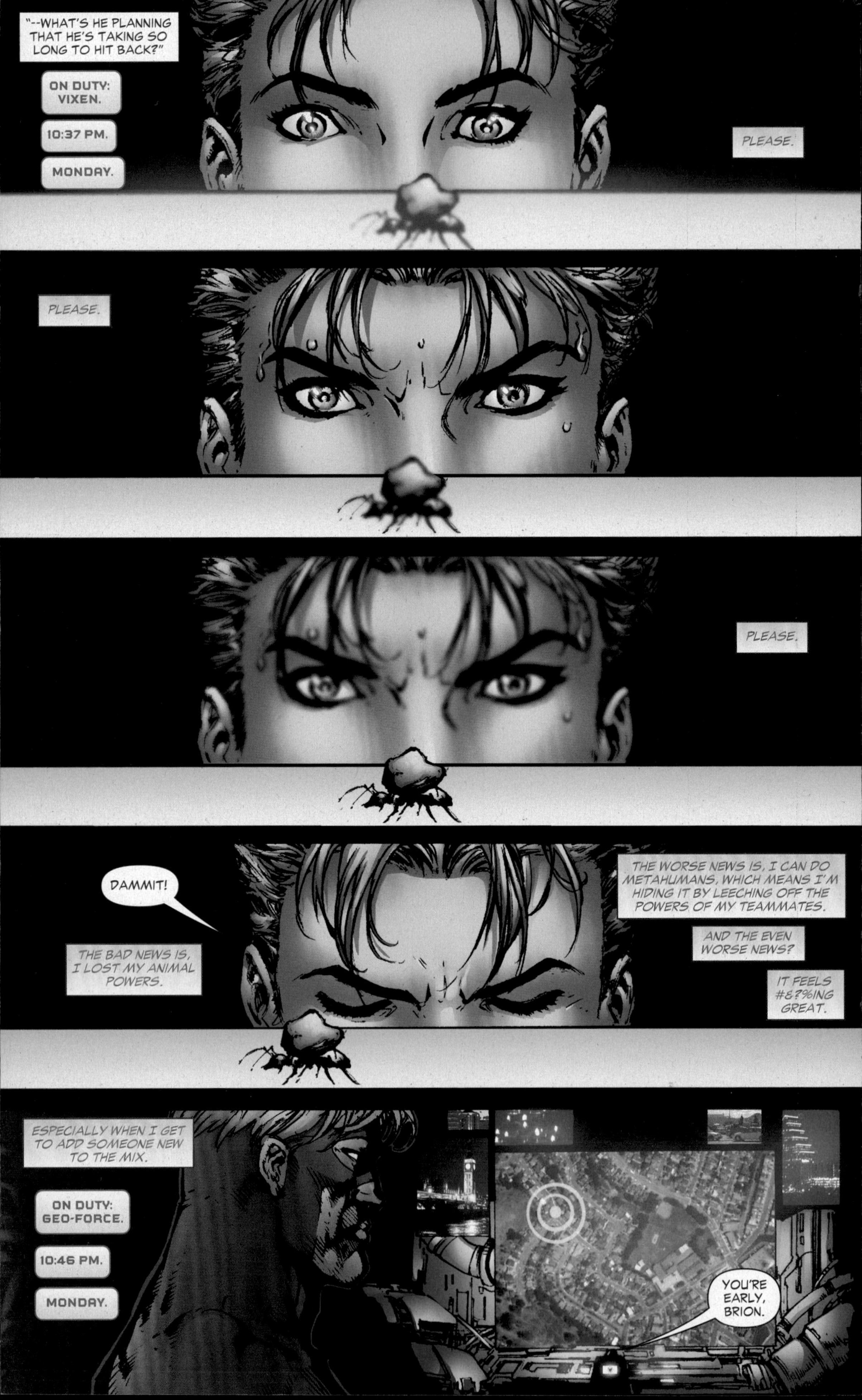
"--WHAT'S HE PLANNING THAT HE'S TAKING SO LONG TO HIT BACK?"
ON DUTY: VIXEN.
10:37 PM.
MONDAY.
PLEASE.
PLEASE.
PLEASE.
DAMMIT!
THE BAD NEWS IS, I LOST MY ANIMAL POWERS.
THE WORSE NEWS IS, I CAN DO METAHUMANS, WHICH MEANS I'M HIDING IT BY LEECHING OFF THE POWERS OF MY TEAMMATES.
AND THE EVEN WORSE NEWS?
IT FEELS #&?%ING GREAT.
ESPECIALLY WHEN I GET TO ADD SOMEONE NEW TO THE MIX.
ON DUTY: GEO-FORCE.
10:46 PM.
MONDAY.
YOU'RE EARLY, BRION.

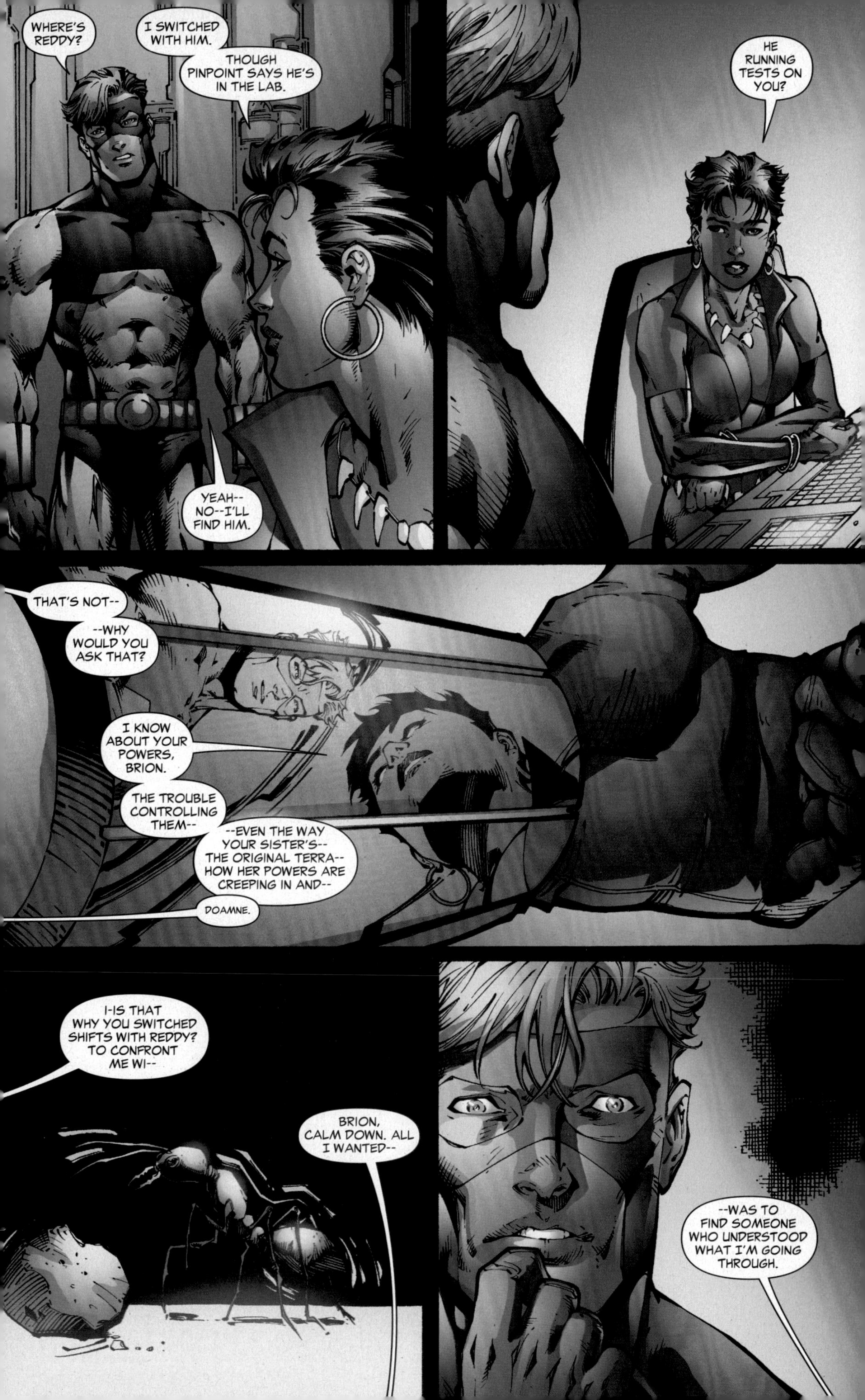
WHERE'S REDDY?
I SWITCHED WITH HIM.
THOUGH PINPOINT SAYS HE'S IN THE LAB.
YEAH-- NO--I'LL FIND HIM.
HE RUNNING TESTS ON YOU?
THAT'S NOT--
--WHY WOULD YOU ASK THAT?
I KNOW ABOUT YOUR POWERS, BRION.
THE TROUBLE CONTROLLING THEM--
--EVEN THE WAY YOUR SISTER'S-- THE ORIGINAL TERRA-- HOW HER POWERS ARE CREEPING IN AND--
DOAMNE.
I-IS THAT WHY YOU SWITCHED SHIFTS WITH REDDY? TO CONFRONT ME WI--
BRION, CALM DOWN. ALL I WANTED--
--WAS TO FIND SOMEONE WHO UNDERSTOOD WHAT I'M GOING THROUGH.

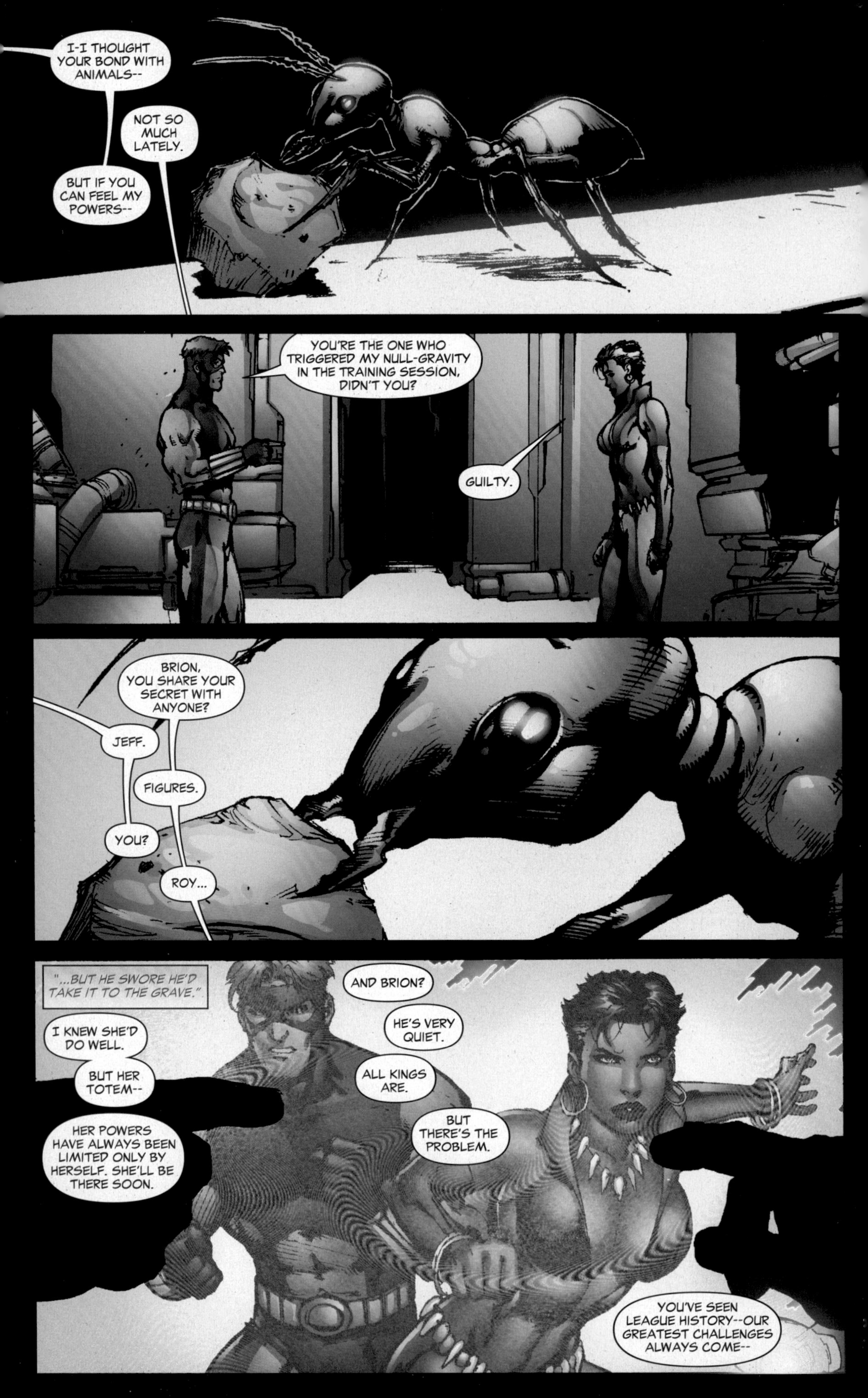
I-I THOUGHT YOUR BOND WITH ANIMALS--
NOT SO MUCH LATELY.
BUT IF YOU CAN FEEL MY POWERS--
YOU'RE THE ONE WHO TRIGGERED MY NULL-GRAVITY IN THE TRAINING SESSION, DIDN'T YOU?
GUILTY.
BRION, YOU SHARE YOUR SECRET WITH ANYONE?
JEFF.
FIGURES.
YOU?
ROY...
"...BUT HE SWORE HE'D TAKE IT TO THE GRAVE."
I KNEW SHE'D DO WELL.
BUT HER TOTEM--
HER POWERS HAVE ALWAYS BEEN LIMITED ONLY BY HERSELF. SHE'LL BE THERE SOON.
AND BRION?
HE'S VERY QUIET.
ALL KINGS ARE.
BUT THERE'S THE PROBLEM.
YOU'VE SEEN LEAGUE HISTORY--OUR GREATEST CHALLENGES ALWAYS COME--

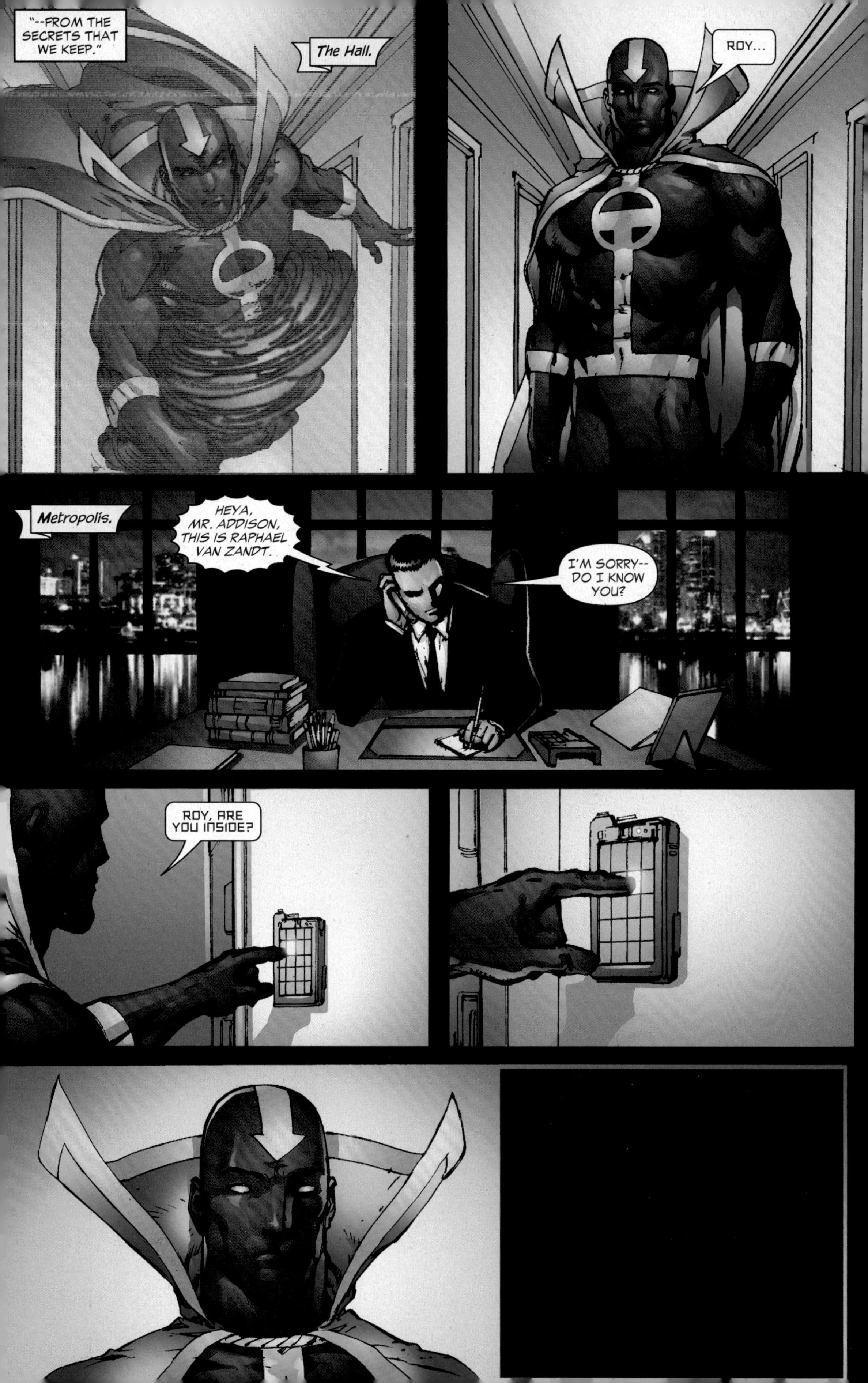
"--FROM THE SECRETS THAT WE KEEP."
The Hall.
ROY...
Metropolis.
HEYA, MR. ADDISON, THIS IS RAPHAEL VAN ZANDT.
I'M SORRY-- DO I KNOW YOU?
ROY, ARE YOU INSIDE?

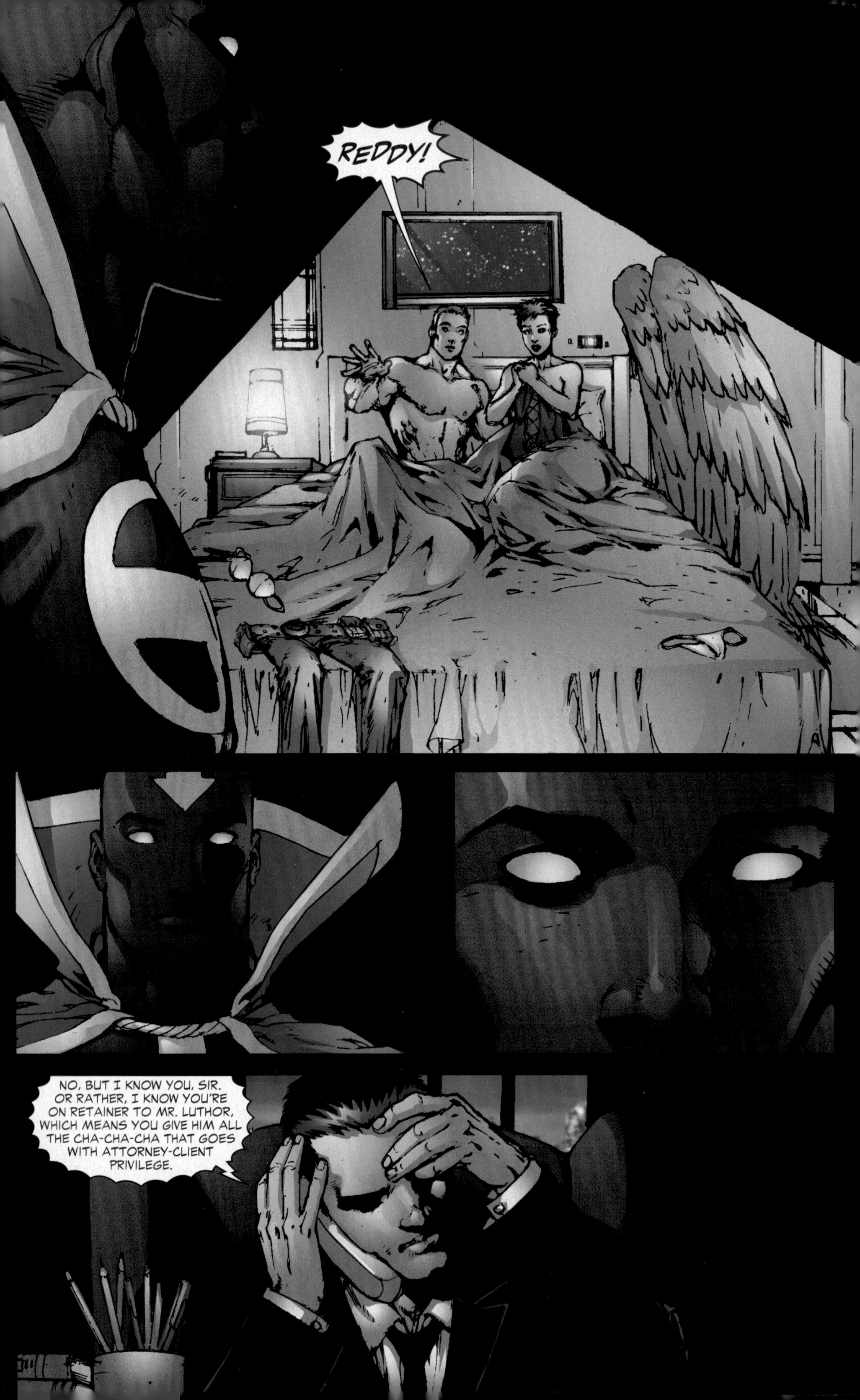
REDDY!
NO, BUT I KNOW YOU, SIR. OR RATHER, I KNOW YOU'RE ON RETAINER TO MR. LUTHOR, WHICH MEANS YOU GIVE HIM ALL THE CHA-CHA-CHA THAT GOES WITH ATTORNEY-CLIENT PRIVILEGE.

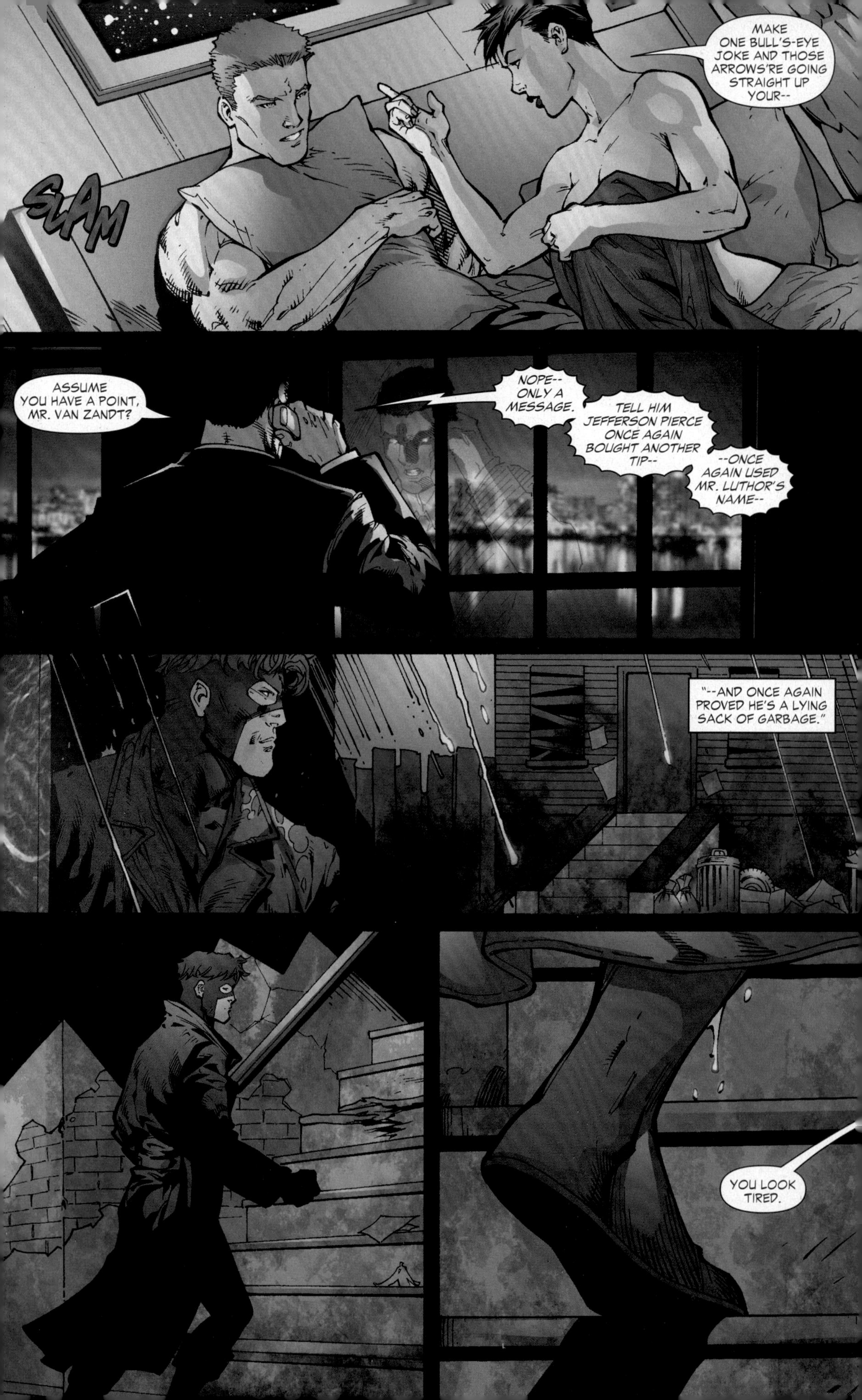

MAKE ONE BULL'S-EYE JOKE AND THOSE ARROWS'RE GOING STRAIGHT UP YOUR--
SLAM
ASSUME YOU HAVE A POINT, MR. VAN ZANDT?
NOPE-- ONLY A MESSAGE.
TELL HIM JEFFERSON PIERCE ONCE AGAIN BOUGHT ANOTHER TIP--
--ONCE AGAIN USED MR. LUTHOR'S NAME--
"--AND ONCE AGAIN PROVED HE'S A LYING SACK OF GARBAGE."
YOU LOOK TIRED.

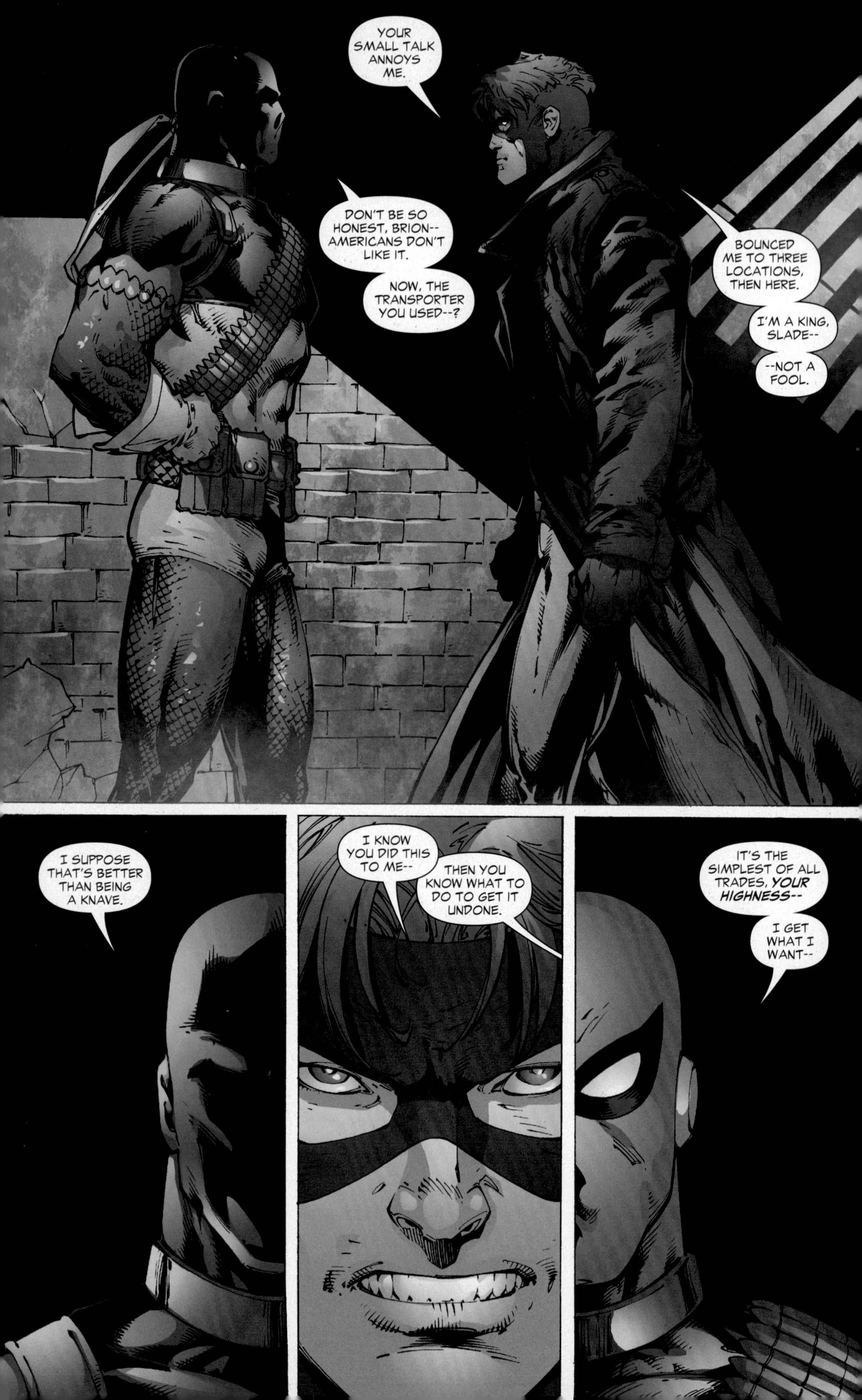
YOUR SMALL TALK ANNOYS ME.
DON'T BE SO HONEST, BRION-- AMERICANS DON'T LIKE IT.
NOW, THE TRANSPORTER YOU USED--?
BOUNCED ME TO THREE LOCATIONS, THEN HERE.
I'M A KING, SLADE--
--NOT A FOOL.
I SUPPOSE THAT'S BETTER THAN BEING A KNAVE.
I KNOW YOU DID THIS TO ME--
THEN YOU KNOW WHAT TO DO TO GET IT UNDONE.
IT'S THE SIMPLEST OF ALL TRADES, ***YOUR HIGHNESS***--
I GET WHAT I WANT--

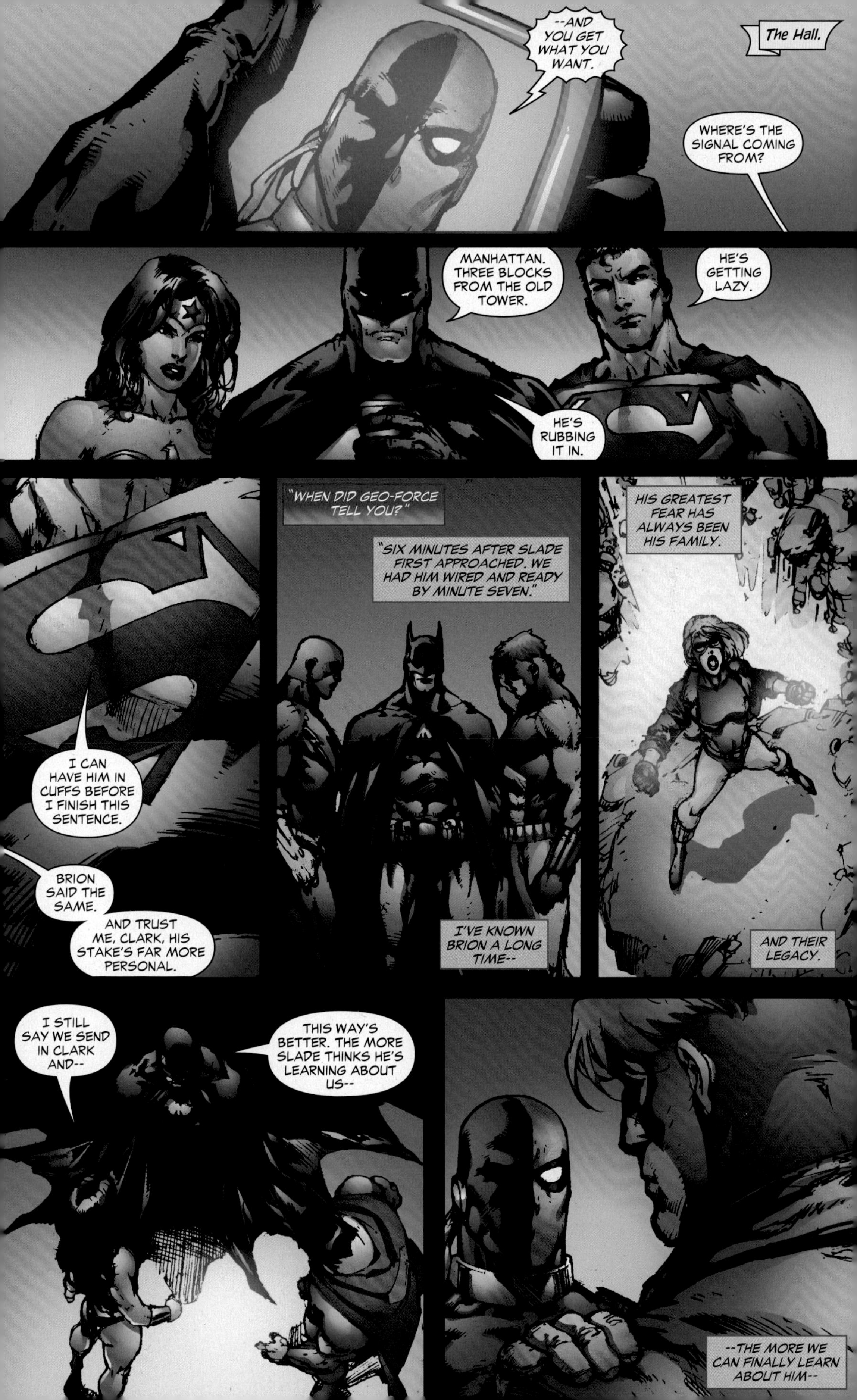
--AND YOU GET WHAT YOU WANT.
The Hall.
WHERE'S THE SIGNAL COMING FROM?
MANHATTAN. THREE BLOCKS FROM THE OLD TOWER.
HE'S GETTING LAZY.
HE'S RUBBING IT IN.
I CAN HAVE HIM IN CUFFS BEFORE I FINISH THIS SENTENCE.
BRION SAID THE SAME.
AND TRUST ME, CLARK, HIS STAKE'S FAR MORE PERSONAL.
"WHEN DID GEO-FORCE TELL YOU?"
"SIX MINUTES AFTER SLADE FIRST APPROACHED. WE HAD HIM WIRED AND READY BY MINUTE SEVEN."
I'VE KNOWN BRION A LONG TIME--
HIS GREATEST FEAR HAS ALWAYS BEEN HIS FAMILY.
AND THEIR LEGACY.
I STILL SAY WE SEND IN CLARK AND--
THIS WAY'S BETTER. THE MORE SLADE THINKS HE'S LEARNING ABOUT US--
--THE MORE WE CAN FINALLY LEARN ABOUT HIM--

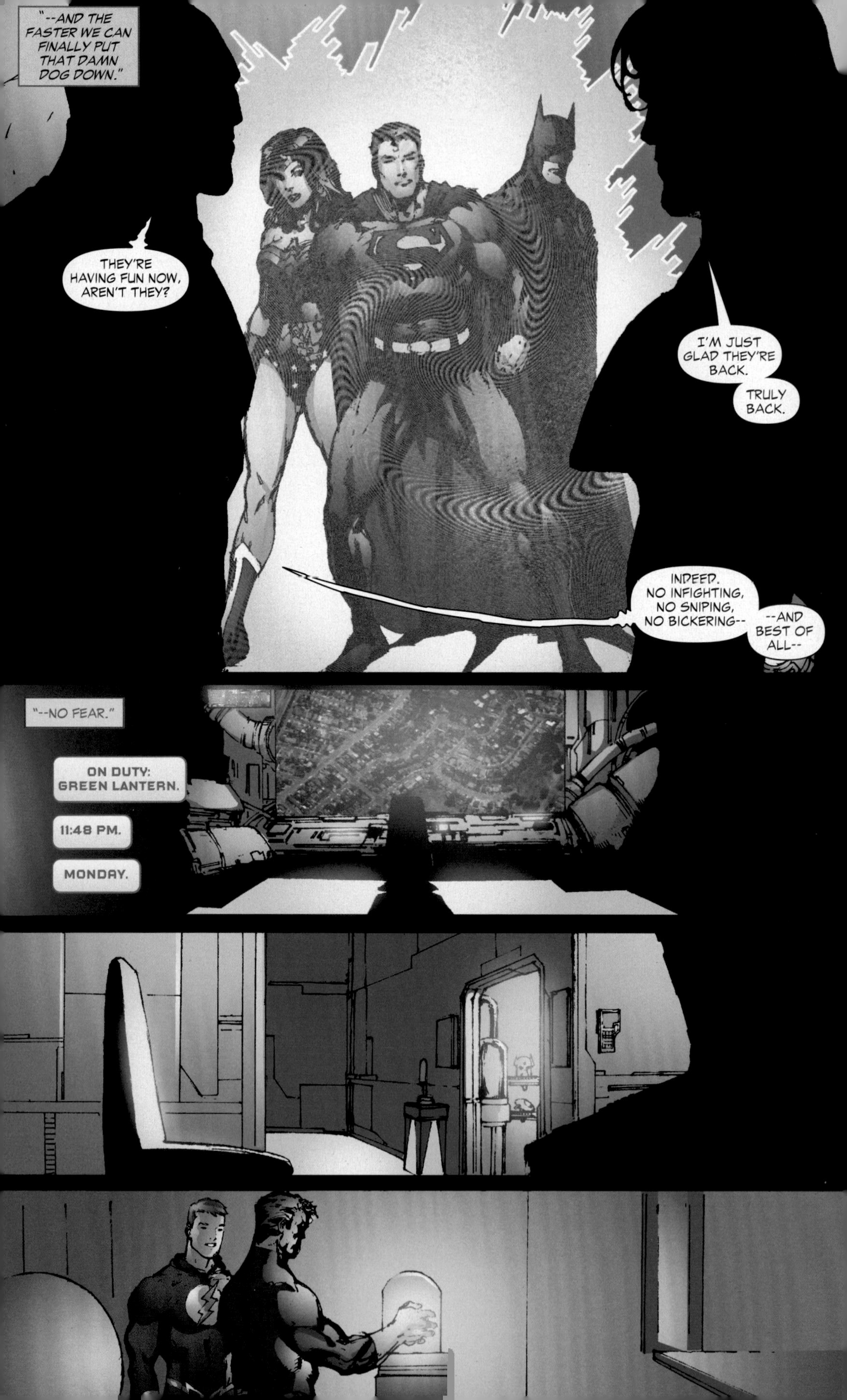
"--AND THE FASTER WE CAN FINALLY PUT THAT DAMN DOG DOWN."
THEY'RE HAVING FUN NOW, AREN'T THEY?
I'M JUST GLAD THEY'RE BACK.
TRULY BACK.
INDEED. NO INFIGHTING, NO SNIPING, NO BICKERING--
--AND BEST OF ALL--
"--NO FEAR."
ON DUTY: GREEN LANTERN.
11:48 PM.
MONDAY.

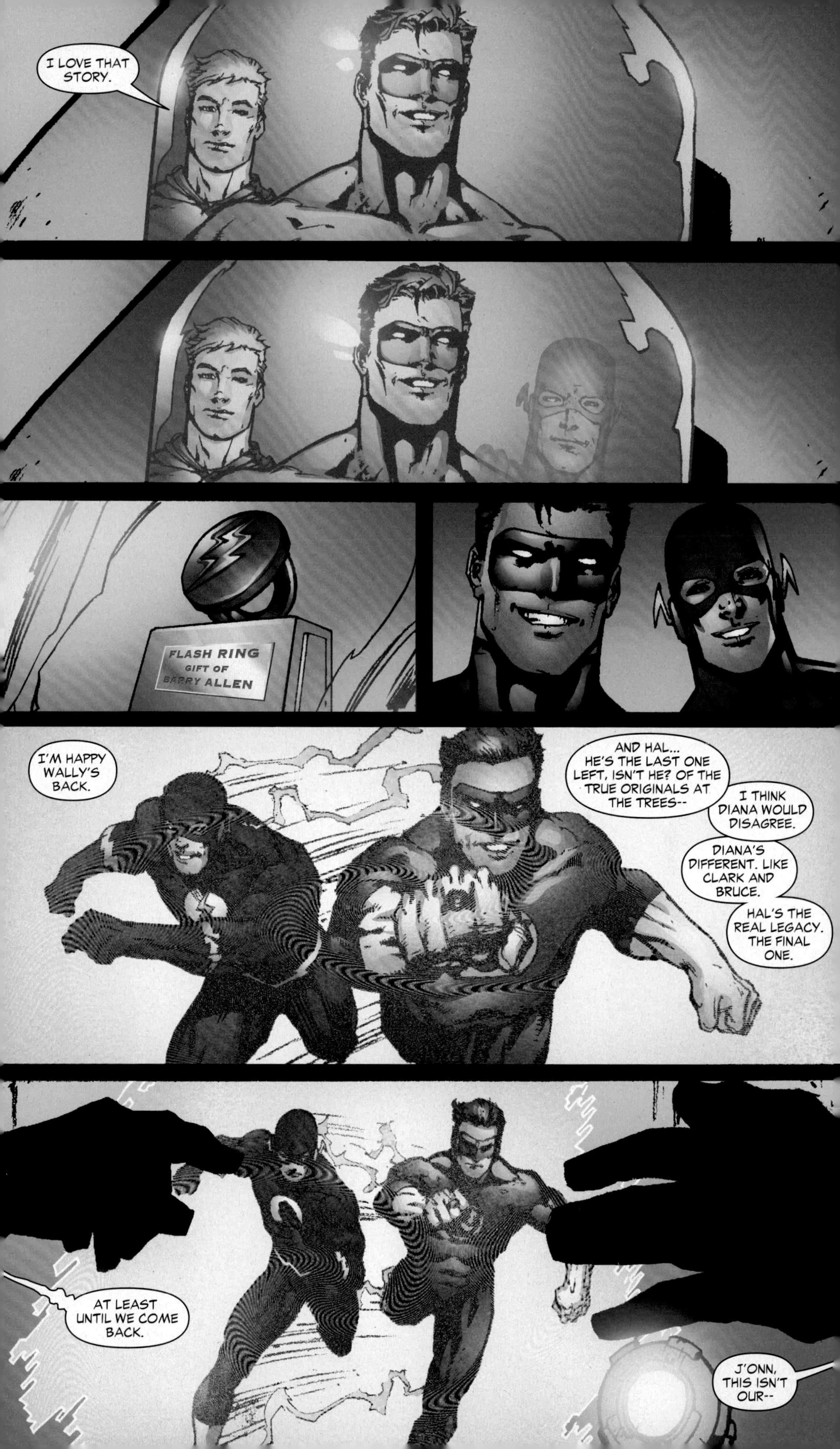
I LOVE THAT STORY.
FLASH RING GIFT OF BARRY ALLEN
I'M HAPPY WALLY'S BACK.
AND HAL... HE'S THE LAST ONE LEFT, ISN'T HE? OF THE TRUE ORIGINALS AT THE TREES--
I THINK DIANA WOULD DISAGREE.
DIANA'S DIFFERENT. LIKE CLARK AND BRUCE.
HAL'S THE REAL LEGACY. THE FINAL ONE.
AT LEAST UNTIL WE COME BACK.
J'ONN, THIS ISN'T OUR--

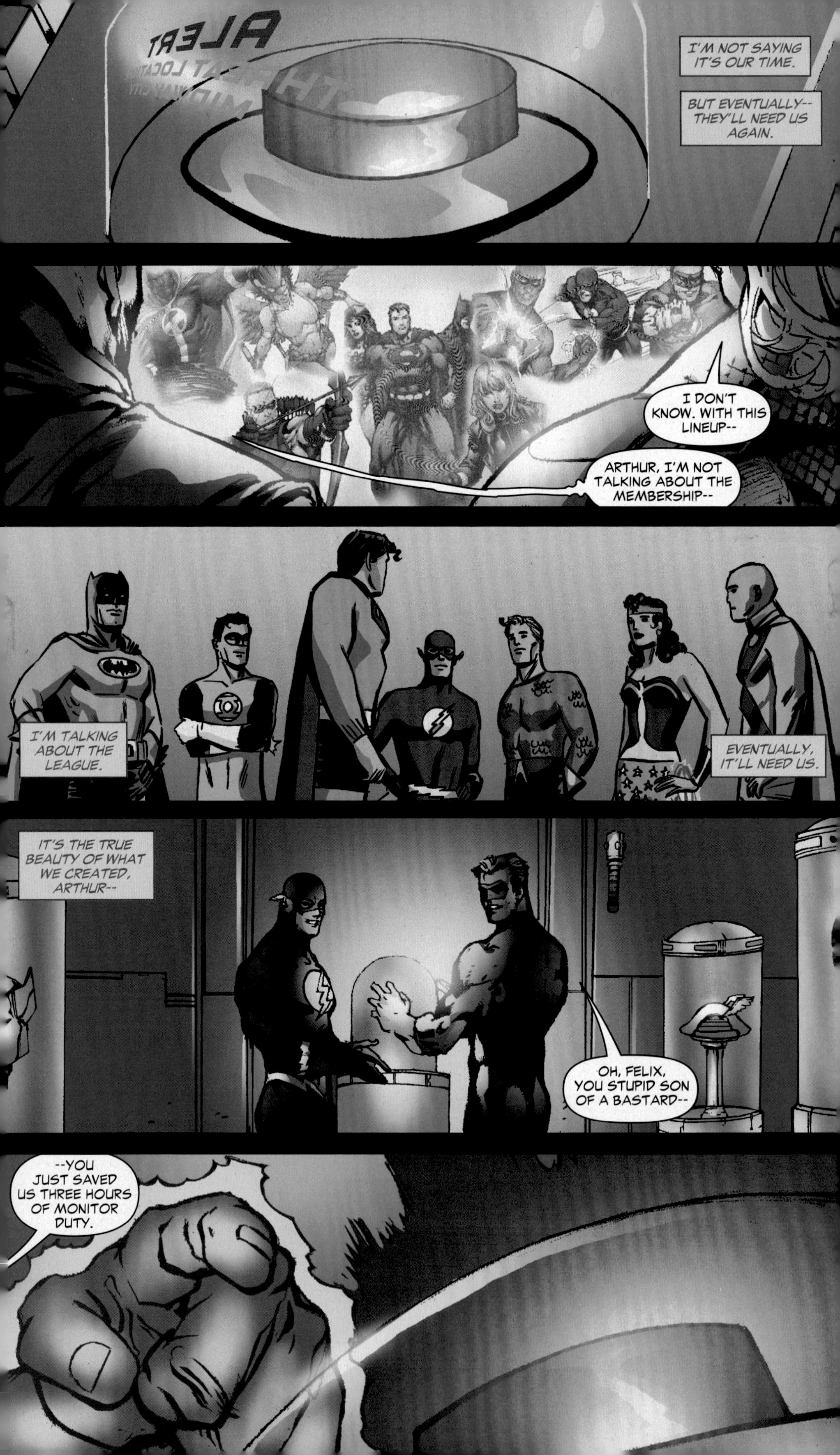
I'M NOT SAYING IT'S OUR TIME.
BUT EVENTUALLY-- THEY'LL NEED US AGAIN.
I DON'T KNOW. WITH THIS LINEUP--
ARTHUR, I'M NOT TALKING ABOUT THE MEMBERSHIP--
I'M TALKING ABOUT THE LEAGUE.
EVENTUALLY, IT'LL NEED US.
IT'S THE TRUE BEAUTY OF WHAT WE CREATED, ARTHUR--
OH, FELIX, YOU STUPID SON OF A BASTARD--
--YOU JUST SAVED US THREE HOURS OF MONITOR DUTY.

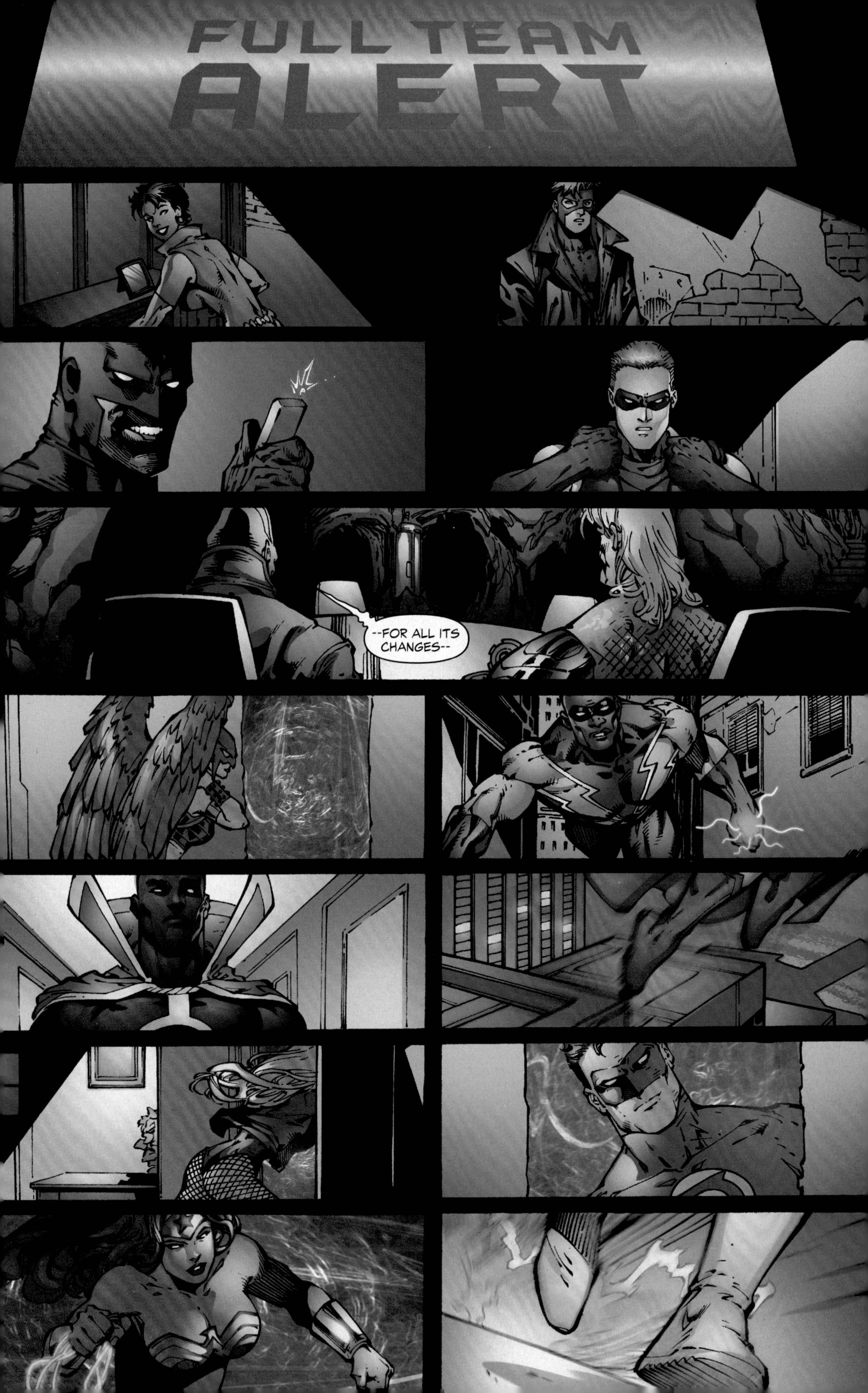
FULL TEAM ALERT
--FOR ALL ITS CHANGES--

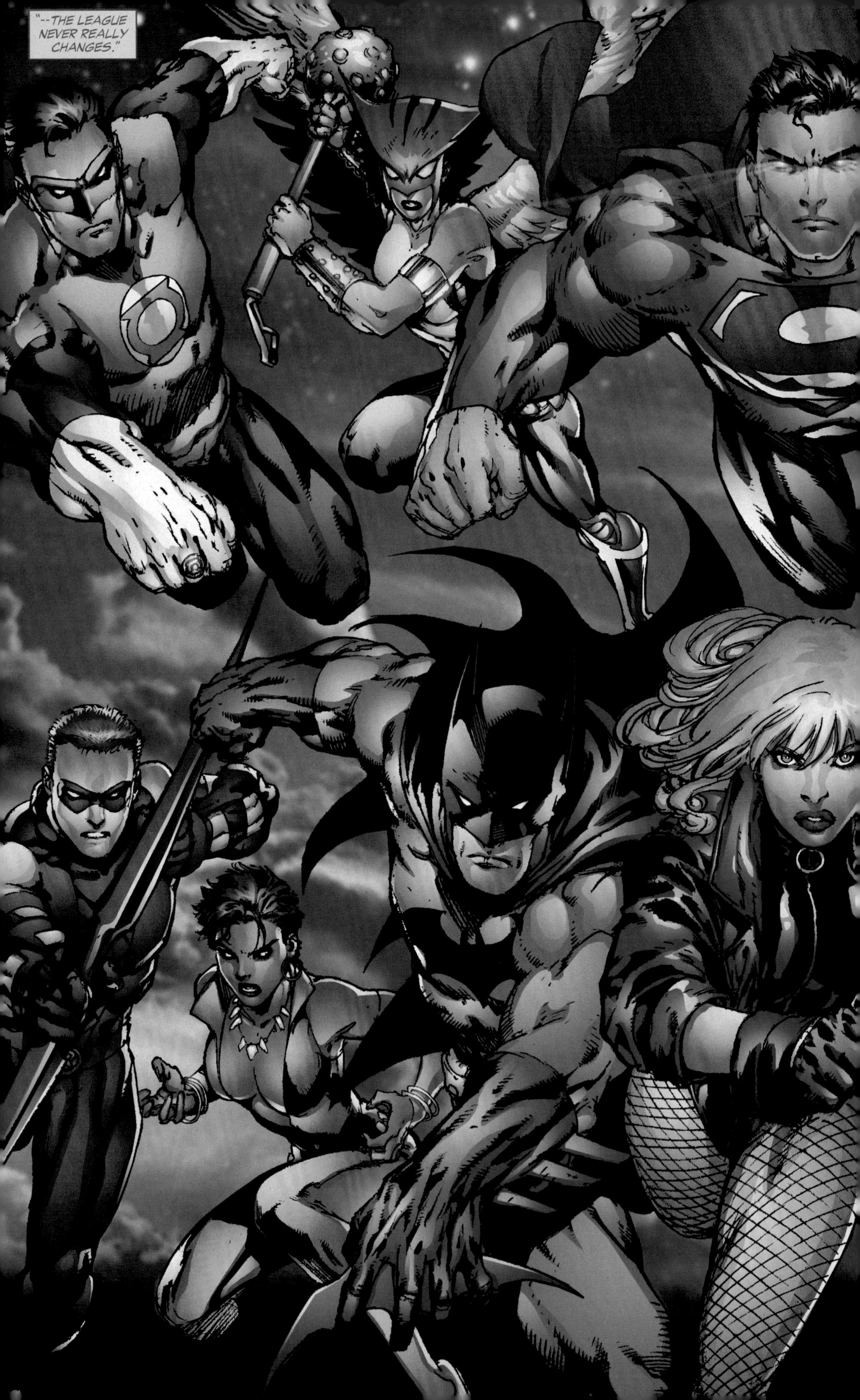
"--THE LEAGUE NEVER REALLY CHANGES."

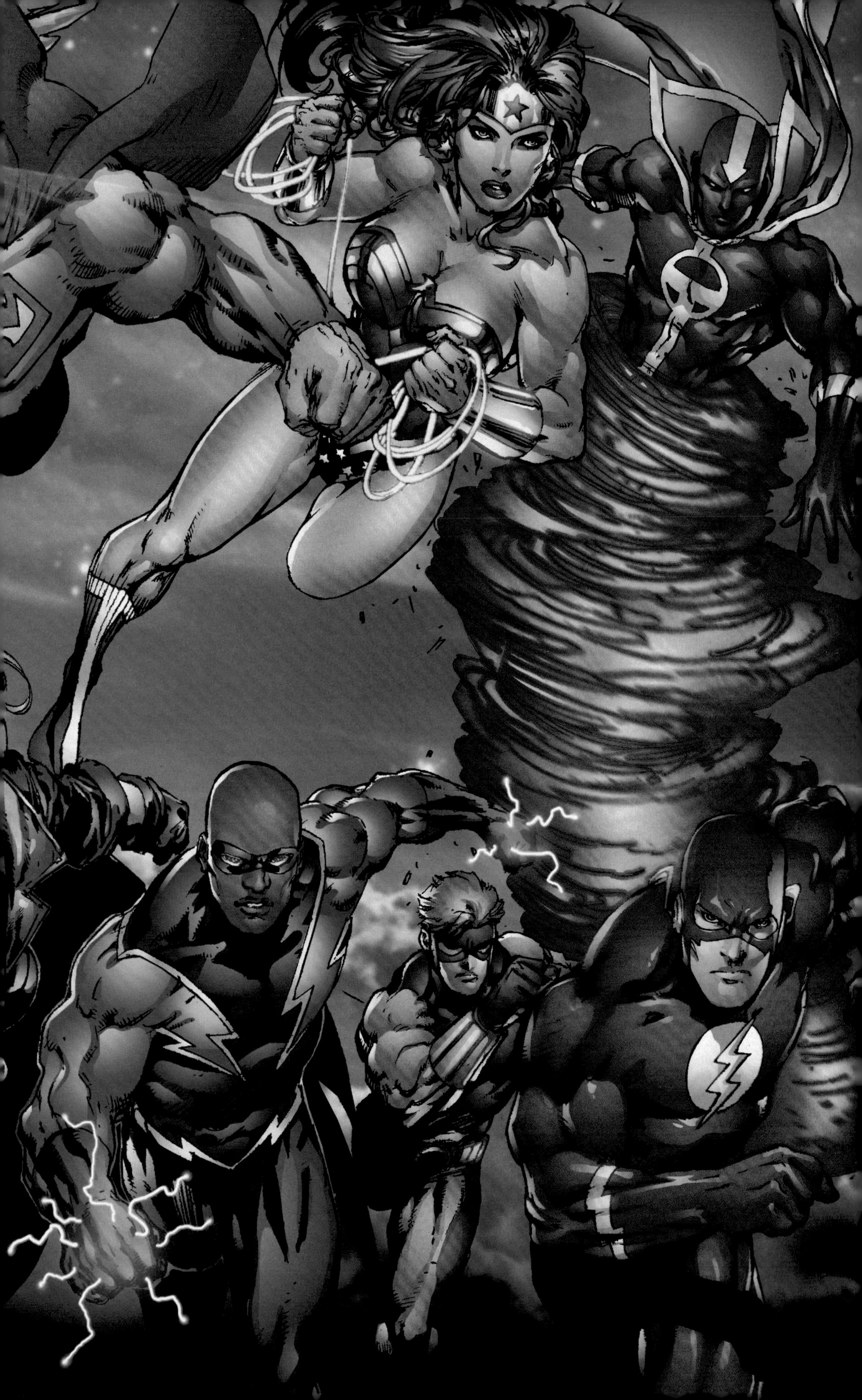

JUSTICE LEAGUE OF AMERICA

And now, at the end, the comic that launched the rebirth of the JUSTICE LEAGUE OF AMERICA

Brad Meltzer
Writer

Eric Wight
Dick Giordano
Tony Harris
George Pérez
J.H. Williams III
Luke McDonnell and Paul Neary
Gene Ha
Rags Morales
Ethan Van Sciver
Kevin Maguire
Adam Kubert
Dan Jurgens and Kevin Nowlan
Jim Lee
Howard Porter and Dexter Vines
Andy Kubert and Jesse Delperdang
Phil Jimenez and Andy Lanning

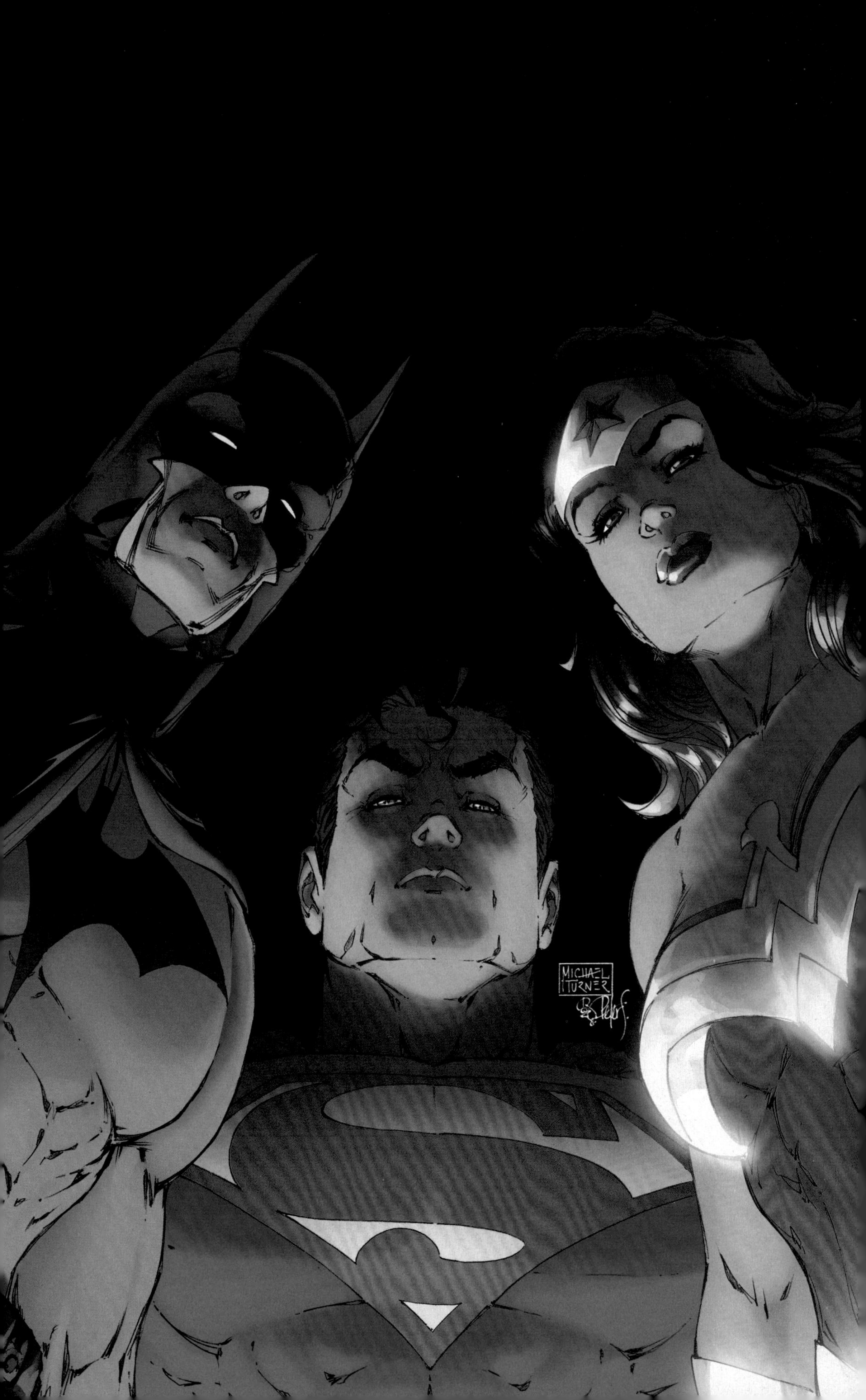
MICHAEL TURNER

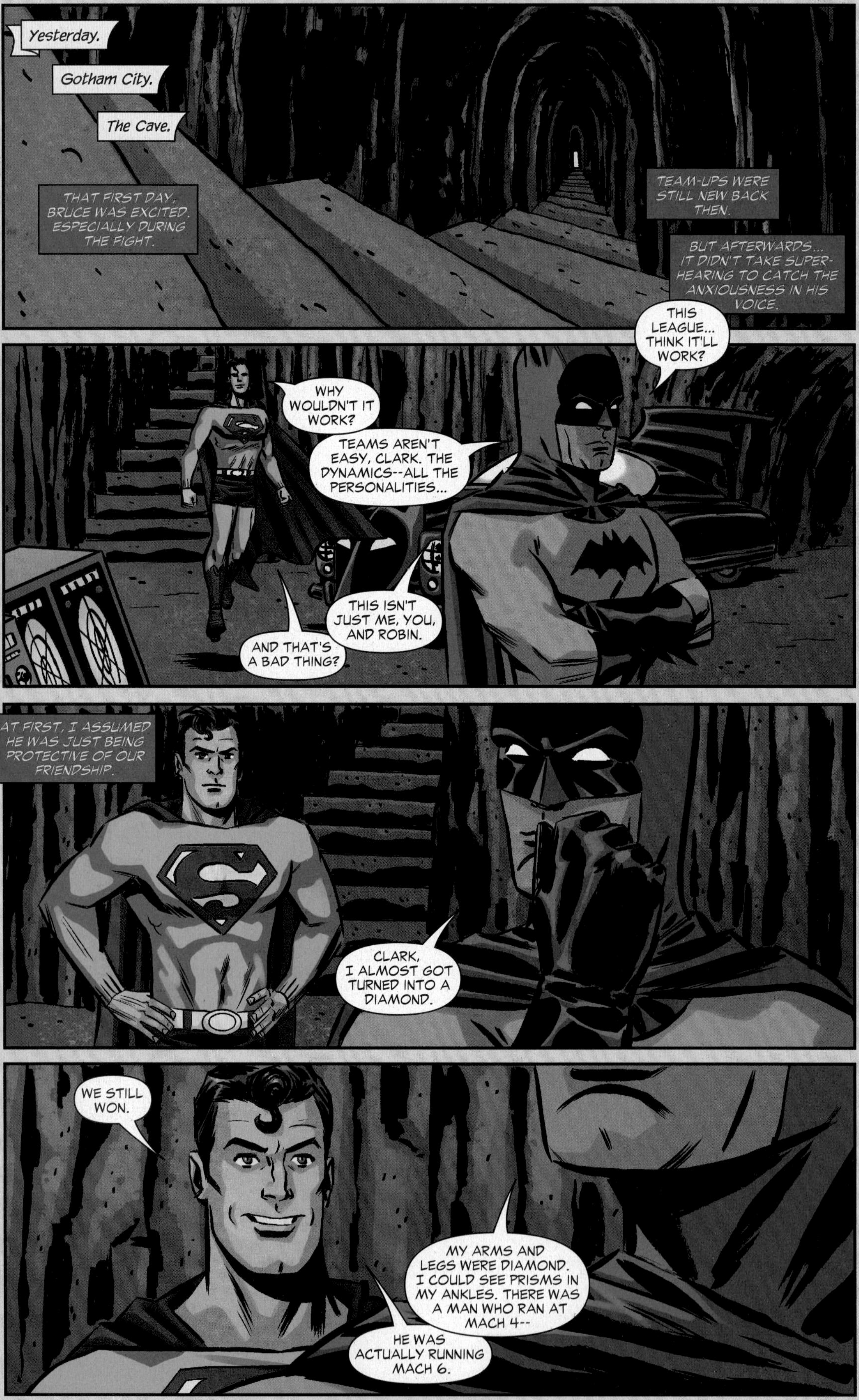
Yesterday.
Gotham City.
The Cave.
THAT FIRST DAY, BRUCE WAS EXCITED. ESPECIALLY DURING THE FIGHT.
TEAM-UPS WERE STILL NEW BACK THEN.
BUT AFTERWARDS... IT DIDN'T TAKE SUPER-HEARING TO CATCH THE ANXIOUSNESS IN HIS VOICE.
THIS LEAGUE... THINK IT'LL WORK?
WHY WOULDN'T IT WORK?
TEAMS AREN'T EASY, CLARK. THE DYNAMICS--ALL THE PERSONALITIES...
AND THAT'S A BAD THING?
THIS ISN'T JUST ME, YOU, AND ROBIN.
AT FIRST, I ASSUMED HE WAS JUST BEING PROTECTIVE OF OUR FRIENDSHIP.
CLARK, I ALMOST GOT TURNED INTO A DIAMOND.
WE STILL WON.
MY ARMS AND LEGS WERE DIAMOND. I COULD SEE PRISMS IN MY ANKLES. THERE WAS A MAN WHO RAN AT MACH 4--
HE WAS ACTUALLY RUNNING MACH 6.

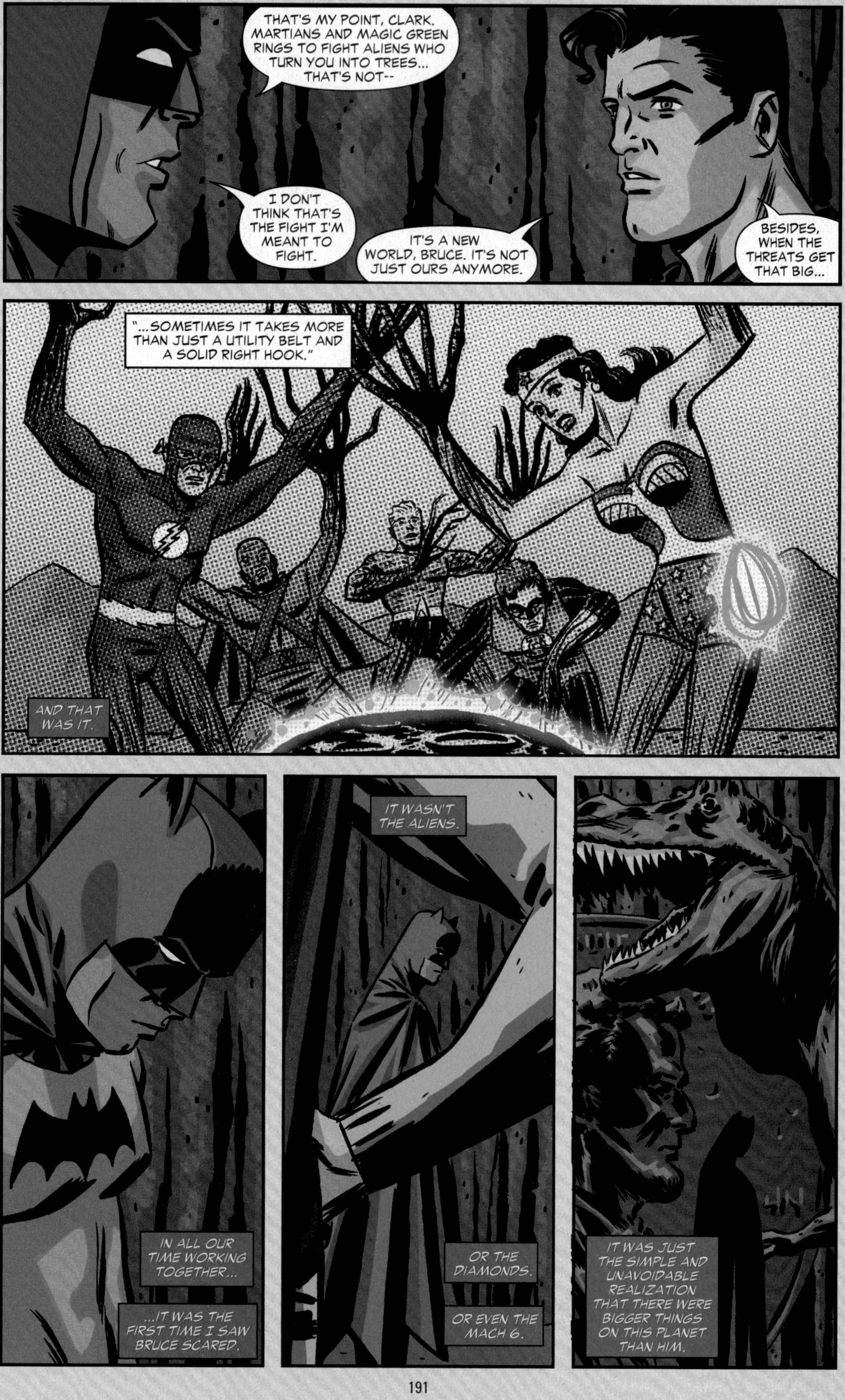
THAT'S MY POINT, CLARK. MARTIANS AND MAGIC GREEN RINGS TO FIGHT ALIENS WHO TURN YOU INTO TREES... THAT'S NOT--
I DON'T THINK THAT'S THE FIGHT I'M MEANT TO FIGHT.
IT'S A NEW WORLD, BRUCE. IT'S NOT JUST OURS ANYMORE.
BESIDES, WHEN THE THREATS GET THAT BIG...
"...SOMETIMES IT TAKES MORE THAN JUST A UTILITY BELT AND A SOLID RIGHT HOOK."
AND THAT WAS IT.
IN ALL OUR TIME WORKING TOGETHER...
...IT WAS THE FIRST TIME I SAW BRUCE SCARED.
IT WASN'T THE ALIENS.
OR THE DIAMONDS.
OR EVEN THE MACH 6.
IT WAS JUST THE SIMPLE AND UNAVOIDABLE REALIZATION THAT THERE WERE BIGGER THINGS ON THIS PLANET THAN HIM.

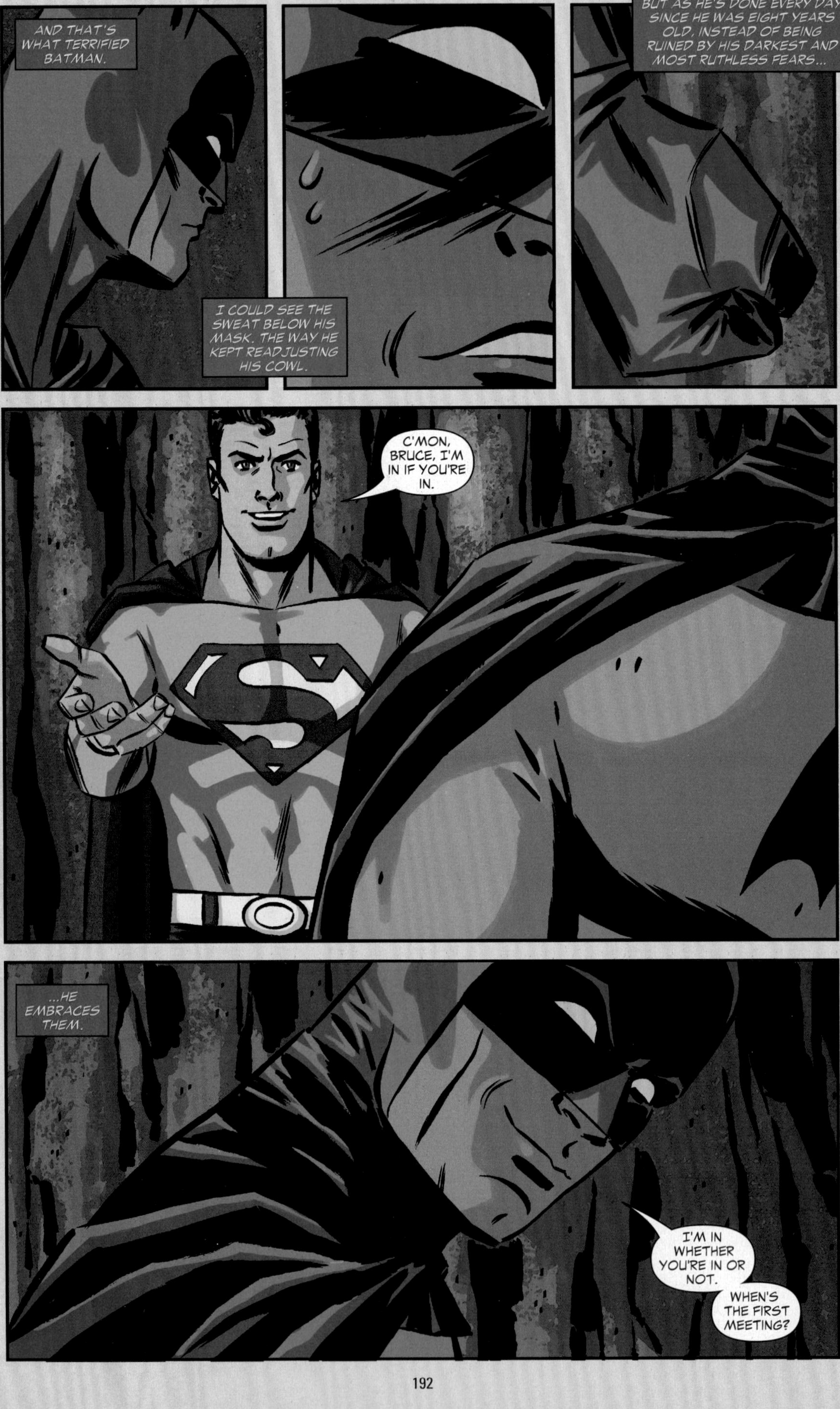
AND THAT'S WHAT TERRIFIED BATMAN.
I COULD SEE THE SWEAT BELOW HIS MASK. THE WAY HE KEPT READJUSTING HIS COWL.
BUT AS HE'S DONE EVERY DAY SINCE HE WAS EIGHT YEARS OLD, INSTEAD OF BEING RUINED BY HIS DARKEST AND MOST RUTHLESS FEARS...
C'MON, BRUCE, I'M IN IF YOU'RE IN.
...HE EMBRACES THEM.
I'M IN WHETHER YOU'RE IN OR NOT.
WHEN'S THE FIRST MEETING?

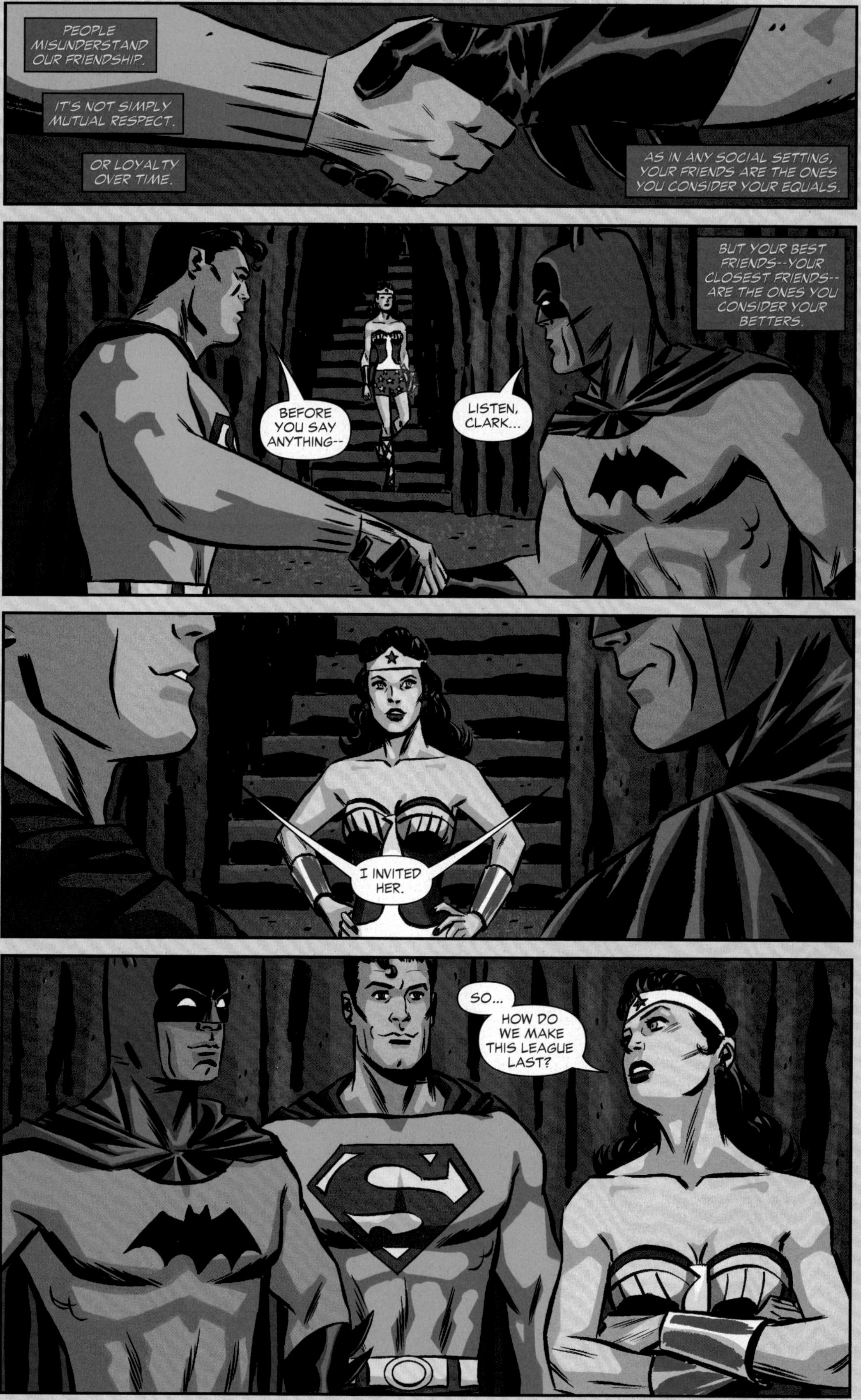
PEOPLE MISUNDERSTAND OUR FRIENDSHIP.
IT'S NOT SIMPLY MUTUAL RESPECT.
OR LOYALTY OVER TIME.
AS IN ANY SOCIAL SETTING, YOUR FRIENDS ARE THE ONES YOU CONSIDER YOUR EQUALS.
BUT YOUR BEST FRIENDS--YOUR CLOSEST FRIENDS--ARE THE ONES YOU CONSIDER YOUR BETTERS.
BEFORE YOU SAY ANYTHING--
LISTEN, CLARK...
I INVITED HER.
SO... HOW DO WE MAKE THIS LEAGUE LAST?

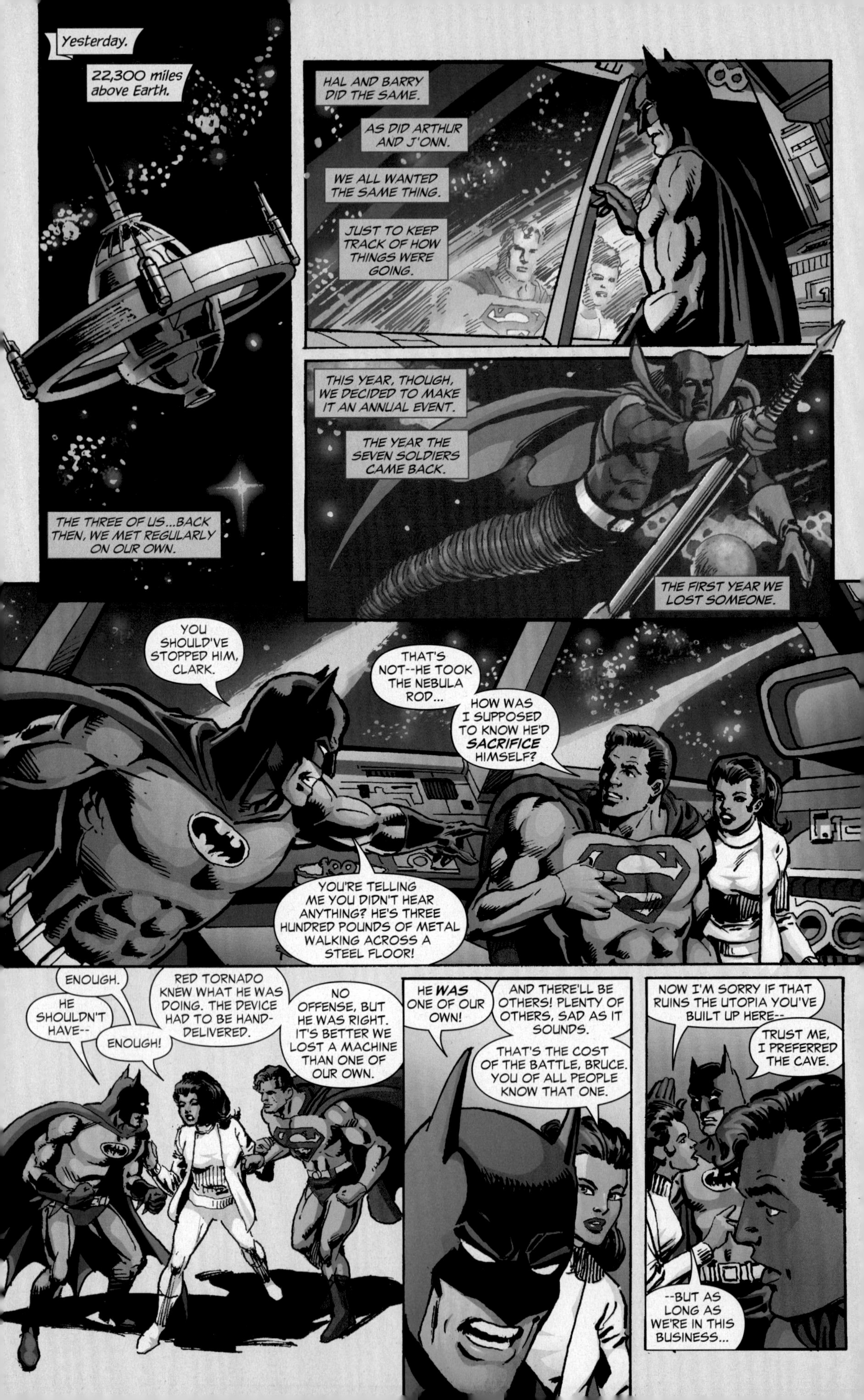
Yesterday.
22,300 miles above Earth.
THE THREE OF US...BACK THEN, WE MET REGULARLY ON OUR OWN.
HAL AND BARRY DID THE SAME.
AS DID ARTHUR AND J'ONN.
WE ALL WANTED THE SAME THING.
JUST TO KEEP TRACK OF HOW THINGS WERE GOING.
THIS YEAR, THOUGH, WE DECIDED TO MAKE IT AN ANNUAL EVENT.
THE YEAR THE SEVEN SOLDIERS CAME BACK.
THE FIRST YEAR WE LOST SOMEONE.
YOU SHOULD'VE STOPPED HIM, CLARK.
THAT'S NOT--HE TOOK THE NEBULA ROD...
HOW WAS I SUPPOSED TO KNOW HE'D SACRIFICE HIMSELF?
YOU'RE TELLING ME YOU DIDN'T HEAR ANYTHING? HE'S THREE HUNDRED POUNDS OF METAL WALKING ACROSS A STEEL FLOOR!
HE SHOULDN'T HAVE--
ENOUGH.
ENOUGH!
RED TORNADO KNEW WHAT HE WAS DOING. THE DEVICE HAD TO BE HAND-DELIVERED.
NO OFFENSE, BUT HE WAS RIGHT. IT'S BETTER WE LOST A MACHINE THAN ONE OF OUR OWN.
HE WAS ONE OF OUR OWN!
AND THERE'LL BE OTHERS! PLENTY OF OTHERS, SAD AS IT SOUNDS.
THAT'S THE COST OF THE BATTLE, BRUCE. YOU OF ALL PEOPLE KNOW THAT ONE.
NOW I'M SORRY IF THAT RUINS THE UTOPIA YOU'VE BUILT UP HERE--
TRUST ME, I PREFERRED THE CAVE.
--BUT AS LONG AS WE'RE IN THIS BUSINESS...

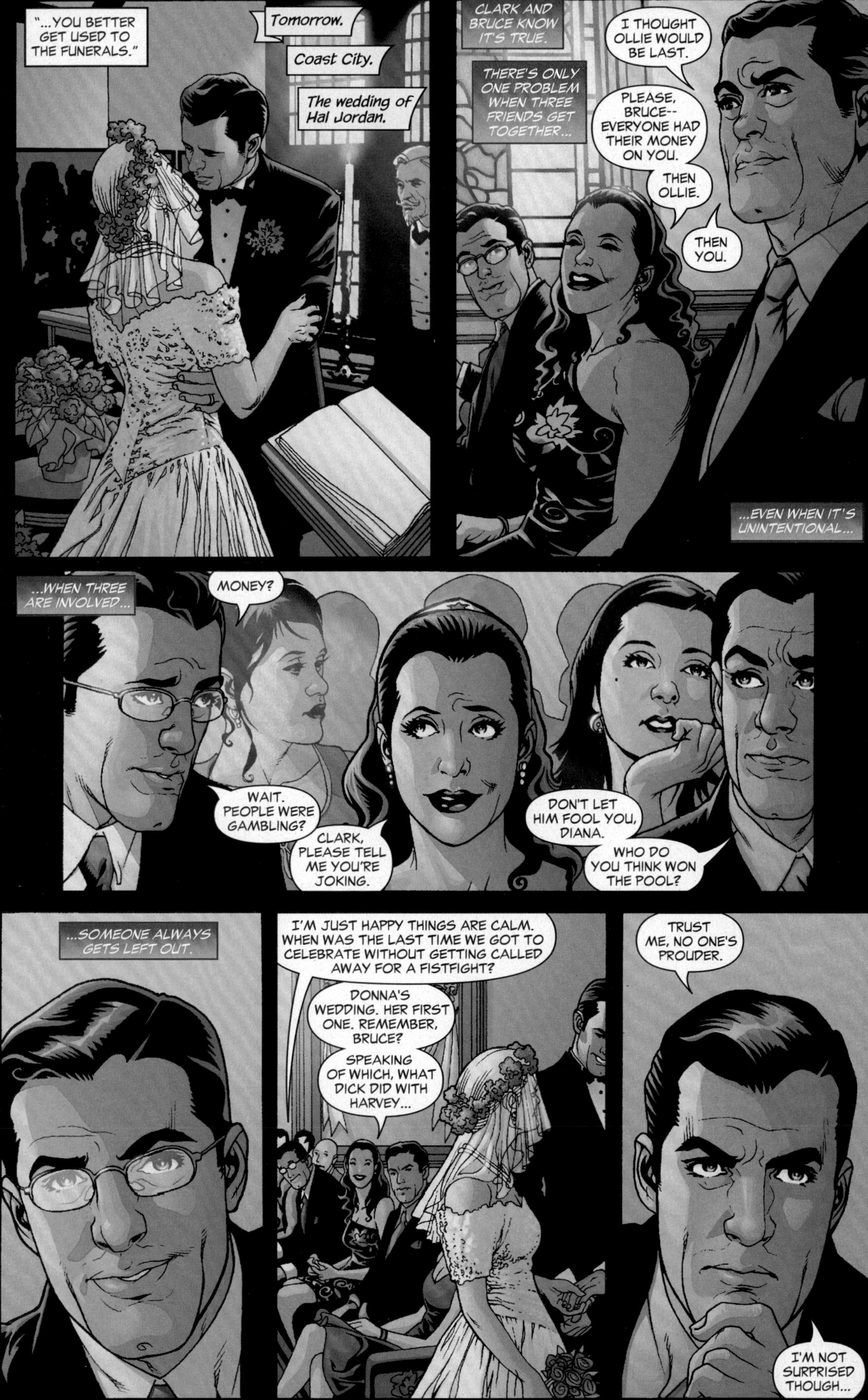

"...YOU BETTER GET USED TO THE FUNERALS."
Tomorrow.
Coast City.
The wedding of Hal Jordan.
CLARK AND BRUCE KNOW IT'S TRUE.
THERE'S ONLY ONE PROBLEM WHEN THREE FRIENDS GET TOGETHER...
I THOUGHT OLLIE WOULD BE LAST.
PLEASE, BRUCE-- EVERYONE HAD THEIR MONEY ON YOU.
THEN OLLIE.
THEN YOU.
...EVEN WHEN IT'S UNINTENTIONAL...
...WHEN THREE ARE INVOLVED...
MONEY?
WAIT. PEOPLE WERE GAMBLING?
CLARK, PLEASE TELL ME YOU'RE JOKING.
DON'T LET HIM FOOL YOU, DIANA.
WHO DO YOU THINK WON THE POOL?
...SOMEONE ALWAYS GETS LEFT OUT.
I'M JUST HAPPY THINGS ARE CALM. WHEN WAS THE LAST TIME WE GOT TO CELEBRATE WITHOUT GETTING CALLED AWAY FOR A FISTFIGHT?
DONNA'S WEDDING. HER FIRST ONE. REMEMBER, BRUCE?
SPEAKING OF WHICH, WHAT DICK DID WITH HARVEY...
TRUST ME, NO ONE'S PROUDER.
I'M NOT SURPRISED THOUGH...

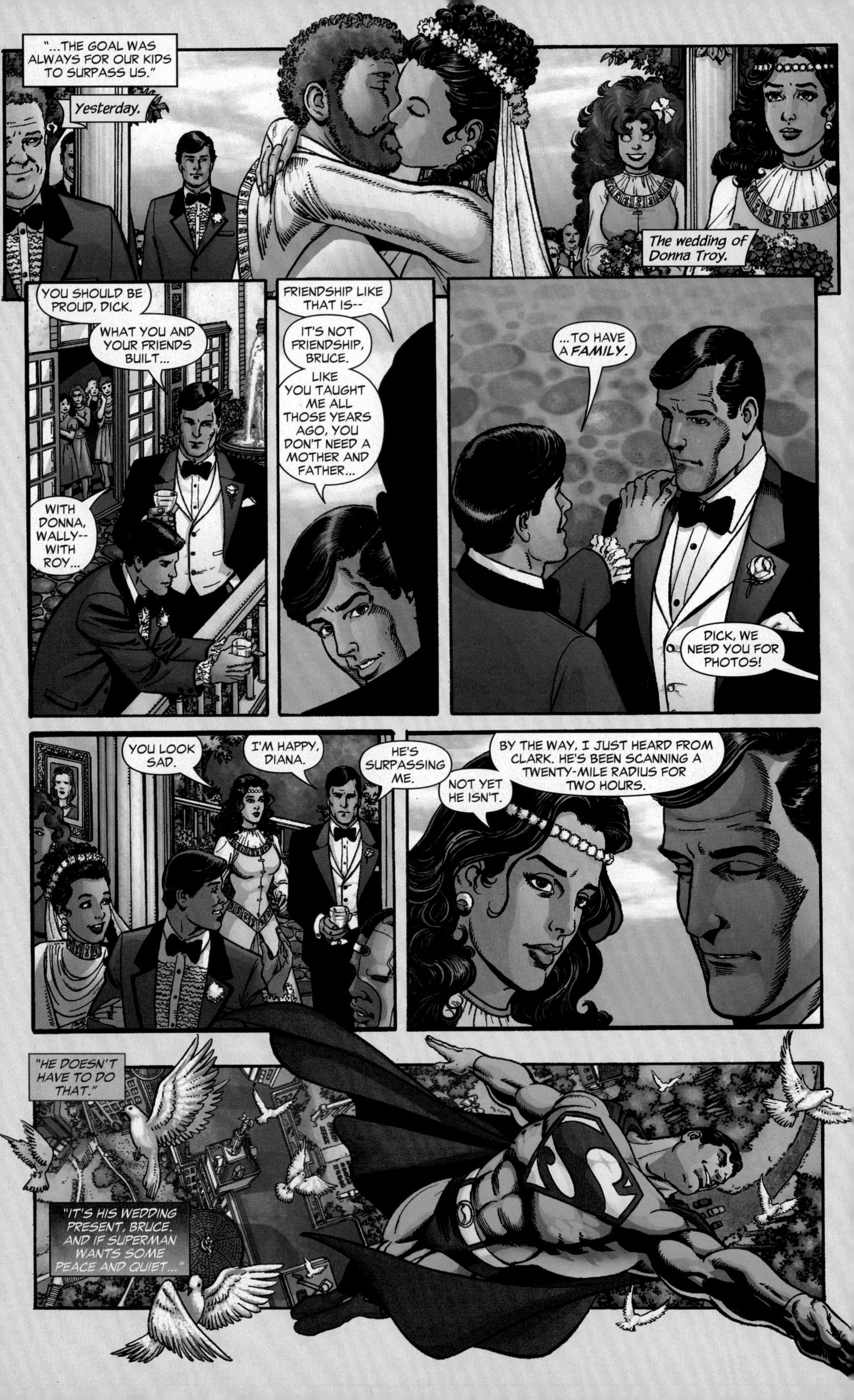
"...THE GOAL WAS ALWAYS FOR OUR KIDS TO SURPASS US."
Yesterday.
The wedding of Donna Troy.
YOU SHOULD BE PROUD, DICK.
WHAT YOU AND YOUR FRIENDS BUILT...
WITH DONNA, WALLY-- WITH ROY...
FRIENDSHIP LIKE THAT IS--
IT'S NOT FRIENDSHIP, BRUCE.
LIKE YOU TAUGHT ME ALL THOSE YEARS AGO, YOU DON'T NEED A MOTHER AND FATHER...
...TO HAVE A FAMILY.
DICK, WE NEED YOU FOR PHOTOS!
YOU LOOK SAD.
I'M HAPPY, DIANA.
HE'S SURPASSING ME.
NOT YET HE ISN'T.
BY THE WAY, I JUST HEARD FROM CLARK. HE'S BEEN SCANNING A TWENTY-MILE RADIUS FOR TWO HOURS.
"HE DOESN'T HAVE TO DO THAT."
"IT'S HIS WEDDING PRESENT, BRUCE. AND IF SUPERMAN WANTS SOME PEACE AND QUIET..."

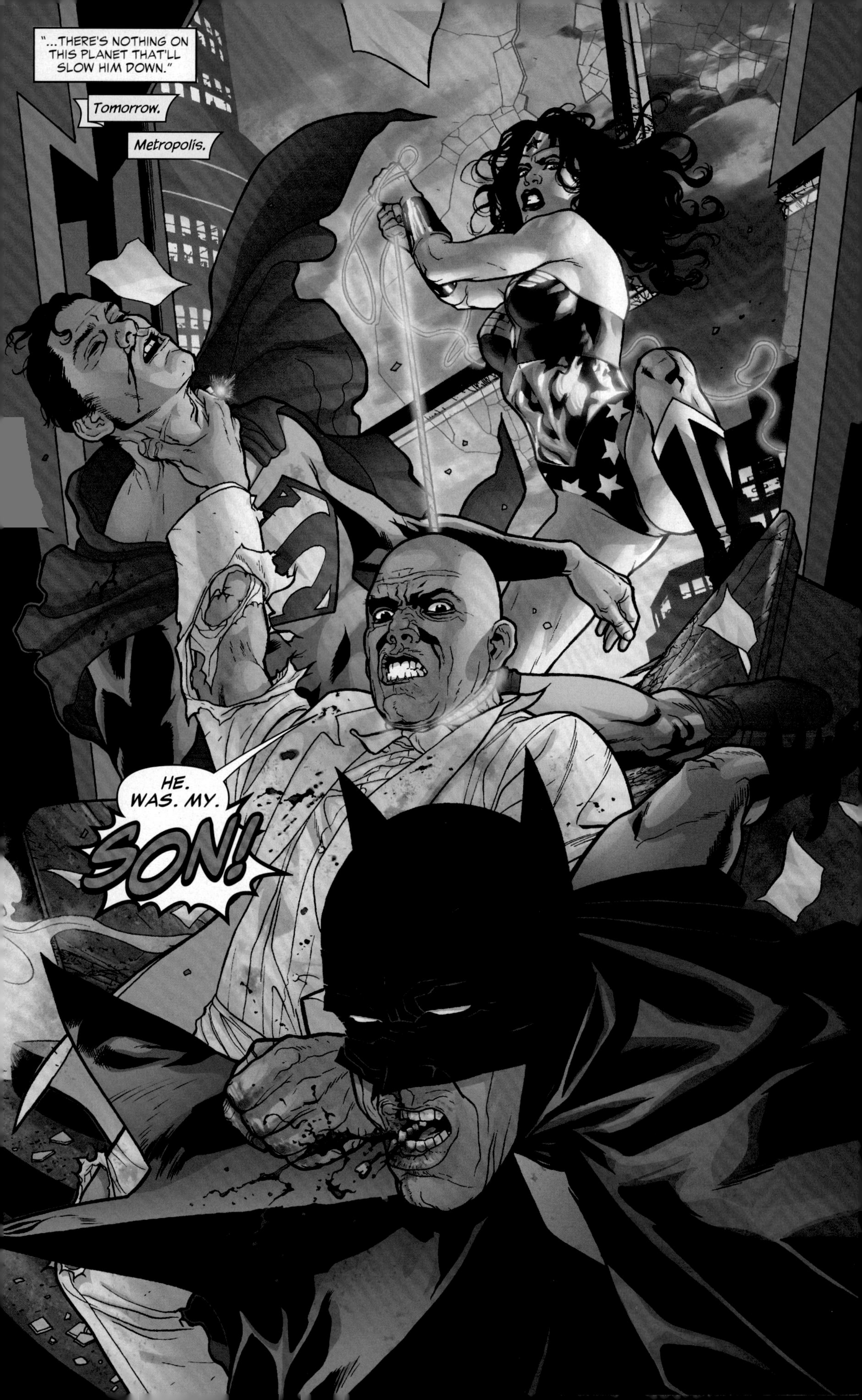
"...THERE'S NOTHING ON THIS PLANET THAT'LL SLOW HIM DOWN."
Tomorrow.
Metropolis.
HE. WAS. MY.
SON!

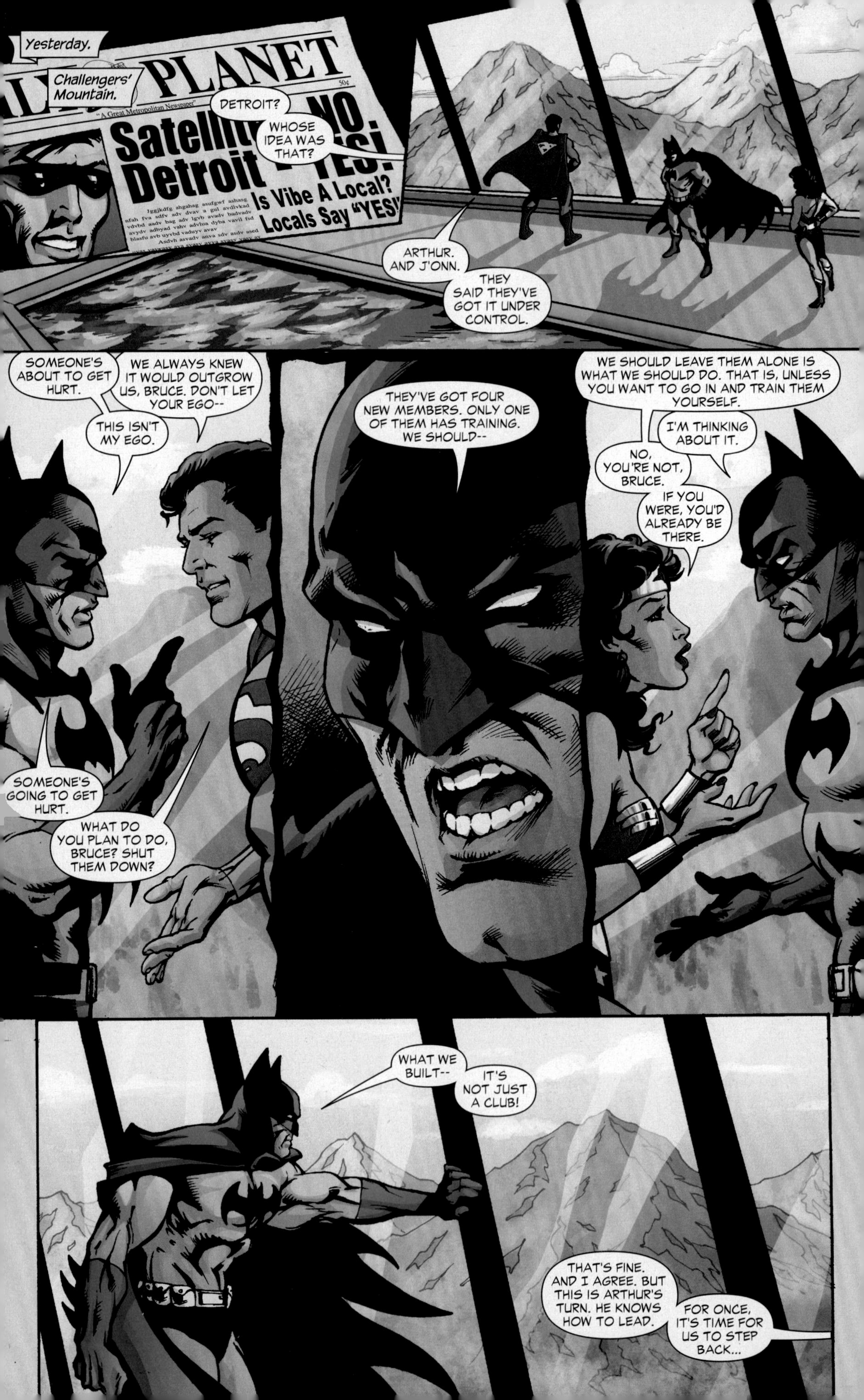

Yesterday.
Challengers' Mountain.
PLANET
50¢
"A Great Metropolitan Newspaper"
Is Vibe A Local? Locals Say "YES!"
DETROIT?
WHOSE IDEA WAS THAT?
ARTHUR. AND J'ONN.
THEY SAID THEY'VE GOT IT UNDER CONTROL.
SOMEONE'S ABOUT TO GET HURT.
WE ALWAYS KNEW IT WOULD OUTGROW US, BRUCE. DON'T LET YOUR EGO--
THIS ISN'T MY EGO.
SOMEONE'S GOING TO GET HURT.
WHAT DO YOU PLAN TO DO, BRUCE? SHUT THEM DOWN?
THEY'VE GOT FOUR NEW MEMBERS. ONLY ONE OF THEM HAS TRAINING. WE SHOULD--
WE SHOULD LEAVE THEM ALONE IS WHAT WE SHOULD DO. THAT IS, UNLESS YOU WANT TO GO IN AND TRAIN THEM YOURSELF.
I'M THINKING ABOUT IT.
NO, YOU'RE NOT, BRUCE.
IF YOU WERE, YOU'D ALREADY BE THERE.
WHAT WE BUILT--
IT'S NOT JUST A CLUB!
THAT'S FINE. AND I AGREE. BUT THIS IS ARTHUR'S TURN. HE KNOWS HOW TO LEAD.
FOR ONCE, IT'S TIME FOR US TO STEP BACK...

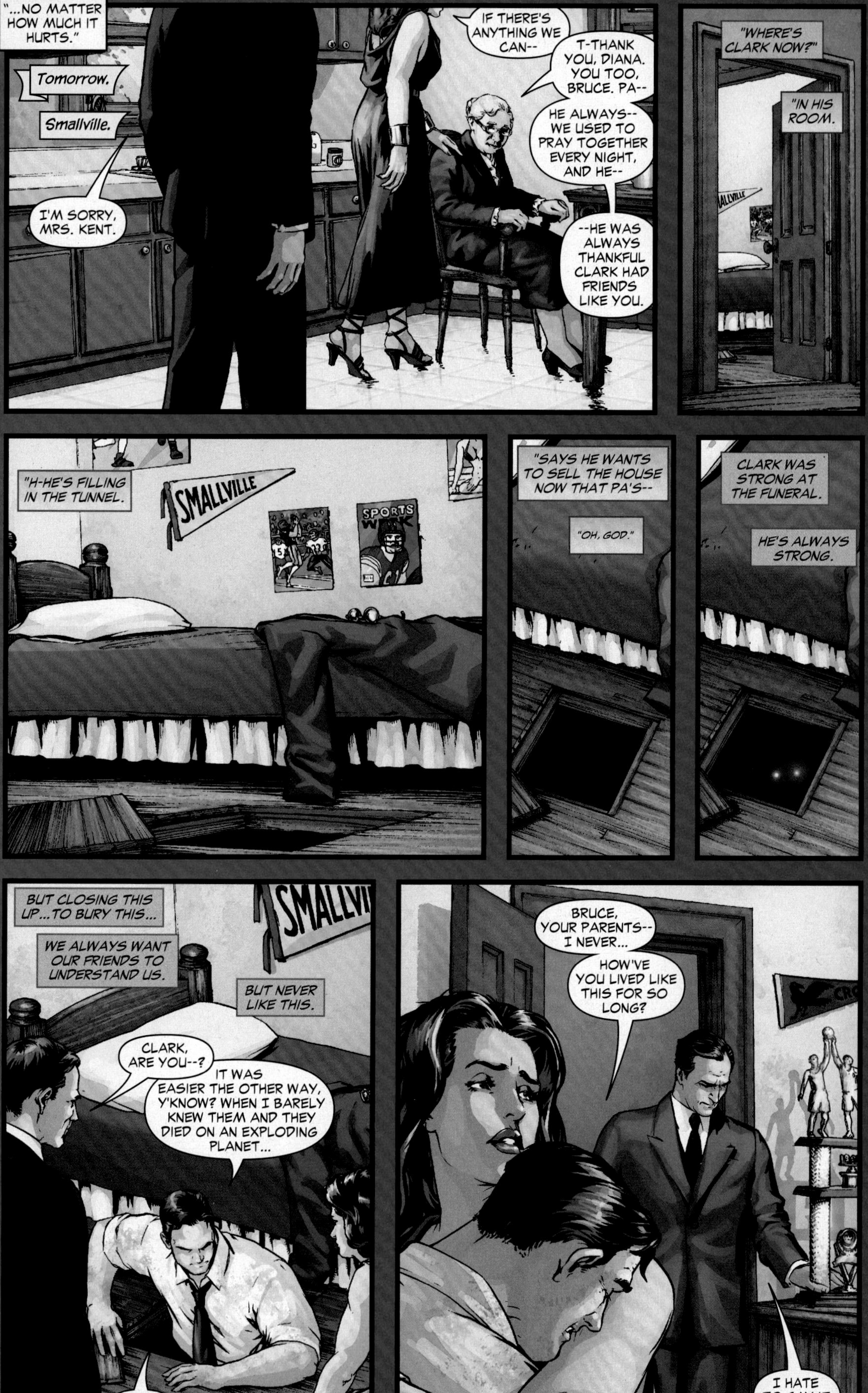
"...NO MATTER HOW MUCH IT HURTS."
Tomorrow.
Smallville.
I'M SORRY, MRS. KENT.
IF THERE'S ANYTHING WE CAN--
T-THANK YOU, DIANA. YOU TOO, BRUCE. PA--
HE ALWAYS-- WE USED TO PRAY TOGETHER EVERY NIGHT, AND HE--
--HE WAS ALWAYS THANKFUL CLARK HAD FRIENDS LIKE YOU.
"WHERE'S CLARK NOW?"
"IN HIS ROOM.
SMALLVILLE
"H-HE'S FILLING IN THE TUNNEL.
SMALLVILLE
SPORTS
"SAYS HE WANTS TO SELL THE HOUSE NOW THAT PA'S--
"OH, GOD."
CLARK WAS STRONG AT THE FUNERAL.
HE'S ALWAYS STRONG.
BUT CLOSING THIS UP...TO BURY THIS...
WE ALWAYS WANT OUR FRIENDS TO UNDERSTAND US.
BUT NEVER LIKE THIS.
CLARK, ARE YOU--?
IT WAS EASIER THE OTHER WAY, Y'KNOW? WHEN I BARELY KNEW THEM AND THEY DIED ON AN EXPLODING PLANET...
BUT THIS...
BRUCE, YOUR PARENTS-- I NEVER...
HOW'VE YOU LIVED LIKE THIS FOR SO LONG?
I HATE TO SAY IT, CLARK...

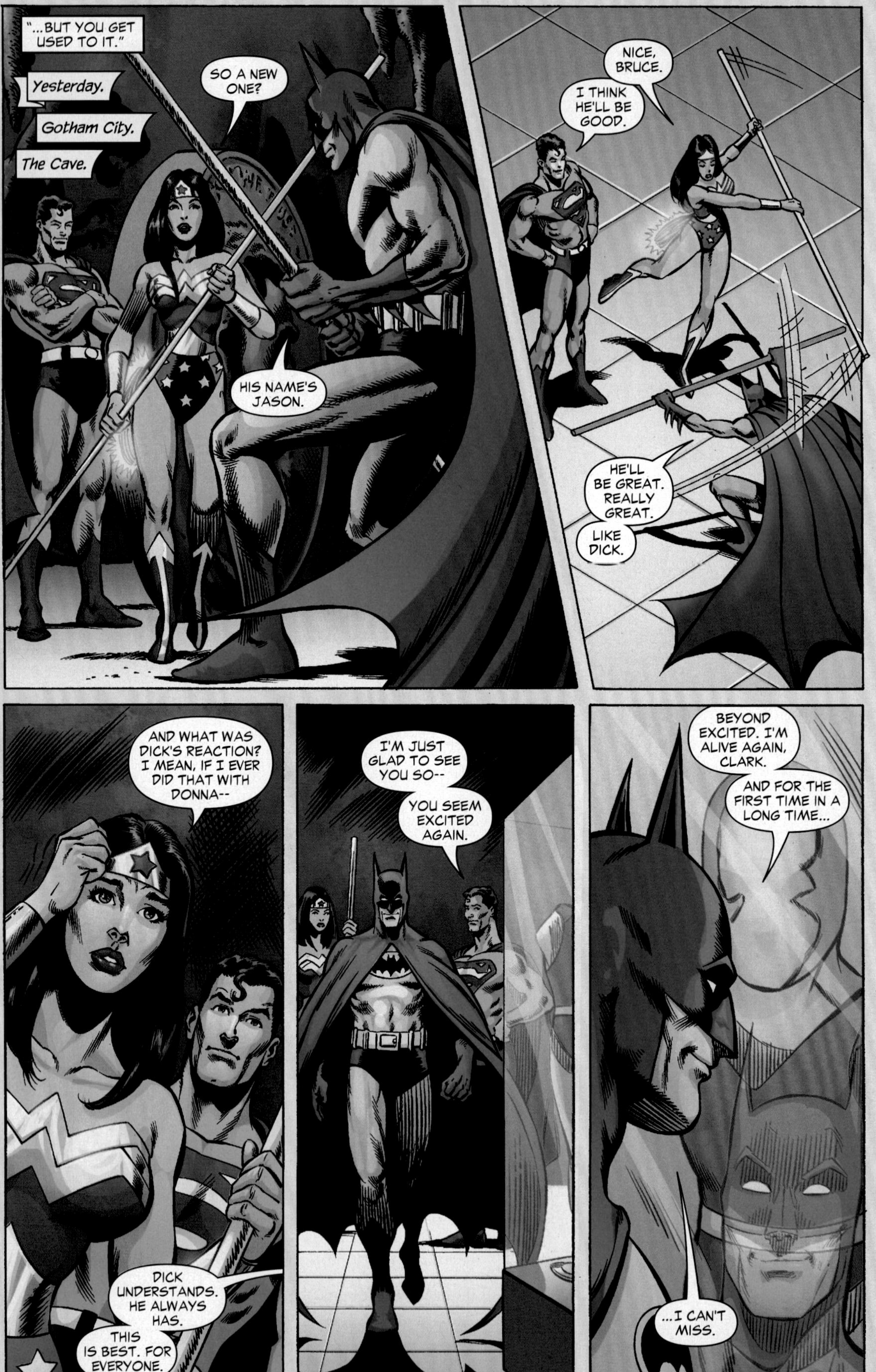
"...BUT YOU GET USED TO IT."
Yesterday.
Gotham City.
The Cave.
SO A NEW ONE?
HIS NAME'S JASON.
NICE, BRUCE.
I THINK HE'LL BE GOOD.
HE'LL BE GREAT. REALLY GREAT.
LIKE DICK.
AND WHAT WAS DICK'S REACTION? I MEAN, IF I EVER DID THAT WITH DONNA--
DICK UNDERSTANDS. HE ALWAYS HAS.
THIS IS BEST. FOR EVERYONE.
I'M JUST GLAD TO SEE YOU SO--
YOU SEEM EXCITED AGAIN.
BEYOND EXCITED. I'M ALIVE AGAIN, CLARK.
AND FOR THE FIRST TIME IN A LONG TIME...
...I CAN'T MISS.

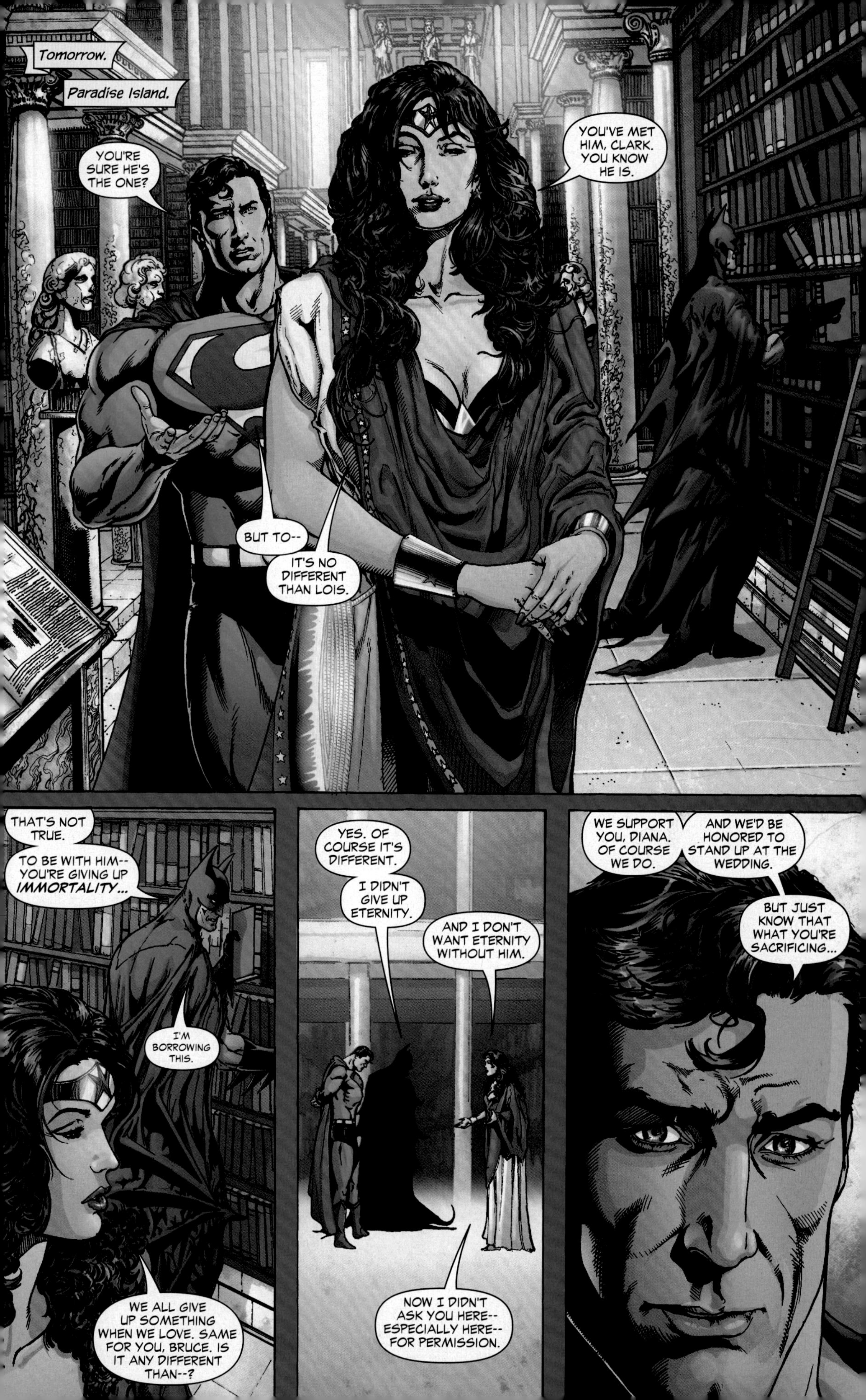
Tomorrow.
Paradise Island.
YOU'RE SURE HE'S THE ONE?
YOU'VE MET HIM, CLARK. YOU KNOW HE IS.
BUT TO--
IT'S NO DIFFERENT THAN LOIS.
THAT'S NOT TRUE.
TO BE WITH HIM-- YOU'RE GIVING UP IMMORTALITY...
I'M BORROWING THIS.
WE ALL GIVE UP SOMETHING WHEN WE LOVE. SAME FOR YOU, BRUCE. IS IT ANY DIFFERENT THAN--?
YES. OF COURSE IT'S DIFFERENT.
I DIDN'T GIVE UP ETERNITY.
AND I DON'T WANT ETERNITY WITHOUT HIM.
NOW I DIDN'T ASK YOU HERE-- ESPECIALLY HERE-- FOR PERMISSION.
WE SUPPORT YOU, DIANA. OF COURSE WE DO.
AND WE'D BE HONORED TO STAND UP AT THE WEDDING.
BUT JUST KNOW THAT WHAT YOU'RE SACRIFICING...

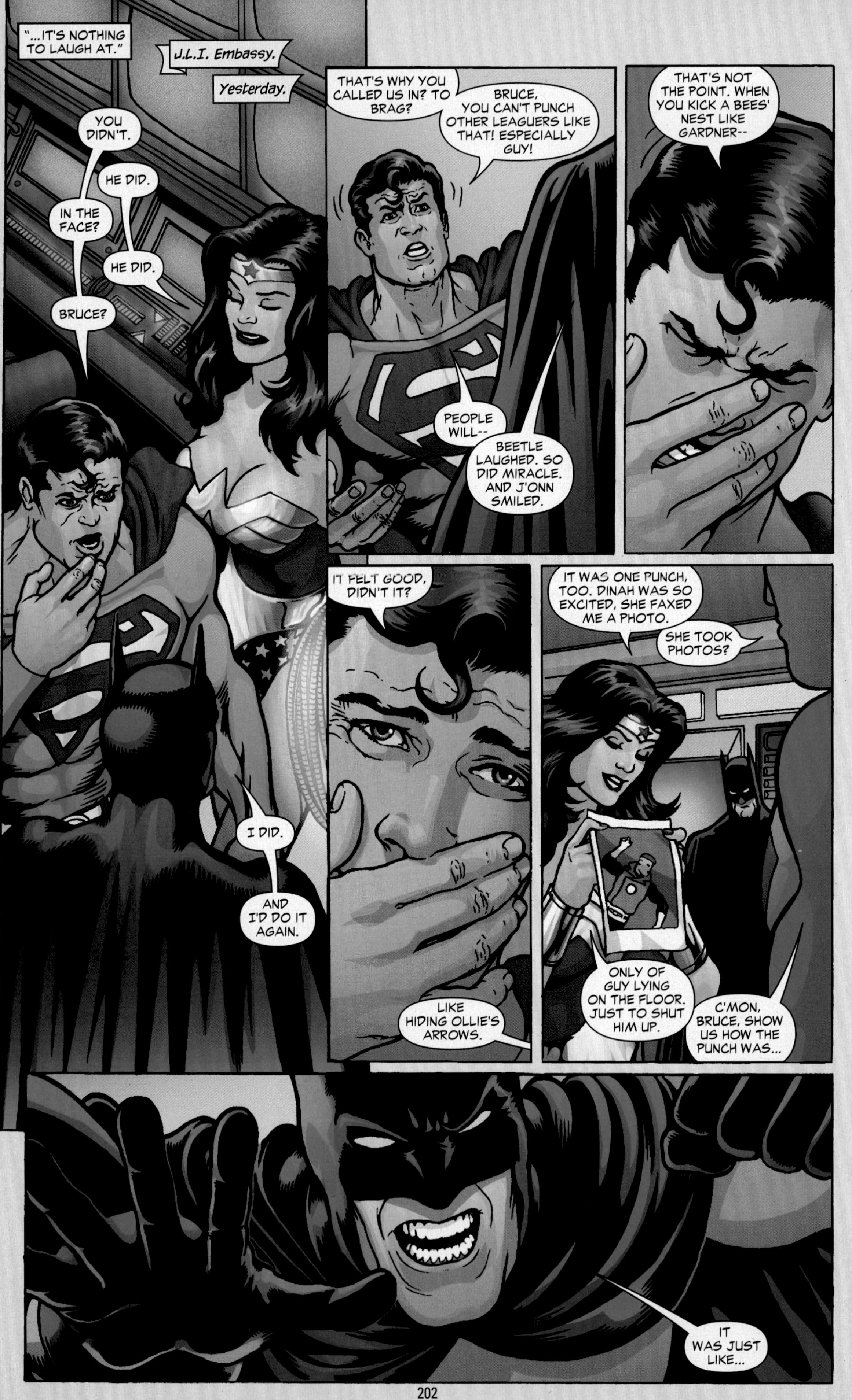
"...IT'S NOTHING TO LAUGH AT."
J.L.I. Embassy.
Yesterday.
YOU DIDN'T.
HE DID.
IN THE FACE?
HE DID.
BRUCE?
I DID.
AND I'D DO IT AGAIN.
THAT'S WHY YOU CALLED US IN? TO BRAG?
BRUCE, YOU CAN'T PUNCH OTHER LEAGUERS LIKE THAT! ESPECIALLY GUY!
PEOPLE WILL--
BEETLE LAUGHED. SO DID MIRACLE. AND J'ONN SMILED.
THAT'S NOT THE POINT. WHEN YOU KICK A BEES' NEST LIKE GARDNER--
IT FELT GOOD, DIDN'T IT?
LIKE HIDING OLLIE'S ARROWS.
IT WAS ONE PUNCH, TOO. DINAH WAS SO EXCITED, SHE FAXED ME A PHOTO.
SHE TOOK PHOTOS?
ONLY OF GUY LYING ON THE FLOOR. JUST TO SHUT HIM UP.
C'MON, BRUCE, SHOW US HOW THE PUNCH WAS...
IT WAS JUST LIKE...

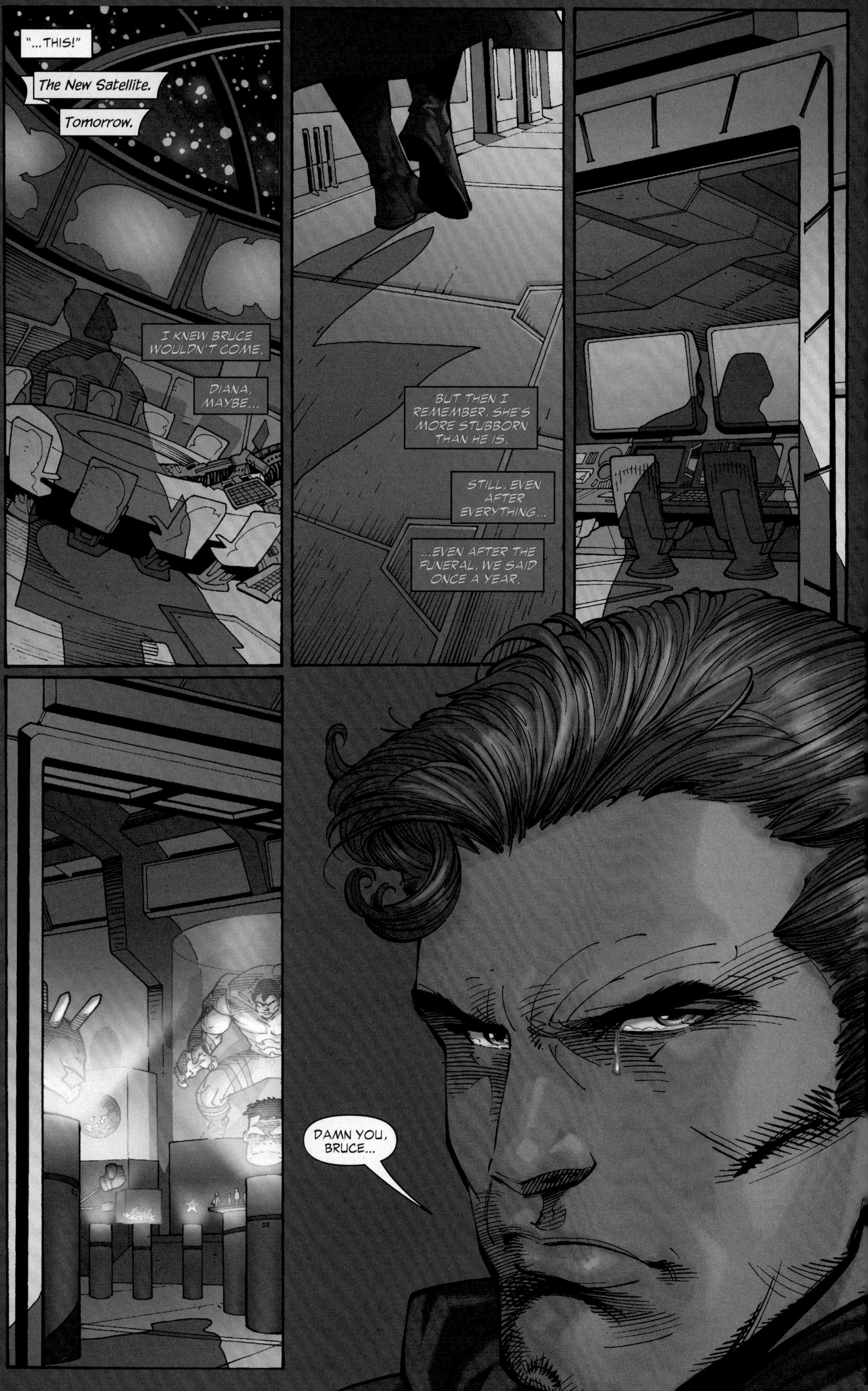

"...THIS!"
The New Satellite.
Tomorrow.
I KNEW BRUCE WOULDN'T COME.
DIANA, MAYBE...
BUT THEN I REMEMBER. SHE'S MORE STUBBORN THAN HE IS.
STILL, EVEN AFTER EVERYTHING...
...EVEN AFTER THE FUNERAL, WE SAID ONCE A YEAR.
DAMN YOU, BRUCE...

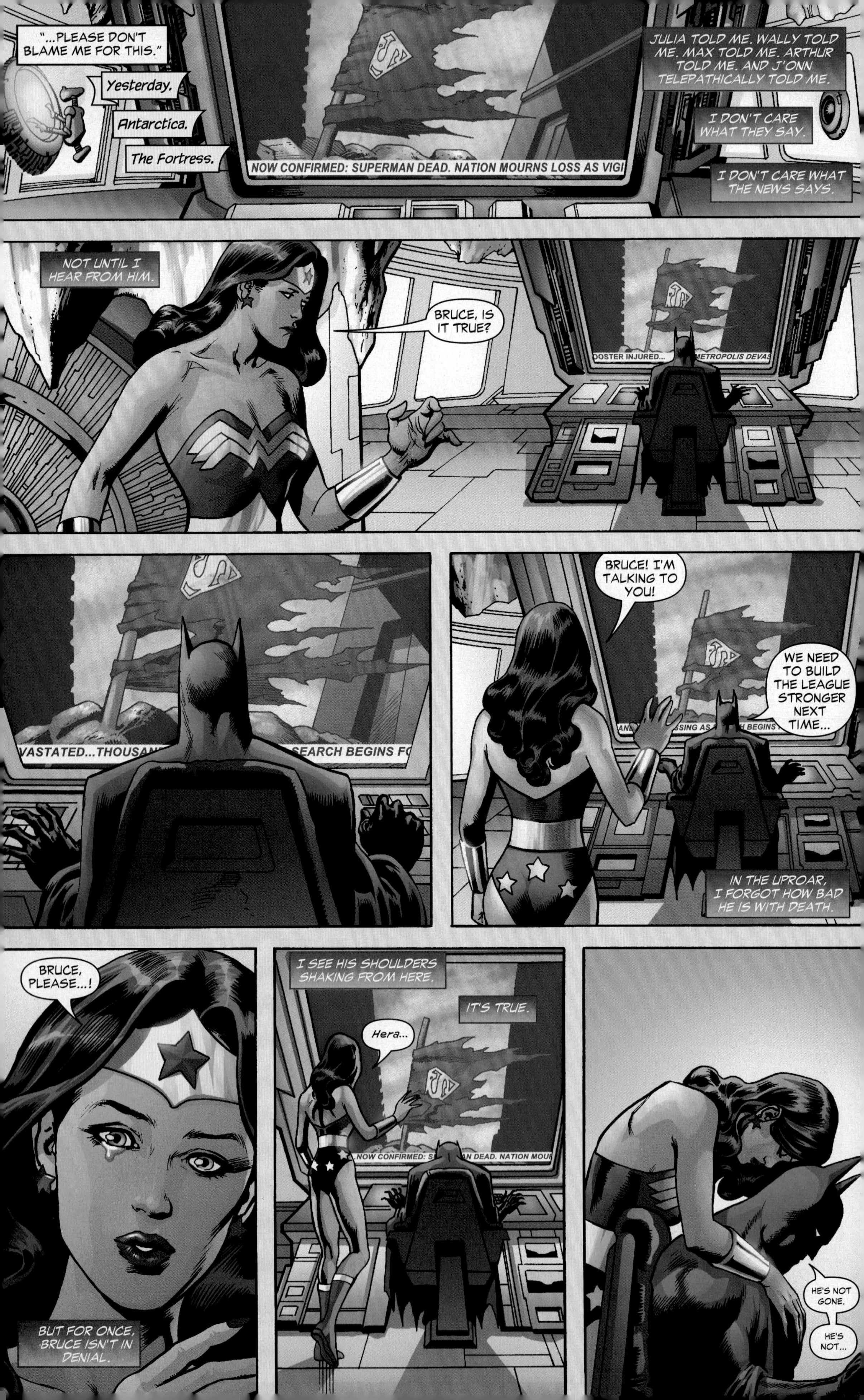
"...PLEASE DON'T BLAME ME FOR THIS."
Yesterday.
Antarctica.
The Fortress.
NOW CONFIRMED: SUPERMAN DEAD. NATION MOURNS LOSS AS VIGI
JULIA TOLD ME. WALLY TOLD ME. MAX TOLD ME. ARTHUR TOLD ME. AND J'ONN TELEPATHICALLY TOLD ME.
I DON'T CARE WHAT THEY SAY.
I DON'T CARE WHAT THE NEWS SAYS.
NOT UNTIL I HEAR FROM HIM.
BRUCE, IS IT TRUE?
OOSTER INJURED...
METROPOLIS DEVAS
VASTATED...THOUSAN
SEARCH BEGINS FO
BRUCE! I'M TALKING TO YOU!
WE NEED TO BUILD THE LEAGUE STRONGER NEXT TIME...
IN THE UPROAR, I FORGOT HOW BAD HE IS WITH DEATH.
BRUCE, PLEASE...!
BUT FOR ONCE, BRUCE ISN'T IN DENIAL.
I SEE HIS SHOULDERS SHAKING FROM HERE.
IT'S TRUE.
Hera...
.NOW CONFIRMED: S
N DEAD. NATION MOU
HE'S NOT GONE.
HE'S NOT...

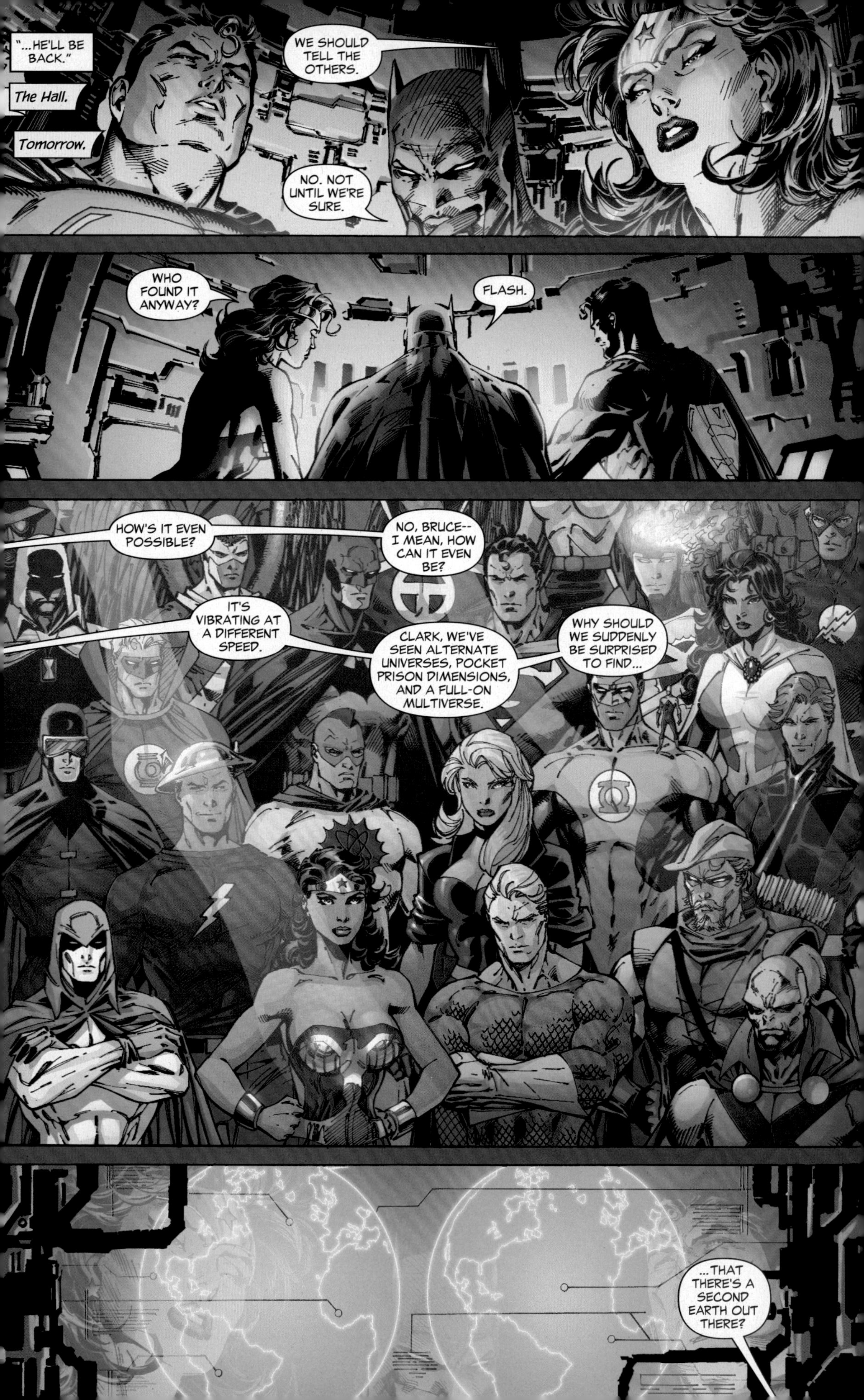
"...HE'LL BE BACK."
The Hall.
Tomorrow.
WE SHOULD TELL THE OTHERS.
NO. NOT UNTIL WE'RE SURE.
WHO FOUND IT ANYWAY?
FLASH.
HOW'S IT EVEN POSSIBLE?
NO, BRUCE-- I MEAN, HOW CAN IT EVEN BE?
IT'S VIBRATING AT A DIFFERENT SPEED.
CLARK, WE'VE SEEN ALTERNATE UNIVERSES, POCKET PRISON DIMENSIONS, AND A FULL-ON MULTIVERSE.
WHY SHOULD WE SUDDENLY BE SURPRISED TO FIND...
...THAT THERE'S A SECOND EARTH OUT THERE?

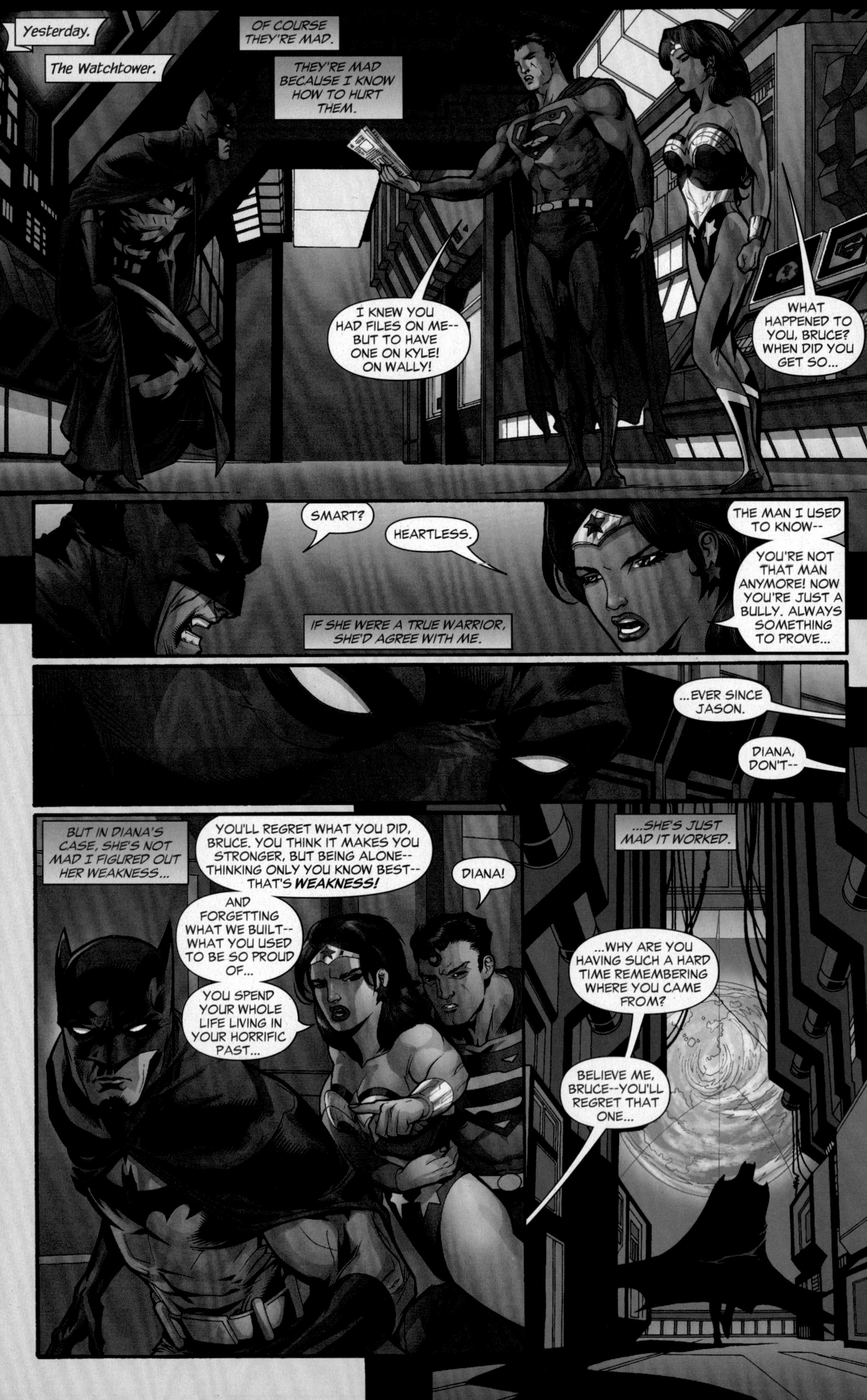
Yesterday.
The Watchtower.
OF COURSE THEY'RE MAD.
THEY'RE MAD BECAUSE I KNOW HOW TO HURT THEM.
I KNEW YOU HAD FILES ON ME-- BUT TO HAVE ONE ON KYLE! ON WALLY!
WHAT HAPPENED TO YOU, BRUCE? WHEN DID YOU GET SO...
SMART?
HEARTLESS.
THE MAN I USED TO KNOW--
YOU'RE NOT THAT MAN ANYMORE! NOW YOU'RE JUST A BULLY. ALWAYS SOMETHING TO PROVE...
IF SHE WERE A TRUE WARRIOR, SHE'D AGREE WITH ME.
...EVER SINCE JASON.
DIANA, DON'T--
BUT IN DIANA'S CASE, SHE'S NOT MAD I FIGURED OUT HER WEAKNESS...
YOU'LL REGRET WHAT YOU DID, BRUCE. YOU THINK IT MAKES YOU STRONGER, BUT BEING ALONE-- THINKING ONLY YOU KNOW BEST-- THAT'S WEAKNESS!
DIANA!
AND FORGETTING WHAT WE BUILT-- WHAT YOU USED TO BE SO PROUD OF...
YOU SPEND YOUR WHOLE LIFE LIVING IN YOUR HORRIFIC PAST...
...SHE'S JUST MAD IT WORKED.
...WHY ARE YOU HAVING SUCH A HARD TIME REMEMBERING WHERE YOU CAME FROM?
BELIEVE ME, BRUCE--YOU'LL REGRET THAT ONE...

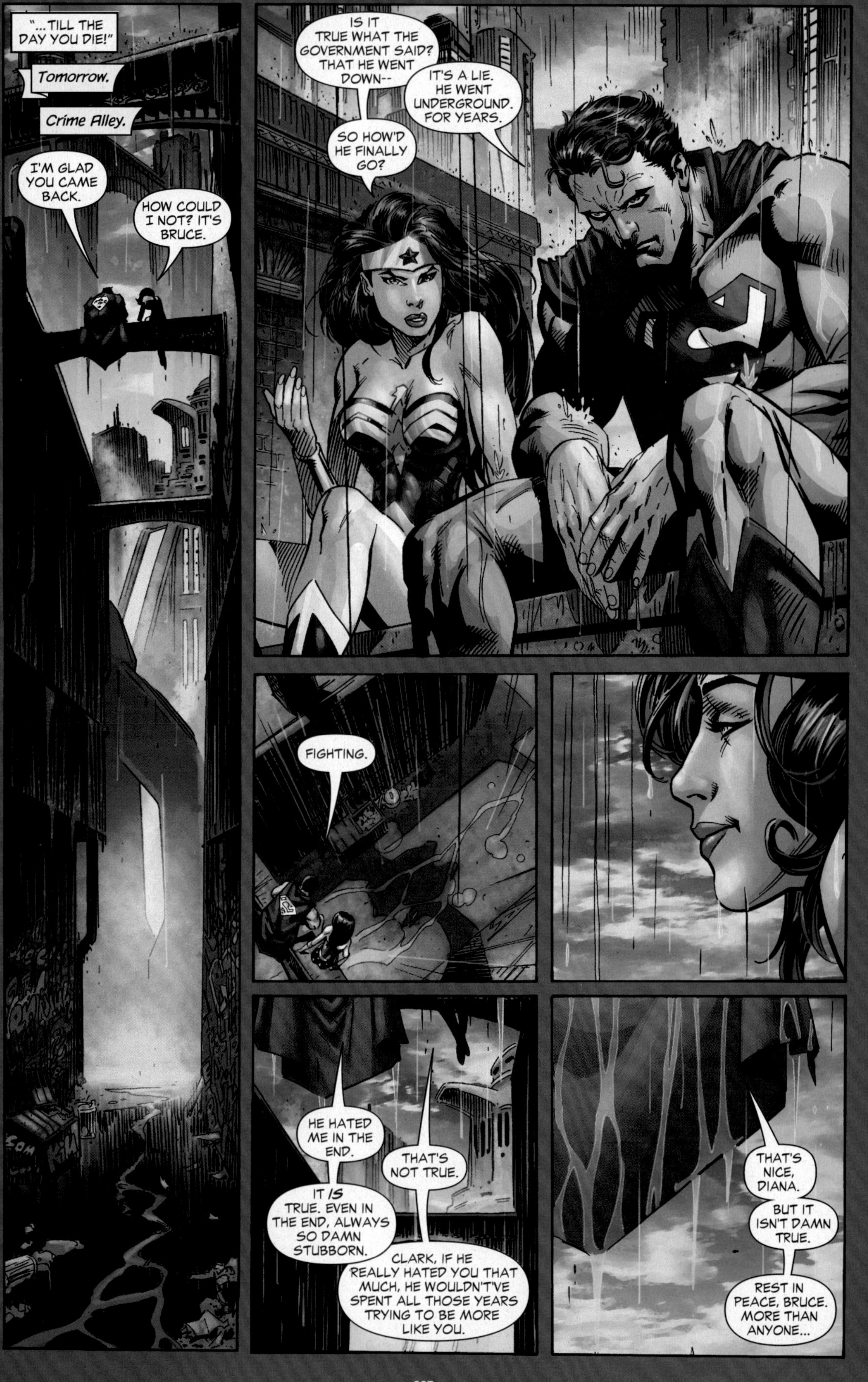
"...TILL THE DAY YOU DIE!"
Tomorrow.
Crime Alley.
I'M GLAD YOU CAME BACK.
HOW COULD I NOT? IT'S BRUCE.
IS IT TRUE WHAT THE GOVERNMENT SAID? THAT HE WENT DOWN--
IT'S A LIE. HE WENT UNDERGROUND. FOR YEARS.
SO HOW'D HE FINALLY GO?
FIGHTING.
HE HATED ME IN THE END.
THAT'S NOT TRUE.
IT *IS* TRUE. EVEN IN THE END, ALWAYS SO DAMN STUBBORN.
CLARK, IF HE REALLY HATED YOU THAT MUCH, HE WOULDN'T'VE SPENT ALL THOSE YEARS TRYING TO BE MORE LIKE YOU.
THAT'S NICE, DIANA.
BUT IT ISN'T DAMN TRUE.
REST IN PEACE, BRUCE. MORE THAN ANYONE...

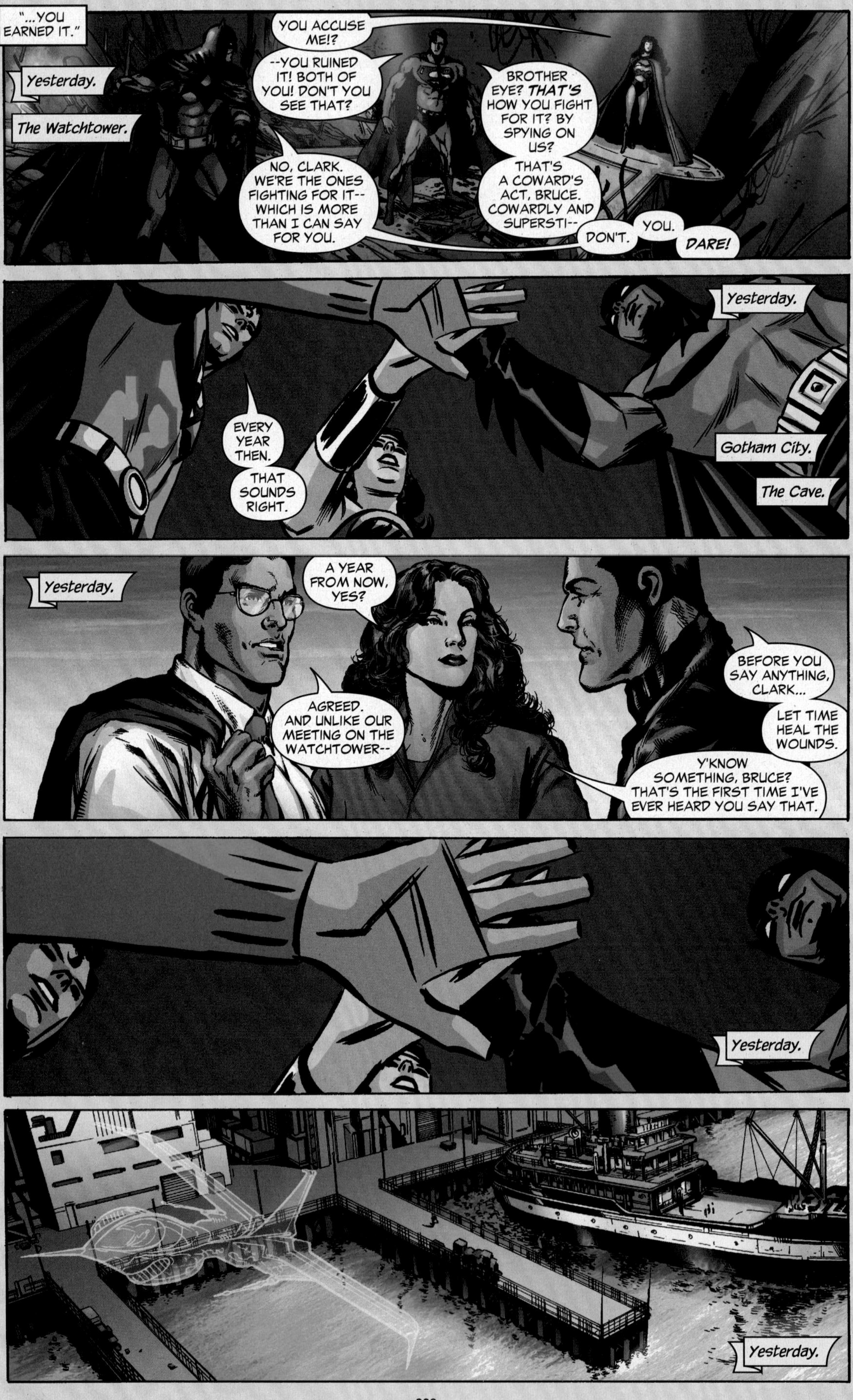

"...YOU EARNED IT."
Yesterday.
The Watchtower.
YOU ACCUSE ME!?
--YOU RUINED IT! BOTH OF YOU! DON'T YOU SEE THAT?
NO, CLARK. WE'RE THE ONES FIGHTING FOR IT-- WHICH IS MORE THAN I CAN SAY FOR YOU.
BROTHER EYE? THAT'S HOW YOU FIGHT FOR IT? BY SPYING ON US?
THAT'S A COWARD'S ACT, BRUCE. COWARDLY AND SUPERSTI--
DON'T.
YOU.
DARE!
Yesterday.
Gotham City.
The Cave.
EVERY YEAR THEN.
THAT SOUNDS RIGHT.
Yesterday.
A YEAR FROM NOW, YES?
AGREED. AND UNLIKE OUR MEETING ON THE WATCHTOWER--
BEFORE YOU SAY ANYTHING, CLARK...
LET TIME HEAL THE WOUNDS.
Y'KNOW SOMETHING, BRUCE? THAT'S THE FIRST TIME I'VE EVER HEARD YOU SAY THAT.
Yesterday.
Yesterday.

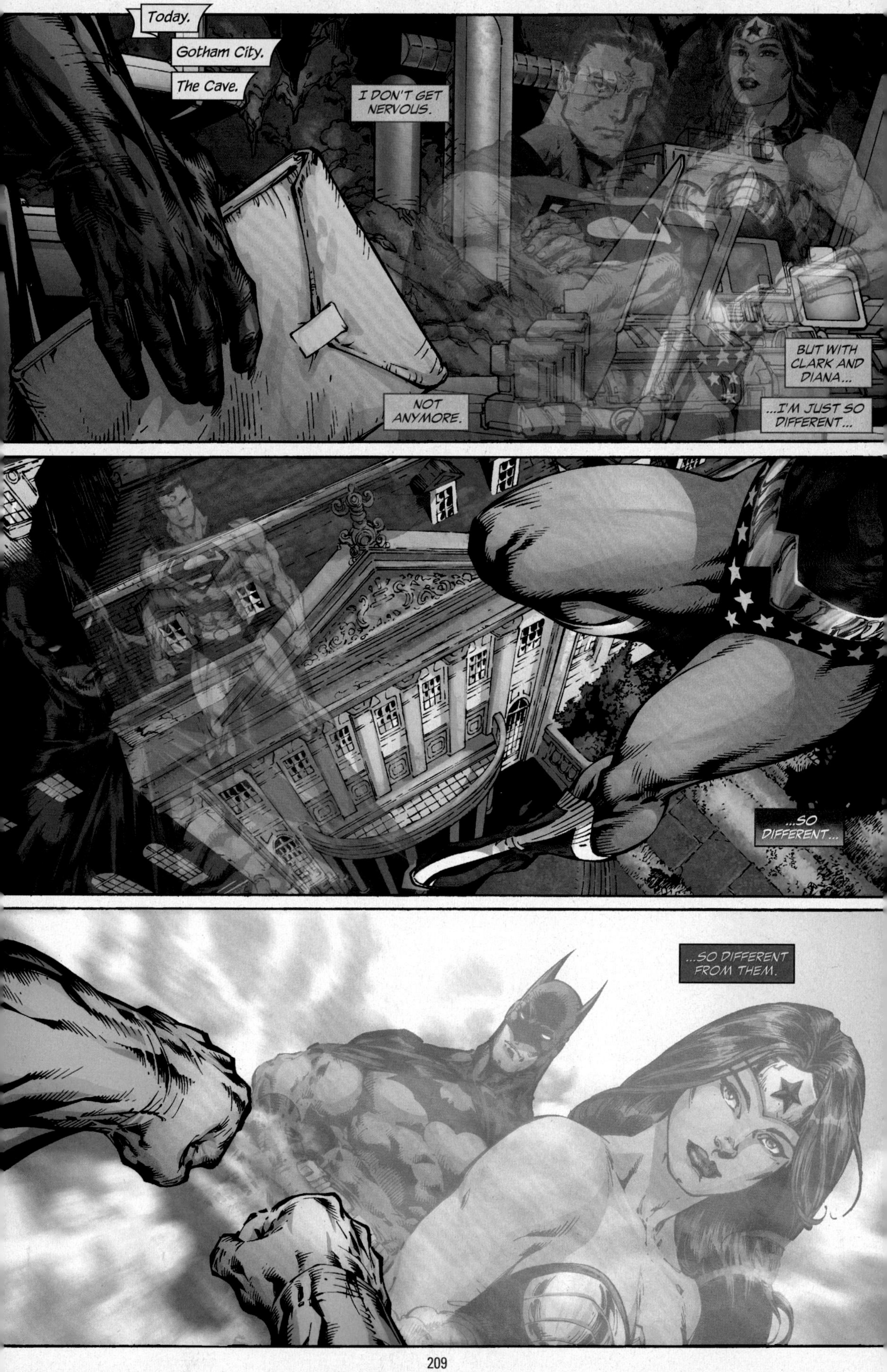
Today.
Gotham City.
The Cave.
I DON'T GET NERVOUS.
NOT ANYMORE.
BUT WITH CLARK AND DIANA...
...I'M JUST SO DIFFERENT...
...SO DIFFERENT...
...SO DIFFERENT FROM THEM.

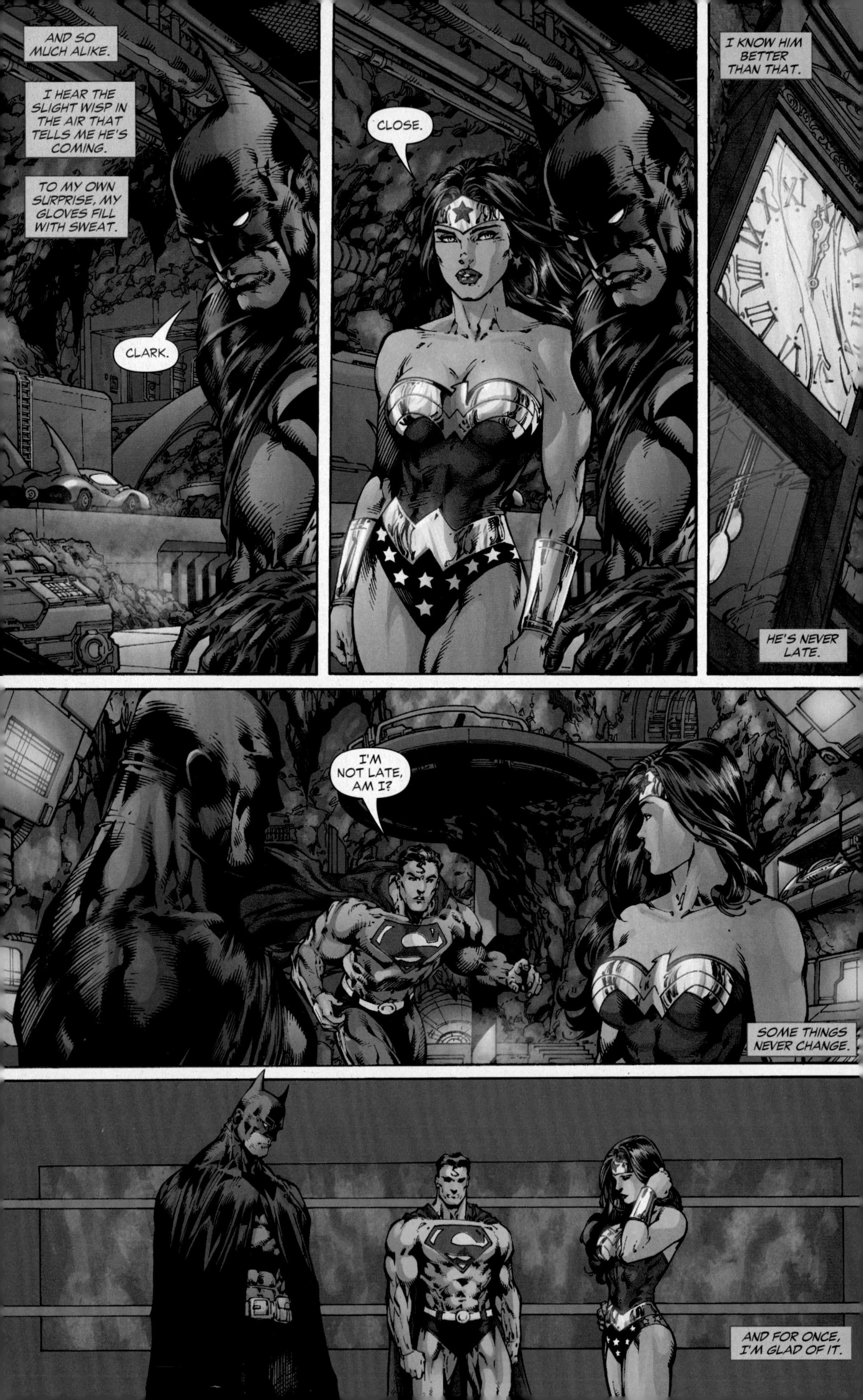
AND SO MUCH ALIKE.
I HEAR THE SLIGHT WISP IN THE AIR THAT TELLS ME HE'S COMING.
TO MY OWN SURPRISE, MY GLOVES FILL WITH SWEAT.
CLARK.
CLOSE.
I KNOW HIM BETTER THAN THAT.
HE'S NEVER LATE.
I'M NOT LATE, AM I?
SOME THINGS NEVER CHANGE.
AND FOR ONCE, I'M GLAD OF IT.

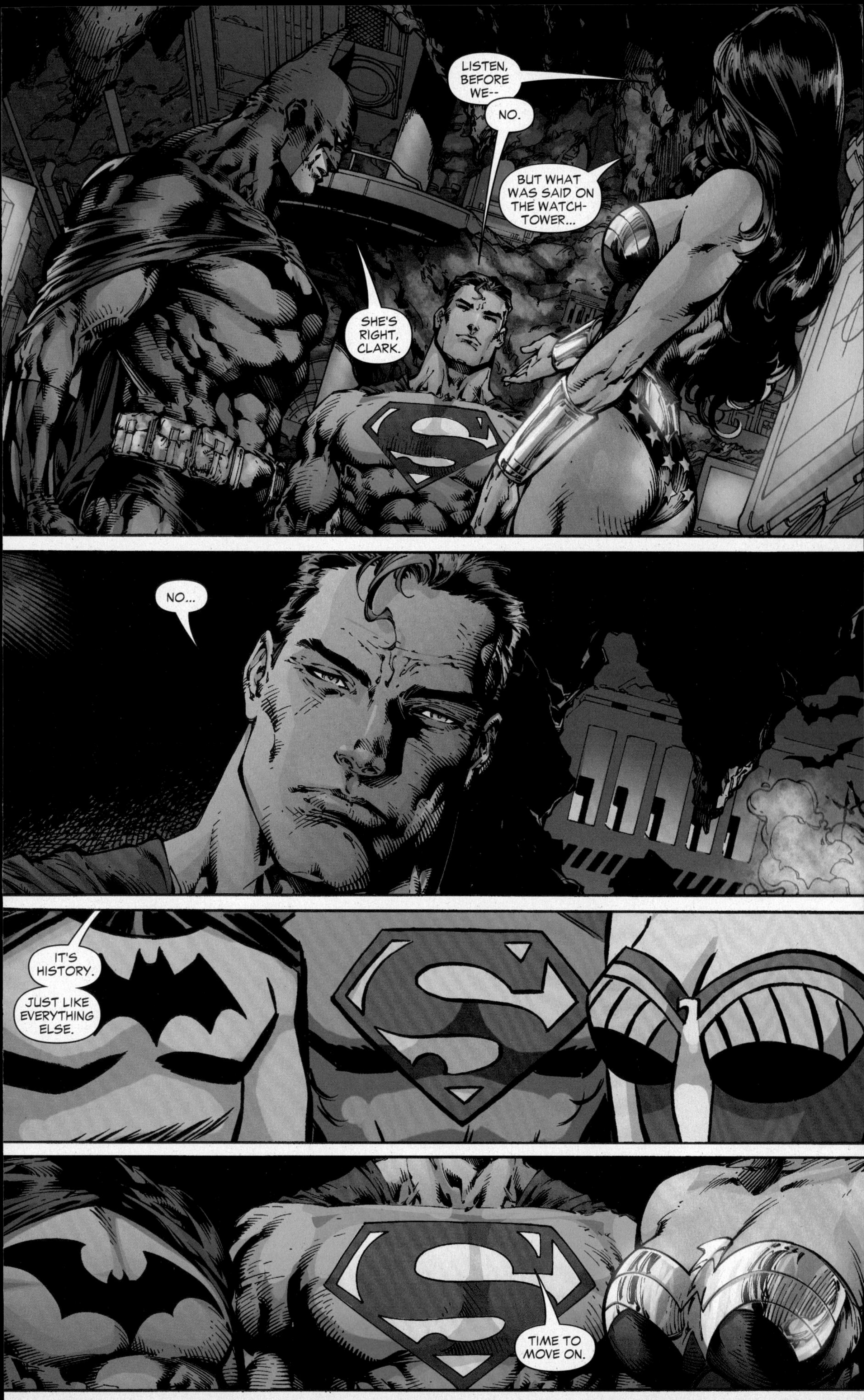
LISTEN, BEFORE WE--
NO.
BUT WHAT WAS SAID ON THE WATCH-TOWER...
SHE'S RIGHT, CLARK.
NO...
IT'S HISTORY.
JUST LIKE EVERYTHING ELSE.
TIME TO MOVE ON.

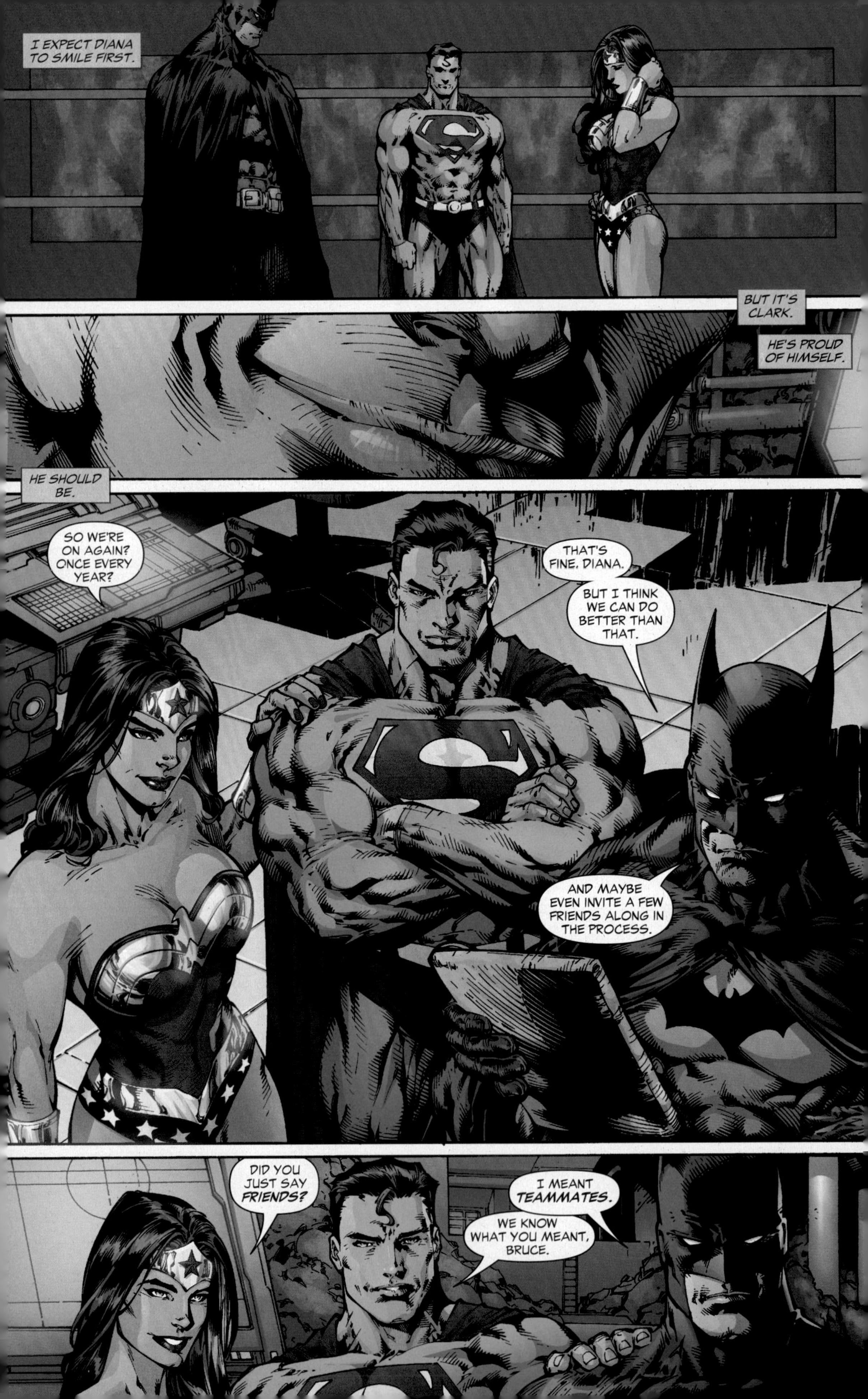
I EXPECT DIANA TO SMILE FIRST.
BUT IT'S CLARK.
HE'S PROUD OF HIMSELF.
HE SHOULD BE.
SO WE'RE ON AGAIN? ONCE EVERY YEAR?
THAT'S FINE, DIANA.
BUT I THINK WE CAN DO BETTER THAN THAT.
AND MAYBE EVEN INVITE A FEW FRIENDS ALONG IN THE PROCESS.
DID YOU JUST SAY *FRIENDS?*
I MEANT *TEAMMATES.*
WE KNOW WHAT YOU MEANT, BRUCE.

YESTERDAY, TODAY, TOMORROW

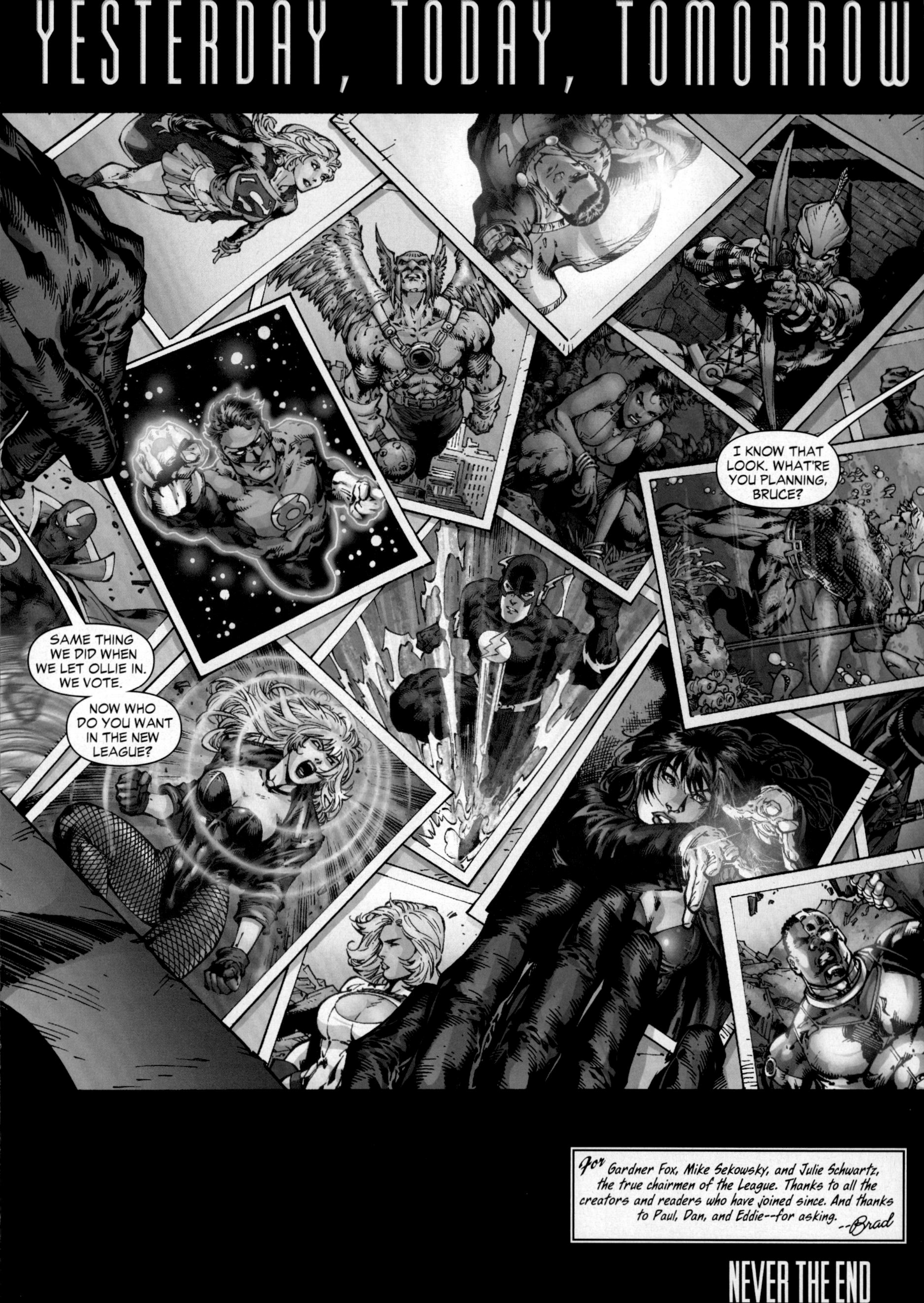
I KNOW THAT LOOK. WHAT'RE YOU PLANNING, BRUCE?
SAME THING WE DID WHEN WE LET OLLIE IN. WE VOTE.
NOW WHO DO YOU WANT IN THE NEW LEAGUE?

For Gardner Fox, Mike Sekowsky, and Julie Schwartz, the true chairmen of the League. Thanks to all the creators and readers who have joined since. And thanks to Paul, Dan, and Eddie--for asking. --Brad

NEVER THE END

JUSTICE LEAGUE OF AMERICA
COVER GALLERY

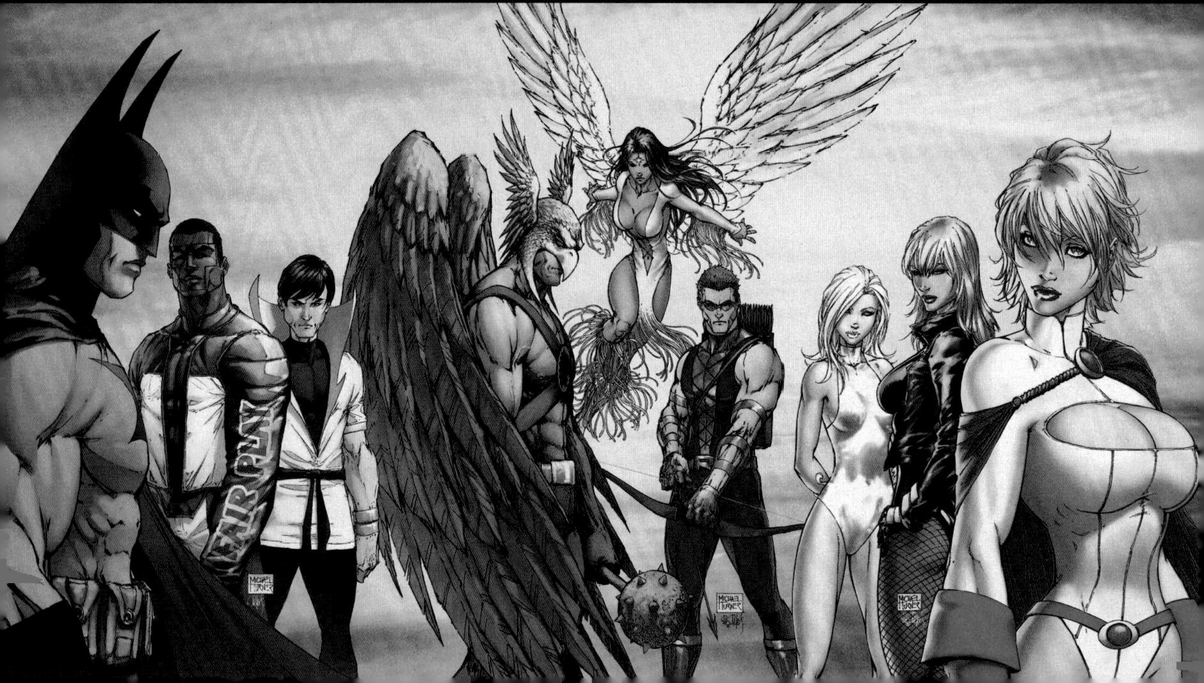
FAIR PLAY

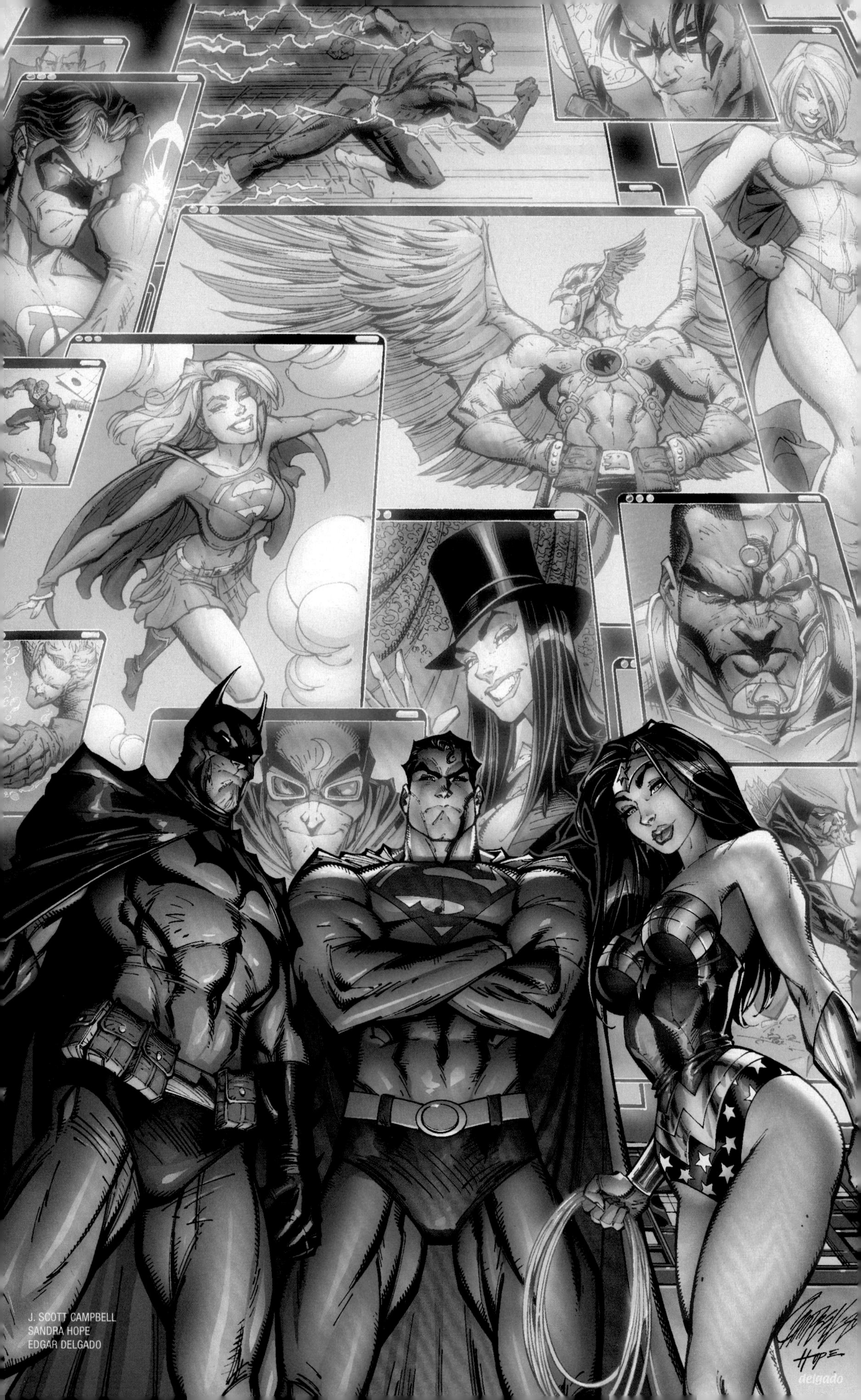

J. SCOTT CAMPBELL
SANDRA HOPE
EDGAR DELGADO

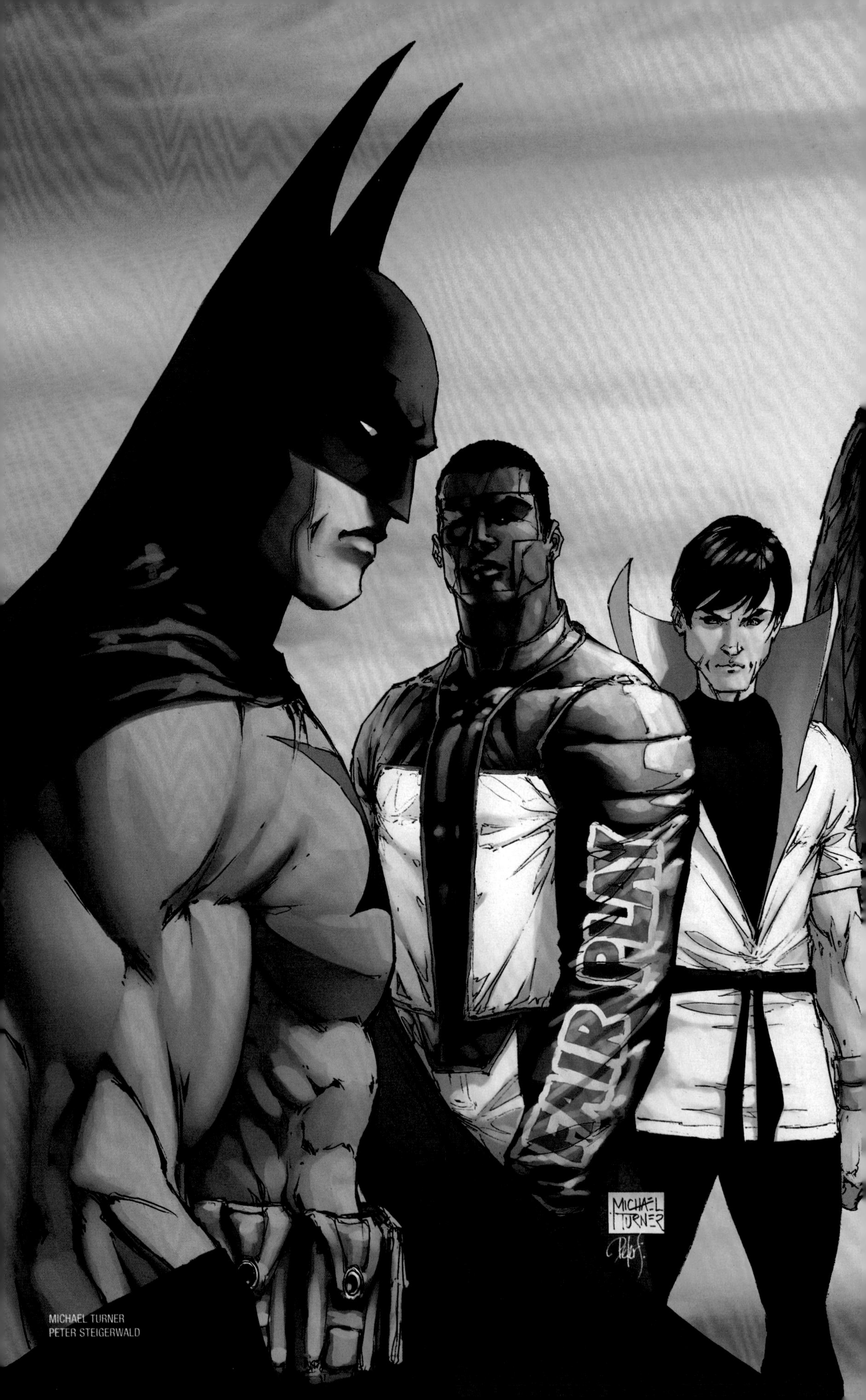
FAIR PLAY
MICHAEL TURNER

MICHAEL TURNER
PETER STEIGERWALD

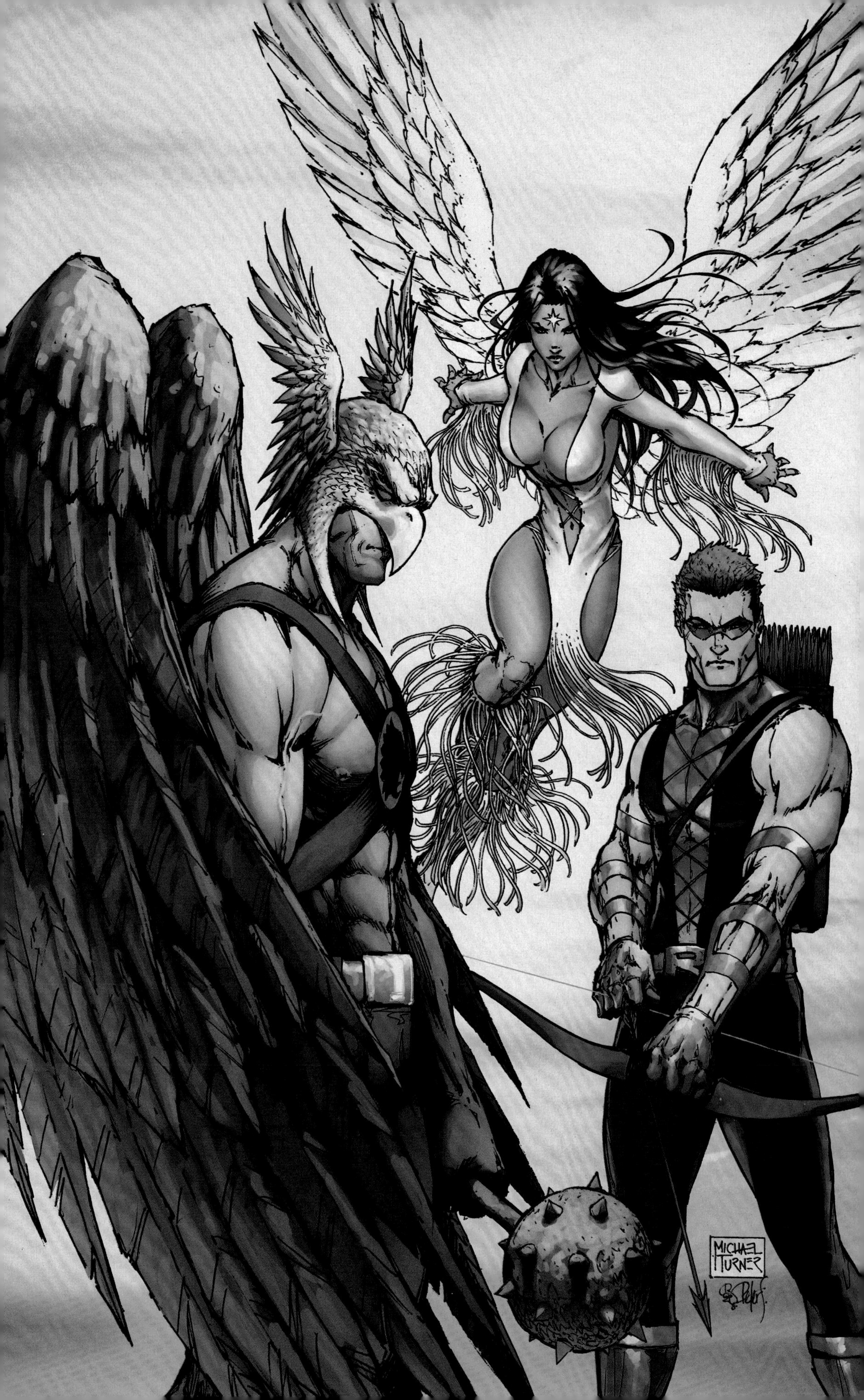
MICHAEL TURNER

MICHAEL TURNER
PETER STEIGERWALD

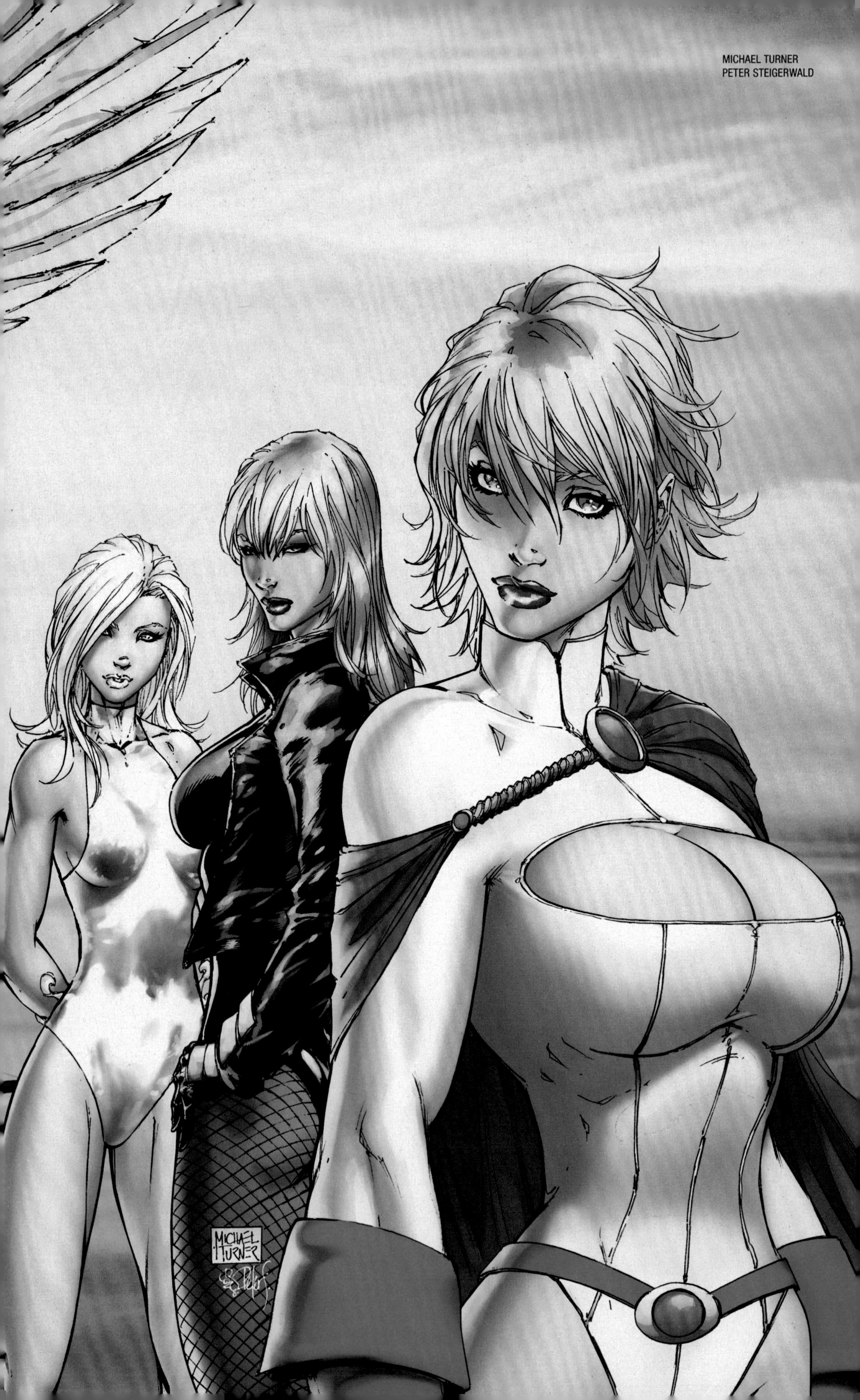

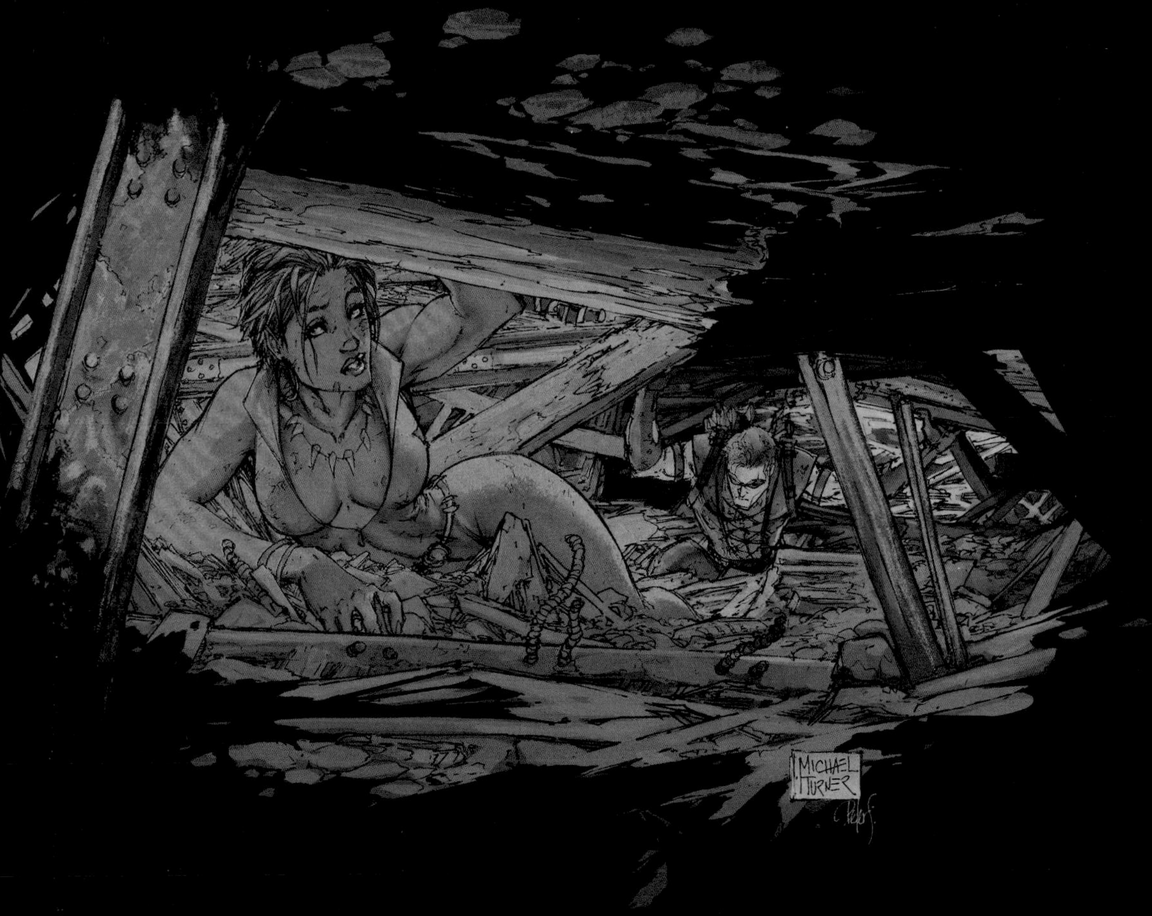
MICHAEL TURNER

MICHAEL TURNER
PETER STEIGERWALD

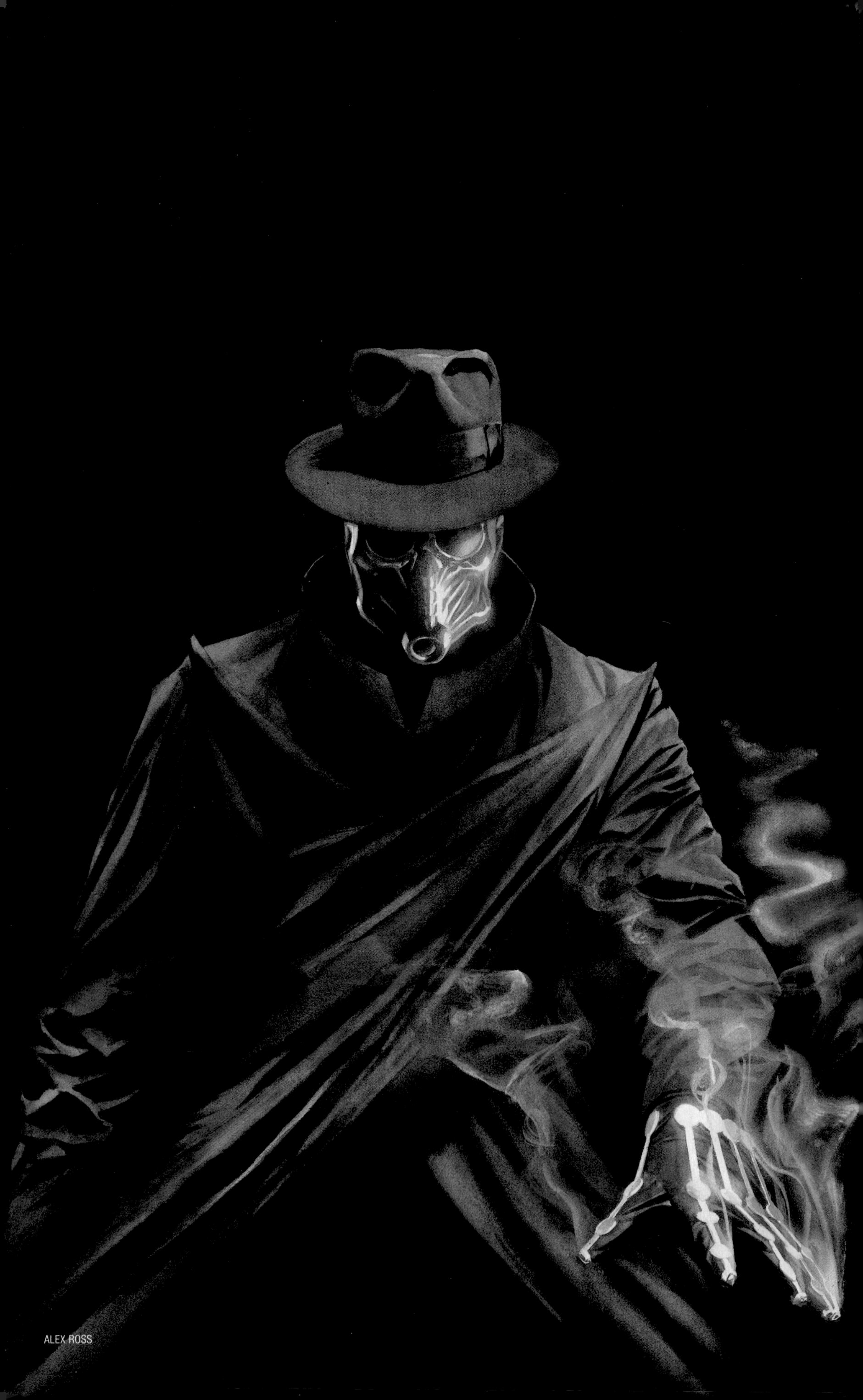

ALEX ROSS

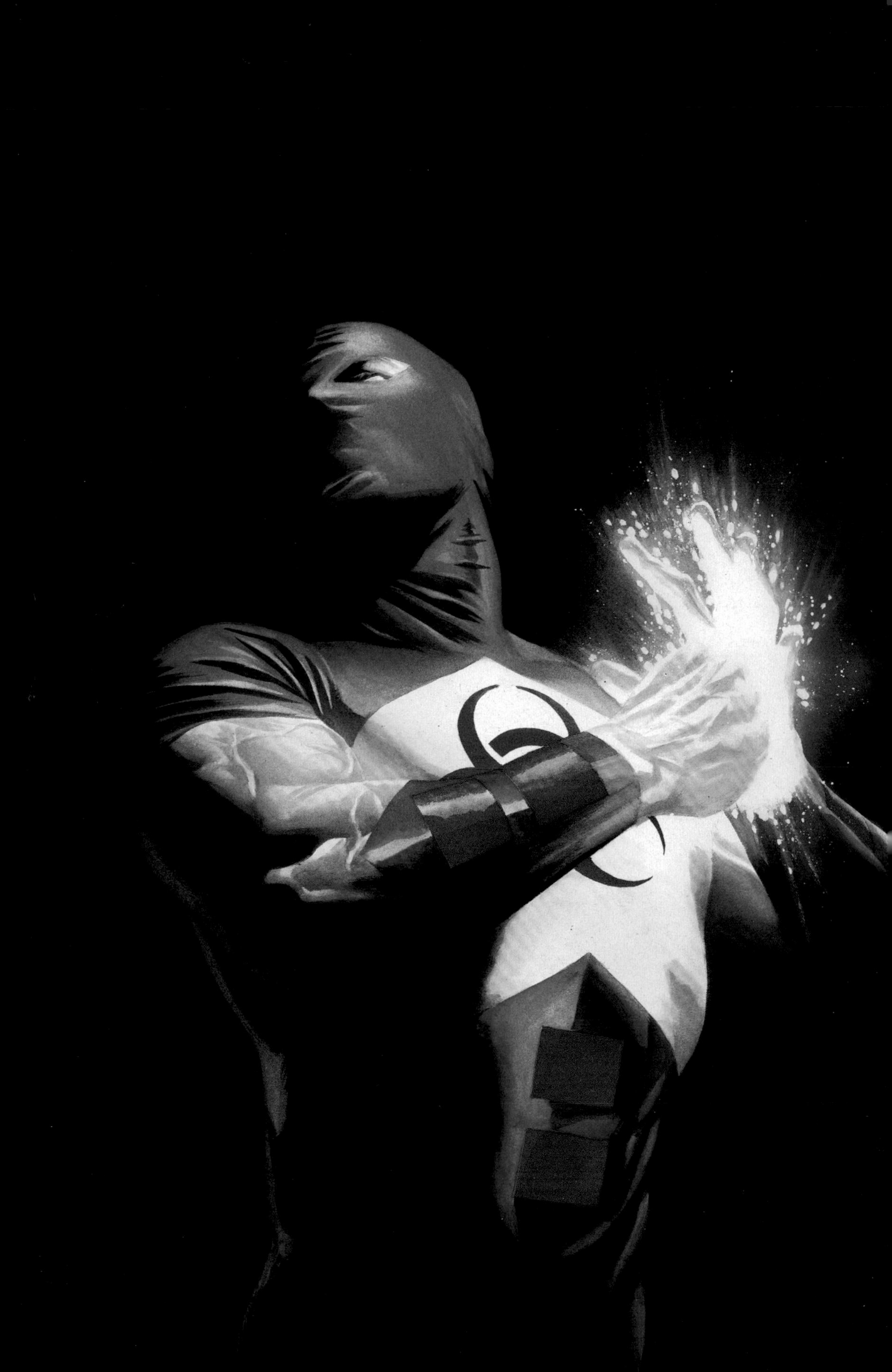

ALEX ROSS

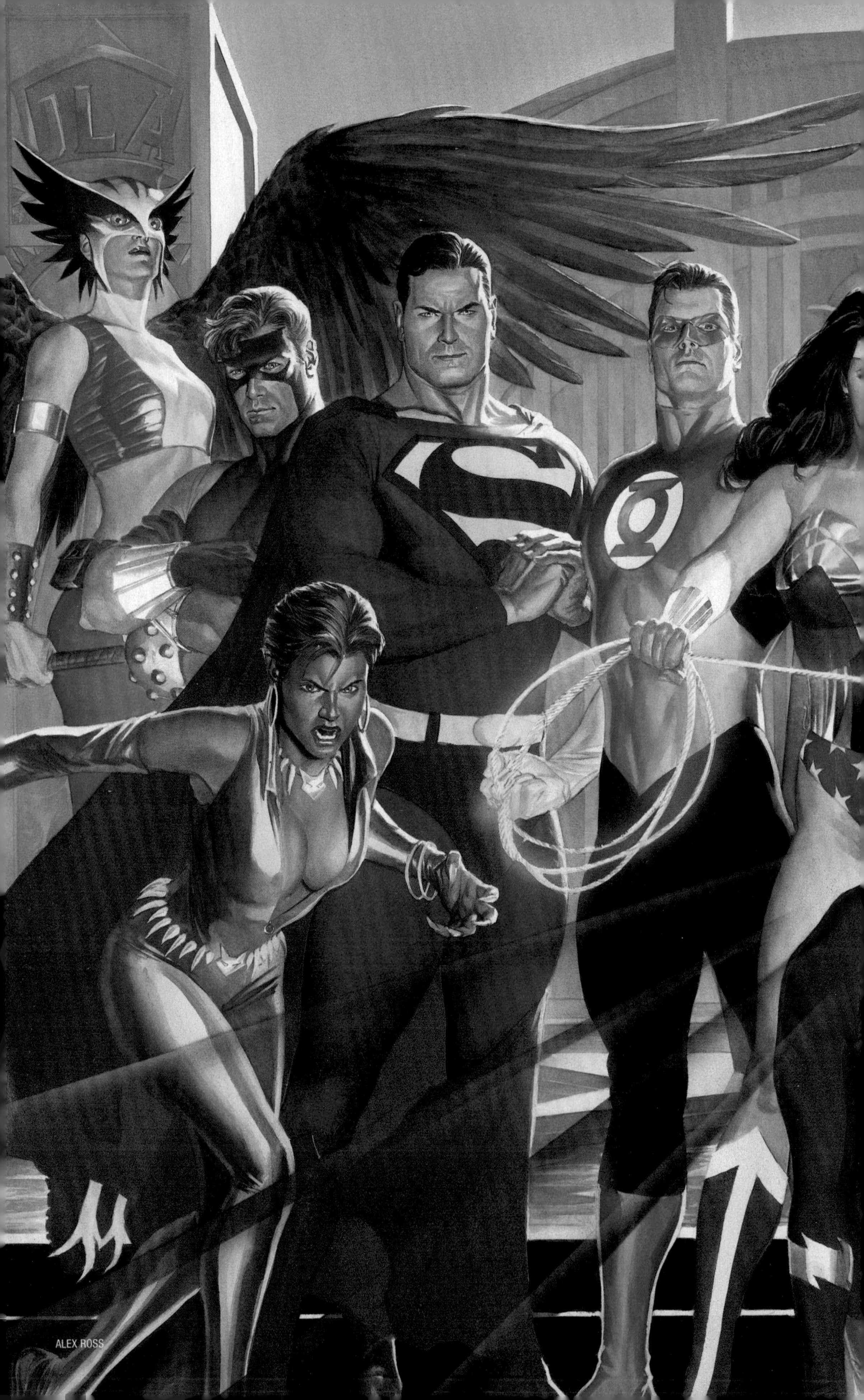
JLA
ALEX ROSS

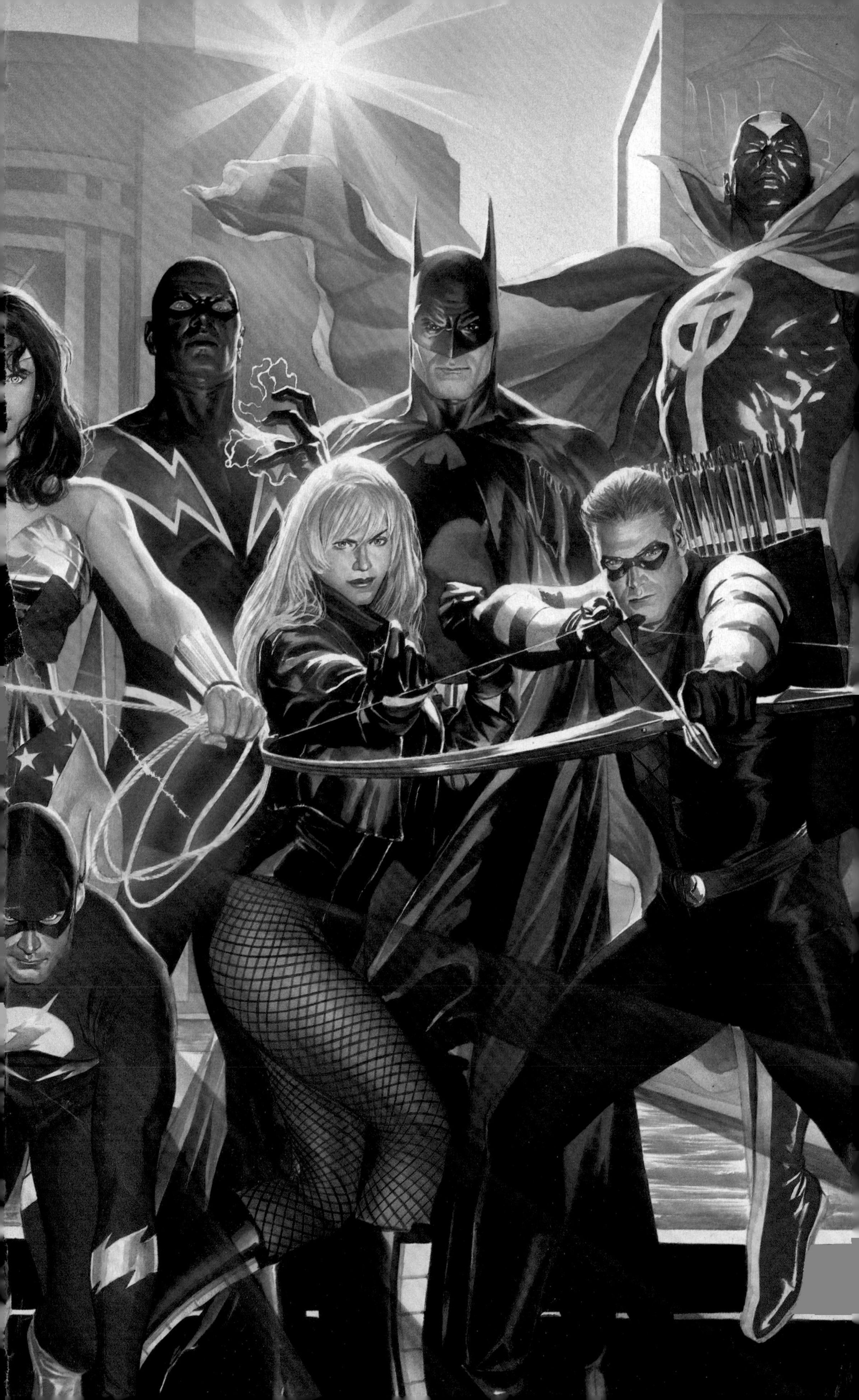

READ MORE ADVENTURES OF YOUR FAVORITE HEROES IN THESE COLLECTIONS FROM DC COMICS:

KINGDOM COME

Mark Waid and **Alex Ross** deliver a grim tale of youth versus experience, tradition versus change and what defines a hero. KINGDOM COME is a riveting story pitting the old guard — Superman, Batman, Wonder Woman and their peers — against a new uncompromising generation.

WINNER OF FIVE EISNER AND HARVEY AWARDS, INCLUDING BEST LIMITED SERIES AND BEST ARTIST

THE GREATEST SUPER HERO EPIC OF TOMORROW!
KINGDOM COME
Mark WAID
Alex ROSS

IDENTITY CRISIS

NEW YORK TIMES BEST-SELLING AUTHOR OF THE ZERO GAME
BRAD MELTZER
RAGS MORALES MICHAEL BAIR
IDENTITY CRISIS
Introduction by JOSS WHEDON, creator of BUFFY THE VAMPIRE SLAYER and FIREFLY
"The IDENTITY CRISIS mystery involves the biggest DC heroes, and uses all of Mr. Meltzer's skills as a thriller novelist."
— The New York Times

BRAD MELTZER
RAGS MORALES
MICHAEL BAIR

CRISIS ON INFINITE EARTHS

CRISIS
ON INFINITE EARTHS
MARV WOLFMAN
& GEORGE PÉREZ

MARV WOLFMAN
GEORGE PÉREZ

DC: THE NEW FRONTIER VOLUME 1

DC: The New Frontier
VOLUME ONE
BY DARWYN COOKE WITH DAVE STEWART

DARWYN COOKE
DAVE STEWART

SEARCH THE GRAPHIC NOVELS SECTION OF

www.DCCOMICS.com

FOR ART AND INFORMATION ON ALL OF OUR BOOKS!

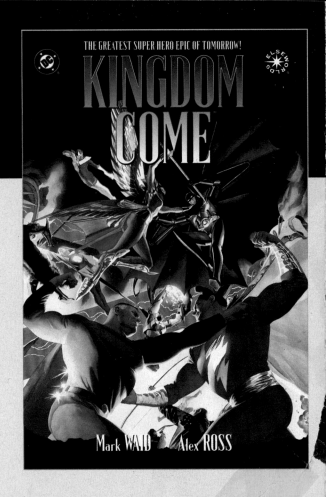

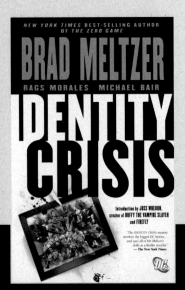

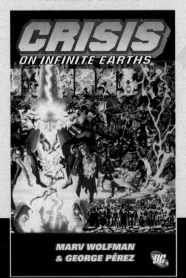

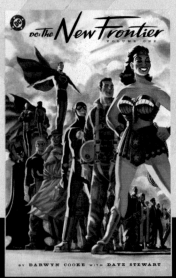